Stirling and Gowan

Stirling and Gowan

Architecture from Austerity to Affluence

Mark Crinson

Published for the Paul Mellon Centre for Studies in British Art by

Yale University Press · New Haven and London

For Asia

Designed by Emily Angus
Printed in China

Library of Congress Cataloging-in-Publication Data

Crinson, Mark.
Stirling and Gowan : architecture from austerity to affluence / Mark Crinson.
p. cm.
Includes bibliographical references and index.
ISBN 978–0–300–17728–2 (cloth : alk. paper)
1. Stirling, James (James Frazer)–Criticism and interpretation.
2. Gowan, James–Criticism and interpretation. 3. Architecture–Great
Britain–History–20th century. I. Title. II. Title: Architecture from austerity to affluence.
NA997.S78C75 2012
720.92'2–dc23
2011042295

A catalogue record for this book is available from The British Library

Frontispiece: Leicester University Engineering Building, 1959–64 (detail of fig. 172).

Contents

Acknowledgements

In researching and writing this book I have drawn heavily on the goodwill and generosity of many people. The following gave me advice, information or guidance: Tim Benton, Alan Colquhoun, Robin Dunn, John Ellis, Peter Fawcett, Adrian Forty, Tom and Carol Frodsham, David Gray, Scot Hein, Dirk van den Heuvel, Malcolm Higgs, Lim Chong Keat, Stephen Kite, Leon Krier, M. J. Long, Jules Lubbock, the late Robina McNeil, Cynthia Manners, Paul Manousso, Eva-Marie Neumann, Clare O'Dowd, David Parker, John Partridge, Joyce Price, Joseph Sharples, Ann-Marie Sigouin, Richard Smith, Elizabeth Stratton, Quinlan Terry, Derek Trillo, Richard Williams, Inge Wolf and David Yeomans. Claire Zimmerman, with whom I have collaborated on a related project, has shared her insights on Stirling and Gowan's work.

I have been able to share my ideas and get valuable feedback through invited lectures at the SAHANZ conference in Adelaide, the College Art Association in Boston, Leicester University, University of East Anglia, Columbia University, University of Greenwich, the Twentieth Century Society, Yale University, the V&A/RIBA Drawings Collection, the Academy of Fine Arts in Vienna and Tate Britain. I am very grateful to the organisers of these events for their invitations: Mike Lewis, Tony Vidler, Teresa Stoppani, Alan Powers, Peter Scriver, Barnabas Calder, Christoph Grafe, John Mitchell, Simon Richards, Marion von Osten, Ayala Levin, Marta Caldeira and Maria Gonzales Pendas. I am also indebted to the skills of three journal editors – Hilary Ballon, Judi Loach and Tom Weaver – who have helped improve my writing.

Work of this kind is not possible without financial support, and I have received generous grants from the Paul Mellon Centre (London), the British Academy and the Canadian Centre for Architecture. The University of Manchester and especially my colleagues and students in Art History & Visual Studies have provided the intellectual and institutional platform for this book. Amongst the many librarians, archivists and curators who have helped, I should especially mention Howard Shubert, the curator whose detailed knowledge of the Stirling/Wilford fonds at the Canadian Centre for Architecture makes life considerably easier for any researcher. Kit Evans, Michael Wilford and Bob Maxwell have generously given full and detailed responses to my many questions. Gillian Malpass, Emily Angus and Emily Lees at Yale University Press have patiently and expertly guided this work through to publication, and Yale's anonymous referees have helped me understand much better what I was trying to do.

Mark Girouard gave me some calm guidance as well as access to his own archives. Lady Stirling opened up her house to me, including her husband's library (now sadly dispersed) and the important documents and photographs in her possession. Above all, I am in debt to James Gowan for demonstrating such faith in this book, showing me his own drawings, and giving me so much time to talk through memories and ideas with him.

Finally, my closest personal debts are to Eva, who reminds me how to live in the present, and Asia, who helps me to see the world better.

Abbreviations

AA – Architectural Association

APRR – Association for Planning and Regional Reconstruction

CCA – Canadian Centre for Architecture (Montreal)

CIAM – Congrès Internationaux d'Architecture Moderne

DAM – Deutsches Architektur Museum (Frankfurt)

LBR – London Borough of Richmond upon Thames

LCC – London County Council

RIBA – Royal Institute of British Architects

RIBAJ – Royal Institute of British Architects Journal

WBC – Wycombe District Council

YCBA – Yale Center for British Art (New Haven)

Introduction

Introduction

And it is now that our two paths cross.

    Both simultaneously recognize his Anti-type: that I am an Arcadian, that he is a Utopian.

    . . . .

    In my Eden we have a few beam-engines, saddle-tank locomotives, overshot waterwheels and other beautiful pieces of obsolete machinery to play with: In his New Jerusalem even chefs will be cucumber-cool machine minders.

(W. H. Auden, 'Vespers', 1954)

The architectural partnership of James Gowan and James Stirling was not long-lived and did not produce many actual buildings. Only nine single buildings or complexes of buildings were finished, and the partnership lasted a mere seven years from 1956 to 1963. Yet their work was horizon-forming. It drew the architectural world's attention to Britain and shifted the terms on which modernism was understood. Challenging the kind of polite modernism that had dominated post-war Britain, it also incubated some of the most influential conceptions of architecture in the second half of the twentieth century. Modernist neo-Palladianism or mannerism, brutalism, Victorian revival, a bricolage aesthetic, and updated versions of such 1920s styles as purism and De Stijl can all be found in this work, and there is no doubt it seeded high-tech and postmodernism. But the flats in Ham Common, the housing estate in Preston and the Leicester University Engineering building, as well as the designs for Churchill College and Selwyn College, Cambridge, are paradoxical in the manner of the best forms of modernism in the arts. They are at once monumental and informal, industrial and bespoke, experimental and historical. They do not fit in yet they seem uncanny; they appear contrary yet they revivify their contexts.

    Among many younger architects in these post-war years there was a belief that modernism had become either over-rational or a mere style, a matter of bureaucracy more than creativity, a moralised faith in the functional that seemed to have lost the challenge, edge and sense of new horizons they associated with the modernism of twenty, thirty or forty years before. This is the period in which rationality, 'no longer the mark of the quintessentially human, had become instead the cause of our alienation from nature and from society',[1] and if this was so then the rationalist claims of modernism had to be reconsidered. Thus, in the post-war architecture these younger architects admired, that of Alvar Aalto and Louis Kahn as well as Le Corbusier's late works, modernism's abstract forms were augmented by a reconsideration of monumentality and institutional meaning, by regionalism and even by primitivism.[2] These architects now actively questioned the idea that modernism was 'an aesthetic of unmediated industrial production'.[3] Yet, as this Introduction will suggest later, if industry could not be blindly embraced nor could it simply be refused.

It may seem obvious, but to understand the achievements of Stirling and Gowan's work we have to treat it as the product of two architects. Authorship in architecture is, of course, a complex thing. In any reasonable consideration it includes clients, engineers, planning authorities and builders, and one might argue that on another level it also involves other architects and previous buildings both near and distant. All these will be given their role in this book. But one of the central problems in studying a partnership is to understand what happens within it, especially when as here the partners both contributed to the designing of buildings. Simplifying the achievement under the name 'Stirling' or assuming that one architect had more significance, as has been done in many previous accounts, if nothing else is to cut out a whole area useful to our understanding of the work. The trouble, therefore, with some of the most influential readings of the partnership's works is that they are premised on a creative arc that only belongs to Stirling. In part this is understandable in a publishing market still dominated by monographs where architects are treated like the romantic image of painters or novelists. After his partnership with Gowan, Stirling first worked on his own (1964–71) and then in partnership with Michael Wilford (1971–92), cementing and then extending his reputation as Britain's most significant post-war architect. The work with Gowan is, then, easily absorbed into this longer trajectory that fits the monographic model. Consider this assessment of Leicester University Engineering building in a much-anthologised article by Peter Eisenman: 'Stirling produced this building as a very definite though less-than-conscious reaction to the mainstream Modern Movement and in particular to Le Corbusier.'[4] Did Stirling design this building on his own, as is more than implied here, or are we to take 'Stirling' as a kind of shorthand for the partnership? And if so, what was Gowan's role in the 'turf-clearing' Eisenman describes? Did Gowan share in the same less-than-conscious aim? Possibly. More likely Eisenman's article, which is such a rigorous reading in many other ways, has no interest in this kind of question and is much more concerned with finding in Stirling a mirror for its own architectural concerns. And for Eisenman, one could substitute many of the critics who wrote on the partnership's work in the years of its greatest influence. To change

1   James Gowan and James Stirling, *c.*1960. Photograph by Sandra Lousada.

this view is not, of course, to say that Stirling's obsessions and motivations do not matter, but that the familiar mythography of the individual creative genius or the celebrity architect may not be the best means of getting at the real creativity of the architecture. Some of the more recent writing on Gowan or on individual buildings has attempted to adjust this, but as yet there has been no sustained attempt to treat the partnership as exactly that, a partnership (fig. 1).[5]

Anyone writing about James Stirling is indebted to Mark Girouard's indispensable *Big Jim: The Life and Work of James Stirling* (1998), a highly readable biography based partly upon scores of interviews with people who knew the architect throughout his life, and partly on access to the then uncatalogued office and family archives.[6] Although Girouard claimed the book was not a study of the buildings, it certainly placed them in vivid relationship with the life, and its assessment of them lucidly considered their failings and the controversies they evoked as much as their achievements. Buildings, projects and ideas are the prime objects of study in this current book, and it does not attempt to add to or correct the biography. This kind of work is now well supported by having Stirling's archives housed, and catalogued, in the Canadian Centre for Architecture (CCA) in Montreal. The scholar researching Stirling is thus able to access one of the largest collections publicly available on any modern architect: some 40,000 drawings, prints and models, 150 linear feet of documents for 105 projects from 1950 to 1992, as well as extensive photographic documentation. The availability of this archive has helped fuel the recent revival of interest in Stirling's work.[7] But, like any archive, this one is partial. Most obviously, its name – the 'Fonds James Stirling/Michael Wilford' – reflects the fact that it is a collection taking its shape from its accumulation by Stirling and then within the Stirling/Wilford practice, augmented by some papers from the Stirling family collection. In writing about the Stirling and Gowan partnership, then, the CCA archive is clearly not sufficient. I have also used interviews, if not as many as Girouard and centred exclusively on issues to do with the architectural practice. Here, though, I have been able to draw extensively from the recollections and papers of James Gowan as a way of balancing what is known from James Stirling's perspective. Research into the partnership's buildings has also benefited from using other archives, notably the 420 drawings that Gowan gave to the Deutsches Architektur Museum in Frankfurt, as well as those still held by the clients, particularly universities and colleges, as well as planning authorities. There is also the rich panoply of published and unpublished sources within the wider architectural culture, and often beyond it, which helps set the partners' work in the context of other buildings and wider debates.

Until very recently, and therefore dominating what was known about the work for many years, the major book-length studies of Stirling all came from his own office.

They took the form of what Le Corbusier called *Oeuvre complète*: in other words, books published under the architect's supervision to catalogue projects through photographs and drawings and aimed, with more than half an eye on history, at creating a coherent body or canon of work. *James Stirling: Buildings and Projects 1950–1974* (1975) and *James Stirling Michael Wilford and Associates: Buildings and Projects 1975–1992* (1994) – or, as they are known because of the colour of their covers, the 'Black Book' and 'White Book' – are the result.[8] Pointedly modelled on the size, shape and layout of Le Corbusier's *Oeuvre complète*, these books are the most complete visual record of Stirling's works. At the same time, though, they play fast and loose with the historical record, sometimes with deliberately waggish effect. Drawings were redrawn or new views invented by the fluid pen of Stirling's collaborator, Leon Krier, who played an important creative role in making the Black Book.[9] Photographs were often edited and doctored following Le Corbusier's own example. Earlier projects were interpreted from the perspective of 1975; while some are exaggerated in significance, others are left out or marginalised. A playful humour relieved the catalogue format's usual solemnity, its irony infecting the most humble and the most ambitious projects. The books attempt to save architecture from contingency and to make it seem instead the product of intention, to keep it away from the large number of middling practices from within which seemingly little claim to cultural significance could be made. Better to preserve the brave fights of near disasters like the Florey building (discussed in Chapter Seven here) than to be seen to have designed and even built something as nondescript as the Kissa house (discussed in Chapter Four).

Stirling's work has also benefited from the attentions of many of the major architectural critics working between the 1950s and the 1990s. Colin Rowe and Reyner Banham in the 1950s, followed by Robert Maxwell, Kenneth Frampton, Joseph Rykwert, Manfredo Tafuri, Peter Eisenman and Charles Jencks – most of whom knew Stirling personally – all wrote about the architecture from positions deeply committed to its symptomatic and its creative possibilities. No historian can ignore the insights and investments in these writings; they are 'operative criticism' of the best kind, explaining the buildings and using them to intervene in architecture's development.[10] This present study seeks to contextualise the architecture, sometimes both more widely and more narrowly than might have seemed relevant to these writers, to get further out from the works as well as closer to the thinking and processes that produced it, and sometimes therefore in ways that do not take the discipline's own wished-for protocols and boundaries for granted.

How does one reinsert Gowan into this account, while at the same time accepting that Stirling's work subsequent to the partnership is far more important? The approach taken here is to place the partnership work at the centre of the book (Chapters Four, Five and Six) but to set its seven years of work within a larger twenty-five-year period that extends from the end of the war to 1970. The first three chapters establish each architect's separate previous experiences of architectural training and practice in an attempt to characterise their formal concerns, intellectual make-up, and understanding of the architectural world prior to their partnership. Thus, Stirling's training as a student at the Liverpool School of Architecture is discussed in Chapter One. Gowan's training and his and Stirling's early experiences in London working in other architects' offices are detailed in Chapter Two. Stirling's contacts with the avant-garde Independent Group and the development of his early ideas about architecture are the subject of Chapter Three. The three chapters on the partnership that follow discuss the nature of collaboration and the various single house projects (Chapter Four), the work for the welfare state and the way it reappraised the Victorian city (Chapter Five), and the university projects including Leicester University Engineering building (Chapter Six). Finally, Chapter Seven, in more summary form, shows how the architects' separate works for a few years immediately after the dissolution of the partnership continued the major themes they had elaborated together.

This book is premised upon the idea that there was a formative relation between the immediate post-war years of austerity and the new kinds of modernism that Stirling and Gowan produced. Another way of saying this is that, as Chapter Three explains it, 'junk, bunk and tomorrow' were all grist to their mill. The result might be called a 'post-industrial architecture'. It should be admitted straightaway that the term 'post-industrial' has certain problems: it was not used at the time, and I want to distance it from its use in 'post-industrial society' to mean a socio-cultural condition deriving from a post-Fordist economy based on the dematerialised labour of globalised financial operations, service industries and computerised interactions.[11] It needs also to be distanced from the associations, loosely made by some postmodernists, between the 'information revolution' of this post-industrial society and the semantic concerns of postmodernist architecture.[12] Rather, post-industrial here means something more like de-industrial or de-industrialising; it is much more closely related to the Industrial Revolution and the buildings, urban forms and engineering structures created during and since that radical paleotechnic shift. Most critically, post-industrial indicates an awareness that the periodic ebb and flow of industrial and economic change had reached a point of systemic crisis in the immediately post-war decades, beyond which a long slump, culminating in the 1970s, was already to be glimpsed in the fortunes of the heavy and manufacturing industries.

The relevant historical facts are well established. Although Britain remained a major manufacturing nation at mid-century, the cracks in its global control of staples like cotton and coal had already appeared while newer kinds of production in chemicals and electronics were rising. Although the cultural significance of the Industrial Revolution to Britain's self-image remained, the damage done to this image by wartime bombing, the extensive reconstruction and replanning of cities, and imperial loss or relative decline was not easily offset by an understanding that the service sector already by 1950 was equal in production and employment to the older manufacturing sector, nor indeed by signs that it was relative decline that was at stake here (Britain's share of world production and exports) rather than absolute decline.[13] The causes of decline in the older industries had much to do with poor investment and the loss of markets, with the effects of massive post-war debt and the consequent *condition britannique* of 'voluntary penury'.[14] None of this was clarified or altered by the kind of reasoning, both then and since, that concentrated excessively on cultural explanations for the lack of technological dynamism, whether of a backward technical education, of 'two cultures', of schooling and trade unions, or of 'the decline of the industrial spirit'.[15]

Within this optic post-industrial does not mean a distrust of industry or a belief that industry had reached some end point, but instead a feeling of changed circumstances concerning not just the forms of industrial production but industry's status in the society at large. While not everyone accepted these changes and their implications, even among the most self-aware modernists,[16] the critic and historian Reyner Banham was one of the most persuasive voices in architecture arguing for the recognition of something fundamentally different in the nature of industry. Influenced by recent American writing on the implications of technological change,[17] Banham hailed the onset of a *second* machine age, ignoring the threatening and often contradictory aspects of this and giving it an entirely positive spin so that it might be encompassed within a revised understanding of modernism.[18] Although he recognised that it was still dependent on industrial production, Banham argued that modernism had to engage now with those new forms of technology that had changed conceptions of the domestic realm, of communications and of consumerism.[19] Banham knew Stirling and Gowan well, and there was some of this kind of concern in their work and writings too. More apparent, however, is a fascination with the possibilities of this moment of decline and discontinuity. They attempted to make architectural use of this post-industrial mindset in a way that was equally as distinct from Banham's second machine age as it was from the taste for ruins and genteel dereliction prevalent within the neo-romantic movement of an older generation.

What I am suggesting in Stirling and Gowan's work, then, is that it set out creatively to exploit a difference between modernity and industrial society without rejecting either. We are, as the sociologist Ulrich Beck has pointed out, 'accustomed to conceiving of modernity *within* the categories of industrial society'.[20] Modernists earlier in the century had certainly not all been blind to the problems of industrialism or averse to making their work out of some critical or sceptical reaction to it. But there was also a strand, arguably particularly strong in later modernist architecture, that conceived of its work as riding the wave of technological change.[21] By the post-war period – and in this sense Britain (and perhaps Italy too) was in a special position – there was already an awareness that, as Beck puts it about a later period, 'modernization *within* the paths of industrial society is being replaced by a modernization *of the principles* of industrial society.'[22] One new modernisation was, effectively, undercutting and changing an older one, opening paths to another modernity.[23] What I find interesting about Stirling and Gowan's architecture, accordingly, is that they seem to understand this and try to find ways of addressing it, of making some architectural sense of the fact that modernity and industrial society were still linked but, because of unintended consequences,[24] the association was no longer inevitable. Their work is on a cusp between what Beck has called first and second modernity, or classical and reflexive modernisation. To put it differently, it sits between the modernisation of tradition (which one might see as a project of modernist architecture at its height in the early and mid-twentieth century) and the rethinking and modernisation of industrial society (which is the task set by some recent architects like Rem Koolhaas).[25] It is in this balancing act, this coming-into-being of a new kind of modernist reflexivity, that one finds the particular ambitions, qualities and even lessons of Stirling and Gowan's architecture.

The post-industrial is rather a descant than a dominant theme in this book. It weaves in and out of the work, at some moments hardly relevant, at others more compelling. Two brief examples of this are useful. Occasionally there was a strategic use of nostalgia, as argued in Chapter Five, in order to make a re-evaluation of the inherited urban forms of the industrial city. The heightened awareness of the fragility of community in the face of de-industrialisation, redevelopment and consumerism was what motivated the architects here. They wanted to find ways of retaining propinquity as well as of illustrating and promoting the transition from the Victorian to the new social democratic society, an 'imperfect' improvement to set beside the abstract 'utopian' forms of the welfare state. At the same time Stirling and Gowan were critical of the downside of the industrial city. Anyone who grew up in 1930s Glasgow or Liverpool, as they did, could hardly avoid seeing the effects of a disease like rickets, for instance, or the prevalence of slum housing. Similarly, Chapter Six argues that the great final work of the partnership, Leicester University Engineering building, affiliates itself both with the nineteenth century and with modernism, and it does this because the building is just as much about representing engineering to the university as it is about housing a community of teaching and researching engineers. The sense of fragile, torn or embattled communities is one of the continuing themes of this architecture. To discount it as sentimental, or to equate and dismiss it with other forms of welfare state modernism, would be the reaction of a later, neo-conservative brand of postmodernism.

If historicism in the nineteenth century was a response to a trauma of change generated by the Industrial Revolution, then the post-industrial attitude might be understood as a similar kind of response to change – this time of the combination of de-industrialisation and the aftermath of war. The aesthetic possibilities here were rich, and in the artistic work of Independent Group members, well known to both Stirling and Gowan, the conditions of rationing,[26] austerity and urban dereliction followed by reconstruction and incipient consumerism became the resources for an art of collecting, reuse and bricolage. In architecture the sources were similar but also included engineering structures, the details of Victorian buildings, and the layout of the Victorian city itself. These are not the only sources of permissive appropriation in Stirling and Gowan's work, and the ways in which they also wrestled with or were inspired by modernist architecture of the inter-war pioneers, of their younger contemporaries and even of the new establishment of modernists in Britain will all be discussed in this book.

We are at a point of reconsideration regarding the architecture of this period. To some extent the controversies surrounding some of Stirling's immediate post-partnership buildings like the Cambridge History Faculty and the Florey in Oxford have settled, partly due to what seem like successful and respectful recent refurbishments. But at the same time many of these buildings have been lost – most of the Preston housing estate, all of the two-phased estate at Runcorn. Some of the buildings are treated as precious objects by their residents or users, while others are at some risk of destructive redesign or serious neglect. The spawn of the brutalist buildings of the 1950s has become the least favoured of modern architectural styles.[27] The critical fortunes of James Stirling have suffered since his death in 1992. Although his work is a constant in any history of the period, there has been very little research or reconceptualising of it in the last twenty years, and to some extent it suffers from the sense that it belongs with the latest major movement to be rejected by the architectural establishment – postmodernism. But the urgency of avant-garde architecture in the period discussed here, and sometimes even its drollery, still offer possibilities and even challenges for our own moment. On one side we have an architecture finding its creative well-spring as much in a post-industrialism of austerity and post-war decline as in a post-industrialism of plenty; on the other, one that plays signature tunes to the dance of private capital even as a new austerity has descended. On one side is an architecture that took seriously its responsibility to community and institution; on the other, one that must perforce do business in a dissipated public sphere.

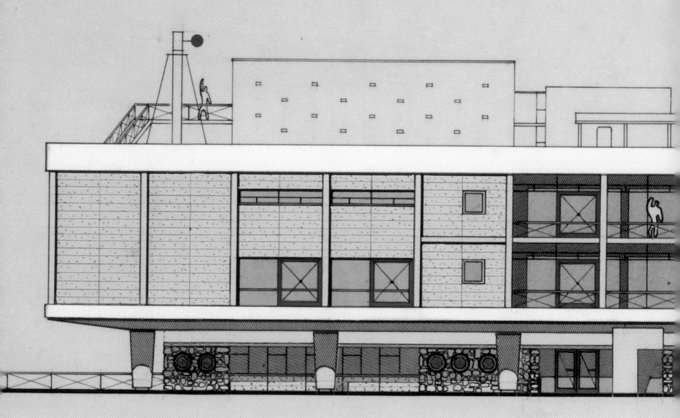

EAST ELEVATION

ONE

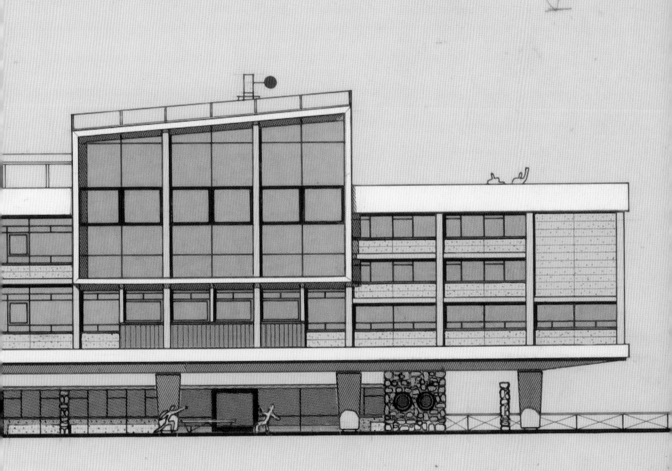

Formulas, Free Plans and a Piranesian City

Everything was shadowy now. The warehouses we passed seemed empty of everything but shadows. A few men – far too few – came struggling over, their day's work over. We arrived at the edge of the Mersey and below us was a long mudbank. The water was a grey mystery, a mere vague thickening of space. . . . I have rarely seen anything more spectral and melancholy. It was hard to believe that by taking ship here you might eventually reach a place of sharp outlines, a place where colour burned and vibrated in the sunlight.

(J. B. Priestley, English Journey, 1934)

To start, a little sortie into autobiography and historical revisionism, and the convenient myths that help either to shape or to damage a career for posterity. In 1965 James Stirling described his student days at the Liverpool School of Architecture, nearly twenty years before, as a time of conflict over the emergence of modernism. 'There was a furious debate as to the validity of the modern movement, tempers were heated and discussion was intense,' he remembered, 'some staff resigned and a few students went off to other schools; at any rate I was left with a deep conviction of the moral rightness of the New Architecture.'[1] Stirling's statement acquired an extra level of significance when used twelve years later by David Watkin as an epigraph for his book *Morality and Architecture* (1977). For Watkin, writing at a time of righteous reaction, Stirling's statement exemplified the arrogance and high-minded certainties in which the social and aesthetic worth of modernism was held. Yet the more we look at what Stirling wrote, the more ambiguous it seems. The statement has perhaps more of 1965 about it and its place of delivery, the RIBA where the 'moral rightness' of modernism was still in the ascendant, than the late 1940s. It certainly shows Stirling's tendency to adjust his stories according to his audience. Only a few years earlier another recollection had entirely contradicted the idea of any 'furious debate'.[2] And rather than a resounding statement by a continuing true believer, Stirling's 'deep conviction' of 'moral rightness' is more of a retrospective description of something that has since changed. Apart from the actual buildings that Stirling made between his Liverpool days and 1965, there is the evidence of the lecture itself. Answering questions afterwards Stirling said that architects were 'cynical about the society which they have got', and that the intense idealism of modernists in the 1920s and 1930s was replaced by disillusionment: 'in the West we have the affluent society, and in the East communism.'[3] Our little sortie has led to the edge of an abyss. So much seems suddenly to be at stake; we cannot settle before we are blown by one blast of ideology or another.

Nevertheless, some historical sense of the peculiar conjunction of conditions and people at the Liverpool School of Architecture and in the city itself must be attempted. The bare bones of Stirling's own background can be sketched from Mark Girouard's vivid biography.[4] Stirling was born in Glasgow where his parents were staying with relatives in that city in 1924. (Even this year of birth, finally established by Girouard, was changed by Stirling to help with his early career.) His often-absent father was a Scottish ship's engineer with the Blue Funnel Line and his mother an Irish-Scots teacher. The family lived in the middle-class suburbs of Liverpool, settling in one of the many inter-war semi-detached houses, and Stirling went to the local secondary school where he did well in art and handicrafts but little else. In his spare time he was a keen bird watcher, travelling out from the city and filling notebooks with his observations. He attended the Liverpool School of Art from October 1941 and, because the idea of 'doing something practical' appealed to him,[5] combined this with working as an office boy for an architect in Liverpool. But any ambitions in this direction were delayed when Stirling enlisted in the army in November 1942. The location of his training camps enabled him to become familiar with buildings by Charles Rennie Mackintosh in Glasgow and with Hardwick Hall in Derbyshire, but the experiences were probably more important in retrospect than at the time. It was apparently during a period of convalescence from war wounds, fortuitously in the Robert Adam-designed Harewood House near Leeds, that he finally decided to become an architect and, with the assurance of an ex-serviceman's grant and the encouragement of a friend who already studied there, he was accepted onto the second year at the Liverpool School of Architecture. In the interim before starting his course he acquired the volume of Le Corbusier's *Oeuvre complète* that covered the years 1929–34.[6]

What kind of architecture school was Liverpool immediately after the war? To some extent it rested on the achievements and eminence it had achieved earlier in the century under Charles Reilly. It was Reilly who had established Liverpool as the leading Beaux-Arts school in Britain and the leading architectural school in the British Empire. He modelled its curriculum on a combination of French pedagogy and theory and the organisation and jury-system of the American schools, throwing in strong links with American practices as well so that students could gain experience in the USA. Students learnt their discipline incrementally. In design the emphasis was on developing the main forms of the plan quickly through an *esquisse* and then elaborating it at length through vast drawings laying out designs according to controlled vistas and axes. Liverpool's graduates took over key positions throughout the architectural establishment: they became heads of schools, chief architects in ministries and local councils, and planners and architects for large tracts of the empire. But Reilly had retired in 1933 and although the momentum he had created continued up until the Second World War, with its failure to attract leading modernists to settle in the school in the 1930s and the emergence of the Architectural Association as a cutting-edge centre for modernist work, by the late 1930s Liverpool's pre-eminence was already draining away.[7]

Like most architecture schools Liverpool emerged from the war rather slowly, its outlook more insular than previously. It was still regarded as a leading school, but most of its staff were relatively old and had missed out on the kind of wartime developments in planning and technology that were beginning to galvanise the British architectural scene. The school's head was L. B. Budden, by most accounts a liberal, likeable man who practised a moderate form of neo-Georgianism. But Budden had no great vision for his subject and was without the charisma of his mentor, Reilly. Other staff included F. X. Velarde and Bernard Miller – 'both wore waistcoats and did churches in a roughly Gothic style, high Catholic. Nobody thought of imitating them.'[8] There was also Giles Gilbert Scott, nationally famous for his designs for the nearby Liverpool Anglican Cathedral, a commission won in 1903 but by 1945 still far from complete. Anyway, as Reader in Ecclesiastical Architecture, Scott did not play a central role in the teaching. Among the less prominent staff were Herbert Thearle, a follower of Erich Mendelsohn and an advocate of a more acceptably urbane modernism. But the most dynamic area of the school, connected directly with ambitious thinking in London, was undoubtedly the Department for Civic Design led by William Holford and initially funded by Lord Leverhulme to promote American 'City Beautiful' town planning. Unlike his colleagues, Holford had played an important role in the wartime years, when he was instrumental in setting up the Ministry of Town and Country Planning. Although he retained a strong loyalty to Liverpool, it is unlikely that Holford with all his national responsibilities was physically often present in the school.[9] Besides which, it is doubtful that Stirling had much if any contact with Civic Design's staff and students, who were very much a postgraduate enclave at Liverpool. It is notable also, as we will see in the next chapter, that when he chose to enrol in a postgraduate course it was that run by the Association for Planning and Regional Reconstruction in London, not Civic Design at Liverpool. Another lecturer worth mentioning is W. A. Eden who largely taught in

Civic Design but was also active in the architecture curriculum. Eden maintained the school's reputation for vernacular architecture, taking groups of students on trips to English villages to make measured drawings.[10]

So Liverpool was in transition, its liberal and eclectic outlook still held together by the Beaux-Arts system, but with a vacuum in terms of leadership. In some aspects this mirrored a wider state of affairs. The universities in the immediate post-war years were changing in ways that often outstripped their own ability to deliver reform. For one thing, they became brim-full of students after wartime lows (Stirling's cohort was more than twice the size of previous years),[11] and many of these students had their life experience accelerated by the war and were older and sometimes less well qualified (as in Stirling's case) than their pre-war equivalents. There were also more female students in traditionally male-dominated subjects like architecture. Although delayed, the expansion of numbers and the wastage caused by the war meant an opening up of opportunities to teach in universities, architectural schools perhaps especially. Finally, although many students were pragmatic, there was also a new spirit of idealism about architecture that was part of a desire to rebuild Britain better than it had been before. So perhaps there was a sense of 'ferment' rather than 'furious debate',[12] a sense that change was inevitable and, if delayed too long, might burst its confines.

One factor that accelerated the confidence of Liverpool's aspirant modernists was the residence of the Polish School of Architecture at Liverpool between 1942 and 1946. This extraordinary situation, a school within a school, was brought about by the collapse of Poland under the twin Nazi and Soviet onslaught in 1939. The remnants of the Polish government and Polish army units that managed to survive and escape the country had re-formed in Britain. This included the faculty of the Polish School of Architecture, who were given a home at Liverpool in 1942 specifically to train their compatriots in the skills necessary for the post-war reconstruction of Poland.[13] The work of the Polish staff and students was more assertive in manner and clearer in its objectives than that of their more numerous Liverpool peers (fig. 2). According to one contemporary, 'the Poles were split, half doing Corb, the others doing a sort of neo-Baroque . . . but both factions drew beautifully.'[14] While Budden

2   Czeslaw Sztajer, Iron Foundry, 1945, elevation.

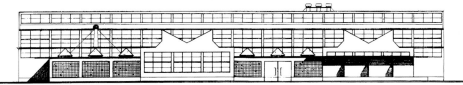

admired their feeling for the monumental, Holford appreciated their confidence and stylishness in taking the lessons of Le Corbusier and other modernists and applying them to historic environments.[15] Although the Poles moved out early in Stirling's time at Liverpool, their influence continued. But despite their mention by all the commentaries on Liverpool at this time, it is difficult to estimate just how much of an influence they had on Stirling specifically rather than on the school in general. They offered an alternative point of authority,[16] and a boost to those wanting to be 'modern modernists',[17] even if some came to feel the Poles oversimplified complicated problems.[18] More specifically, an important part of the Polish students' work was the design of industrial buildings, a subject rarely tackled by Liverpool students. Many of these are reproduced in *The Polish School of Architecture 1942–1945* (1945), which Stirling owned.[19]

In its general lines, if not its content, Liverpool's curriculum when Stirling started there in 1946 was not unlike its curriculum thirty years before. The *Prospectus* laid out what Stirling might expect: 'The study of design, beginning with exercises of an elementary order, is finally carried to a stage at which it involves the solution of large and complex problems'; 'from the third year onwards students are required to develop carefully studied schemes with the detailed and working drawings necessary for a contract'; 'stress is laid on logical planning as the basis for good architecture and a large proportion of the subjects set in the school studios are planning problems.'[20] To do these things meant time spent in the studio, and this rose from slightly less than half of all the students' time in the first three years, to nearly two-thirds of their time in the fourth year, rising to five-sixths of it (twenty-five out of thirty component units) by the fifth year.[21] The studio was thus central to the curriculum while almost everything else – construction, history, theory, structures, services – was delivered by lectures. These were, however, rarely as integrated or parallel with the studio as the prospectuses promised. The prospectuses, which often provide the only record of what architectural schools taught, are filled with lists of courses and indications of reading. But what mattered most to the experience of learning architecture were the hours spent in the studio, usually under the direction of younger or less senior staff. The degree at Liverpool was essentially a species of officer training. Students would leave not with any substantial knowledge of how to build anything, but instead with the artistic skills of design and presentation and the executive skills in communication (which would include history and theory) to serve high up in the ranks of the construction industry. Further years spent in postgraduate study and as assistants in offices were necessary before they could see anything through to the construction site.

History and theory were interrelated but separately taught parts of the curriculum. History was taught over the first four years and attempted to cover everything from the Egyptians to Le Corbusier, favouring continuities rather than depth of analysis. There was a point to this that connected with the studio; history, or at least certain parts of it, was still understood to provide precedents for good design. Theory was also only taught over the first four years and had a strongly Beaux-Arts flavour, with the definition of 'primary and secondary elements' early on followed by all the main components of composition: programme, *parti* (that is, the broad conception of the whole building), symmetry, axes, proportion, style and so on. The key text here was Julien Gaudet's *Eléments et Théorie de l'Architecture* (1904), recommended to students throughout their first three years. This was supplemented by Atkinson and Bagenal's *Theory and Elements of Architecture* (1926) and Howard Robertson's *Principles of Architectural Composition* (1924), both essentially distillations of Gaudet's text if updated and with some examples from what was becoming a canon of modern buildings. Only in their fourth year, after the apparently rigorous framework and mindset of the Beaux-Arts had been inculcated, were students guided to such writers as Ruskin and Morris as well as Le Corbusier (*Towards a New Architecture*, 1927) and Gropius (*The New Architecture and the Bauhaus*, 1936), the reading held together, presumably, by the recommendation of Pevsner's *Pioneers of the Modern Movement* (1936).[22] Whether this non-Beaux-Arts theory was regarded as antagonistic towards it (which was the intention of these authors) or whether it could be encompassed within its eclectic broad church (as Reilly and others believed in the 1930s) probably depended on the individual student and lecturer, and might even change from year to year. But Gaudet's ideas were still meant to be paramount, just as they were in most architectural schools of the English- and French-speaking world. They are best described by the architectural thinker who came into most pointed contact with their legacy at Liverpool, Colin Rowe.

The theory's success was based on its combination of doctrinal clarity and eclectic allowance; there were rules, but there was flexibility in the style that could be applied to them. As Rowe summarises, Gaudet claimed that his approach was founded on the underlying elements on which all good architecture was based. He privileged function, structure and composition, seeing these as 'the embodiment of continuously present, underlying and rational principles'.[23] For Gaudet it was the plan above all that was the generator of architectural design. The plan was the primary focus for composition, its ideal form was a 'concentric one, implying generally a grouping of elements about a central space or void'.[24] These 'elements' are, then, the basic units of architecture, assembled to enable function and meaning.[25] Beyond these principles Gaudet's allowance for eclecticism – for style as a kind of afterthought – was intended to enable the universality of his theory: in Rowe's gloss, 'at all times and in all places, the architect's motivation is purely rational and formal' because it was able to draw from 'all centuries and all countries . . . a reservoir of possible motifs of composition . . . to discover in all periods the presence of a common denominator which is conceived as transcending style'.[26] Thus, style was actually treated as an irrelevance, 'purely a matter of taste and personal bias'.[27] This helps explain the evolution Liverpool went through under Reilly so that by the 1930s its students were turning out various versions of modernism accommodated within the irrefutable rules of Gaudet's theory. Nevertheless, Rowe argued, these eternal compositional principles were nothing more than 'an *a posteriori* academic formula' radically unlike the ideas that had generated form in such modernist movements as cubism, constructivism and De Stijl.[28]

In 1946 Stirling would not have understood these theoretical accommodations. Instead he, like other reasonably idealistic ex-servicemen, was mildly baffled by what he was expected to do: 'Renderings were executed on stretched Whatman paper, flood-washes were used and graded shadows were normal';[29] 'we did renderings of classical orders followed by the design of an antique fountain and at the end of that year we had to design a house in the manner of C. A. Voysey.'[30] Unfortunately, nothing survives from Stirling's first year at Liverpool (the second year in terms of curriculum) so we have no sense of what any non-modernist work by him might have looked like. Second-year design projects that year included a fishing lodge, a poster for the *Britain Can Make It* exhibition (then showing at the Victoria and Albert Museum), a beach pavilion in Barbados, a branch bank (to replace a Liverpool bank destroyed in the war), a pub in a satellite town, a golf clubhouse and a village social club.[31] Each was given out with basic instructions, a sketch design was produced the same day and then a more developed design made within a two-week period. Apart from the gradually growing scale of these projects, what is interesting about them, as well as Stirling's memory of what he learnt, is their parochial and almost entirely pre-war concerns. There was no urgency here about getting students to address early in their course the new problems of reconstruction, for instance, or the emergence of modern building types or new technologies of prefabrication. Yet although these subjects and Stirling's memories of his early years at Liverpool seem to bear out his contention that 'to succeed, one had to be good in many styles',[32] the evidence of Stirling's projects, at least from this moment on, is rather different.

Third-year projects in 1947 to 1948 were a deliberate test of students' versatility. They included a pier, a terminal station for a mountain railway, a memorial loggia and various tourist buildings. There were also projects for several mid-size projects: a nursery school, a fashion house and a furniture museum.[33] The first surviving design by Stirling, a nursery school, was particularly approved by his tutors (fig. 3).[34] It established the main units of the school in three different volumes, suggesting in

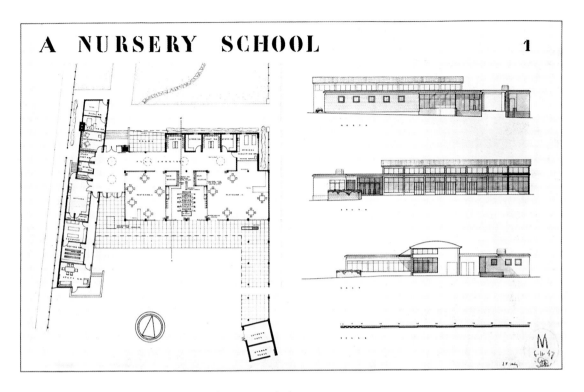

3   James Stirling, Nursery School, 1947, elevations and plan.

its rigour of planning and lightness of mass that Stirling had seen reproductions of some of the early Hertfordshire schools, then forging new methods of construction.[35] Playrooms were located in the largest volume, a high clerestoried block with a curved roof and doors opening directly onto a canopied play area. A lower slab to the north housed a 'play corridor' and various amenity rooms, while a third, longer block, canted to line a road to the east, accommodated offices and utility rooms. The entrance was placed between the canted block and the other two blocks and ran through a foyer to a garden on the north side. The various components of the school were cleverly locked together; modest exteriors were perked up on the entrance court with the classical proportions of the playroom block. The design resourcefully provided different kinds of spaces and ways of relating interior and exterior without losing a sense of discipline.

The fashion house was an immediately attractive design, aiming for an elegance and lightness of effect (fig. 4).[36] The accommodation was arranged in an L-shaped plan on a corner site, with a 'mannequin parade ground' taking over the courtyard.

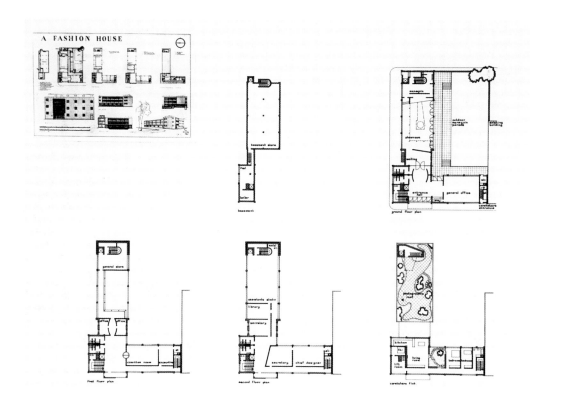

4   James Stirling, Fashion House, 1947, plans, elevations and perspective.

Skittish devices enlivened the plan, like a playfully laid-out 'photographer's roof' (an outdoor studio) and an oval passage between offices on the first floor. The latter, surely cribbed from the elliptical space on the second floor of Le Corbusier's Villa Stein/de Monzie, is the first of many Corbusian borrowings to come. But the fashion house's façades were restless, losing any metropolitan suavity in sudden transitions between different wall treatments, over-emphatic attempts to portray minor differences of function within the building.[37]

The furniture museum had a simpler *parti* and was the least liked of these designs by Stirling's tutors (fig. 5).[38] Two contrasting slabs were set at right angles, one seemingly sliding under the other, with an entrance at their inner angle. The architectural language here now seems more obviously an attempt to reconcile certain aspects of Mies van der Rohe and Le Corbusier. One slab housed the main galleries on a first floor which was lifted on *piloti* above a recessed ground floor containing library and office spaces; the other was a lower block housing a lecture theatre and framing a

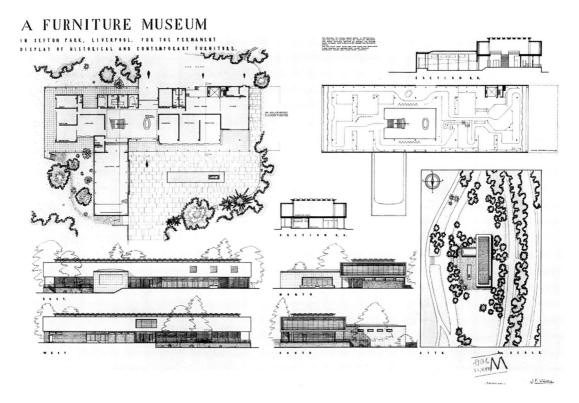

5   James Stirling, Furniture Museum, 1947, plans, elevations and sections.

courtyard with a pool and sculpture. The stairs emerging into the middle of the upper floor allowed a number of temporary gallery shapes to be suggested in the big rectangular space, including even an octagon. The gallery was lit by an attic clerestory as well as by entirely glazed walls at either end, freeing the long east wall so that a window could be placed to emphasize the entrance below, even if a little weakly for Beaux-Arts tastes.

All three of these designs are attempts, not uncommon at the time, to bring together abstracted elements of classical architecture, the clarity of Beaux-Arts planning, and newly informal and less overtly hierarchical relationships between the various components of a building. An inkling of something distinct may be discerned in a taste for playing up these contrasts, not allowing elements to become too blended or repetitive and, as is most apparent in the window forms, delighting in a widening repertoire. Yet, for all that, these are recognisably deviations and contrasts within a contemporary manner.

As laid down by the school, the period from the summer before the fourth year to the end of the first term of that year was spent gaining experience overseas. This was one of the most influential of Reilly's innovations, not only for the chance it gave Liverpool students to travel and experience different architectural cultures but also for the sense that it promoted of the world as the students' oyster. Students went to Canada, South Africa, Sweden, Finland and Switzerland,[39] but usually the largest number, like Stirling, went to the USA. Arriving in New York in August 1948, Stirling spent the next six months working for the firm of O'Connor and Kilham, whose principals had both been educated in American Beaux-Arts schools. Much later Stirling dismissed this work as 'hacking in a commercial office',[40] but some reassessment is due. The firm's reputation for college buildings, libraries and museums (they designed an extension for the Metropolitan Museum of Art at this time) introduced Stirling to the building types in which he would later make his name. Stirling helped with the firm's work on the Firestone Library at Princeton, underway since 1944, and specifically on the open access shelving system.[41] Whatever Stirling's actual role in this, the design and arrangement of the shelving were central to how this huge library functioned. Furthermore, with the building nearing completion, this was probably Stirling's first serious experience of visiting a building site. The library's modern interior, with the bulk of the building underground, was belied by the Firestone's neo-gothic exterior designed to match its collegiate surroundings,[42] a difference between interior and exterior that Stirling was later to exploit in his School of Architecture at Rice University in Houston (1979–81).

Outside his work Stirling used New York as a base to visit other cities. He was usually underwhelmed, or if overwhelmed unimpressed, but the language he used slipped from the joshing to the near histrionic. He found Princeton, where he worked for O'Connor and Kilham, full of 'sham, sham Oxfordian Gothic'.[43] New York itself was 'a ghastly monstrosity . . . the shadow the skyscraper casts is more significant than all beside . . . sliding, edging, nicking and crowding, tier up tier a soulless shelf, box on box beside boxes, black shadows below with artificial lights burning all day long in little caverns and squared cells, prison cubicles . . . the skyscraper, that stupendous adventure in the business of space making for rent . . . it's only the first three floors which are important . . . relentless commercial engine, architecturally the skyscraper is a nonsense.' New York's contemporary architecture seemed superficial; although it lacked the 'philosophizing and fanaticism' of European modernism, what it had instead was ephemeral style-mongering and 'constipated breath'. It was far too close to the commercial world of fashions. This sniffiness about American vulgarity was typical of its time,[44] but the excitableness of Stirling's prose shows that he was almost as much attracted as appalled.

There were architectural pluses, moreover. Stirling admired the engineering of the George Washington Bridge as well as the Art Deco of the Chrysler building.[45] Most especially he raved about a Frank Lloyd Wright house he visited for a weekend in Long Island – 'the finest building I have ever been in. . . . I have never felt such emotion before it's really beyond description, it was worth coming to America for this single experience.'[46] The only possible candidate for this house is the Rebhuhn residence, built in 1937 for husband-and-wife publishers. This is a reworking of Wright's Usonian houses, cruciform in plan with a double-height living room and low-angled roofs extending in spectacularly wide eaves. Stirling used his free time to visit other Wright houses as well as such modernist buildings in the Boston and Philadelphia areas as Alvar Aalto's newly finished Baker Dormitory at MIT, Howe and Lescaze's PSFS building in Philadelphia, and houses by Gropius and Breuer near Boston.[47]

One of the products of this stay in the USA was a design for a community centre for a small town in the Middle West, signed and dated 'J F Stirling New York 1948' (fig. 6). This picked up several of the features of the furniture museum design. Again

6   James Stirling, Community Centre for a Small Town in the Middle West, 1948, plans, elevations and section.

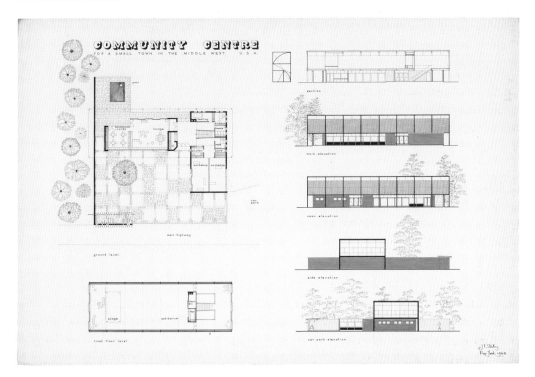

7   James Stirling, Organic Chemistry Laboratories for a Northern University,
1949, photograph of model.

the contrasts of an L-shaped plan are exploited, and again the entrance is placed at
the meeting of the two slabs, with the largest communal space on the upper floor
of the main block. The emphasis on the grid of the exposed structural frame as the
primary visual device perhaps shows Stirling less constrained by the weight of Liverpool's tradition. But the attractive paving pattern reveals a displaced interest in
decoration, and the diagram of the golden section is not the only indication of an
attempt to think through the proportions of the building. If the building is 'American' in any way, then it might be in the apparent lightness of its components and
the clarity of relation between frame and infill, both reminiscent of Mies's work at
the Illinois Institute of Technology (started in 1939).

Back in Liverpool, Stirling's progress can be measured by his fourth-year project
for organic chemistry laboratories for a northern university, dated 17 February 1949
(fig. 7). The brief has similarities with the building Stirling eventually made his name
with, the Leicester University Engineering building. Workshop laboratories and
research laboratories needed accommodation as well as offices, a library and a lecture
hall. Again the approach expressed these functions in the shapes and elevation treatments of the different volumes. One can sense here the influence of Lubetkin and
Tecton, the most prominent contemporary modernist practice in Britain, and particularly their Spa Green Estate then nearing completion in London. Like several of

A FOREST RANGERS LOOKOUT STATION

8   James Stirling, Forest Ranger's Lookout Station, 1949.

Stirling's previous schemes, the main block was lifted up on *piloti* so that other elements could seem to slide in or out, in part framing entrances or views onto paved areas and decorative elements like sculpture. The main horizontal slab of his earlier student projects was now grown to five storeys, while one-storey office slabs and a lecture theatre emerged as if from underneath it. If Stirling's tutors thought anything could be made of the 'northern university' part of the title, then Stirling does not seem to have considered it.

A short (one day) fourth-year project allowed Stirling a whimsicality that seemed banned from his laboratories. For a forest ranger's lookout station he designed a hexagonal pavilion perched on a rocky outcrop, while a fly-like helicopter with a plaid-shirted boffin-pilot at its controls buzzed above (fig. 8). As intimated in the Midwest community centre design, the lookout station shows an interest in lightweight structure; while the pavilion is linked to its site by rubblestone core and buttresses, its light upper storey is held to the ground by guy wires.

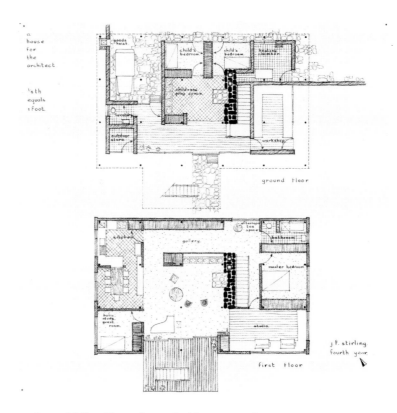

9   James Stirling, House for an Architect, 1949, plans.

Also surviving from Stirling's fourth year is a design for a house for an architect, and this was awarded one of the top marks in his cohort (fig. 9).[48] The plans are simply yet elegantly drawn with a confident placement of handwritten, lowercase captions, while the little model that Stirling made is delicately constructed out of card, cork, string, metal pins, balsa and hessian (fig. 10). The house suggests a certain bourgeois dream of open plan living spaces lightly lifted above the ground, of having every pleasure of a domestic and cultivated lifestyle organised within easy reach – carport, large kitchen/dining room, workshop and studio, gallery, hearth, grand piano, deck, pool and children. These are all neatly fitted within the box's perimeters; the upper floor is made to straddle the garden wall, and the centred entrance is made less formal by the off-centred canopy and windows above. The plan shows Stirling's developing propensity to fill every area with different textures – rubblestone, tile, wooden floorboards. He also uses primary colours to heighten certain building parts – yellow window surrounds, red doorframes, and dark blue panels. Incongru-

10   James Stirling, House for an Architect, 1949, model.

ous by contrast with the semi-detached suburban family home where Stirling was actually living at this time and certainly with austerity Britain, the House for an Architect is a form of wish-fulfilment, a fantasy world of mobility, culture and American comforts: the houses of Paul Rudolph or Marcel Breuer as filtered through *Architectural Forum* or *Arts & Architecture*.

~

The new maturity of Stirling's work in his final year at Liverpool may be due to his stay in America, but there was at least one other major factor as well. The 1949–50 *Prospectus* lists for the first time 'C. F. Rowe' as 'Lecturer and Studio Instructor'. The introduction of the magnetic intellect of Colin Rowe was to have a profound effect on Stirling and other students. Rowe was only two years older than Stirling, and as well as tutor for his final year thesis he also quickly became a friend. The two had already met in the army, and Rowe himself had completed a degree at Liverpool in 1945. In 1947, while studying for a PhD at the Warburg Institute in London, Rowe

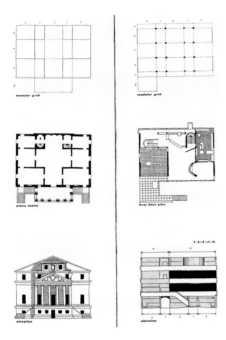

11   Colin Rowe, illustration from 'The Mathematics of the Ideal Villa: Palladio and Le Corbusier Compared', 1947.

published an essay that was to have wide impact – 'The Mathematics of the Ideal Villa: Palladio and Le Corbusier Compared'.[49] The essay was largely an exercise in close formal comparison, deriving its analytical intensity and its interest in neo-Palladian proportions from Rowe's Warburg supervisor, Rudolf Wittkower.[50] Mainly through a comparison of Palladio's Villa Malcontenta and Le Corbusier's Villa Stein/de Monzie at Garches (fig. 11), Rowe presented Le Corbusier as an inheritor of the classical tradition, in provocative contrast to his reputation as a maker of machines for living in or a purveyor of cubist form and the space-time *zeitgeist*.

Rowe's article has several important resonances with Stirling's work and his attitude to modernism, although the implications of some of these were not to emerge until much later. History was now to be an active element in understanding modernism. While Rowe saw this as a deep history ranging from 'Virgilian nostalgia' to the natural beauties of geometry and proportion shared with the classical tradition, it was also, more influentially, a history of formal procedures and resemblances based on gridded elevations and plans. This appropriation of history abstracted it from anything else that might make the past seem different – patrons, social customs, technologies. Abstracted, and therefore all the more assimilable.[51] Rowe's comparisons thus set aside any avant-garde aura surrounding Le Corbusier's work as well as any assumption that it had primarily issued from some spirit peculiar to modern times. Related to this, and here Le Corbusier's case stood for modernism more widely, was Rowe's sense of distance from modernism's high point twenty or more years before, of modernism itself as part of history and, as a consequence, of the dimming and loss of its utopian promise. Finally, the key modernist architect was not a functionalist ascetic, as many in Britain perceived him,[52] but instead 'the most ingenious of eclectics'.[53] 'With Le Corbusier', Rowe suggested, 'there is always present an element of wit, suggesting that the historical reference has remained a quotation between inverted commas, possessing always the double value of the quotation, the associations of both old and new context.'[54]

Rowe's other important article of this time was 'Mannerism and Modern Architecture', published in *Architectural Review* in 1950.[55] At the core of Rowe's understanding of mannerism was the idea of 'deliberate inversions' of the existing architectural language, motivated by 'the very human desire to impair perfection'. Mannerism was thus lightly psychoanalysed: it was both a 'state of inhibition' and 'an attitude of dissent'. Rowe starts by seizing on the 'suave' and 'ravishing' features of Le Corbusier's early house, the Villa Schwob (1916), a work left out of Le Corbusier's *Oeuvre complète*. This wilful move is matched by a contrariness Rowe finds in the building itself, especially the anomalous blank panel dominating the entrance façade (see fig. 43). Encompassing 'systematically opposite values', this panel was ravishing in the finesse of its details but also disturbed normal expectations of other elements. The panel's ambiguity, Rowe contended, paralleled the 'complexity and duality of emphasis' in late sixteenth-century mannerism.[56] Most of the rest of the article explored resemblances between the geometries of modernist and mannerist space. Thus, the Bauhaus building was found to be mannerist, Michelangelo's Capella Sforza was related to Mies van der Rohe's Brick Country House, and Vignola and Ammannati's Villa Giulia was seen to correspond to Mies's Hubbe house.

These revelations about modernism's relation to the past must have coursed through Rowe's teaching.[57] They were pedagogically inspired anyway, motivated by his fundamental criticisms of Gaudet's theory and its continuing centrality in the curriculum. As he argued a little later, because Gaudet '[is] unable to comprehend the internal individuality of particular styles, he is also unable to explain the phenomena of historical differentiation. Able by reason of his criteria to explain *appearance*, he is not able to explain the intimate and irrational preoccupations on which appearance is based. . . . Gaudet's method ends by destroying the logic of the historical process, while insisting on the value of historical precept.'[58] Rowe saw that the main challenge to Gaudet was a tradition of ethical thinking about form. This counter-tradition, running through the nineteenth and twentieth centuries and encompassing modernism, was based on 'defining forms of indisputable integrity, so that an architecture generated from such a basis is believed to possess an objective significance which is denied to forms ensuing from the mere existence of visual preferences'.[59] But Rowe dodged both the universalising logic of one tradition and the ethical drive of the other, instead restoring the idea of style that both traditions had rejected as mere character, or psychology, or decoration. By contrast, 'modern architecture is a style, as disciplined, as legitimate, and as limited as any of the great styles of the past'.[60] Rowe here drew from Immanuel Kant's philosophy of immanent critique to justify this view: 'In the last analysis, the authentic process of artistic creation is also unconsciously a critique of history, the intuitive recognition that at the moment of creation only a limited range of possibilities can claim a real legiti-macy'.[61] Style is formed 'without thought of style, but by means of a positive posi-tion with regard to history'.[62] This engagement of the present with the past explains why, for example, Rowe would often bring copies of Palladio's *Quattro Libri* and other historical sources into his teaching and expect his students to relate them to contemporary architecture: 'to infect them with mannerism,' as Robert Maxwell has since explained, 'to encourage a kind of postmodernism on the drawing board'.[63]

It has been said that Rowe's teaching encouraged cribbing as a serious activity;[64] that it bred an eclectic and, for a modernist, somewhat unconventional interest in the architecture of the past; and that it justified the pleasures of 'setting up a set of formal rules and then contradicting them'.[65] Rowe certainly encouraged Stirling to become acquainted with modern architecture by other routes than Liverpool's cur-riculum, and his earlier passions for Mackintosh and Hoffman were now replaced by the work of the Italian rationalists Giuseppe Terragni and Cesare Cattaneo.[66] Rowe also nurtured Stirling's interest in pre-modernist architects and subjects that were not part of the Beaux-Arts curriculum. One prized book was Saxl and Wittkower's *British Art and the Mediterranean* (1948), and it may be that in recommending the book Rowe was just as interested in its imaginary Britain of country houses and gardens as in how its suggestive juxtapositions of images taught the lessons of Brit-ain's own cultural relation to classical civilisation. Linked to this was Stirling's growing interest in the English baroque architecture of Hawksmoor, Vanbrugh and Archer.[67] He had already, before he encountered Rowe's teaching, criticised a modernism of 'philosophizing and fanaticism'.[68] More profoundly, students like Stirling may have wanted to emulate, or aspired to emulate in the future, what Rowe enjoyed in man-nerism: the 'dilemma of dual significance', 'deliberate architectural derangement' and 'an attitude of dissent . . . [demanding] an orthodoxy within whose framework it might be heretical'.[69]

Part of the reason for Rowe's impact, apart from his personality and intellect, was surely the lack of any firm sense of what modernism stood for at Liverpool. Deriving design ideas from certain modernists like Mendelsohn and Dudok seems to have achieved grudging acceptance in the 1930s, but the library was dubious about acquir-ing Le Corbusier's *Oeuvre complète* until quite late into the 1940s,[70] and if students experimented in too committed a manner with Le Corbusier they might risk fail-ure.[71] The situation could change from year to year, especially as younger studio staff came and went,[72] but the gradually growing confidence in addressing modernism within the school that characterised the 1930s had certainly dissipated or flickered intermittently by the 1940s. Importantly, with Holford away for much of the war and relatively marginal when he came back in the Department of Civic Design, there was no one of intellectual weight and modernist credentials among the staff who could effectively proselytise its key tenets. What students got, then, was either diluted or derived at second-hand from their own looking and reading in magazines, and much of the debate was, until the arrival of Rowe, among the students themselves.[73]

The second-hand nature of this encounter with modernism is noteworthy. Stirling later described how the volumes of Le Corbusier's *Oeuvre complète* were pored over, 'utilised as catalogues' in the manner of Renaissance treatises.[74] Another Liverpool student, Robert Maxwell, did not actually see any Le Corbusier buildings until several years after his studies,[75] and even the Poles' knowledge of Le Corbusier and other modernist work was almost entirely paper-based. Qualities of material, subtleties of light and colour, and the experience of space were unlikely to be understood by such means. Or perhaps they were to be creatively misunderstood. Stirling himself described the encounter as more intellectual than emotional,[76] and one of its off-shoots in his case seems to have been his heightened interest in the image of archi-tecture. But might modernism be understood from British examples? For Stirling this was a limited experience: 'with the exception of the buildings of Lubetkin there were few others in this country which could be visited and therefore assimilated emotionally.'[77] Limited it may have been, but the mention of Lubetkin here indicates one British modernist to whom, as already shown, Stirling certainly was attentive in his student work.

It was crucial for Rowe's own character and approach as a critic, based as they were on distancing himself from the programmatic functional, social and techno-logical agendas of modernism's pioneering first generation, that the architecture school at which he first taught had no real understanding of these agendas except at best in a woolly or piecemeal manner. For the students that were most drawn to him, therefore, what they learnt was an antithesis before they had properly taken in the thesis. If they understood Rowe properly they would be modernists, but sceptics rather than disciples. To be a modernist was the only possible state for an architect, but at the same time modernism's heroic period had already come and gone; it was itself history, second-hand. As Rowe later described his time at Liverpool, 'while an old guard still clung to anti-modern architectural propositions, while a middle guard was able to devote itself to the propagation of allegedly far out performance, there was coming to exist, embryonically, a species of vanguard, increasingly concerned with the vacuity of content which modern architecture was beginning to reveal.'[78] To fill the vacuum modernism was to be perceived, from even before the start of the vanguardist's career, not as a fundamental break with past architecture but as having deep connections with it; not as a dour vehicle of social amelioration but as an artistic and formal medium; and not as the inevitable outcome of a calculus of

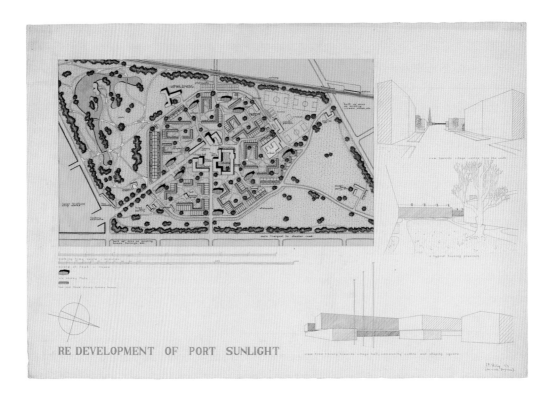

RE DEVELOPMENT OF PORT SUNLIGHT

12   James Stirling, Redevelopment of Port Sunlight, 1949, site plan and perspectives.

technology and programme but as an instrument of intellect, allusion and playful-ness. And although this anti-pedagogy might be buried under the humdrum of work and professional contingencies in large offices in the next few years, it would surely eventually come out.

∽

The culminating project of Stirling's degree was his thesis, but before this he was set several challenges he had not faced before, designed to push him and other final-year students to a larger scale of considerations. One such project was a scheme for the Redevelopment of Port Sunlight (fig. 12), a one-week programme intended to make students address the urban scale without thinking too much about the form of individual buildings. Stirling's Port Sunlight is, perhaps surprisingly given its mod-ernist language, not a place so very different from the late Victorian model village for soap industry workers that already existed. What is immediately apparent from its plan is the large variety of shapes given to its two- and three-storey terraces and its (mostly) centrally located communal buildings, by contrast to which the rhom-boid-shaped blocks of six-storey flats offer the relief of at least some regularity. The aim was clearly to give some sense of urban scale and density, but the perspectives that Stirling offered to one side of his plan scarcely dispel the impression that he had simply stuffed too many dissimilar creatures into his garden city menagerie. But perhaps this was the point: juxtaposition, proximity, lack of resolution, rather than the zoned aridity of post-war planning.

The idea of a final-year thesis was a Beaux-Arts invention that continues still today in most architecture schools. Students chose their own subject, were given instructions on what range of drawings or models might finally be presented, and then, with often minimal guidance from a tutor, were let loose to spend most of their year on the work. Other thesis topics in Stirling's year were an 'Arts Centre at Whitehaven', a 'Maritime Museum for Liverpool', a 'National Theatre, London' and a 'Hotel at Ludlow'.[79] Though culturally ambitious in their way, none of these and few of the others had the same scope of urban and social betterment that can be seen in Stirling's choice of topic and that some have seen as linked to a 'Polish' expectation about the scale of ambition for architecture.[80] In fact, one of the least noticed (or most denied) aspects of Stirling's early career – right up to the late 1960s – is the high proportion of public sector, socially conscious work that he did, despite only briefly working in a public sector office, and the thesis topic is an early sign of this inclination.

Stirling took the social and local aspects of his thesis extremely seriously. He chose as his subject Newton Aycliffe, designated in 1947 as a new town in County Durham. The town was largely to provide housing adjacent to an existing industrial estate, and the site was a stretch of gently undulating agricultural land.[81] Like the nearby Peterlee new town, Newton Aycliffe was an essential part of government attempts to reverse the pattern of industrial decline in the area. Stirling visited the site and took photographs of it as well as drawing two landscapes in neo-romantic mode, owing something in their spiky, graphic qualities and a centralised rock motif to the contemporary paintings of Graham Sutherland (fig. 13). These drawings might have helped Stirling reflect on the nature of the local stone and the shapes of the landscape, something that W. A. Eden at Liverpool had strongly encouraged.[82] Stirling copied out careful notes on local construction from one of his sources: observations, for instance, on the local pitched roofs 'finished with two courses of slate or split stone slabs at the eaves. . . . there is often a small cornice or at least a projecting brick course below the gutter; overhanging eaves are not generally used.'[83] He also visited two of the already canonic buildings of British 1930s modernism,

13   James Stirling, Aycliffe Landscape, 1949.

Gropius and Fry's Impington Village College in Cambridge and Owen Williams's Peckham Health Centre in London, and he claimed to have visited Le Corbusier's Pavillon Suisse in Paris and his *Unité d'habitation* in Marseille, the latter then still unfinished.[84] He read government reports on redevelopment, Thomas Sharp's writings on town planning and Ernö Goldfinger's summary version of *The County of London Plan*, as well as various contemporary texts on urbanism by Le Corbusier, José Luis Sert, Eliel Saarinen and Siegfried Giedion.[85] He was clearly exercised by the issue of how to realise or represent community, his bibliography containing four books on the subject including Walter Gropius's *Living in Communities*. But most of all, Stirling drew extensively from the report prepared for the Aycliffe Development Corporation by the Grenfell Baines Group, with whom he had met, which laid out a master plan for the town but left the town centre itself as a blank rectangle. It was this empty space that Stirling's thesis was designed to fill, though he was guided by the principles for its development laid out by the Baines report. These are very much the principles that had quickly come to seem common sense to planners in the wake of the plan for Coventry and its post-war rebuilding. There

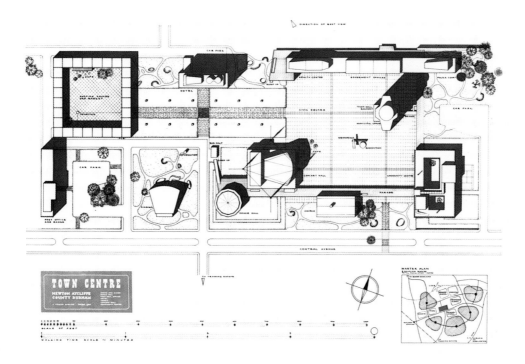

14   James Stirling, Newton Aycliffe Town Centre, 1950, site plan.

was to be a central pedestrianised area, development would occur outwards and upwards, intimate shopping precincts would contrast with a dignified civic square, and the scheme would predominantly be populated with contemporary architecture, though not to the absolute exclusion of 'revivalist designs for special purposes assuming their standard was high enough'.[86]

Stirling was anxious to cater for some kind of popular culture in his scheme, and by this he envisaged more a folk culture than a mass culture. 'There is in English social life', he quoted from the Baines report, 'a tradition of public assembly, procession and pageantry which survives with some strength in the politically conscious north-east region.'[87] Accordingly, he envisaged the town centre as a stage enabling the culmination of processions in spectacles or meetings that could be of a religious or civic nature (fig. 14). There would be a building to house such meetings as well as spaces for outdoor concerts; speeches, plays and pageants would be planned. In a preliminary scheme a parade area was shown in the form of a paved rectangle with a space for pageantry in an open court.[88] If this was the scheme's 'social function', there were also administrative, educational and shopping functions to provide for as well.

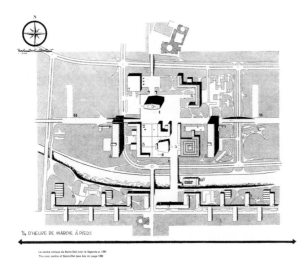

15   Le Corbusier, Saint-Dié Civic Centre, 1945,
site plan.

Stirling catered for all of these and more in an urbanistically ambitious scheme. Isolated, individually shaped buildings were linked across a somewhat austere precinct by teasing off-centre axes and asymmetries, grids partial and suggested. While the plan developed from several detailed studies of what Stirling called circulation 'forces',[89] it also bore the evident stamp of Le Corbusier's more recent planning schemes, such as the civic centre of the 1945 scheme for rebuilding Saint-Dié (fig. 15). The town centre combined discipline and informality where before, in the Port Sunlight design, there had only been informal disorder. Perhaps with the example of Le Corbusier's meditations on the Acropolis in mind,[90] Stirling set this approach in opposition to the layout of Renaissance and Georgian cities: 'each structure should have its own setting and . . . each should be capable of being viewed as a whole in itself – though of course each building would have a definite space relationship with the rest. . . . each building will have its own fundamental shape (ie cube, cylinder, wedge etc).'[91] Stirling followed this to the letter. There was a wedge-shaped cinema, a circular dance hall, a square terrace of shops, a rectangular auditorium (hung from 'compression-mast' pylons),[92] a cruciform tower for municipal offices, and so on, many of them based on similarly shaped buildings in the Saint-Dié scheme. The outer buildings were simpler and more rectilinear in shape, framing the centre but having some of their severity reduced by softer landscaping around them. The whole town centre was positioned alongside a dual carriageway, and Stirling took a road feeding into this as the link into his complex.

The key building here, and the one that Stirling worked up in detail, was the community centre (fig. 16). Again the Baines report provided the roster of necessary functions, and after researching other centres Stirling planned his own to contain a multi-functional hall, restaurant, library, art gallery, museum, lecture theatre and classrooms. It was, therefore, in its programme a combination of those two great pre-war modernist buildings, both of which Stirling had visited: the Impington Village College and the Peckham Health Centre. But the result was physically and visually very different: a multifunctional slab block with entrances from several

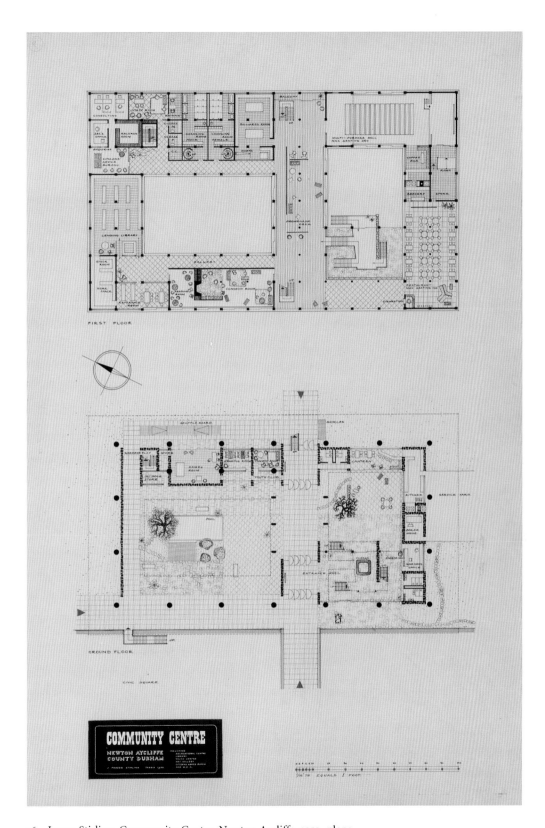

16   James Stirling, Community Centre, Newton Aycliffe, 1950, plans.

directions and containing two courtyards of contrasting character. It used two different structural systems: a monolithic frame held up by tapering piers with cantilevered first and second floors, and a system of weight-bearing walls for the ground floor. Many rooms were intended to be flexible through subdivision; there were promenade decks on the first floor, and the roof – which connected with a gymnasium – was intended for recreational purposes including, somewhat optimistically, sunbathing. In his design Stirling aimed for both a sense of permeability with the surrounding civic spaces and buildings, and what he called a domestic character: 'while sacrificing the external appearance of the building to harmonise with its neighbours, the interior, with its intimate courtyards, smallness of scale and brightly coloured finishes, has, I think, this essentially domestic character.'[93] The colour scheme internally included dark red, lemon yellow and dark green, as well as orange/brown and purple. One aspect of the centre that was clearly important to Stirling was the treatment of flooring and paved surfaces that, in their variety, might be seen as a microcosm of the mixed materials across the town centre. Stirling specified 'reconstructed stone slabs on hardcore', a pool with 'cobbles bedded to Portland cement' and paving of 'selected random rubble open jointed on hardcore'.[94] These, together with the 'battered wall of coursed rubble' connecting the ground-floor youth hostel with the square, as well as the trees and boulders marked in the courtyard landscaping, all show Stirling conceiving of his ground-level materials contextually in relation to the landscape studies he had made as well as in strong textural contrast to the materials higher up on his building. The range of textures and colours here may have been learnt from some of Lubetkin's schemes, but they bear witness to an entirely independent attempt to give a sense of layered, archaeological denseness.

It is the elevations of the community centre that have been most often reproduced but without usually attracting detailed comment (fig. 17). Stirling gave them a jaunty, regatta-like air, and figures even wave from parts of the building as if from a departing ship. On the ground floor the rubble walls were given portholes and the roof kitted with slender chimney flues suggesting masts, each marked with green weather vanes (a similar device would later feature prominently in the Florey building in Oxford) and held by guy wires. Where Le Corbusier in his *Unité d'habitation* had presented such elements as part of an abstract landscape of forms, Stirling treated the flues as rooftop tackle, unmistakeably part of the building's service equipment. Particularly revealing is the relation between the elevations of the thesis and those of the southern block of Le Corbusier's Pavillon Suisse (fig. 18). As shown in the *Oeuvre complète*, the pavillon's elevation is far more severe than it was in the original building. The massive curved supports seem thinner, and the contrasts in the eleva-

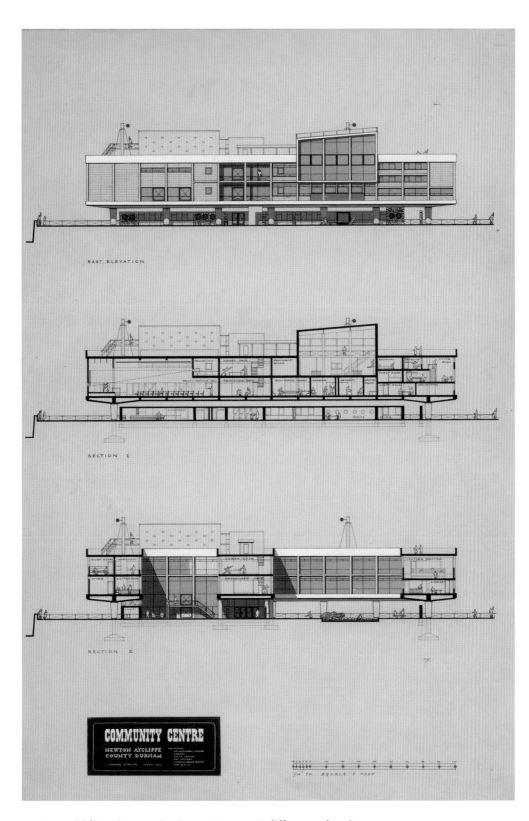

EAST ELEVATION

SECTION 1

SECTION 2

COMMUNITY CENTRE
NEWTON AYCLIFFE
COUNTY DURHAM

1/16" TH EQUALS 1 FOOT

17   James Stirling, Community Centre, Newton Aycliffe, 1950, elevations.

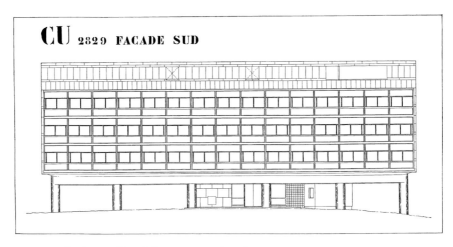

18   Le Corbusier, Pavillon Suisse, 1930–33, elevation.

tion above are largely bleached out of the line drawing. Instead, it is the tripartite division of the façade that strikes one, with the regular grid of the student rooms clearly dominant over the other two elements. By comparison Stirling's elevations, while retaining the primary ordering device of Le Corbusier's, are more fidgety, a combination of the patterned façade compositions he would have seen in Lubetkin's work and the sense of layered grids in Terragni's.[95] It is as if the energy of community activities housed inside the building must find its equivalent on the outside.[96] Partly this is a result of the variety of window types seen also in other student projects by Stirling; partly it derives from the tapering piers and the angling of the frame they support on the outer bays of the building by contrast with Le Corbusier's more soberly rectilinear frame. Partly, too, this comes from a desire to suggest internal volumes through insets and projections on the outside, sometimes marking them in different colours, and sometimes even making them visible through the outer walls; thus, for instance, the sloping floor of the auditorium in one drawing is made to appear as if plainly visible on the north elevation.[97] Again this last is a device that would be taken up by Stirling three years later in the competition design for Sheffield University. Finally, the elevations make clear that the centre's relation to the rest of the plaza would be mediated by the sizeable plinth on which it stands, like a ship moored at dock, another association that was to take on great importance in later buildings. These points were amplified in the witty perspectives of the scheme that Stirling asked Robert Maxwell to do. Then taking his Diploma in Civic Design, Maxwell was a Rowe acolyte who became Stirling's friend and, later, an important critical advocate of his work in Britain and the USA.

Le Corbusier's work was substantially appropriated in Stirling's Newton Aycliffe. Stirling's confidence in handling the Swiss master's material was surely closely aided and abetted by Rowe, but it was also modified by his own experience of modernism in the USA and Britain. From the Saint-Dié scheme Stirling tried to apply the idea that the centre itself should be a place of repose with no strong movement in any one direction.[98] Unlike Saint-Dié, Newton Aycliffe was not a town devastated by warfare, and there was no need to relate new buildings to surviving ones. The Newton Aycliffe scheme did not include housing, so there was no chance for Stirling to show if he approved of the multi-storey housing blocks – the *Unités* – planned for Saint-Dié. But the main building, the community centre, was laid out using elements of a *plan libre*, and its roofscape displayed the sculptural forms demanded of any *Unité* (a *Unité de culture* in this case). Unlike his peers, Stirling had the confidence to treat the *Unité* or the Pavillon Suisse as either formal solutions or embodiments of community, but he also adapted their forms inspired by details from the work of Breuer, Mies and the Eameses.[99] As for the *plan libre*, again Stirling was distinctly undutiful towards his source. He later wrote of how in his community centre 'rooms and circulation were intermixed and no doubt compromised each other functionally, which is always the case with a *plan libre*.'[100] Yet this was a free plan merely in its components; free-standing *piloti* only suggested the flow of space, because wherever a specific function was required it was given its own room.

There was, finally, another area of Corbusian influence. 'Circulation is excessive', Stirling wrote, 'and varied types of accommodation are fitted into a rectangle; "compressed" is a more operative word, describing the forcing of volumes as different as restaurants, assembly hall, libraries, offices, into a constricting box.'[101] But this constricting box could also be seen as a dematerialised cube. As described by Rowe, modernism relished 'the prismatic quality of the cube; and at that same time [was] an attack on the cube, which by disrupting the coherence of its internal volume, intensifies our appreciation of both its planar and its geometrical qualities'.[102] Stirling's community centre was thus firmly in that modernist tradition of using the basic datum of a building-container as the starting point for a series of exercises, exploiting a structure based on Le Corbusier's Dom-ino system to clothe the building in different materials, fit glass walls, extend internal spaces outwards through balconies or open up walls entirely to the air, and to work similar operations on the ground floor and roof.

The thesis shows Stirling displaying his aptitudes in several different directions, but even in the role of a thesis, a culminating project of the largest scale in a student's course, Stirling's work was remarkably ambitious. He gave himself a town planning problem, a problem in the characterisation of civic institutions, and a problem in the detailed realisation of a multifunctional community centre. Already there is a love of layered references to other modernists, as well as a delight in variety – of shape, materials, colour – that pushes beyond programmatic justification. What the thesis does not show, and this despite the dutiful nods in its text towards local building forms, is any strong sense that the town centre was conceived as having some inevitable relation to the north-east. The precinct is essentially a way of establishing correspondences and distinctions which are to do with the internal relationships between institutions of the town centre as well as, overreaching the locality, relationships with a larger world of modern town-making. Unlike Lubetkin in his work on the new town of Peterlee, then being planned for a site not far from Newton Aycliffe, Stirling was uninterested in fathoming the interests and dispositions of his potential users or in representing them in a way that took seriously their relationship to the local topography.[103] The idea of the 'pageant' was only a weak nod in this direction.

Stirling graduated with a Diploma in Architecture in July 1950. His course had been of the same length and content as those who graduated with a degree, but only a Diploma could be given to those who had not entered with the right level of qualifications.[104] Overall, in the university's own terms, Stirling was a good if not outstanding student. His marks show that he was in the lower half of a cohort of just over a hundred students for much of his time at Liverpool. The fourth year was particularly weak with Stirling struggling in his studio work and in a course on reinforced concrete, which he failed twice.[105] But in his final year he turned this round, perhaps because there was more design and less lecturing, perhaps because like many bright students it was only then that the combination of finding like-minded peers and the pressure to complete pulled the best out of him. In his final exams he came in fifteenth in his cohort, and for the thesis itself only seven students did better.[106]

In the summer following graduation Stirling entered a competition for the Honan Scholarship, run by the Liverpool Architectural Society, with a design for a Merseyside Film Institute (fig. 19). Here an office block over the entrance foyer was played off against the lower body of the film institute stretching back across the site, and there is a hint of a 1920s cinema about the stepped frontage to the side road. The scheme is treated as a tight-knit group of different buildings related by two axes across the site, suggestive of the collage-like urban schemes that Stirling would develop twenty years later. The most interesting aspect of this project was the treatment of the main façade as dominated by the steel exoskeleton of the building, so that the largely glazed office elevation was articulated by a screen of seven steel

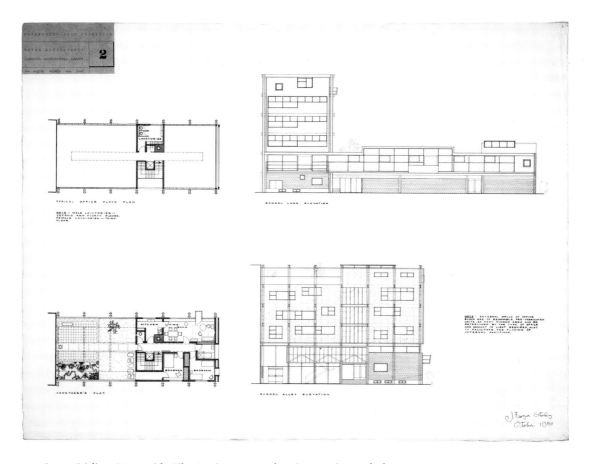

19   James Stirling, Merseyside Film Institute, 1950, elevation, section and plans.

columns, each apparently made of pairs of girders. The contrast with the thesis project is startling, revealing an entirely different architectural approach. Stirling had argued in the same year against placing vertically aligned buildings on piers: 'To put a box on edge (that is with greater height than breadth) on stilts is to contradict its verticality, this form should plunge into the ground like a spear.'[107] The extruded structure of the Honan entry avoided this problem and also enabled hangar-like interiors: not so much free plans as the universal spaces of Mies van der Rohe. But perhaps the interest in how walls in tight urban frontages could be opened up to light owed less to Mies than to Liverpool's own history of warehouse and office design, and particularly to the daring façade treatments of the Victorian architect Peter Ellis. In Ellis's work, as we will see, iron piers were sometimes positioned just behind the largely fenestrated façade. In several other Liverpool examples, of which

20   Office building on the corner of Tempest Hey
and Quakers Alley, Liverpool, c.1855.
Photograph c.1950 by James Stirling.

Stirling was certainly aware (fig. 20), partially extruded piers running the whole height of the building were used to create as much window space as possible on the façades.

~

Liverpool was, of course, far more than just the architectural school, and this chapter cannot finish without estimating the city's impact on Stirling. There is little doubt that the city itself had a big part in his architectural education, if more through personal initiative and fascination than formally.[108] He had grown up in the middle-class suburbs, three miles from the city centre, and the city's docks and warehouses must have seemed both part of his birthright yet also 'magical places . . . extremely exotic . . . huge objects that slithered around'.[109] The most obvious monuments to Liverpool's global significance, in the 1930s the docks that extended twenty miles along the river Mersey were busy and exciting places redolent still of the sense that Liverpool was particularly tied by trade and location to New York: Stirling called it '[the] most American city in Eng[land]'.[110] The feeling was underlined by the American-style offices and banks, mini-skyscrapers, that clustered on the Pier Head and in central Liverpool.[111] Yet there was also ample evidence of the city's poverty in the decline and overcrowding of its inner-city Georgian terraces, the 'dockline of slums', as Charles Reilly called it.[112] Furthermore the inter-war years saw significant changes to Liverpool's economy, and these were deepened by the recession when many shipping firms moved their headquarters to London. Competition from other countries' shipping increased, the Lancashire textile industry declined, and other British ports expanded their share of passengers and trade.[113] Liverpool suffered ninety bombing raids between 1940 and 1942, most intensively in May 1941.[114] The docks were extensively damaged, and major buildings like the Customs House, which lost its cupola and was eventually demolished, stood in a wrecked state for several years after the war ended. Here were the intimations of a post-industrial state of things. But despite the evident tragedy of such scenes, economic decline was not steady from this time onwards. Indeed, after recovery from wartime damage, Liverpool's trade returned to its earlier levels; the real decline did not set in until the late 1960s.[115]

Colin Rowe, much later, described some of the effects of the city in his own encomium to Stirling's architecture. It was 'grim but grand. It was dour, squalid, improbably Piranesian and, characteristically, it was equipped with an apparently endless series of smokily stratified sunsets (light filtered through alternating layers of humidity and dirt) which served, occasionally, to contribute to a highly poignant magnificence.' Having broadly brushed this scene, Rowe then picked out a few highlights of Liverpool's architecture – St George's Hall, the Customs House, the Cotton Exchange, the two cathedrals. His account was calculated to evoke the conditions from which Stirling emerged, and its leading adjectives may suggest a portrait of him as much as of the city – 'abrasive . . . showy . . . largeness . . . brash . . . self-confident.'[116] Rowe pointed to the dramatic Cyclopean architecture of the Liverpool docks – the Liverpool of granite setts, sheer red brick walls and cast iron columns – as an architecture which would induce either fastidious academicism in response to it or, surely with Stirling in mind, a 'highly experimental open-mindedness'.[117] Oddly, the tradition of inventive office buildings that attracted Stirling's strong interest was hardly mentioned by Rowe.

Stirling continued to cherish the architecture of Liverpool long after he had moved to London in 1950. His journal from the mid-1950s shows him noting the titles of books about the city, jotting down some of its architectural features, relating his observations to major developments in nineteenth-century American architecture, and trying to make Liverpool take its place in Henry-Russell Hitchcock's and Siegfried Giedion's accounts of modernism's pre-history.[118] Liverpool, as recollected in London, is a site of scholarly interest and conservationist regret for the wartime and post-war destruction of architectural heritage.[119] There is also nostalgia for the loss of architectural possibilities: 'The attitude and noble approach of the style, united with the railway and dock achievements, ie the Lime Street cuttings, denote a sweep and vigour of approach which today we show not the slightest sign of recapturing.'[120] What we find in Stirling's attitude to Liverpool is, then, a post-industrial understanding of the city, a sense of separation from its great industrial past that often relates directly to a sense of separation from the high point of modernist achievement. There would be at least two important effects of these feelings of separation: one is manifest in flashes of nostalgia, often of a critically productive sort; the other is a freedom to pick from the past, to mix and match and make some newly eclectic resolution.

LEFT 21   Blacklers department store, Liverpool, *c.*1910.
Photographs *c.*1950 by James Stirling.

ABOVE 22   Warehouse in central Liverpool. Photograph *c.*1950
by James Stirling.

Stirling kept some of his early pictures of Liverpool right through his career, and
when he later revisited the city he would often add to his stock of photographs. In
the 1960s he regarded his photographic activity in his home town as sufficiently
important to apply for permission to photograph in the dockyards.[121] Stirling's photographs seem to have had several purposes: as *aide-mémoire*, design stimulus,
perhaps even as talisman. He mostly photographed the city's industrial structures:
ships, docks, iron chains and other dockside gear, but especially nineteenth-century
offices and warehouses, as well as the occasional architectural oddity.[122] He was often
looking for something that he could relate to his own architectural efforts. There is,
for instance, a photograph of the Blackler's department store on Great Charlotte
Street, with its ground floor stripped back to its steel structure as a result of fire
bombing (fig. 21). The stripping away creates something unusual out of an unremarkable building, something that clearly intrigued Stirling. Two and a half images
of the building were included in the thesis, stuck onto the back of a photograph
showing a model of the Newton Aycliffe community centre. The conjunction suggests some association between Corbusian *piloti* and this blitzed Edwardian hulk.[123]

More common among the pictures Stirling kept are images of Liverpool's warehouses. In one we see a street corner in central Liverpool and a detail of the opening in a warehouse nearby across a narrow alley (fig. 22). Almost certainly Stirling's eye was drawn to the peculiar and mysterious configuration of this opening. It seems to frame a pair of taking-in doors rather than a window and was clearly a later adaptation of an early nineteenth-century building. There is a horizontal slit that seems to be an integral part of the new opening and might have been used for the projecting arm of a hoist, and the whole arrangement is repeated below. Other details might also have intrigued: the drainpipe set into the wall, the iron lintels, and the bull-nosed bricks framing the window to lower left. Another photograph shows the south warehouse block at Stanley Dock built by the engineer Jesse Hartley in 1852–54 (fig. 23). Stirling must have been drawn to the sheer brick surfaces of the gable, and especially to the huge rounded corner of the building which is echoed in the thick, curved piers – more like guard houses – of the gate. This is an architecture that seems both idiosyncratic

23   Jesse Hartley, Stanley Dock, Liverpool, 1852–54, south warehouse block. Photograph *c*.1950 by James Stirling.

and functional, indestructible yet ruggedly adaptable, intimating classical sources but also a product of the Industrial Revolution.[124] Again the image seems to revel in the evidence of change in the rebuilding of the upper parts of the structure; indeed it had been robbed of its original function when it was cut off from the water by the filling in of part of the dock in the 1890s to make space for the tobacco warehouse visible in the upper left of Stirling's photograph.[125] In both pictures there is something more than a bird-watcher's delight in recording for its own sake. These are densely layered buildings, rich in contrasting textures and the visible results of different moments of their history.

As the example of the Honan entry shows, even from this early date Stirling wanted to incorporate lessons from and references to Liverpool's industrial architecture in his own designs. But what these photographs also affirm is the sense of Liverpool as a battered and exhausted industrial city. This was not the Athens of the north, full of the civic monuments that Rowe picked out, but a city whose work had been done. Unlike Rowe's description, Stirling's photographs do not separate the poignant post-industrial aura from the architecturally intriguing; these are one and the same thing for Stirling. They do not portray Liverpool's warehouses and wharfs as busy with workers or crammed with goods and shipping. More often they focus on signs of decay and disuse. As portable reminders of Liverpool, a memory stock of images, they were often drawn upon by Stirling in later years, especially when lecturing on his career or on the sources for some particular building.[126] The most obvious instances of this are the images that Stirling made of offices designed by Peter Ellis in Liverpool,[127] which again he seems to have taken in his student days and kept carefully for the rest of his career. The architect himself, still intriguingly obscure, fascinated Stirling, and he pieced together details concerning his inventions and early suicide.[128] Ellis's Oriel Chambers (1864) and No. 16 Cook Street (1864–66) both have façades divided by slender stone mullions rising the full height of the buildings and helping to free up their façades for repeated window bays – the Honan type (fig. 24). Oriel Chambers, which had its structure exposed by bomb damage in 1941,[129] also has an almost entirely glazed courtyard façade achieved by setting the supports inside the façade and arranging the glazing in horizontally facetted bands. Without decoration the result gives one of those shivers of premonition, of a building ahead of its time, by which modernists were particularly aroused. In Cook Street the courtyard is also largely glazed, now stepped back as it rises, and rammed into the corner of this tight space is a startlingly frank cantilevered spiral staircase faced with panels of iron and glass (fig. 25).

$\sim$

In academic terms Stirling was not the outstanding student of his time at Liverpool, yet he was without doubt the most important architect to have studied there. Inevitably, then, hindsight colours our estimation of his student work. And it was with hindsight, too, that Stirling interpreted and reworked his student days in commentary later on. He certainly exaggerated the 'furious debate' about modernism, and although he never disavowed it, he was hardly ever, from at least the time of his first serious encounter with Colin Rowe in 1949, as deeply convinced of the 'moral rightness' of modernism as his later statements might have implied. Or, at least, if there was a 'rightness' about it this need not mean an absence of humour, irreverence or perspective on it, or a sense that all other architecture was negated and made irrelevant by it. It is abundantly clear that from his third-year projects onwards Stirling was convinced that his architectural language was essentially modernist and

LEFT 24   Peter Ellis, Oriel Chambers, Liverpool, 1864. Photograph *c.*1955 by James Stirling.

RIGHT 25   Peter Ellis, No. 16 Cook Street, Liverpool, 1864–66. Photograph of courtyard *c.*1955 by James Stirling.

that his destiny was, like so many of his contemporaries, to work for the new welfare state. Rather than '[oscillating] backwards and forwards between the antique and the just arrived Modern Movement',[130] as he later claimed, his development as a student was remarkably consistent, especially given both an environment that encouraged the skills of pastiche and his own eclectic range of historical interests. A largely abstract box was his prime datum with other boxes sliding under, breaking into, or extending outwards from this. Textures, colours and the shapes of minor forms elaborated on these fundamentals without challenging them. Stirling's experiences in the USA gave him a sense of the way that modernism could enhance bourgeois lifestyle but also a scepticism about mass culture and the jarring effects of the modern (American) city. His contact with Rowe helped him to articulate an understanding of modernism as by now an established architecture with its own history and also a more relaxed, even dialogic, relationship with previous architecture than seemed possible to older generations of modernists. It was partly this that might reconcile his strong personal attachment to the architecture of Liverpool, his admiration for modernism, and his sense of being part of an as yet barely articulated avant-garde.[131]

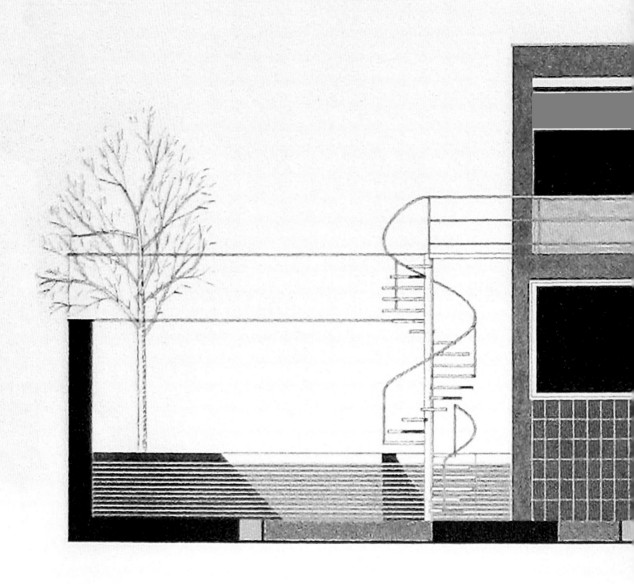

S E C T I O N A L   E L E V A T I O N   O

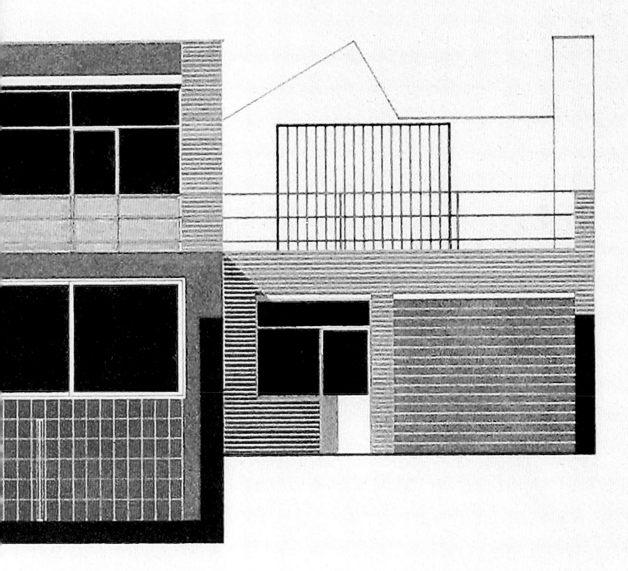

TWO

LINE CC

Third Generation

Man has no mean; his mirrors distort;
His greenest arcadias have ghosts too;
His Utopias tempt to eternal youth
Or self-slaughter. . . .

I've lost the key to
The garden gate. How green it was there,
How large long ago when I looked out,
Excited by sand, the sad glitter
Of desert dreck, not dreaming I saw
My future home. It foils my magic:
Right the ritual but wrong the time.
The place improper.

(W. H. Auden, *The Age of Anxiety: A Baroque Eclogue*, 1948)

In the early months of 1951 a strange object began to rise above the pavement on London's South Bank. This was the 'Skylon' (fig. 26). Part architecture, part sculpture, the Skylon took the form of a large cigar or perhaps a small up-ended Zeppelin or perhaps, for art lovers, a more regular version of one of Brancusi's *Bird in Space* sculptures. Slender and pointed at both ends, the whole construction was 300 feet tall and consisted of a twelve-sided latticed steel frame clad in aluminium louvres and supported fifty feet above the ground by cables held between three steel pylons so that it seemed to rest, weightlessly, on the bottom-most point of its long, elegant form. The Skylon was intended as a landmark and symbol of what the Festival of Britain was about, and was visible by day, as the festival's most prominent vertical feature, and by night lit up from within. It was designed by Hidalgo Moya and Philip Powell, with the help of the engineer Felix Samuely. And working in Powell and Moya's office at this time was the young James Gowan. Gowan did the initial drawings and made a balsa wood model, discovering in the process that the model would not take the stresses from the thread used to stand in for the eventual cables.[1]

26   Powell and Moya, Skylon, Festival of Britain, South Bank, London, 1951.

The work of designing the buildings on the festival's main South Bank site was given to a particular kind of architect: people like Hugh Casson, Leslie Martin, Robert Matthew, Ralph Tubbs, Maxwell Fry, Wells Coates, H. T. Cadbury Brown and Basil Spence. This new establishment, rapidly becoming 'be-medalled veterans',[2] mostly belonged to what was called a 'second generation' of modernists. These were architects born in the century's teens who had studied in the 1930s, come into practice either late in that decade or in the 1940s, and quickly risen to positions of influence as modernism became mainstream in the 1940s. Behind them was also a numerical superiority: three-quarters of architects in the early 1950s were over forty years old.[3] They were second generation also in a more profound sense because their approach depended on what a pioneering first generation of continental modernists had already achieved. The festival buildings celebrated many different things, but central to the architects themselves was a coming of age for modernism in Britain. It had become the architecture of the state, as suitable for its new housing schemes as for a national celebration. In the eyes of the second generation, and those of their political patrons, modernism was now 'architecture as public service':[4] official, popular and inevitable. These festival pavilions could point back to the Great Exhibition of 1851, its engineering achievements, industrial might and surge of national goodwill. At the same time they implied a Britain that had emerged from the war and the disciplines of post-war austerity refreshed and invigorated, not held back by any Victorian clutter of styles; a Britain that would retain its place in the world not by old imperial powers, by deferential monuments and hierarchies, but by a new informality combined with the romance of technology as it was thought to be embodied in modernism. The festival site was laid out as a kind of modern, picturesque model town. It certainly had its big pavilions (like the Dome of Discovery and the Royal Festival Hall), but these were not allowed to dominate their surroundings. Visitors would wander upstream and downstream, coming across unexpected vistas, resting on the plentiful outdoor furniture to take in the surprise sights of public art. The pavilions themselves displayed their new materials of concrete, aluminium, steel and glass, and were decked in the primary colours of the national flag. Playful devices gave the pavilions a light, 'engineered' character: there were perforated, curved, tetrahedral and abacus-like screens, raking tubular steel struts and masts, canopies that seemed unsupported, and suspended offices like 'carry cots'. This was a 'new empiricism', claimed as a distinctly British, light and populist form of modernism.[5]

It was all too much for those of the third generation of modernists born between the two wars.[6] For the ambitious younger architect or critic, the festival was something on which to cut one's new avant-garde teeth. Stirling was certainly dismayed. 'After the Puritanism of my academic conversion,' he later wrote, 'I found [the South Bank Exhibition] a nasty experience, finickity, decorative and inconsequential compared with Asplund in '36, or Paxton in 1851.'[7] Stirling's specific mention of Paxton is obvious in its implication that a spirit of daring technical adventure had not been revived with the centennial of the Great Exhibition. By 'Asplund in '36' he must have meant the Stockholm Exhibition of 1930, known for its lightweight metal structures and the conviction of its socially accessible style. Both associations were desired ones for the festival organisers, but not of course in terms of these critical comparisons. As Colin Rowe explained it, 'both the substance and the ambition of 1951 were local, chauvinist and intolerably restricted. . . . apart from all this . . . [it] unabashedly proclaimed the Picturesque.'[8] Looking back on it, Reyner Banham, one of Stirling's new London acquaintances, took Lionel Esher's phrase 'flimsy and effeminate' as the title for his essay on the festival.[9] And Colin St John ('Sandy') Wilson also attacked the festival's model estate, Lansbury in Poplar, for its 'extraordinary effeminacy'.[10] All of these adjectives are telling. They speak of a sense that a tougher (more masculine), more serious and rigorous modernism, more international in outlook and without the foibles of certain despised national traditions (mere jingoistic rhetoric in Banham's view), had been abandoned in pursuit of a seductive populism foisted upon architecture by an older generation gone soft.

It is unclear whether the Skylon was included in these criticisms, and it was not specifically mentioned by any of them. The competition for the Skylon had been understood by Casson, the festival's architectural director, as intended for those architects who had missed out on the main commissions for the site,[11] and at least in age Powell and Moya were closer to the third generation than the second. But the Skylon was consistent with the festival architecture's attempt to express a sense of lightness;[12] indeed, if anything it provided the keynote. Gowan himself took a different view of the festival from his generational peers. For him it was 'spirited' and the Skylon itself was a major engineering achievement; if it could be accused of artiness that did not mean it was either inconsequential or finickety.[13] As this indicates, Gowan was to take some time to connect with those of his generation who found the need for a distinctive form of modernism in the post-war period, a form that might even seem anti-modernist in order to do this. Gowan's career was to become bound up with Stirling's, the two working in partnership together from 1956 to 1963, and for long after that tied to the reputation of what he and Stirling had achieved together. They met while both were working for the firm of Lyons Israel Ellis, but before this, earlier in the 1950s, their careers followed occasionally similar tracks, sometimes crossing as they had related experiences or entered the same competitions. This chapter reconstructs Gowan's early training and career and, by taking Stirling's career forward to the mid-1950s, it pursues some of these parallels, including the experiences of both architects in other architects' offices. But it also focuses on some of the early designs by Stirling that explored how 'austerity' itself became something to be expressed rather than something to be magically dispelled as the festival had done.

~

Gowan was born in 1923 and studied architecture at the Glasgow School of Art and at Kingston School of Architecture. As with Stirling, there were no architect precedents in his family (his father had run a butcher's business); he was directed towards the profession by a careers counsellor impressed by his artistic abilities.[14] Like Liverpool, the Glasgow School of Art was originally one of the country's leading Beaux-Arts schools. Indeed, it had some claim to being Britain's first Beaux-Arts school, and because of the presence there of Eugène Bourdon, it drank more directly from the Parisian vintage than any other British school.[15] But Beaux-Arts pedagogy had become diluted and routine by the time of Gowan's wartime studies there between 1940 and 1942: Bourdon had died a quarter century before, and 'most of the teachers had disappeared and the lights were dim.'[16] With the war on, Glasgow was reduced to one lecturer who taught both studio design and architectural history, while technical studies were done at the Royal Technical College.[17] According to Gowan, although not to its originators' lofty ideals,[18] the approach was geared to produce 'docile labour, schooled and conditioned by the narrow needs of the offices'.[19] In other words, the school supplied Glasgow's architectural offices with students who were skilled, disciplined draughtsmen and who had no necessary commitment to classicism or any other style. So although much of the time was spent making copies of plates in books like Arthur Stratton's *The Orders of Architecture* (1931), or free-hand copies from casts, or studying the historical styles via Bannister Fletcher's indispensable survey, the design work was relatively free: 'you could be sparing with the ornament, or you could have none at all really.'[20] The system, in Gowan's view, was benign: 'you were not expected to put the Orders on everything you did.'[21] One result can be seen in his design for a gazebo, a short second-year project for a 'pavilion in brickwork' (fig. 27).[22] Entirely without social or technical concerns and intended simply to develop a taste for mass, proportion and line, the design was impressively accomplished for a student then only eighteen, particularly so in its easy absorption of the manner of Edwin Lutyens.

Gowan was fascinated by aspects of Glasgow's architectural patrimony. Unlike Stirling at Liverpool, this was less the industrial past than the work of Charles Rennie Mackintosh (in whose Glasgow School of Art building Gowan worked daily) and Alexander 'Greek' Thomson. The latter's St Vincent Street church intrigued him for the way its strong urban presence was achieved by stacking the building's volumes above the steeply sloping street level: a 'classical pile-up' of tower, temple front and aisles, all on top of a tall stylobate or podium (fig. 28).[23] At the same time, almost equally interesting was the lack of integration between these elements. Appreciation for Thomson was, for Gowan, a natural extension of the standard Beaux-Arts compositional exercises (fig. 29). These tests of drawing skill and knowledge of ornament

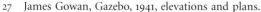

27   James Gowan, Gazebo, 1941, elevations and plans.

28   Alexander Thomson, St Vincent Street church, 1857–59.

and the orders were often later characterised by modernists as one of the Beaux-Arts system's stalest and most unnecessary features. But for Gowan there was something suggestive in the way they forced the student to compile and arrange classical details in one drawing, to make a kind of summation that was also a 'pile-up', put together without need for plausible integration. We have, then, two indications already of formal obsessions to come: the building on a plinth and the building as a collage of elements.

Like Stirling, Gowan's formal architectural training was broken up by the war. His return to architecture after four years working as a radar technician was described by him in terms that also echo Stirling's: 'When the Second World War ended in 1945, we returned to the schools full of energy and enthusiasm, eager and impatient

29   James Gowan, Composition, *c.*1940.

to build a new world but with no knowledge whatsoever of how to go about it.'[24] To return was also to discover new possibilities: 'We read everything, desperately trying to recapture lost time. Giedion's book, with its Swiss format, evoked the precision, whiteness and smoothness of the new style, but the manifesto which accorded most closely with how we felt, social-reforming artists as scientists, was the Etchells translation of *Vers une architecture.*'[25]

Gowan's understanding of Le Corbusier's influence on him is notably different from Stirling's, and although in some ways more typical of his generation it was also strikingly insightful. For him the key elements in *Vers une architecture* were its enthusiasm for ship engineering, its examples of new ways of planning space, and its relation to the classical past. Ships were exemplary, at least as Le Corbusier presented them, because of their clean lines and simplicity and especially because of the delight that could be found in their plain presentation of functional gear. And related to this was Le Corbusier's advocacy of car production as a model both aesthetically and technically for house construction. With planning, Gowan explained, 'Le Corbusier had dropped a bomb on conventional house plans and the pieces scattered.'[26] Interestingly, this is less a description of the free plan than of the rearrangement of normal expectations of a house's different levels. '[Le Corbusier's sections] read like anatomical drawings', wrote Gowan. 'They are packed with an activity which could never be gleaned from the plans.'[27] Finally, what struck Gowan about Le Corbusier's musings on classical architecture was his understanding of the telling detail: 'A fraction of an inch comes into play', he quotes Le Corbusier. 'The curve of the echinus is as rational as that of a large shell. The annulets are fifty feet from the ground, but they tell us more than all the baskets of acanthus on a Corinthian capital.'[28] Gowan also discovered the *Oeuvre complète* volumes by Le Corbusier at around this time. And here again he took a different position from some of his peers: 'Most of my contemporaries escaped from the technical problems of architecture by aligning themselves with Corbusier or Mies', he wrote. 'They found no need to discuss architecture on a technical basis because, when confronted with a problem, they pulled out the Corbusier volumes and knew exactly where the detail was for a particular set of conditions.'[29] His own response to this was confessedly Presbyterian: 'this seemed to be a reprehensible way of behaving . . . a form of intellectual obeisance.'[30]

By contrast with Glasgow, Kingston School of Architecture, where Gowan finished his studies between 1946 and 1948, was directed like 'a Bauhaus version of a puritan grammar school'.[31] Immediately after the war Kingston had the reputation of being, if briefly, the most radically modernist of all British architectural schools.[32] The local deity was Walter Gropius – all his writings were recommended – while the functionalist aspects of Le Corbusier's legacy were revered. Kingston professed a clean start for its students: there was no history teacher and Gowan had studio teachers like James Cubitt and Peter Chamberlain, both only a little older than he was. They were enthusiastic but lacking any experience of teaching modernism. Indeed, Gowan felt that modernism seemed to have no pedagogy or design method, apart from meeting the needs of the programme and the personal tastes of these teachers.[33]

Gowan's final-year thesis, while it declared its modernism emphatically, was also strikingly different from Stirling's thesis in almost every other respect, starting with its modest scale and demeanour. His subject was a house for a sculptor, ostensibly to be built in the Cheyne Walk area of Chelsea (fig. 30). This had deliberate and direct connections with first generation modernism as it had been transposed to 1930s Britain. Down the road in Chelsea stood a house by Erich Mendelsohn and a house by Gropius, built side-by-side in 1936 and designed with RIBA-approved partners

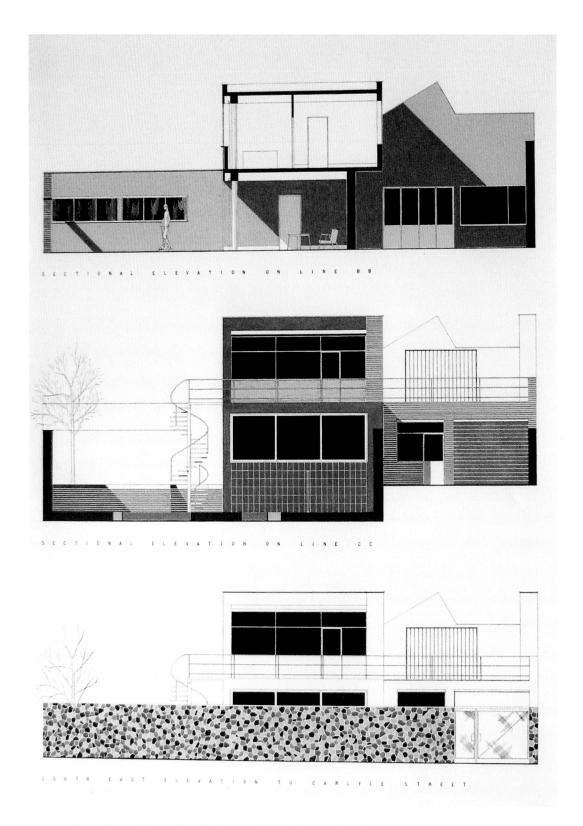

SECTIONAL ELEVATION ON LINE BB

SECTIONAL ELEVATION ON LINE CC

SOUTH EAST ELEVATION TO CARLYLE STREET

30   James Gowan, House for a Sculptor, 1948, elevations and section.

BREUER'S HOUSE · LINCOLN · USA

ABOVE 31   James Gowan, House for a Sculptor, 1948, interior view.

RIGHT 32   James Gowan, Living Room in the Gropius/Breuer House, Lincoln, Massachusetts, 1947.

during the architects' brief sojourns in Britain. But although Gowan's design took up the same close, harbouring relation between façade and retaining wall found in these houses, the distinctive proportions of his windows had more in common with the house Gropius and Breuer designed slightly later (1937) in Lincoln, Massachusetts.

The thesis was mostly a study in interior design (fig. 31). The sculptor's house was largely hidden from the street by a wall; its studios, workshops and generous living spaces were fitted rectilinearly within its oblong site. Gowan had spent much of the summer of 1947 filling a sketchbook with rather stylised drawings from reproductions of living rooms across the ages, including those in houses by Mies, Neutra and Le Corbusier, as well as the living room of the Gropius and Breuer house in Lincoln (fig. 32). Like Stirling in his house for an architect design, Gowan in his thesis was drawn to the example of continental modernism as transposed to the USA. Context was irrelevant: 'this was Bauhaus objectivity', Gowan said of his, 'the site didn't matter.'[34] Where Stirling had produced a concentrated image of a life given conspicuously multiple aspects through ease of consumption, Gowan's ideal sculptor's house was dominated by spaces for physical work and contemplation. Despite its courtyard and pool, the Chelsea house had an industrial edge to its external spiral stair and angled roof lights. What mattered to Gowan was a spirit of experiment: in colour (pink tiles, grey render, yellow panels and a multicoloured garden wall) against monochrome, in elegant modes of presentation, in the compatibility of an artistic and a domestic life. And in these ways it made its own protest against Kingston's Bauhaus ethos.

At the same time as his Kingston studies, to support himself Gowan worked as an architectural assistant. Between 1946 and 1950 he was employed on an occasional basis by Brian O'Rorke. A New Zealand-born modernist, O'Rorke was first generation in age and had built up a strong line in the design and furnishing of ship interiors for the Orient Line, often with highly specialised joinery requirements. More important for Gowan was the occasional help he gave the émigré architect, Karl Jelinek, who had worked in Paris and Algeria and, at the time of Gowan's contact with him, mainly designed exhibition stands and shoe shops. He was also the first modernist of continental pedigree Gowan had encountered.[35]

After Kingston Gowan found his first full-time job through his friendship with Geoffrey Powell (later of Chamberlain, Powell & Bon) when they were both working as assistants for Brian O'Rorke. Powell recommended Gowan to Philip Powell (no relation), who was teaching at the Architectural Association, and the latter invited Gowan to work for him and Hidalgo Moya after he had finished at Kingston.[36] Gowan made drawings for houses in Chichester and for the practice's curious 'Newton-Einstein house' (1950), an aborted Festival of Britain project in the form of a rotating panopticon demonstrating scientific forces. At this time Powell and Moya were still building the huge Churchill Gardens Estate in Pimlico, and Gowan helped with drawings and costings (fig. 33). The partners had, sensationally, won Westminster City Council's competition in 1945 at the respective ages of 23 and 24.[37] By 1951, the year of the Festival of Britain, they already had a standing that few if any of their peers could match. Thus, they blurred a distinction that aspirant avant-gardists seemed to need: they were of the third generation and yet already working on a major welfare state scheme. In a sense, then, all notion

33   James Gowan, Kitchen in Churchill Gardens (Powell and Moya), *c.*1950.

of being thrust inevitably into a position of antagonism towards an establishment that was betraying early ideals or diluting modernism was as alien to the partners as to their assistant, Gowan. It is also notable that the strongest modernist influence on Gowan at this time was probably Dutch rather than Swiss. At Kingston he began to develop a taste for Van Doesburg and the work of the De Stijl group, as a counter-weight to the Gropius and Le Corbusier disciples around him, and through Powell and Moya this was deepened; the Churchill Gardens Estate itself was directly inspired by Dutch pre-war schemes. The Dutch influence helped Gowan to develop his feel for sheer brick surfaces, evident as early as the gazebo design, the articulation of terraces by stepped set-backs and, as he put it, '[simply] arranging objects in a legible and dynamic fashion'.[38]

After a year with Powell and Moya, Gowan left in 1952 to work for Stevenage New Town Corporation, whose architectural head, Clifford Holliday, hired Gowan 'sight unseen' because of his previous work.[39] The experience was almost entirely disheart-ening, the common reality of public sector work after the exceptional experience of Churchill Gardens. Holliday was a product of the Liverpool School of Architecture, another interesting crossing point with Stirling. He had studied there just after the First World War and then worked as an architect and planner in the Middle East and Malta, although this work was entirely unknown to Gowan. For his part, Hol-liday's preconceptions about Gowan as a product of a dynamic London practice were rudely disturbed by the latter's honest opinions on the humdrum environment he observed at Stevenage.[40] Gowan worked on prototype industrial buildings, mostly low factories (of which one was built), with an entrance foyer and offices in front and a shoe-box shaped factory behind. These were made of concrete frame and infill, flat-roofed and with long ranges of standard windows. Occasionally the type was varied with big clerestory windows and pavilion-like entrances at the front (fig. 34). He also picked up two commissions for private houses in and around Stevenage, run

34   James Gowan, Factory Prototype, 1952, perspective.

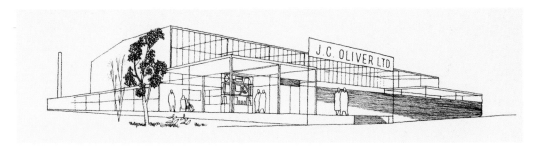

35   James Gowan, House in Stevenage, 1952, perspective.

of the mill work for its time but competently carried out using the contemporary suburban idiom (fig. 35). Almost from his arrival (part of the deal was a place to live in) he was disheartened by the lack of imagination in the town's layout and housing design: 'it lacked any modulation, to put it at its mildest. There were acres and acres of serpentine roads, moving a little this way and a little that way. It just went on and on.'[41] The experience was repeated when Gowan visited the New Jersey suburbs a decade later: 'it looks as if it could all be blown away tomorrow', he observed.[42]

The positive effect of Stevenage was to motivate his desire to engage architecture more tenaciously and meaningfully with its site and place. But Gowan floundered in other ways at Stevenage, recognising the need for the public provision of cheap housing but unable to find a way of making his work intellectually adventurous or creatively satisfying against the 'doctrinaire bureaucracy and the cold hearts'.[43] His time there put him off public sector employment for life, if not working as a private architect on state commissions.

Like Stirling in the early 1950s, Gowan put considerable effort into entering competitions. The first was in the autumn of 1951 for a new medical school for Edinburgh University. He entered the competition with two Kingston contemporarfies, Peter Eldon Jones and Eric Towell, submitting a design that was far more Bauhaus than Beaux-Arts. The only record is a poor reproduction of an elevation in the *Architects' Journal* (fig. 36). In response to the site, a long narrow plot on the north side of George Square which the organizers specified should be kept as an 'architectural unit'

36   James Gowan, Peter Eldon Jones and Eric Towell, Competition Design for Edinburgh Medical School, 1951, elevation.

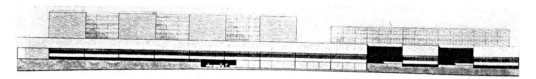

in relation to the rest of the square, most entries established obvious contextual references through Georgian windows or even temple fronts. Gowan and his partners, however, devised a scheme of stunning simplicity that was partly a response to the possibilities of a two-phased building campaign.[44] Following the existing height of the buildings on the square, they set up a giant rhythm with a façade that in its higher administrative blocks projects and recedes across the frontage like a lower version of Le Corbusier's *à redents* (or meander-patterned) towers or perhaps, more relevantly, one of several Dutch schemes (the Oceanboulevard apartments, by J. J. P. Oud, for instance). In front of

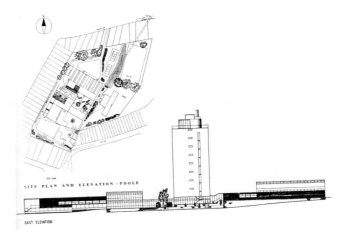

37   James Gowan, Peter Eldon Jones and Peter Gordon, Competition Design for Poole College of Further Education, 1951, elevation and site plan.

this a lower entrance slab partially screens these meanders. However, half-way across, the façade stops and reverses itself so that the lower entrance block now meanders while the administrative storeys hold themselves reticently above. A similar device, of turning a block through 180 degrees to vary a frontage, would be used in the Preston housing that Gowan designed with Stirling some eight years later, as well as in some of Stirling's later schemes.[45]

With Peter Eldon Jones and Peter Gordon, Gowan also entered the Poole College of Further Education competition in 1951. They produced a design that was intended to elevate the main part of the building above the mundane two-storey housing that surrounded the site, obtaining views of the nearby Poole Harbour via a tower block (fig. 37). A plinth was used below this tower to house workshops and to link the college's various parts across the sloping site. The contrast of point block and base was further enhanced, at least on the east and west elevations, by the solidity of the one and the near transparency of the other. But the scheme was to be built in parts,[46] and Gowan's entry may have seemed incapable of transcending this condition to produce a more memorable unity than was suggested in the elevations.[47]

What is notable about Gowan's architectural experiences up to the early 1950s is how varied they had been but also how they lacked the kind of charismatic theoretical input that Stirling had received from Colin Rowe. Gowan had first-hand knowledge of the kind of opportunities for modernism that were normally the preserve of the second generation, but he had begun to develop a critical distance from the pioneering modernists, a distance that Rowe had helped Stirling, too, to appreciate. Gowan had also, unlike Stirling, an established family life by the early 1950s that, whether as symptom or cause (the infamous 'pram in the hall'), helps explain a much less restless attitude towards his chosen metier.

~

With his choice of subject for his Liverpool thesis Stirling had hedged his career bets. He seemed on course to be a planner or an architect, or perhaps one of the new type of super architect-planners along the lines of William Holford or Stirling's own hero, Le Corbusier. His next step was towards planning and London: 'England was shrinking by the 50s,' he later explained (meaning in terms of municipal life), 'so I made for London.'[48] In 1951 he enrolled on a course at the school of Planning and Research for Regional Development based in London's Gordon Square. The school was set up by the Association for Planning and Regional Reconstruction in 1946 to train planners for reconstruction, with a specialism in the training required for planners in the colonies. When Stirling was there its head was E. A. A. Rowse, who had played a prominent role in the Architectural Association's pre-war modernist struggles, and its staff included such planning luminaries as Jacqueline Tyrwhitt, Colin Buchanan and Percy Johnson-Marshall.[49] Stirling found almost immediately that he had made a mistake and was unsuited to the school's aim to train its students 'to appreciate the wider issues of the economic and political situation'.[50] He left after only a year of the two-year course, having, as he put it, 'learnt everything except 3d physical'.[51] 'It was so boring – all about sociology not architecture,' he wrote,[52] and more tellingly, 'they rarely got down to urban planning, being more concerned with national and regional problems, which I thought unrealistic as decisions at that level are more likely to be political.'[53]

What survives from Stirling's time on the course is a design for St Albans town centre, dated 1952 (fig. 38). The rationale was to provide the town with a set of new cultural buildings, to improve certain aspects of the public realm, and to locate new flats and housing. It seems a bitty, half-hearted design. Any remnants of the medieval town were largely lost to street widening and straightening as well as the introduction of buildings of an unprecedented scale with little overt relation to what was left of the town. Most of these new buildings were located around a group of four precincts and include a museum whose plan was plagiarised from Le Corbusier's Mundaneum project. Although more tightly clustered than the layout of Newton Aycliffe, Stirling's St Albans shared with that thesis scheme a desire to frame public space around new pedestrian-centred civic spaces, leaving transport provision virtually

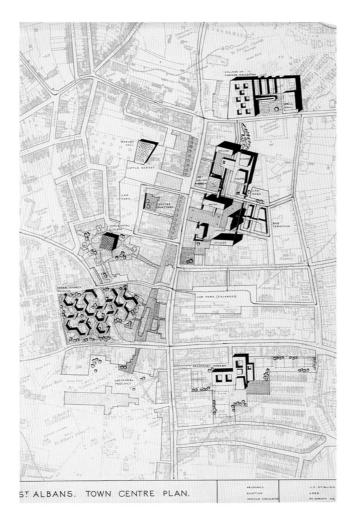

38   James Stirling, St Albans Town Centre, 1952, map of town
with new additions marked.

unaltered. Most interesting here is the estate of three-storey housing like the fragment of a honeycomb, an informal disposition implying growth and change and
indicative of a desire, shared by other young architects in the 1950s, to break from
rectilinear housing arrangements.[54] The city centre changes were part of a larger plan
that envisaged the town growing to a much bigger size.[55] Three new neighbourhoods
were sketched out, each of 10,000 people, as well as, immediately outside the civic
centre, six twenty-storey blocks each housing a thousand people. This was the kind
of scope to which the new architect-planner should aspire.

The logic of the course was to feed planners into the Planning Division of the London County Council's Architect's Department, then probably the largest architectural and planning office in the world. Stirling was taken on but stayed only for five weeks. His time at the LCC was summed up laconically in some lecture notes: '5 weeks LCC record room, pools, girlie'.[56] (He was, apparently, sacked for staring out the window at passing secretaries.)[57] Sandy Wilson, whose friendship with Stirling dated from this time, seems to have flourished in the semi-autonomous teams set up by the LCC's Housing Division and in the sense of playing a part in actively rebuilding Britain.[58] By contrast, Stirling must have felt the Planning Division to be both uncreative and lacking in the kind of architectural glamour he craved.

He had now arrived at a crossroads. With the end of the APRR course and the failure of his attempt to work in a public office, the most common career at that time for an architect of his age, Liverpool School background, and metropolitan ambitions was closed off to him. Partly this was owing to lack of application, a dislike of routine and teamwork, but partly to a realisation – one which Gowan was also reaching in the early 1950s – that the public sector's necessary bureaucracy and its rationale of a social architecture at the lowest cost simply did not suit him.[59] Instead, he embarked on a period of employment working for several private firms, each practising a form of middling modernism.

This needs more explanation. It is easy to polarise the post-war period, partly on the basis of what has been said about the Festival of Britain, as consisting of two mutually antipathetic camps: the second generation and the third generation, or more pointedly the establishment modernists and a new avant-garde, and the next chapter will look in particular at the latter. But valuable work by several historians has recently helped to introduce a broader range of tones into this picture.[60] The idea of a polarity, while certainly useful to some architects at the time, tends to break down when considering how new ideas were often fostered within public sector offices (the group of architects around Sandy Wilson in the LCC's Housing Division is only the most obvious example of this).[61] Also, while there were still many approaches or styles practised other than modernism, modernism itself had cut more facets onto its rough stone. Its adherents had acquired more self-awareness of its history, there were clients who wanted different things from it, and there were different paces of change in the transmission, take-up, or resistance to new modernist trends. Reconstruction, the recovery of the economy, and increased funding in areas like university buildings all encouraged the setting up of new, younger practices in the early 1950s, or the diversification of older practices and the injection of youthful designers into them. So 'middling modernism' (distinct from the 'high' modernism of the pioneers) or 'mainstream modernism' (because of the nature of the commissions) seem good terms to describe this expanding area of modernist practice,[62] between the cutting edge dissidents (to be discussed in the next chapter) and the defenders of a now old faith, yet often in contact with both. All of the firms that Gowan and Stirling worked for in the early 1950s might be described in this way.

The first of these private firms for Stirling was James Cubitt and Partners, with whom he stayed for about six months from the time of his aborted employment at the LCC in the early summer of 1952 until February 1953.[63] Cubitts was known for its West End shops and showrooms as well as for its schools and government buildings in the British colonies, and it practised an accomplished form of modernism, never cutting edge but often distilling the better elements of the movement. One of its most reproduced designs at this time – and one which Stirling probably had no contact with – was for the South Africa Travel Centre, presenting a simple glazed front to Piccadilly but a beautiful range of colours and materials within, all held together visually by an undulating, Aalto-inspired ceiling of wooden slats.[64] Cubitt, who had taught at Kingston, distanced himself from designing work in the office but had several talented architects working for him, most notably the Hungarian émigré Stefan Buzas.[65] Stirling kept a drawing he did for a staircase bay on a science block, dated 6 June 1952,[66] and it is likely that this and the other work he was given was for one of the many West African educational projects that Cubitts had in the office at that time: one contemporary remembers Stirling 'working on designs for schools in Ghana'.[67] This is not an aspect of Stirling's early career that has ever been much noticed and it would have been taken for granted at the time, but the large amount of colonial work still coming into London's architectural offices in the 1950s and his experiences at Liverpool and at the APRR, which both had numbers of colonial students studying at them (and in the APRR's case was actually geared to those students), show how taken-for-granted these colonial connections were in the architectural culture of the time. In common with many of his generation, Stirling probably regarded empire and decolonisation as an irrelevance, something going on in the background but otherwise a mystery.

Whatever the reasons for the termination of Stirling's appointment at Cubitts, at the very least the experience – and that of the other private offices – was more important to his own identity as an architect than he later admitted. He moved next to Gollins Melvin Ward, with whom he stayed for some nine months from early 1953 to around September of that year. At that time Gollins Melvin Ward was still a small firm but expanding from house conversion work to housing for Lambeth Borough Council and schools in Hertfordshire and Kent. They were beginning to deploy a diluted Miesian vocabulary ideal for a fit-for-purpose contemporary styling typical of middling modernism. It is not known what Stirling worked on, and certain myths have grown up surrounding his time there.[68] He may well have stayed longer had not his independent entry into the Sheffield University competition (which will be discussed later in this chapter) created a conflict of interest with his employers' own entry to the same competition.

~

At this point the narrative of training and employment needs breaking. Architecture exists also as an aspiration, as a promise of creative fulfilment in articulating what the culture has not yet realised about itself. At least this is what many of the third generation believed. The next chapter will examine how Stirling sought to do this through his activities within a newly emerging avant-garde. Here though, two competition designs, both carried out in spare time free from either the grind of training or the labour of helping to produce other architects' designs, will be discussed. Competition entries, of course, have a long history of being used by young architects not just to launch independent careers but also to announce distinctive visions of what architecture should be about.

Like Gowan, Stirling also entered the Poole competition in 1951.[69] His design returned to the device he had used several times at Liverpool of two virtually freestanding slabs, one of eight storeys and the other of three, linked here by a raised walkway (fig. 39). But this obvious similarity might obscure the new directions that are found elsewhere in the design, and that were articulated in an argument made in the report written to accompany the entry.[70] This argument did not point to an impoverishment of materials and spaces, but used a notion of 'economy' to introduce different kinds of potential in the architecture. On the one hand, brick construction was re-evaluated as a local British material and as 'skin clothing the façade',[71] with all that implied about frame and infill and especially about the ornamental potential of brick now that it was free from structural purposes. On the other hand, Stirling used 'economy' to create some distance from Le Corbusier's free plan and instead placed a new emphasis on the corridor as an important element in its own right, as 'something of fundamental organizational significance'.[72] This argument justifying a spatial layout from the basis of economy was new to Stirling at this time but repeated elsewhere during the decade.[73] There are certainly several notable visual elements in Stirling's Poole – the angled outline of the lecture hall clearly visible at the end of the lower slab in one drawing; the 'industrial' elements apparent in the slanting volume on the top of the building and elsewhere[74] – but the two devices with most potency both sprang from this argument about economy. First, the variegated window openings on the upper floors of the higher slab, a variety also found on the end walls

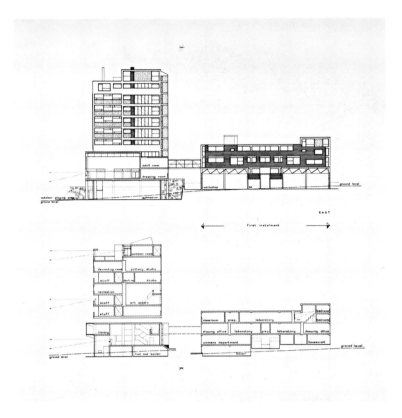

39   James Stirling, Competition Design for Poole College of Further
Education, 1951, elevation and section.

of the lower slab, created a pattern justified by the different kinds of room functions
behind them. The pattern was heightened by the darker bricks used on this part of
the façade, which Stirling saw as emphasising the non-structural character of the
brickwork.[75] Second, in its complex sectional treatment Poole shows how Stirling
exploited his criticism of the free plan to develop a new area of architectural thinking in his work. Corridor sizes were attenuated as the traffic using them diminished
higher up the tower. The tower itself was divided on its upper levels so that while
on one side a series of rooms of the same height jut out of the façade like trays
pulled at different lengths, on the other side all the variation is done in the room
heights, so providing single, double and one-and-a-half height spaces.

To be economic, to restrict, to ration, to use cheaper materials; all of these were
familiar exhortations in this period when post-war rationing was still in force and
the British economy in a state of 'voluntary penury'.[76] (To save and to reuse are

similar themes that will be taken up in the next chapter.) In this regard, apart from its justifications in terms of materials and spaces, and what that meant for ornament and the abandonment of the free plan, economy also pointed to a larger feature of Stirling's relationship to modernism at this time. He had also argued in his report that new materials and untested structural techniques would be avoided, again because of the argument around economy (they might increase the building costs). But, as before, this was not just expedience. One of the tenets central to avant-garde modernism in its first generation incarnation, and still held if in diluted form by the second, was the idea that modernism had to exploit new materials and techniques if it were to fathom truly and express modernity.[77] In using and expressing these means, modernism would be driving new forms of cultural expression; it would be experimental and it could be utopian. New materials and technologies guaranteed modernism's relation to modernisation, its harmony with the idea of constant revolution in industrial processes. So to abandon this – as the argument for Poole did – was to abandon something that seemed to lock modernism together with industrialisation.[78] To abandon it was not just practical. It was necessary if a different kind of contemporary modernity was to be expressed – a post-industrial austerity.

Many of Poole's formal elaborations are announced in the monumental foyer space that runs across the full depth of the block at the lower levels. Here, in the first instance we have of a much later redrawing of Stirling's early work, Leon Krier's 1974 drawing of the foyer space emphasised what had previously been more buried in the sectional drawings and barely remarked on in the report (fig. 40). Everywhere people look down and across this space and out of it towards Poole Harbour. Grand double-height columns pace down the length of the foyer, and pockets of people underline its different qualities down in the ground-floor vestibule, up behind on the rear gallery, on the solidly serene staircase and in the concourse itself. Where the sections implied that this space might be something like the Royal Festival Hall's wall-to-wall foyer space, Krier's image draws from the great transitional zones of Schinkel's Altes Museum in Berlin to celebrate a kind of model Poole citizen-student in harmony with the public realm that has swept inside the building. And yet, there are perhaps good reasons – apart from the absence then of Krier's persuasive pen, and apart from its anachronistic classical resonances in a pre-postmodern time – why a similar image could not appear part of the Poole entry in 1951. After all, this is the grand generosity of open space that the free plan also enabled, and to present such an image in 1951 would seem to deny much of what Stirling had argued for in his report.

The Sheffield University competition was announced in February 1953 and was at that point the most important post-war competition for university buildings. In common with other universities, Sheffield was faced with a huge increase in stu-

40   James Stirling, Competition Design for Poole College of Further Education, 1951, interior view. Drawing *c.*1974 by Leon Krier.

dents – some three times more than pre-war numbers – and the plans for expansion made before the war were inadequate to these demands.[79] Competitors were required to provide designs for two phases of extension to the university: the first was for detailed designs for a library and buildings for arts departments and administrative accommodation, the second a layout design mostly for science departments. Among other conditions they were required to avoid enclosed courtyards and to provide elevation treatments that were 'contemporary in character'.[80] Stirling's entry was made jointly with Alan Cordingley, another one of Colin Rowe's acolytes from Liverpool (fig. 41). It was unplaced, but Stirling saw it from the very first as his most significant design up to this date. One sign of this is the effort he made even two years later to have the designs published outside Britain, going so far as to importune Le Corbusier – whom he had neither previously met nor corresponded with – to use his influence to persuade André Bloc, the editor of *Architecture d'aujourd' hui,* to publish the scheme.[81]

Although this was not to be a campus building of the Oxbridge quad type and certainly not of the demurely mirroring contextualism that Stirling had found in

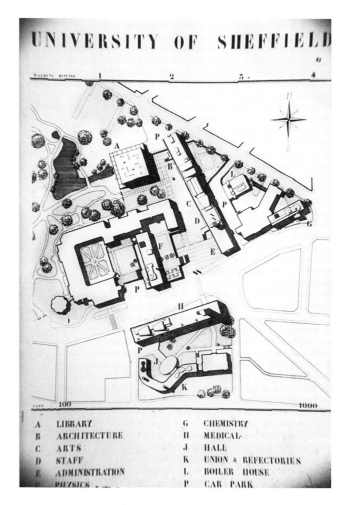

41   James Stirling and Alan Cordingley, Competition Design for
Sheffield University, 1953, site plan.

Princeton five years before, nevertheless there are evocative urbanistic and architectural dimensions to the Sheffield design. These have hardly been discussed before,
but they are important not least because they show thematic aspects of the post-
industrial attitude: the licence to range into pre-industrial urbanism and architecture, to evoke ruination, and to espouse an aesthetic of repair.

The collaborators divided the work simply: Cordingley 'did the square library
building I did the long one', according to Stirling.[82] The accommodation was arranged
in these two strongly contrasting blocks, according to what Stirling called 'physiologi-
cal counterpoint':[83] a library block to the north of the existing main university build-

ings, and a long rectangular block housing the administrative functions and the arts departments. The library, which was square in plan and elevation, was to have a 'static quality' like a 'centralised church plan of the Renaissance',[84] while the site on which the two first-phase buildings were to go was 'thought of as having a Renaissance quality about it (superficial resemblance to St Marks Venice)'.[85] The Arts and Administration block, 'essentially a wall (perforated) seldom seen in its entirety',[86] lined this long piazza with the older university buildings opposite. The block was angled so that it exaggerated the perspective recession of this piazza towards the 'natural climax of the scheme', the isolated, smoothly surfaced library.[87] Contrast between the two buildings would be increased by the smooth materials of the library against the raw concrete of the Arts and Administration building, the latter intended to stain 'like rust on a battleship'.[88] What this also indicates is a set of related ideas emerging in Stirling's thinking at this time. If the library was a renaissance church, the Arts and Administration building was baroque: '[baroque architecture] does not rely on sun but on the juxtaposition of solid and void and the resulting pattern, also because of the amount of wet and dirt, our buildings must be of such a powerful domination that dirt and staining do not matter.'[89]

The urban aspects of the Sheffield design are significant if usually unnoticed.[90] For all that the long block evoked Corbusian precedents, it was never intended to be as free-standing as the *Unité d'habitation*, and its bulk would never have been as aggressively self-sufficient as any similarity with the *Unité* might suggest.[91] In fact, this block was hardly longer than the rear range of the existing university buildings on the site, and in height it would not have exceeded these and other surrounding buildings. The implications of the site were carefully thought through in other respects too, and these show how distant Stirling's design was from the contemporary calls for a picturesque modernism. It was not regionalist in any obvious way, it did not seem to cultivate 'idiosyncrasy', and it was not particularly concerned with monumentality – all crutches of the new picturesque thinking in *Architectural Review* circles.[92] By contrast, Sheffield's layout seems generated by the existing contextual conditions. The long Arts and Administration building, which provided a covered way on its ground level from one end of the site to the other, placed the architecture department at the north end of the long block (for the light) and the administration at the south end (for access to the main entrance). The second phase of the building campaign was suggested by rectangular blocks to the north and south of the road that cut through the university, and these, too, continued the urbanistic thinking. A block to house physics on the north side was to provide the third arm of a courtyard opening onto the road while, on the other side of the road, a long block housing the medical school framed the street as a corridor, and then a more informal space was opened up behind it by a student union block folding itself around the space. Finally, a chemistry block to the east gave point and edge to the acute angle of the site. This subtle, layered response to the existing context is usually considered to be a feature of a much later period in Stirling's career (and it is, one might add, a response that would have knitted the campus together far better than the aloof buildings and baggy, windblown spaces that resulted from Gollins Melvin Ward's additions over the next twenty years). Just as it is not picturesque, 'townscape' modernism, so it is distinctly not the kind of urban planning that Stirling had learnt at the APRR (as evidenced in the St Albans plan), and there is no evidence of a similar approach in either the Port Sunlight extension or the Newton Aycliffe town centre that he did at Liverpool. All of these layouts strove to be clearly one kind of entity – whether garden city or Corbusian modernist – whereas Sheffield introduces deeper layers of historical complexity as well as the desire to take the measure of the properties of whatever his buildings stood next to.

To be post-industrial, then, might mean evoking the pre-industrial, or at least the less-than-pristine: dirt and staining do not matter; a building is intended to stain like rust on a battleship; modern libraries evoke renaissance churches; in Sheffield, the steel town, one finds something of Venice, the once maritime empire; perspective helps to bind and enclose, to repair what is incomplete. While Stirling's architectural forms were unmistakably modern, there were other dimensions and affinities that he wanted to evoke that were far from the idea of an inevitable, exclusive bond between modern technologies and modern architecture that was at the heart of an amnesiac modernism. And these resonances can be further sounded in the scheme's main building.

Stirling's Arts and Administration building, especially its much-reproduced elevations (fig. 42), quickly became a kind of manifesto of what the architect could do. Most evidently, the outlines of eight lecture halls, stacked in two syncopated groups of four in the middle of the block, were revealed in all their interlocking angularity. The emphatic expression of this device may have been encouraged by the constructivist designs of Konstantin Melnikov, but given the obscurity of Melnikov's work at this time this seems unlikely, and, anyway, such exposed theatres were already suggested in the community centre thesis design and in the Poole competition entry.[93] As with Stirling's response to the site, the discordant (even proto-brutalist) qualities of the design have tended to be emphasised at the expense of what it shares with Stirling's experience at Liverpool, as well as how it echoes the urbanistic concerns outlined earlier. Essentially, the building was conceived as a six-storey, *piloti*-carried container for academic and administrative departments, taking the idea of the *Unité*, stretching it out and exposing its inner organs. As a container or open-sided box,

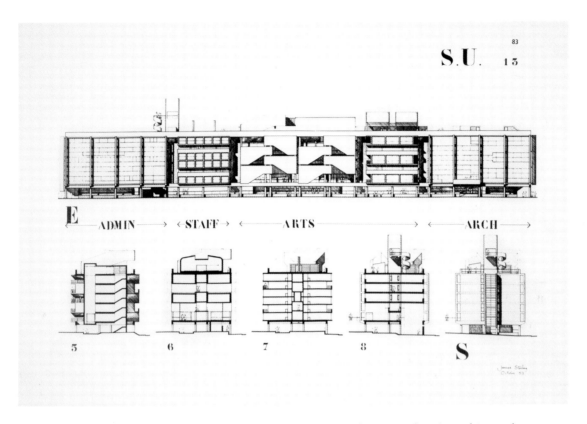

42   James Stirling, Competition Design for Sheffield University, 1953, elevation and sections of Arts and Administration building.

all issues of formal unity were resolved by the overall frame of the building rather than a unifying façade treatment or a form of structural expression. The inner organs – lecture theatres, seminar rooms, staff rooms, offices – were organised in groupings of shared function either side of a central axis of circulation directing the flow of people and spaces, the groupings separated by clustered shafts of vertical circulation which were expressed on the outside as recessed elements. The long building thus became articulated like a composition (ABCCBA), conjugated and resolving dualities in the Beaux-Arts manner by the strongly distinct repeated shapes contained within its frame. There is something similar here to the combination of deference and assertion relative to its site that characterises Gowan's Edinburgh Medical School design. The Arts and Administration building might even be seen as a mannerist composition in Colin Rowe's sense, in that the strong containing structure is like a classical frame for the variations in a set of components.[94] Rowe's mannerism was more a matter of elevations than plans, unlike the way Stirling's avant-garde contemporaries understood Wittkower's neo-Palladianism at this time.[95]

The complexity and duality of Rowe's mannerism, its interest in 'deliberate architectural derangement',[96] is to be found, therefore, in these elevations of rhythmically repeated, large-scale abstract forms. This is to claim also that the post-industrial anxiety about history and progress is paralleled by the kinds of anxieties that Rowe found in the Counter-Reformation and 1920s modernism. In effect, Rowe's projection of a post-war 'state of inhibition' onto these historical periods is returned to the present in Stirling's Sheffield design.[97] The 'derangement' at Sheffield consists both in repetition itself and in the voids that are repeated. Abstracted from the language of classicism but held in by its compositional rhythm, the repeated forms become more like objects – lecture hall objects, for example, – than architecture. One detail is telling here. The grouping of lecture theatres superficially evokes the decorative patterning of façade elements that had become characteristic of Berthold Lubetkin's work, but there are more subtle visual effects at work. Under their sloping undercuts each lecture theatre has an expanse of glazing providing light onto the central corridor, but as this glazing is rendered in grey on the drawings these areas cannot help but be read as cast shadows (even if from two different light sources). These 'shadows' imply that the lecture boxes project out at different distances from the surface plane of the building, whereas they are actually flush with each other, and this effect is exaggerated further by the recession to either side of the banks of lecture theatres. Such effects might be compared with Rowe's interpretation of the perplexing qualities of the Villa Schwob's blank panel (fig. 43). Like that panel, the bank of lecture theatres is the resolution of a duality that has been set up elsewhere on the façade. Like the rich, incisive detail of the frame around the Schwob panel, the visual ambiguity of the 'shadows' around the lecture boxes and the 'real' cast shadows to either side of them point up the 'activity of emptiness' of the lecture boxes themselves. As with the panel, we could say with Rowe that the bank of lecture boxes 'draws attention to itself; and yet, without apparent content, it at once distributes attention over the rest of the [building].' Emptiness and repetition deny the expected hierarchy; 'derangement' threatens to make objects of all architectural arrangements. There is 'both a disturbance and a delight', to use Rowe's words; we are 'both ravished and immensely irritated'.[98] Or, to use his comments on Le Corbusier's Salvation Army building, 'plastic elements of a major scale are foiled against the comparatively minor regulations of the glazed wall. . . . Disturbance is complete.'[99] What Sheffield brought together in direct and productive tension, then, was the mannerist modernism Stirling had learnt from Rowe and his interests in what this book calls the post-industrial.

43   Le Corbusier, Villa Schwob, La Chaux-de-Fonds, 1916. From Colin Rowe,
'Mannerism and Modern Architecture', 1950.

One tendency is to see these elevations as a kind of X-ray of the building's innards. Indeed Stirling himself was to describe Le Corbusier's villa at Garches as 'something positive in a physical sense, rather like X-ray photos of the gut after swallowing coloured liquid.'[100] Stirling saw the Sheffield volumes in relation to ideas about the solidification of spatial voids. This was a borrowed theory, one that was elaborated almost entirely on the basis of historical rather than modernist examples. It is worth quoting Stirling at length on this, from his contemporary report:

A few years ago, Luigi Moretti illustrated in *Spazio* the plaster castings taken from inside accurate models of certain historical buildings. By treating the external surface of the inner constructions of a building as a three-dimensional negative or mould, he was able to obtain solidified space. If space can be imagined as a solid mass determined in shape and size by the proportion of a room or the function of a corridor, then an architectural solution could be perceived by the consideration of alternative ways in which the various elements of the programme could be plastically assembled. It is not assumed that every element should be expressive, but it is important that a hierarchy of the most significant volumes is recognisable in the ultimate composition. Within practical limits, room shapes are variable and the different ways of assembling accommodation, circulation etc., may be almost infinite; nevertheless a design will start to emerge in the imagination when the relationship of spaces appears to have *coherent organizational*

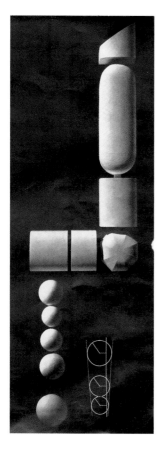

44   Luigi Moretti, model of
1952–53 showing spatial
sequence in Palazzo Thiene.

pattern. At this moment of coagulation, however, the cerebral exercise loses its abstract value as it is necessary for it to materialise as substance; and a successful transition from organizational pattern into structure and materials is dependent upon the author's structural vocabulary. Through its selection the method of support should assist the ideogram of the space organization.[101]

What the Sheffield jury would have made of this can only be imagined. It did not help Stirling to win. By some distance it is the most abstract piece of theorising he had done up to this point, indeed he rarely matched it after this date. The Italian architect Luigi Moretti and his magazine *Spazio* certainly had avant-garde credentials of a new post-war kind: *Spazio* had even published a dismissive review of the claims that the Festival of Britain embodied a new, British version of modernism.[102] Stirling seems to have learnt about Moretti and the magazine he edited from two of his Liverpool friends, Thomas (known as 'Sam') Stevens and Robin Dunn.[103] In the article mentioned in the Sheffield statement Moretti had used plaster models to render the contained interior volumes of famous historical buildings (Hadrian's Villa at Tivoli, St Peter's, buildings by Palladio, Michaelangelo, Sangallo, Guarini and Frank Lloyd Wright) as moulded solids (fig. 44).[104] The images accompanying the article had startling qualities – familiar buildings rendered into abstract sculpture, corridors become dense matter, structure dissolved into void – that suggest far more than the mere re-evaluation of spatial sequences Moretti had attributed to them. Indeed, as Moretti's rendering of a sequence of rooms in Palladio's Palazzo Thiene shows, the spirit of this investigation must have had something of the same appeal, in its imaginative dialogue between history and modernism, that Stirling had learnt from Colin Rowe. The Palazzo Thiene's formal arrangement of rooms, now a set of lumpy beads on some stiff necklace, is transmuted into interchangeable units ready for plastic assembly and reassembly until they achieve what Stirling calls 'coherent organizational pattern' or 'the ideogram of the space organization', to which the structure and materials are implicitly secondary. To treat space as a casting is to treat it as merely the other to something solid, as the negative to a positive, in effect as just another architectural property. All this acts as some kind of rationale for the most immediately striking aspect of the Sheffield design – the way that a long horizontal box contains volumes of different shape and size.

Stirling argued later that both his Sheffield and Poole designs attempted to deal with the problem of 'excessive circulation and compromised room usage' that the *plan libre* and his own thesis design had bequeathed.[105] Instead, circulation in both competition designs was emphasised, restating it as 'the dynamic and motivating element of the building' by treating it as more than just corridors and instead 'an armature or skeleton on which rooms fastened'.[106] In the Sheffield case this entailed a spine like 'a driving axle on to which rooms were connected, like a mechanized assembly' with functional groupings linked by shafts of vertical circulation.[107] In reacting against one hallmark Corbusian space Stirling had turned to another. The 'driving axle' of Sheffield was nothing less than the interior streets running through the centre of the *Unité*. In fact, this image of a 'driving axle', rather than the less striking and more indebted notion of interior street, should perhaps be seen more as a later

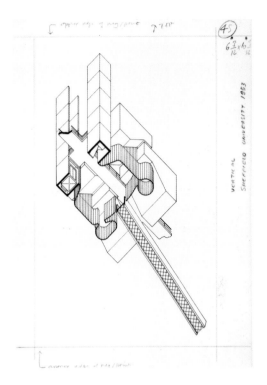

45   James Stirling, Competition Design for Sheffield University, 1953, axonometric of detail of Arts and Administration building. Drawing *c*.1974 by Leon Krier.

reworking of Sheffield's intentions rather than a mark of how Stirling actually saw it in 1953.[108] The later idea is similar in its effect to the drawing that Krier made in 1974 (fig. 45): a worm's-eye axonometric that picks out a section of the Arts and Administration building with lecture theatres and lift towers attached to a length of the corridor, the whole imagined as a kind of floating abstract sculpture. This now is more 'driving axle' than internal street, exaggerating the difference between what Louis Kahn had not yet in 1953 begun to call 'served and serving spaces', and seeming to expose the 'serving' stacks far more than they had ever been on the original designs. Perhaps, too, Krier's drawing was also generated by a hindsight desire to rival the Sheffield competition entry by Peter and Alison Smithson and their famously long, exposed, tube-like corridor (see fig. 51). The drawing cleverly implies the continuation of Stirling's corridor, stopping short of the inconvenient fact that in the original design the corridor varied in width after this point, narrowing, widening and sometimes becoming more room-like as if to mirror the changes of function to either side of it.[109]

Stirling and Cordingley did not win the Sheffield competition, and their design was not even placed. The winners, announced in December 1953, were the very firm that Stirling had been working for – Gollins Melvin Ward.[110] The falling out with his employers, glossed over by Stirling on the rare occasions he referred to it and fallen into obscurity since, marks an important if perhaps inevitable stage in Stirling's career. This stage, involving greater self-consciousness about the independence of his architectural ideas, will be discussed further in the next chapter. For now, more needs to be said concerning that falling out. Late in the period of the competition, in September 1953, Stirling wrote to the secretary responsible for the process. He had been employed by Gollins Melvin Ward for much of the past year, Stirling explained. Privately he had been working on the competition for which his employers were also developing a scheme but without his assistance:

> On Thursday 9th September, it was decided to bring me into the scheme working on the Firm's design whereupon it was disclosed that I was doing it privately. On Friday 11th September, Mr Melvin said in an interview that I may have been influenced by the firm's scheme and asked me to withdraw my design or lose my job. In reply I asked him to inspect my drawings to ascertain any similarity and this he refused to do.[111]

Stirling wanted to know if he would be disqualified from competing on a personal basis because of his employer's involvement. The main building in Gollins Melvin Ward's scheme, a sleek Miesian tower block with a curtain wall hung in front of its structural frame, was utterly unlike Stirling's Arts and Administration building. However, the winners-to-be housed their library in a low square slab located just north of the existing university buildings – the same basic building shape and almost exactly the same location designated by Stirling and Cordingley for their library. Whether this was coincidence or whether Stirling, who had certainly seen the design,[112] had borrowed the idea from his employers and they had some inkling of the similarity, will probably never be known. Such borrowings were and remain part of the currency of architectural practice, though in this case there is nothing specific enough in the two library designs to determine that one must have been dependent on the other. The general area for situating the library was laid down in the competition conditions.[113] And there was certainly nothing wrong with Stirling entering the competition privately while working for a firm who were also competing, as is clear from the secretary's reply.[114] In the end Stirling decided to go ahead and enter, at the same time losing his job.

~

Stirling's final and most lengthy employment as an assistant was in the practice of Lyons Israel Ellis where he worked from 1953 for about two and a half years until early 1956. Gowan joined the practice in 1954, drawn to it by the odd mistake of thinking that one of its partners – Edward Lyons – was Eric Lyons, who was then just beginning to build an interesting career as a developer-architect of middle-class housing estates.[115] Lyons Israel Ellis tried to attract the most promising young architects to work for them, and these assistants in their turn were drawn by what Alan Colquhoun (who joined later in the 1950s) has called the practice's 'refreshingly down-to-earth quality, free from the picturesqueness and whimsy that typified modern architecture in Britain in the wake of the 1951 Festival of Britain'.[116] They had a reputation for a highly professional and serious-minded approach, and this resulted in a stream of well-detailed school buildings that mirror the changing trends of the high end of architectural culture during this period. Their office practice and approach to designing these buildings is known from accounts left by some of the assistants. All three partners drew and there was often overlap of roles among them, but they kept responsibility for design largely to themselves and away from the assistants. The assistants were usually assigned to one project for its duration (a school, for instance, would require one partner and one or two assistants), and required to produce many different schedules for the same items, to refine details (with technical precedents provided by the practice's previous jobs), to draw up working drawings, and to help with supervision on site.[117] Outline designs were produced quickly and often at home by one or other partner, while the long development phase, the 'real production in the office',[118] was regarded as the most important and often entailed weeks spent on certain details.[119] This resulted in designs that were often less interesting in their overall concept and planning than in their details.

Design proceeded according to a practised formula. With the school designs the brief was immediately analysed and divided into a hierarchy of accommodation needs: communal spaces, repeated units like classrooms, special functions like gymnasia. These were then grouped as pavilions around linking corridors, 'either predominantly linear or pinwheel, in response to a reaction to the site',[120] and staircases and other such matters were positioned and refined 'in an effort to inject another level of architectural intention.'[121] This approach was regarded as pragmatic and rational, a process of decomposition in order then to find expressive unity in the conditions of the brief and the site, rather than in some preconceived compositional entity. As such, and probably without much rationalisation within the Lyons Israel Ellis office, it offered both Stirling and Gowan the working principles of a middling

Above: Site plan. Key: **1** main entrance, administrative and classroom block **2** kitchen etc. **3** assembly halls and dining area **4** classroom block **5** classroom block **6** housecraft and needlecraft **7** gymnasia **8** staff and maintenance rooms **9** tools **10** cycle shelter **11** tools and greenhouse **12** caretaker **13** parking space **14** playcourt

46   Lyons Israel Ellis, Peckham Girls' Comprehensive School, 1956–58, site plan.

47   Lyons Israel Ellis, Peckham Girls' Comprehensive School, 1956–58, water tower designed by James Stirling.

modernist practice. The Peckham Girls' Comprehensive School (1956–58), on which both Gowan and Stirling worked, can be seen to epitomise the results. The school was divided into six blocks, each housing a different function and all grouped around a central assembly hall (fig. 46). Low, wide corridors linked those blocks not directly connected with the assembly hall, the whole forming a pinwheel plan with the blocks spaced more or less evenly across it.[122]

Stirling fitted into this office environment far better than in any of his previous private practices. The reason for this was partly to do with the personal interest that Tom Ellis took in him. Becoming a partner in 1949, Ellis was the youngest of the three partners, in age occupying the gap between the second and third generations. In part he saw his role as keeping the partnership abreast of current architectural developments. He thus helped with that appropriation and sometimes taming and refinement of new ideas typical of the middling modernist practices. As a 'fierce Corbusian' wedded to notions like the 'discipline of the route',[123] Ellis needed the kind of up-to-date engagement with Le Corbusier's work that Stirling could supply (this will be discussed in the next chapter), as well as the young assistant's design talent.[124] Stirling's lack of aptitude for the stuff of building before he came to Lyons Israel Ellis was compensated for by his experience within the practice, in particular Ellis's technical briefings. His work on the Peckham school included responsibility to design the water tower and a staircase beside it (fig. 47).[125] Colin Rowe described the pavilion on the roof at Garches as 'a temple of love and the bridge of a ship',[126] and this water tower has something of the same dual qualities. It is a little Corbusian folly: a concrete framed structure of two levels, the lower glazed and infilled, the upper open and canopied. By contrast with Ellis's relation to Stirling, Gowan was treated like any other assistant in the office – as obedient drawing labour with very little chance for design input on

48   Holford & Creed, St Thomas's Hospital Flats, Royal Street, Lambeth, London, 1957.

the practice's work. He helped with the Peckham school, assisted with drawings for the second phase of the Northfleet school in Gravesend, and supervised a private house that Israel had designed for his sister in Barnet.

Stirling also did occasional moonlighting at this time; at least, that was the case with a design he made in December 1953 for a block of flats for St Thomas's Hospital on Royal Street, a redeveloped site in Lambeth. Stirling's sketch design for these nurses' flats was a piece of outwork for the office of Holford & Creed, a private office run by Holford parallel to his public work.[127] The flats were built, with some modifications,[128] by 1957 and might be seen as an anglicised version of the Corbusian *Unité d'habitation* (fig. 48). In this case, as befits a rapidly produced design for another firm, they were much closer in spirit and form to the Corbusian prototype and without the post-industrial elements that have been found in the competition entries. Stirling designed a nine-storey slab with a structural grille of maisonettes. The design can be related to the Bentham Road flats in Hackney (1951–56) (fig. 49), an important free-standing slab of council flats with which Stirling was closely acquainted through

49   London County Council, Bentham Road Estate, 1951–56.
Photograph *c*.1955 by James Stirling.

visits during construction and because several friends in the LCC Housing Division, like Sandy Wilson, were involved in their design. Bentham Road has claims as the first *Unité*-type slab to be built in Britain, and its tough-looking rigour of design certainly marked a new departure.[129] But again the differences between the Royal Street flats, Bentham Road, the *Unité*, and Lubetkin's slab block schemes are almost as telling as the similarities. Unlike the unrelenting façade of Bentham Road, Royal Street's maisonette side is broken two-thirds of the way along Stirling's design by a staircase that almost seems to split the building in two. The remaining third of this side is then taken up with three distinct façade treatments as different sizes of accommodation (one- and two-bed flats) and different solid to void relationships are expressed; the manner recalls some of the carpet-like patterning that Lubetkin had deployed for the façades of his Priory Green housing in Finsbury (1937–51). Like the Newton Aycliffe community centre, while Royal Street is lifted on sturdy supports it also houses distinct functions in a ground floor treated as if sheltered under the main mass. The building lacks a roof garden and has access walkways instead of internal corridors, placing these, as was customary with LCC neo-Georgian inter-war flats and as Bentham Road had done, on one side of the building. As a result this side, despite the building being free-standing and fully visible on all sides, immediately assumes the status of the rear. Stirling's early design clearly laid the template for the building and shows again that, even though he had just seemingly abandoned any aspirations to work as a public sector architect, he was still seen as having the skills to organise a design for this kind of large-scale housing block.

Oddly, by comparison with Stirling's competition designs, if understandably given its circumstances of production, Royal Street demonstrates how avant-garde awareness was necessary to the mainstream – whether public or private office – because such knowledge helped to develop modernism through an idea of linear change generated by the absorption of new trends. But what both Poole and Sheffield indicated, parallel with Gowan's experience, was that linear change was now beginning to seem an irrelevant model for both young architects.

~

This chapter has deliberately dwelt longer on a stage that in most architects' careers is usually passed over rapidly, whether retrospectively by architects themselves or by historians. It has also introduced James Gowan much earlier into the account than has been done by other writers on Stirling; indeed, Gowan's evolving architectural thought as well as his direct input into architectural design will continue to play a strong role in this book.

Each architect's choice of thesis topic gave him early directions that had to be changed. The ambition for work of a scale and public nature announced by Stirling's thesis topic was all too quickly dented by his lack of aptitude and interest in the more mundane tasks as well as the political awareness required of the architect-planner. Urbanistic thinking, when it reappeared in his career, would take an entirely different turn: smaller scale, allusive, witty and contrary. The close focus on domestic interiority and artistic intensity evident in Gowan's thesis was then confronted with what Stevenage represented in terms of housing production. In a sense, for both architects, the experience of working for private practices, and particularly Lyons Israel Ellis, was a necessary correction to excessive early ambitions. But, of course, architecture is not just what an architect is paid to do, and competition entries gave both architects the chance to develop architectural ideas outside the office environment. Of these designs, the aspirations represented in Stirling's Poole and Sheffield designs were the more important, having something subversively anti-modernist in their potential. For that reason they were not likely to be achieved, but their implications were to run through Stirling and Gowan's later partnership and even beyond that.

THREE

Junk, Bunk and Tomorrow

The symbol of this mood is London, now the largest, saddest and dirtiest of great cities with its miles of unpainted half-inhabited houses, its chopless chop-houses, its beerless pubs, its once vivid quarters losing all personality, its squares bereft of elegance, its dandies in exile, its antiques in America, its shops full of junk, bunk, and tomorrow, its crowds mooning round the stained wicker of the cafeterias in their shabby raincoats, under a sky permanently dull and lowering like a metal dish-cover. . . . what we are really witnessing is the collapse of the Industrial Revolution, of that British Empire which was founded on geographical position, business daring, foreign investments, cheap labour, food and goods, wise administration, coal, iron and sea-power. We are decadent only if we fail to replace it by another. . . . if we could only produce a great architect, a man or a group who could create a new three-dimensional poetry in a material suitable to our climate and our time, then the whole nightmare of war-destruction, housing schemes, ruin and dilapidation would vanish. . . . since we have no real idea as to what are the values of our present civilisation we cannot get an architecture which embodies them.

(Cyril Connolly, 'Comment', *Horizon*, April 1947)

Stirling's preoccupations in the early 1950s were sometimes richly interconnected, and sometimes rendered up little more than suggestive fragments. Chapter Two described his work for private practices of the middling modernist kind, as well as his entries into two competitions for educational institutions. The present chapter is concerned with the same period but with a more theoretical and experimental side of his architectural thinking, showing how it related to the contemporary avant-garde. There are several unfolding developments and commitments that will be discussed here: his understanding of contemporary architectural possibilities as con-fided in his architectural journal; his relation to the Independent Group; his engage-ment with a number of related ideas about vernacular, regional and post-industrial architecture; and, finally, his complex and anxious commitment to Le Corbusier's work even as that work itself radically changed in the 1950s.

What brings all these matters together is the continuing emergence of a distinct aesthetic attitude. 'Junk, bunk and tomorrow' is a useful tag for this and one perhaps not unfamiliar to Stirling as a regular subscriber to Cyril Connolly's *Horizon*.[1] The first two terms indicate waste and nonsense, disregarded aspects of the past as well as disdained ways of thinking about it. The third term links to *This is Tomorrow* (1956), a seminal exhibition in which Stirling participated. The ambiguous referent of 'This' in that exhibition title matches the ambiguity of 'tomorrow' as a commodity in Connolly's London shops. Knowing that Connolly and Stirling were both frequent visitors to second-hand shops gives this phrase an extra dimension.[2] Both enjoyed the sense of potential discovery and reuse, and the memory of previous life in the worn and discarded. At the same time the proliferation of such shops was, for Connolly, symptomatic of a wider dissolution and decay, of a post-industrial and post-imperial civilisation in entropic deceleration. Connolly pointed to architecture as a way out of this situation, though he wrote little about it. Stirling had expressed a similar sense of an architectural vacuum.[3] The kind of 'three-dimensional poetry' he envisaged during the early 1950s might be called 'junk, bunk and tomorrow'.

This chapter argues that, in effect, 'junk, bunk and tomorrow' was layered onto Stirling's earlier modernist mannerism just as the latter began to diminish in interest for him. He wrote in 1957 that the neo-Palladian approach 'probably reached its peak in 1950–54'.[4] What he saw as both a replacement and a reaction to this was 'a reassessment of indigenous and usually anonymous building and a re-evaluation of the experience embodied in the use of traditional buildings and materials'.[5] The reasons for this turn to vernacular sources were a 'decline of technology' as well as 'economy, practicability and policy', meaning by 'policy' the lack of planning approval for modernist houses.[6] But, as the chapter suggests, this theory and its sources went wider than what is usually perceived as vernacular to 'other' architecture of various kinds,[7] to a bricolage approach, and to the beginnings of what would later be called 'an archaeology of the present', unearthing and reusing the layered remnants of the architectural past.[8] This was the period of Stirling's most intense involvement in theory, or at least the closest he came to coherent theoretical elaboration of his thinking about architecture. Not only did he keep an architectural journal, he also emerged in the mid-1950s as one of the more prominent of younger commentators on Le Corbusier's contemporary work. But 'junk, bunk and tomorrow', perhaps by its very nature, could not be a fully fledged aesthetic approach in architecture. It was more a number of related interests that, if never quite cohering at the time, would energise later architecture.

~

Stirling started his 'Black Notebook', or architectural journal, probably sometime late in 1953, continuing to make notes in it until 1956. Judging from the opening pages, which consist of quotes and commentary on Le Corbusier's *Modulor* (1951), it was probably started to initiate a kind of imaginary dialogue with something of importance, to project the writer into the company of those he esteemed. Also significant is that the journal starts with Le Corbusier because the Swiss architect remains one of its main, preoccupying subjects. So the Black Notebook was mainly a sounding board for Stirling's reflections on architectural theory and represents his first, if short-lived, forays into writing architectural criticism. The journal records Stirling's continuing struggles to understand and get some critical purchase on Le Corbusier's work. These efforts amount to an 'anxiety of influence', an obsessive need to come to terms with and to find a way around a dominant predecessor.[9] But whether quoting from Le Corbusier's writings and making notes on his buildings, jotting commentary on his reading and looking or speculating about broad architectural developments, there is a common focus to the journal. Stirling was driven to create some historical and critical space for working in, to define in non-pragmatic terms, outside everyday office work, what contemporary architecture should be doing and what his own role in that could be.

This is found early on in the journal when Stirling uses passages from Bruno Zevi's book, *Towards an Organic Architecture* (1950), to reconsider what the pioneering modernists had achieved as well as what had happened since the 1920s and early 1930s. The first period had produced 'programmatic' architecture, and since then a second generation, led by architects like Terragni, Asplund, Moretti, Aalto and Duiker, had devoted itself entirely to diffusing and harmonising these lessons: 'Since there has been no architecture of this category (programmatic) built in Europe between 34–53, therefore the great lack of vitality in that period.'[10] Most of the 'vocabulary' of modern architecture had descended from a small group of buildings designed by Le Corbusier, Mies van der Rohe and Frank Lloyd Wright. But there had not been a programmatic building put up since the 1930s, 'therefore the apathy': 'It will probably be left to the third generation to continue (we hope) programmatic development.'[11]

What this might mean is indicated only a page or two later when Stirling reflected on the exhibition of entries to the Sheffield University competition early in 1954. First he reduced the entries he considered worthy of comment to those by four of the younger practices: he and Cordingley, Sandy Wilson and Peter Carter, Alison and Peter Smithson, and John Voelcker. Then he gave his second and third impressions. Wilson and Carter's design for the Arts and Administration building consisted of a ten-storey slab building with curtain walling (fig. 50). Inside, the building housed the same variety of functions as in Stirling's design, but these were only acknowledged on the exterior of the building at those points where the curtain walling was

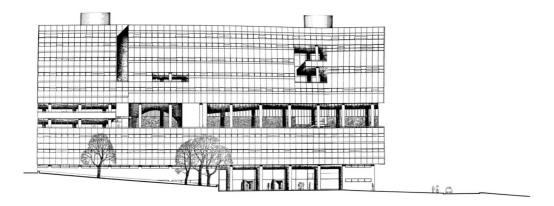

50   Colin St John Wilson and Peter Carter, Sheffield University Competition Entry, 1953, elevation.

cut away to reveal *piloti* and a further 'skin' inside the building surrounding the bigger, double-storey functional units within. The Smithsons' design struck out in two angled ranges of buildings that met to encompass a triangular piece of green parkland (fig. 51). Its most striking aspect, and one emphasised in the accompanying report,[12] was the theme of 'connection' here articulated at deck level, a circulation level running right through the buildings but also across the site and spearing through the existing buildings via an elevated and tube-like corridor or 'people-aqueduct'. The positioning of academic functions was decided partly with a view to feeding the busy-ness of this route.

The winners – Gollins Melvin Ward – Stirling described as 'the best of the safe, understandable moderns',[13] but he and some of the other young architects stood for something different in that all four of their designs were based on an 'idea'. Stirling identified Wilson's design as more architectural, 'more intelligible and acceptable' to a jury, but it was especially in its greater refinement that Stirling staked his own difference from Wilson.[14] Stirling characterised the approach of 'refining a principle which I had already worked out' as a kind of 'reaction'.[15] Instead, he wanted to push his development as far as possible, and as a consequence, he admitted, 'what I do appears to lack completion.'[16] 'I consider it desirable', he wrote, 'that the vocabulary and the development of contemporary architecture be extended and continued, ie anti-Mies, pro-Corb.'[17] This is clarified in Stirling's third impressions of the exhibition. His problem with Wilson's work was that 'it is regarded entirely legitimate to give an overall single expression to a block which has such highly diverse accommodation, by running a glass curtain wall in front of the structure so "disguising" the nature (function) of the accommodation behind.'[18] This was related to Mies,

51   Peter and Alison Smithson, Sheffield University Competition
Entry, 1953, axonometric.

whose architectural language allowed him to 'combine the Farnsworth house and the
drive-in restaurant, inflate to a gigantic size and make it a national theatre'.[19]

So the lessons of the competition were clear. Continuing with an architectural
form like the curtain wall regardless of the differing demands of function or programme led only to 'refining a principle' or a merely architectural solution. Equally
undesirable was the approach that effectively consisted in the building declaring 'I
have an idea', particularly to be found when the idea consists in an obsession with
a structural system or a strong method of circulation.[20] By contrast, and this is what
Stirling saw in Le Corbusier and presumably in work like his own Poole and Sheffield designs, it was better to reach for new forms of expression to match the functions of the building even at the risk of these not being fully worked out. The midway
point was to be found in the Smithsons' entry: '[somewhere] between total functional expression and complete subjugation of functional expression'. But the Smithsons '[make] the frame as such the most important, and [their] scheme is simple

52   Le Corbusier, *Unité d'habitation*, Marseille, 1946–52. Photograph *c.*1955 by James Stirling.

53   Skidmore, Owings & Merrill, Lever House, New York, 1949–52.

and unfunctional from the point of circulation.'[21] Stirling thus chose to focus on the reinforced concrete frame of the Smithsons' design, rather than its more radical handling of layout and circulation.

This intense scrutiny and reconsideration of his contemporaries' designs is one way by which Stirling tried to distinguish a third generation approach. But although he started out by seeming to want to renew the programmatic aspect of the first generation of modernists, by the end despite the licence granted for functional expression the discussion had become strangely unresolved. In fact, Stirling had come to accept that lack of resolution or incompletion was a kind of virtue. His next step, or set of ruminations, mapped an old dichotomy in architecture, between art and technology, onto a new geographical contrast, between Europe and America.

The central comparison here was between the expressive, 'artistic' means of Le Corbusier, represented by his *Unité d'habitation* (fig. 52), and a new impersonal, technology-led architecture that Stirling saw as emerging in America, exemplified by Skidmore, Owings & Merrill's Lever House in New York (fig. 53). They both continue high modernism but one path is academic or 'art architecture', the other is techno-logical or 'non-art architecture'. Stirling saw these paths as expressions of a fundamental split in modernism, one that had been latent before but never entirely manifested. One path 'exploits the technological advance (scientific discovery), is designed by a team, is anonymous in "character" and functional only in relation to its construction (factory fabrication) not functional in regard to its occupants'. The other path 'is reactionary in as much as there is no constructional advance, indeed it was built by mass labour (this is even more manifested by Corb's India buildings), it is designed by one man and has the imprint of prima donna architecture. It completely rejects the factory. It is functional in regard to its occupants (circulation, privacy of each dwelling unit).'[22]

The opposition is obviously highly simplistic and at first seems to load the dice in favour of the technological path. Possibly this is because Stirling's newer architectural acquaintances, like the critic and historian Reyner Banham, would have favoured this as the more dynamic path of development (embodied by Buckminster Fuller, Luigi Nervi and Albert Kahn). Yet there is tension in the rhetoric because all Stirling's other inclinations – whether in Rowe's teaching or Le Corbusier's buildings or in the other architects he lists on this side (Moretti, Wright, Mies) – had made him more sympathetic to the path of art architecture. One explanation for this is that the term 'academic' is not as negative as its usage in other contexts to mean rule-bound or stultified might suggest; in fact, as Stirling points out, its specific meaning here derives from Banham himself, who used it to stand for a belief in a style for the age (academic) rather than styles that change according to attitude and the 'permanency of technological change' (non-academic).[23] In this sense Stirling himself was academic, as he practically admitted: 'In architecture, the use of regulating lines, balanced asymmetry, proportion, any mathematical basis (including the Liverpool neo-Palladians) is considered "Academic". Non plan-grid architecture (ie AA tendencies), factory functionalism, is considered non-Academic.'[24] And, as he also argued, although a technological or 'non-art' architecture might once have been possible in Britain (he mentions the Crystal Palace and bridges by Telford), it could not succeed any more because of 'social conscience . . . our surplus of population, guilt complex, combined with a decline in wealth'.[25] The welfare state seemed to sponsor an academic modernism in Britain, but this did not have to mean one of the diluting, second generation sort. The solution instead was located in Le Corbusier's recent, post-war architecture: '[it] has been called classical, academic, antique, with justification as it is definitely anti-technological, though it is in every way progressive, indeed it is he more than anybody who has solved the schism in our own day.'[26] This way forward was also to be found in the 'conscious imperfectionists' among the second generation Europeans.

As we saw in the previous chapter, this 'programmatic development' would be a very different thing from that of its first generation forbears. It would break any connection between advanced architecture and new technology, and its functional expression would push it towards the mannerist reworking of anterior forms of architectural expression and urbanism. The new element the journal shows Stirling thinking through is the idea of functionalism in relation to work that seemed inconsistent, puzzling and even disruptive of previous expectations. This was not so much a group of architects as a number of works by architects of a similar generation, all belonging to the European 'art' camp but all distinct from what Stirling called 'academic perfectionists'. In particular, it was buildings by the contemporary architects Jaap Bakema, Peter and Alison Smithson, Luigi Moretti and André Wogenscky. He described their work as that of 'conscious imperfectionists'. It was romantic, even schizophrenic, 'reflecting the generally unsettled, financial and national aspects of many European countries', whose equivalent in Britain was the post-industrial condition.[27] The architecture was a product, then, of Rowe's 'state of inhibition' as well as what he called 'deliberate inversion' motivated by 'the very human desire to impair perfection'.[28]

Perhaps the most obvious of these 'imperfectionists' was Luigi Moretti and his lyrical, expressive modernism (fig. 54). Moretti used features like strangely rusticated basements, fragments of sculpture, and surfaces presented as if newly exposed or peeled off. Even Reyner Banham, in an article that Stirling must have known, had to admit to the 'disturbing quality' and baroque elements in Moretti's work.[29] There were memories of classicism in his compositions, and great drama in their deployment of looming, uninflected masses suddenly cut through with deeply shadowed voids. Moretti's buildings may well have indicated how modernism might find its way back to those historical sources, particularly the baroque, that Stirling had begun to admire under Rowe's tutelage.

Stirling's reaction to Bakema's work is more unexpected. Peter Smithson's response to the house Bakema designed for himself (fig. 55), for example, entirely missed the contradictions that Stirling found in it: 'the whole thing is designed

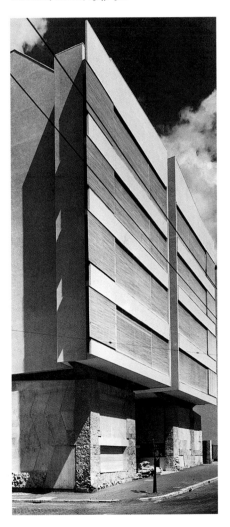

54   Luigi Moretti, Casa del Girasole, Rome, 1947–50.

55   Bakema and Van den Broek, Bakema House, Rotterdam, 1954, rear elevation.

with conviction, detailed with knowledge and supervised with care', Smithson wrote. 'It is the only post-war house in which I have felt anything other than despair. Here architecture lives.'[30] By stark contrast the same house for Stirling is 'the ideal of the romantics'; its structure is not just unclear but deliberately contrary:

> Is it a frame structure or a weight bearing wall building? (Three sides one and one side the other). The rear wall which has all the appearance of a poured concrete structure (a frame structure – Poissy) is actually weight bearing brick – rendered! – and worse insult it has long horizontal slit windows necessitating long and heavily reinforced lintels to convey big areas of brickwork over, all of which is rendered. What happens to the circular steel columns at the ceiling? Do they pick up beams which span back to the brick wall?[31]

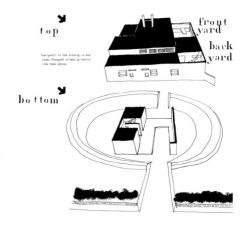

56   Peter and Alison Smithson, Bates's Burrows Lea Farm, 1953–55.

Here is an early example of a typical ruse in Stirling's writing. He is drawn to the very things that others might reject. He points to contradictions and raises unanswered questions, mulling over those features that fascinate him for their obscurity or idiosyncrasy.

Stirling wrote that he found these same qualities in the Smithsons' Bates's Burrows Lea Farm (1953–55) (fig. 56), but because he did not detail them in this case some speculation is needed. It may have been, for instance, the fact that neither the light steel frame nor the internal accommodation was expressed on the exterior, which instead had what seems an entirely idiosyncratic pattern of fenestration including inset glass bricks, all cut into seemingly load-bearing walls.

57 André Wogenscky, Wogenscky House, St Rémy-les-Chevreuse, 1954.

Finally, the house that André Wogenscky designed for himself at St Rémy-les-Chevreuse (1954) is one that Stirling visited and photographed at this time, mentioned in the Black Notebook and reproduced in the article on Ronchamp that he published in 1956 (fig. 57). Like the equally cave-like Bakema house, Stirling was drawn to the 'arbitrary' lack of fit between inside and outside in Wogenscky's house, particularly because the exterior seemed to disregard the double-height volumes within. And, again, previous values are ignored and become precarious: 'the flight from the "academicism" of pre-war modern is questionable when it produces an architecture of the irrational',[32] he wrote in the published article, while these effects and possibilities clearly also intrigued him.

Another eccentric who was undoubtedly aligned with the 'imperfectionists' in Stirling's mind was his friend and fellow Liverpool student, Christopher Owtram. Stirling stayed in contact with Owtram, visiting him in his converted oast house in Kent for a weekend in 1954. The visit impressed him deeply, and in the journal he lays it out as a formative event, an intense encounter of two romantic spirits. Owtram's studio was full of models, and it was lit by a huge 'zeppelin window' he had cut into the ceiling. The models included one for a house in the mountains of Arizona.[33] Owtram's designs had something of the uncompromising if overdramatic quality attributed to Howard Roark's work in Ayn Rand's novel, *The Fountainhead* (1943). They were full of jagged shapes looming hugely and vertiginously over the landscape (fig. 58), no floor or ceiling was set plumb, and a wide range of different angles was deployed (though it should also be said that in character Owtram, apart from his obsessiveness, was almost entirely the opposite of Roark's *übermensch*).[34] Stirling describes the designs as starting from an expressionist response, but then they 'go down a geometricising "production line"'. He continues:

> I imagine the conception might completely alter during this phase, plans, sections, elevations spring from a series of triangles or a selection of angles which he gets

58   Christopher Owtram with a model of his
design for the Queen Elizabeth Theatre,
Vancouver, 1955.

from an analysis of the planes that occur in the platonic solids, octahedrons, dodeca-hedrons etc. This gives him a variety of angles (how many? Guess 15) to which every plane in his architecture conforms. Thus a building is a grouping together of a number of points (or intersections) from which all his angles depart (or converge). By doing this on the vertical as well as the horizontal and in depth, he maintains he is truly three dimensional.[35]

Owtram was thus an odd combination of the terms that Stirling was deploying at this time: technological, but only in his devotion to mathematics; imperfectionist in his desire always to push solutions beyond what was reasonable; and romantic in his big-hearted, generously creative attitude towards his metier. Both for an idea of what an utterly committed architect could be, and for his strange, expressionist yet mathematically derived designs, Owtram seems to have remained in the back of Stirling's mind for some time. A decade or so later, on some of the conceptual sketches for the Florey building, he inscribed the name 'OWTRAM' almost as an admonition to think daringly.[36] But in 1954 Stirling was clear that while Owtram represented some direction striking out from the heart of modernism, it was not one that he could follow.

~

The neophyte architect glimpsed in the journal is one who, perhaps inevitably, seems introverted, bookish and absurdly ambitious given how little he had actually done. And unlike retrospective accounts of this period, the journal largely ignores those avant-garde circles which Stirling was a part of at this time; they seem marginal to his personal discoveries and swotty analyses. There is hardly a mention of discussions or meetings, apart from the stay with Owtram, a note of a passing comment by Edward Lyons, and mention of an Architectural Association lecture. Where signs of a sympathetic interlocuter might be expected – his collaboration with Cordingley on the Sheffield design, for instance, or the fact that when he visited the Maisons Jaoul in Paris he was accompanied by Alan Colquhoun – there is nothing. There is only one mention of Reyner Banham, and the references to such active young architectural fellow travellers as Sandy Wilson and Peter and Alison Smithson are strangely detached, as if denying Stirling's personal knowledge of them. On the one hand, there is the intensity of the journal with barely a hint of Stirling's links to any group, and, on the other, the undoubtedly close social and intellectual links that Stirling had in these same years with members of the most avant-garde grouping of the time. This is not to question the significance of what has since become known as the Independent Group (a term hardly used at the time) to Stirling; more to doubt its paramount importance. It was not his only reference point for what might constitute avant-garde activity and advanced thinking about architecture.

The nature of that activity justifies the descriptor 'neo-avant-garde'. The term has been much debated, especially by art critics, since Peter Bürger gave it currency in the mid-1980s.[37] It relates to a contemporary perception that a radical spirit had re-emerged in certain aspects of post-war architecture.[38] But 'neo-avant-garde' seems particularly relevant in describing the Independent Group's close, fascinated and ambivalent relation to the new forms of commodity or consumer culture, as well as the group's hyper self-consciousness about its relation to the historical avant-garde of earlier in the century (similar, as already seen in Chapter One, to Colin Rowe's position). Rather than Bürger's idea that the neo-avant-garde was actively complicit in nullifying the potential of the historical avant-garde, there was the sense, felt very strongly by the Independent Group, that the historical avant-garde's radical ideas had become institutional, ossified either by its own ageing members or by a succeeding, second generation. The spirit of that avant-garde needed reviving but also updating.

The Independent Group had started in the early 1950s, first through informal meetings of friends and sympathisers, and then through a symbiotic if rebellious relation to the Institute of Contemporary Arts.[39] Formalised in 1952, this relationship enabled the group to hold its own meetings and exhibitions at the ICA. Usually opposed to the newly official version of modernism, whether promoted by the 'old Surrealists', Herbert Read and Roland Penrose (who had founded the ICA),[40] or by Nikolaus Pevsner and other established cultural arbiters, the ideas of the Independent Group ranged widely across artistic, architectural and wider cultural matters, and its members were involved in groups like Team 10 and were to sponsor movements like New Brutalism. The membership was also broadly drawn, from critics like Reyner Banham and Lawrence Alloway, to artists like Richard Hamilton and Eduardo Paolozzi, and architects like Alison and Peter Smithson. Many of these members were from the provinces, several had been on active service or taken on technical roles during the war, all were of the same generation, and some even had working-class backgrounds. Stirling was one of a wider circle of supporters and participants, and his contact came primarily through that 'invisible college',[41] or talking shop, constituted mainly by gatherings in Reyner and Mary Banham's north London flat. Mark Girouard has detailed some of the complexities of this social network and Stirling's place in it.[42] He was on the margins of the group anyway. If he was a frequent attendee at the Banhams' mornings, he infrequently attended anything more formal than this: he later described the group as 'more social than intellectual. . . . the semi-public meetings were secondary for me'.[43] Of the latter it is only known for certain, for instance, that he attended Sandy Wilson's 1953 ICA lecture on 'Proportion and Symmetry'.[44] These provisos are important to what follows, in which four key Independent Group interests are described and Stirling's relation to them is plotted.

The first of these concerns ideas about high and low culture. As has often been discussed, the attempt to come to terms with new forms of mass and consumer culture (for which read American culture) was critical to the Independent Group. Paolozzi, Alloway, Banham and Hamilton were fascinated by, if equivocal about, many aspects of consumer culture even before it had properly emerged in Britain, their attitude lacking the snobbery or reflex condemnation typical of an older generation of modernists.[45] Hence Paolozzi's famous 'Bunk' epidiascope show at the ICA in 1952 based on his collection of comics and ephemera, Hamilton's paintings of cars and white goods, Banham's reviews of new product design, and the many Independent Group meetings devoted to mass culture. All of these were committed to analysis of the new phenomenon, often playful, often seeking creative inspiration, and never blandly celebratory. Whether Stirling was sympathetic towards much of this is open to some doubt. As discussed in Chapter One, he was intrigued by American mass culture in the late 1940s but also largely dismissive. Unlike Stirling, however, none of the inner core of members had actually visited the United States until 1955,[46] and it seems likely that his experience in the United States, conveyed through informal slide talks, contributed to the group's understanding of American culture.[47] Perhaps, though, American culture was more exotic when diffracted or seen from a distance through the media of film, advertisements and comics.

The second of these Independent Group interests is the issue of epochal change, the idea that the post-war years were witness to some fundamentally new form of modernity. Banham's own thoughts on this would result in his *Theory and Design in the First Machine Age* (1960), based on the PhD he worked on through the 1950s. His premise was that this first machine age, the age of the pioneer modernists of the first generation, could now be better understood from the perspective of a fundamentally different relation to industrial production – 'an epoch that has variously been called the Jet Age, the Detergent Decade, the Second Industrial Revolution'.[48] There was no sense of decline in Banham's mind. His progressive technological outlook (famously, the architect had to 'run with technology')[49] had no room for the historical dialogues, nostalgic musings and scepticism about technological advance that were present in Stirling's post-industrial outlook at this time, or indeed for the retro- or revivalist modernism that were later to be seen as the first indicators of postmodernism. Banham's was a profoundly, even aggressively positive attitude; new transformations in science and technology 'have powerfully affected human life, and opened up new paths of choice in the ordering of our collective destiny'.[50] It has been suggested that this attitude, shared by some other Independent Group members, played a legitimising role in relation to those interlinked policies encouraging consumption, rearmament and new technologies, and known as 'Tory Futurism',[51] though if this were the case then it would have gone against the group's avowed leftism. Arguably, the emphasis on these emerging technologies also played a sustaining part in some of the gathering myths of a post-industrial world free of the heavy industries, a world of immaterial labour.[52] This would lead, on the one hand, to ideas like information technology taking over all positions of power and, on the other, to the notion stemming from Marshall McLuhan of a new egalitarianism in the very technology of the new media. But above all, for Banham, it was in everyday and family life – in its disposable objects, domestic electronics (television bringing mass communication and entertainment into the home) and synthetic chemistry – that the effects of the new second machine age could be found.[53] As yet, Banham argued, we had still to find appropriate new ways of conceptualising this and were 'freewheeling along with the ideas and aesthetics left over from the first [machine age]'.[54] Of course, this was only the lens through which Banham saw the 'first' period of modernism, but there was equality in this very numbering of ages (rather than Pevsner's use of the term 'pioneers'). His revision of the canon of modernism in that first age was intended to draw out those lost elements which might best support the second age's new drives and impulses: futurism, expressionism, the inventions of Buckminster Fuller. If Stirling was interested in the same kind of revisionism, he shared few of Banham's enthusiasms. Instead, it was the constructivists (barely mentioned by Banham), De Stijl, and the late work of Le Corbusier who were the pioneering or first machine age elements of most interest to him. His lack of interest in technological utopia is epitomised by his remarks on his Poole entry or his journal comments on the two paths (the European art architects or the technologically driven American non-art architects). Although far from suggesting an architecture of resistance, at the same time Stirling's attitudes were not assimilable to Tory Futurism.

The third of the Independent Group interests is the idea of an anthropology of modernity. This relates to the Smithsons' famous Urban Re-identification Grid, exhibited at CIAM 9 in 1953, in which they challenged the dominant modernist organisation, the Congrès Internationaux d'Architecture Moderne (CIAM), and its approach to city planning. The Smithsons' grid presented a nested relationship of anthropological spaces based on terms like house, street, district and city, in contrast to CIAM's more abstract zoning of urban functions. The Smithsons' thinking was certainly aimed at revaluing working-class life, but not to the same extent as Stirling, who, later in the 1950s, attempted to do this by remaking the most potent embodiment of that life, the Victorian terrace (to be discussed in Chapter Five). Stirling's inclination here was in line with his own interest in nineteenth-century industrial and urban structures: he had, for instance, a particular interest in the backs of Georgian and Victorian terraces. In a sense this was a little too like Richard Hoggart's account of working-class culture – *The Uses of Literacy* (1958) – and perhaps not enough like the Independent Group's more favoured sociology of East End life, Willmott and Young's *Family and Kinship in the East End* (1957). Both texts were as much antagonistic to the sweeping powers of post-war reconstruction as to the condescension of the cultural elite, but Hoggart's in particular also saw the threat as coming from American-style consumerism, and with this Independent Group thinkers like Banham disagreed vehemently.[55]

Stirling developed rural versions of the Smithsons' anthropological modernism, but his interest in the vernacular veered close to the folk culture normally despised by Independent Group members. The first manifestation of this was a 1955 design for a house in Woolton near Liverpool (fig. 59).[56] The Woolton house took the form of two ranges of rooms with a group of lean-to roofs arranged dynamically in four different directions and at different angles above. Stirling presented this as a 'new interpretation of vernacular',[57] and described Woolton as 'traditional building . . . similar to the indigenous appearance of some recent European architecture',[58] no doubt thinking about the contemporary Danish houses discussed in his journal.[59] Like many of those Danish designs, Stirling made great play of the sloping ceiling by centring the Woolton house on a double-height living room with a gallery running for much of its length (fig. 60).[60] In describing the house as 'the reflection of a devitalised technology and . . . a reversion towards cosiness in domestic life',[61] he used terms that echo the post-industrial rationale for his Poole design. These sentiments would be repeated the following year when he wrote of how prefabrication and mass production 'no longer appears acceptable either at an aesthetic or at a practical level, and creative thinking is now mainly directed towards the utilisation of existing building methods and labour forces.'[62] It is not known how Stirling got the Woolton

ABOVE 59
James Stirling,
Woolton House, 1955,
model.

LEFT 60
James Stirling,
Woolton House, 1955.
Drawing c.1974 by
Leon Krier.

commission,[63] but it says a lot about his conception of regionalism that the site was only two miles from his family home in Liverpool, that he compared the design with Cotswold (!) farm buildings,[64] that Woolton itself was an area of already considerable suburban development, and finally that the house was never built because of the discovery of a tin can dump under the site.[65]

The village housing project was a hypothetical design (fig. 61). Conceived in 1955, it became one of seven display grids presented by the British contingent at CIAM 10, held in Dubrovnik in 1956.[66] This contingent was effectively the new Team 10 group, several of whom – like Stirling – overlapped in membership with the Independent Group.[67] (As it turned out Stirling could not attend the meeting, and his concern at the way the Smithsons presented all the British grids as variations on their own thinking led to a lasting estrangement from them.)[68] All seven grids were based on the idea of 'cluster', conceived in relation to different 'scales of association' according to generic locales and types of community.[69] Most closely associated with the Smithsons, 'cluster' was a principle by which a community was to be renewed by extending its already existing form, underlining that form as a basic anthropological datum for community.[70] The principle opposed the CIAM establishment's urban and rural thinking that aimed to subdivide by function. Rather than propose a new estate on the edge of the village or even rethinking the idea of a village, Stirling used Thomas Sharp's *The Anatomy of the Village* (1946) as his guide to rural spatial anthropology. For this third 'scale of association' he designed a scheme for linear housing parallel with the village street. Like the Woolton house, this housing was based on three structural walls, particularly a central, longitudinal wall off which were aligned parallel ranges of rooms and lean-to roofs. Variegated roofscapes and internal planning were created within this basic schema by differences in the provision for one- and two-storey accommodation, by differing land levels, or by different subdivisions of the parallel ranges.[71] The village housing was not regionalist in any specific sense, and there was no pretence it was based on study of actual cases, but it was an attempt to define vernacular not as a style or as a kind of representation but as a mode of repeated spatial form that offered certain aspects of flexibility. The scheme supplied a model that could be carried through in different situations by the available labour and materials,[72] whether traditional or industrial.[73] The vernacular was therefore seen as a broad orthodoxy encompassing and allowing aspects of dialect as they came to hand. Regionalism was not so much designed into the building as allowed for in the construction.[74]

Returning to Stirling's relation to the Independent Group, the fourth and final area of shared interest is the idea of the 'as found'. Broadly, in relation to a culture of austerity, the 'as found' was a bracing engagement with the everyday and a re-evaluation of objects as things to be used, cared for and reused rather than consumed

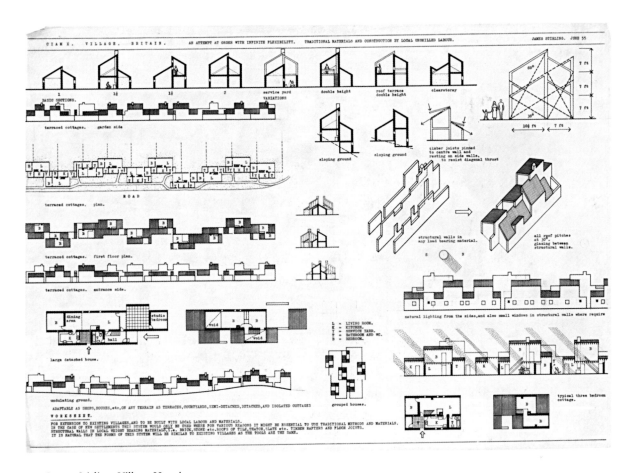

61   James Stirling, Village Housing, 1955.

and discarded. But at least three distinct positions on the 'as found' can be discerned, identified with Banham, the Smithsons and Stirling. As used by Banham in 1954 to describe the Smithsons' Hunstanton School, the 'as found' was an approach in which 'every element is truly what it appears to be',[75] and the lineage here went back to the Dadaists, 'who accepted their materials "as found"'.[76] Indeed, for Banham the 'as found' was a key element in a movement he was then defining – the New Brutalism – centred on 'memorability as image, clear exhibition of structure, valuation of materials as found'.[77] The 'as found' was neither 'truth to materials' nor the *objet trouvé*; both of those attitudes involved a kind of transcendence of ordinary expectations, whether in the bringing out of a material's essential qualities or the magic of chance discovery. For Banham the 'as found' had a strongly moral aspect, a quality of direct unvarnished truth that could, as at Hunstanton, insist on exposed plumbing

62   Peter and Alison Smithson, Hunstanton School, 1949–54.

to show, with edifying directness, how water got into and out of a sink (fig. 62).[78] For themselves, the Smithsons published little directly on the 'as found' at the time, although their planning notes for the *Parallel of Life and Art* exhibition reveal their thinking. Photo-enlargements would be shown of 'material belonging intimately to the background of everyone today. . . . [it is] so completely taken for granted as to have sunk beneath the threshold of conscious perception.'[79] Looking back in 1990 they defined the 'as found' as 'both about the specifics of a place and "a new way of seeing the ordinary",[80] an attentiveness to things that would raise them from their ignoble state. As found objects had a grand function: they were 'remembrancers in a place', and they could 're-energise our inventive activity . . . [and] re-energise the existing fabric'.[81] In a sense the 'as found' was an alternative to Rowe's mannerist modernism in seeking to find aura in the face of mass production, but instead of history it would be the immediately everyday that would be the source.

For Stirling the 'as found' was probably too closely linked to Banham's writing on the Smithsons for the term to be used extensively, and he seems not to have given the concept the Smithsons' sense of almost epiphanic powers of intensity. Stirling's use of materials 'as found' is, anyway, more properly discussed later in this book in relation to his work with Gowan. One root for it was, as discussed earlier, the turn to the vernacular and against attempts at prefabrication and mass production in the building industry. It was against this latter, a failure aesthetically and practically, that he posited the 'exploitation of local materials and methods',[82] and this was to extend to off-the-shelf products in his partnership with Gowan. The work of Charles and Ray Eames provided one model here (fig. 63). This certainly interested the Independent Group,[83] particularly the distinction between steel frame and 'as found' infill often seen in their work,[84] but Stirling – who claimed to have visited the Eames house in 1948, and certainly visited it later in the 1950s[85] – was drawn to a particular aspect of their work that he seems to have understood earlier than others in Britain.[86] This was the ad hoc and often playful use of materials and components manufactured for other industries, 'such as marine and aircraft fittings and factory building

63   Charles and Ray Eames, Eames House, Venice, California, 1949. Photograph by
James Stirling (?).

units . . . ranging from agricultural sheds to cast iron staircases'.[87] These might
provide, Stirling suggested, 'the basic components for houses composed as a *collage*
of existing products'.[88] Tellingly, his own photograph of the house gives no setting
or sense of volumetric presence, instead flattening its forms onto the picture plane,
like a piece of synthetic cubism. It was this interpretation of the 'as found' as involving serendipitous combination that was to spur Stirling and Gowan's use of disregarded materials and components often made for different purposes than those they
put them to.

For this chapter there is a more immediate example of the 'as found' in Stirling's
work. The swansong of Independent Group activities was its participation in *This is
Tomorrow*, an exhibition held at the Whitechapel Art Gallery in 1956.[89] The show was
organised as a collection of twelve exhibits, each put together by groupings of three
or four collaborators from the different arts. No consistency was intended; indeed,
according to Alloway the displays were meant to be dissimilar and even deliberately

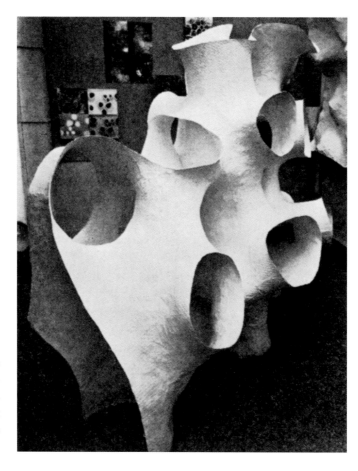

64   James Stirling,
Michael Pine and
Richard Matthews,
Group Eight
exhibit for *This is
Tomorrow*, 1956.

contradictory like the chaos of a city street.[90] Stirling's contribution was as part of
Group Eight with the two sculptors Michael Pine and Richard Matthews (fig. 64).
Their work was one of the simplest of those on display; it was certainly little noticed
at the time and subsequently.[91] It took the form of a free-standing sculpture inspired
by an investigation of detergent bubbles and consisting of a membrane made out of
papier mâché on chicken wire. It was biomorphic in shape and punctuated by
roughly regularly sized holes. The work can be understood as an attempt to make a
sculptural equivalent of the 'surface of discontinuity' in soap bubbles and of their
clustering effects, all beautifully described in D'Arcy Wentworth Thompson's *On
Growth and Form* (1917), a cult book among Independent Group members.[92] The
basis of the Group Eight work was underlined by exhibiting photographs of bubbles
on the walls around the sculpture,[93] thus pointing to the process of making the
bubbles, the action of then photographing them, and the translation from detergent

via photograph to papier mâché. There was also a contemporary aspect to Group Eight's work that can easily be missed in retrospect. This was *detergent* (the word was used on some of the photographs), rather than mere soap. Detergent was then coming into such widespread domestic use that the period, as we saw with Banham, was sometimes called the 'Detergent Decade'.

The collaborators in their accompanying notes made several gestures towards high modernism but couched them in the mock-breezy puffs of the salesman. The arts were absorbed into one – 'why clutter up your building with "pieces" of sculpture when the architect can make his medium so exciting'; romanticism was dead – 'the painting is as obsolete as the picture rail. . . . The ego maniac in the attic has at last starved himself to death'; and finally, artists were in a managerial culture – 'if the fine arts cannot recover the vitality of the research artists of the twenties . . . then the artist must become a consultant, just as the engineer or quantity surveyor is to the architect.'[94] Possibly more seriously, Group Eight suggested, the 'breaking down of conventional form' that had already occurred in the fine arts had not yet happened in architecture: 'the wall at least is beginning to go. The next step will be the volume of the building.'[95] Using an image evocative of Stirling's Aycliffe landscape drawings, the arts should come together 'in the landscape with no fixed composition but made up of people, volumes, components – in the way that trees, all different, all growing, all disrupted into each other, are brought together in an integrated clump'.[96]

Group Eight's work might simply be regarded as an avant-garde experiment in which Stirling's input was absorbed into the collaborative enterprise.[97] But it was more interesting than this suggests. The work's reflection on its own processes, for instance, offered a parallel to the collaboration of photographer, sculptor and architect in the way it moved from two-dimensional image, to sculptural fabrication, to room-size 'architecture'. It might also be seen as a kind of poker-faced comment on Le Corbusier's famous statement that 'a building is like a soap bubble', by which he exemplified a functional aesthetics.[98] But perhaps apart from its obvious organic analogy or morphology,[99] the Group Eight project is best understood as a manipulation of the 'as found', an experiment on ordinary materials. An act of amateurish, kitchen-sink science was practised upon a group of barely disguised everyday objects: chicken wire, newspaper and domestic detergent. Among the critics who ignored Group Eight's work was Reyner Banham.[100] Banham was far more interested in the work of Group Two (Hamilton/McHale/Voelcker) and Group Six (Henderson/the Smithsons/Paolozzi) and the twin, apparently opposed poles within which these works seemed to make sense: between the pleasures of mass consumption and the spectacle of ruined consumption in the post-apocalyptic dwelling. More 'austerity' thriftiness than 'affluent' consumption, Group Eight's work had none of the immedi-

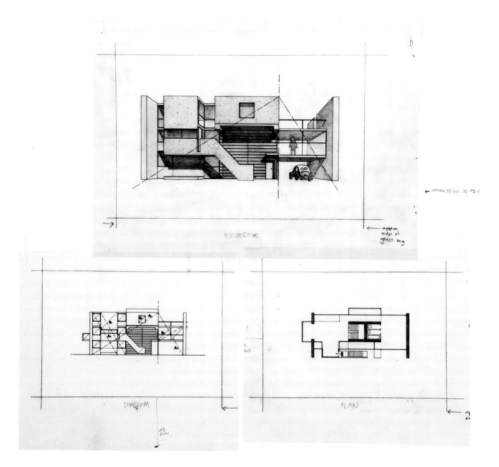

65   James Stirling, Core and Crosswall House, 1951, elevation, section and plan.

ate visual impact of these somewhat theatrical exhibits. But if it lacked the Independent Group's interest in image-making, it was also different from the pure, form-making concern of other exhibits.[101]

∼

This is a period of contradictions and possibilities, and part of 'junk, bunk and tomorrow' for Stirling was accepting these as part of the compost of a future architecture. Alongside his paid work and his competition entries in the early 1950s, there was also the occasional house project that shows him practising a kind of retro-modernism. The Core and Crosswall house (1951) is one of these (fig. 65). The design slung all of its accommodation between two widely spaced party walls and an H-shaped core. Any façade was largely dissolved within an elevation of stairs, glazed balconies and a parking bay. Unrelated to any commission, the design seems largely an exercise in purism, as if the garden façade of the villa at Garches had been reconsidered as a front. The regulating lines in Stirling's drawings demonstrate this Corbusian allegiance, but also a reworking of Rowe's neo-Palladian mathematics.[102]

Another equally propositional design is the so-called Stiff Dom-ino housing (1951) (fig. 66). Although Stirling evoked Le Corbusier's Dom-ino housing in the title and when he presented the project later,[103] the similarity only rests on the idea of the repeatable structural type. In Stirling's design four rectangular units were wrapped around a central staircase, each virtually free-standing with its own post and lintel system of trabeation (presumably giving the 'stiff' moniker).[104]

66   James Stirling, Stiff Dom-ino Housing, 1951, axonometric.

This kind of retro-modernism can also be found elsewhere. Stirling's design for a prototype table was shown at the ICA's *Tomorrow's Furniture* exhibition in 1952, and was a feature in his own flat (fig. 67).[105] Like a Marcel Breuer table reproduced in that classic modernist book *Bauhaus 1919–1928*,[106] Stirling's table had the same 'floating' glass surface and steel frame with curved corners, though it also had a slate surface set below and at right angles to the main glass pane. It is a notably elegant, high modernist, and therefore retardataire production compared with, on the one hand, the heavy, inscribed concrete slab that gave an existentialist edginess to the table made by Paolozzi and Terence Conran for the ICA two years before,[107] or, on the other hand, the furniture by Festival of Britain designers Ernest Race and Robin Day that also featured in *Tomorrow's Furniture*.

A little later, Stirling also worked on a design for a house that had De Stijl characteristics – the so-called house in north London (1955) (fig. 68). Brick in structure, in plan this took the form of two intersecting cubes with rooms arranged either side of a central hall and stair. Unlike some of Stirling and Gowan's designs in the later 1950s, Stirling did not exploit this configuration to set up spiralling levels within the

67   James Stirling, Table, c.1951, photograph taken in Stirling's black-painted flat.

house, preferring instead to design the whole of the first floor as one large area. The designs show a crisply cubic house, with slot and square windows as well as columns of windows rising the full height of the building on three sides, all deliberately designed to create a juxtaposition of bright and dark walls inside. It is a deceptively simple design but one that reminds us how even De Stijl and Corbusian purism could each be regarded as an architecture of fragmentation. Stirling conceived the design as either stand-alone or multiplied as a terrace – a kind of modern urban vernacular.[108]

Such modernist houses, Stirling came to conclude, were doomed never to be built because 'the building industry of this country cannot subscribe to "modernism" in the design of the "one-off" house.'[109] Instead of nostalgia for a modernist utopia, or even a transhistorical dialogue of modernist and mannerist, he was already looking to the possibilities of 'junk, bunk and tomorrow': of the vernacular and the 'as found' – as we have seen – but also of the industrial, of baroque relics and of the possibilities opened up by Le Corbusier's more recent buildings.

The interests in industrial buildings and in baroque architecture that Stirling had developed at Liverpool continued and expanded in the early 1950s and were joined by other, pre-modern architectural concerns. This was less an unfolding or tight-knit set of preoccupations than an activity of eclectic stockpiling of ideas and images. The best-known contemporary equivalent to Stirling's industrial architecture interests was the long campaign led by the *Architectural Review* to promote what it called the 'functional tradition', by which it largely meant early industrial structures and gear: factories, warehouses, dockyards, and mills especially, but also watermills, windmills and oast houses. The campaign's peak was reached in the special issue of 1957 in which Eric de Maré's photographs picked out the 'simple,

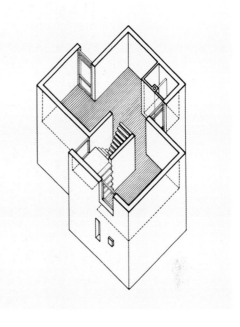

68   James Stirling, House in North London, 1955, axonometric.

robust detailing' of granite setts, steel plates and stone steps,[110] while J. M. Richards emphasised the 'range and subtlety of aesthetic effects' in the buildings.[111] There was a sense of loss for the 'long anonymous process' of reaching solutions based on generations of experience and skill,[112] but there was also a desire to reconcile the public with modernism by showing its continuity with the already familiar: as Richards put it, 'to allay the feeling that there is anything alarming or subversive in our preoccupation with functionalism'.[113]

Stirling sympathised with some aspects of this approach. He shared the idea that such buildings were 'unselfconscious and usually anonymous',[114] and his own interests at this time included oast houses and, of course, dockyards and mills (de Maré had even photographed Stirling's beloved Albert Dock). But he also criticised the *Architectural Review*'s idea of the 'functional tradition' for being 'a little narrow, faintly Georgian, and too nearly confined to early industrialism. It could have included fortifications, village housing and early office building.'[115] Fortifications in fact became one of his biggest interests at this time, with photographs of castles and earthworks in England, Ireland, France and even Mexico kept in his possession.[116] And unlike the *Architectural Review*, these pursuits were not maintained because of a campaign to sell modernism by showing how it shared functionalist attributes with already admired buildings, or even through some preservationist instinct. Instead, they were about providing equivalents, prototypes, inspirations and justifications; they existed for Stirling essentially as formal resonances and hardly at all as historical justification. One example of this is the trope of the rounded mass, the big, bulging cylindrical or conical form that keeps on recurring in his photographs from this time. He found and recorded it in castles at Herstmonceux and Restormel, in lighthouses and Martello towers, in the walls of Carcassone and at Albi cathedral, in Loire châteaux and Irish round towers, in oast houses and in Liverpool dock buildings.[117]

The sculptural attraction of such forms may also explain Stirling's continuing interest in the baroque. It was the success of the 'plastic' qualities of architects like Archer, Hawksmoor and Vanbrugh, he wrote around 1954, which pointed the way ahead for British architects in the future. Furthermore, 'Baroque or heavily sculptured architecture is [suitable for Britain], as it does not rely on sun but on the juxtaposition of solid and void and the resulting pattern, also because of the amount of wet and dirt, our buildings must be of such a powerful domination that dirt and

69   Thomas Archer, St John's, Smith Square, London, 1714–28, as photographed in 1943 after bomb damage.

staining do not matter (they will be inevitably), thus although Seaton Delaval and Archer's Westminster church have burnt out innards and damaged exteriors, they are such dominating and powerful designs that they are today still two of the most magnificent buildings' (fig. 69).[118] If 'bombing performed collage',[119] then this was how Stirling also saw Hawksmoor's 'facility to collage elements from the past'.[120] Generally, baroque architects had an 'ad hoc technique which allowed them to design with elements of Roman, French and Gothic – sometimes in the same building'.[121] The baroque resisted weather and war, and had a rugged relation to history; a liking for it was not to be conflated with the neo-romantic 'cult of ruins'.[122]

More recent industrial buildings also interested Stirling. The signs of wear and tear lovingly focused upon by the *Architectural Review*'s photographers were largely absent from most of Stirling's images of these buildings. Stirling photographed floating landing stages, weatherboarded riverside sheds, and the workings around gravel pits with cross-braced

LEFT 70   Gravel pit shack and workings. Photograph *c*.1955 by James Stirling.

BELOW 71   Mosley Common Colliery. Photograph *c*.1955 by James Stirling.

shacks faced with corrugated iron like some rough version of the Eames house (fig. 70). He was drawn, most notably, to the Mosley Common Colliery near Wigan, then recently nationalised and at the peak of its production (fig. 71).[123] From his photograph it is clear that the colliery offered Stirling the big volumes that he liked in the form of the stout concrete cylinder and funnel of the ventilation tower juxtaposed almost violently with the main building. It also had an exposed structural frame and angled sheds containing conveyor belts. The main building here – the coal cleaning plant – is lifted up above the ground so that cleaned coal could drop through screens into trucks below, and its layout and form probably also offered Stirling a frisson of recognition, a *Unité* in the Lancashire coalfield or perhaps even a premonition of

72   Harry S. Fairhurst & Son, York House, Manchester, 1911. Photograph *c.*1957 by James Stirling.

the Sheffield design. He was also drawn to York House, a distinctively shaped warehouse in Manchester, and photographed it in the late 1950s (fig. 72). Like the Mosley colliery, York House was by no means an old building – the architects Harry S. Fairhurst & Son had designed and built it in 1911. Many of Manchester's textile warehouses had almost entirely glazed rear elevations to provide as much light as possible for purposes of display and cloth inspection, but in addition here a narrow inner city site (it was originally hemmed in but neighbouring buildings had been destroyed in the war), legislation protecting rights to light and the availability of steel glazing bars had encouraged Fairhursts to adopt a seemingly idiosyncratic solution by stepping back and glazing the entire rear façade.[124] Again this becomes a formal source, inspiration or justification, as will be seen in Chapter Seven, for the Cambridge History Faculty building.

If the Mosley Common Colliery is related to Sheffield, then it is reconceived both as *parti* and as form – a scheme of a building elevated above the ground and served by various sculptural shapes, its bits and pieces reimagined as angled stairs and *piloti*-bearing substructure. The Manchester warehouse is reconceived as if its terracotta ornament and showcase functions did not exist; instead, it is a cascade of faceted plate glass. Both have their industrial functions stripped out of them as they are remade – picturesquely and arbitrarily – into university buildings.[125] To use today's jargon, the knowledge economy is seen to rise out of the industrial heritage.

What is happening in these and other photographs is a revaluing of these buildings as found objects separate from their functional or historical existence. Partly this is accorded to the photographs themselves, kept carefully in Stirling's possession throughout his career, but partly also this is expressed in terms of a fetishistic industrialism, a formalism that is both aesthetic and anaesthetic. Even though both the colliery and York House were still active working buildings (indeed, the colliery had recently been nationalised and was at the peak of its production), when Stirling photographed them they were treated as if liberated from their everyday locations and functions. The pictures tell us next to nothing about how these buildings function, who works in them and why they take the form they do. There is also – unlike the *Architectural Review*'s 'functional tradition' – a curious ambiguity about the meaning or lessons of such buildings, as if they resonate only within a personal image bank where gravel pit shacks can evoke the Eames house. Some justification for this can be found in Stirling's essay, 'Regionalism and Modern Architecture' (1957). As with his Poole design, he related architectural expression to mid-century industrial changes:

> In this country, the decline of technology, particularly in Building and Civil Engineering, is forcing Architects away from the radical or science fiction outlook. One only has to compare the Crystal Palace to the Festival of Britain, or Victorian railway stations to recent airport terminals to appreciate the desperate situation of our technical inventiveness in comparison to the supreme position which we held in the last century.[126]

This is also why Stirling's fascination with industrial structures evokes first generation modernist interest in things like grain silos and ships but at the same time is cut off from such a pattern of sourcing. The sense of industry neglected or decaying, coming to an end or simply sidelined but now noticed by the aesthetic imagination, is more apparent. Tellingly, the illustrations accompanying this article were largely Stirling's own photographs of nineteenth-century industrial structures, photographed as remnants of a dead civilisation (fig. 73). Indeed, the article barely disguised itself as a portrait of Stirling's own attitudes: today, he wrote, such structures 'may be appreciated picturesquely and possibly used arbitrarily'.[127] Yet Stirling was also plainly disturbed by this and engaged his own inclinations in a piece of implied self-critique: he quoted W. R. Lethaby attacking 'derivative ideas of what looks domestic, or looks farmlike . . . things that look like things but are not the things themselves'.[128] He saw his interests as related to the contemporary 'New Movement' in literature (writers like Kingsley Amis, John Wain and Philip Larkin) but at the same time realised that they both shared a certain nationalistic, 'cottage culture' attitude.[129] The article ends, however, by invoking Eliot's 'The Waste Land' as an almost forgotten modernist work: 'how much more *modern* it seems than anything being written now.'[130]

Both Stirling and Rowe were admirers of T. S. Eliot's poetry and Rowe seems also to have admired his critical essays. For Rowe, as Anthony Vidler has written, Eliot 'was a champion of the virtues and values of the ambiguous and the difficult'.[131] For Stirling, invoking Eliot seems like a way of dealing with the fetishistic and parochial. What was specifically ambiguous and difficult in Eliot's work was the meaning of the relation between elements of myth, previous poetry, vernacular language, kitsch

Figure 1a Early warehouse in Liverpool

Figure 1b Late nineteenth century warehouse in
Liverpool

Figure 1c Late nineteenth century office building
in Liverpool

Figure 1d Martello tower on the south coast

Figure 1e Tile kiln in Staffordshire

73   James Stirling, photographs of industrial
buildings from 'Regionalism and Modern
Architecture', 1957.

and high poetic diction that were all brought together in his poetry. In other words, what 'Eliotic modernism' included was *both* Rowe's mannerist conflation of the high artistic traditions of the past with the present *and* (despite Eliot's mandarin reputation) the linking together of the previously segregated realms of ordinary, vernacular, even kitsch diction with those of aristocratic tradition. This was not a bare, austere modernism but one that embraced the oceanic variety of literature; it did not declare war on the past but fingered the past's differences lovingly, and it did not develop by stripping away to the essence of the medium but by accreting and collaging 'as found' images and languages.

Another example of a practice of using found objects was the work of Eduardo Paolozzi. Stirling was close to Paolozzi in the mid-1950s, and they shared similar experiences of growing up near areas of blighted dockland. Around 1957 Stirling stayed with the sculptor in his cottage at Thorpe-le-Soken in Essex.[132] In the photographs Stirling took of the studio, Paolozzi appears as a shadowy or marginal presence while the studio itself is the main subject (fig. 74). A bag of plaster sits in the middle, drawings and reproductions are tacked onto the far wall, and a bare bulb shines down on the detritus of work all around. In the mid-1950s in this same studio, Paolozzi began to make sculptures that combined several wax reliefs, each encrusted with the shapes of found objects pressed into the original clay. He listed some of these objects: 'dismembered lock, toy frog, rubber dragon, toy camera, clock parts, broken comb, parts of a radio, an old RAF bomb site, natural objects such as pieces of bark, gramophone parts and model cars'.[133] A little later Paolozzi explained that it was the process of transformation that intrigued him, and that 'in the finished casting the original *objets trouvés* are no longer present at all, as they are in the Dada and Surrealist compositions of this kind. They survive in my sculptures only as ghosts of forms that still haunt the bronze, details of its surface or its actual struc-

74   Eduardo Paolozzi in his studio, 1957. Photograph by James Stirling.

ture.'[134] This was, then, not the preservation, displacement or juxtaposition of junk for its convulsive potential; nor was it a mere record of its previous life – after all, what interest was there in the life of mechanical gadgets or circuit boards? Rather, it was a record of junk going through a 'metamorphosis of matter'.[135] The items – not so much blasted as petrified – were treated as 'ready-made phrases',[136] found then reconfigured as entirely different objects: 'A MAZE OF PARTS AND PERSONS like an avant garde POWER PLANT'.[137]

Writing about Paolozzi's work in 1956, Lawrence Alloway described its frame of reference as reaching far beyond the studio. It was not the collected images in themselves, Alloway argued, that were Paolozzi's inspiration. Rather, these images belonged to an undifferentiated field of visual material, one which was familiar to earlier modernism but which no theory or formal rules, in the manner of the Bauhaus, would now constrain: 'Paolozzi approaches the material from the opposite direction; to him motion studies, microphotography, illustrated magazines, are "natural sources". To him Moholy-Nagy's *Vision in Motion* is not a grammar, but just another collection of images, in line with *Life*.'[138] In other words, the high modernism of Moholy-Nagy was another form of junk, part of the recyclable mass of cultural detritus, the manure in which another art would grow. According to Alloway, Paolozzi's approach entailed a new, 'multi-evocative' way of 'seeing wholes': 'the head is a head, a planet, an asteroid, a stone, a blob under a microscope; it is big and small, one and many.'[139]

Stirling was certainly interested in his friend's work, though there is very little record of what he thought about it beyond a tantalising comment that it, like the work of the De Stijl artists and the constructivists, 'presents images and symbols for the use of constructors'.[140] Alloway's views on it clearly resonate with Stirling's work. A ragbag of images and interests seem to have operated as a kind of mystic architectural writing pad for Stirling like the junk captured in Paolozzi's lost wax process: architecture and building, modern and pre-modern, industrial and vernacular were all drawn from. Imperfection was valued; something like a 'multi-evocative' whole would result. And if there was an architectural equivalent for this that Stirling could latch onto, it was in Le Corbusier's contemporary buildings.

~

From the time when he first encountered it in the late 1940s, Le Corbusier's work had played a central role in Stirling's thinking about architecture. More surprisingly, even before he could put his name to any building of his own, Stirling had acquired a certain status and certainly a distinct voice as a public commentator on Le Corbusier. In 1955 he shared a platform at the ICA with the eminent architectural historian Henry-Russell Hitchcock,[141] in 1955 and 1956 he published two influential articles on Le Corbusier's post-war buildings, in 1958 he lectured on the same evening at the Walker Art Gallery, Liverpool, with the equally eminent John Summerson,[142] and in the following year he shared a radio panel discussion with his mentor Colin Rowe and the modernist pioneer Berthold Lubetkin.[143] It is in his two articles that Stirling reached his most coherent exposition of the new developments in Le Corbusier's post-war architecture. Envisaged as a pair, the articles clearly emulate Rowe's two articles of 1947 and 1950, also published in *Architectural Review*, but in addition they challenge mannerist modernism by confronting it with Le Corbusier's new interests in the vernacular and the metamorphosis of base materials.[144]

Stirling writes as a third generation modernist separated by age and war from the pioneering years of the movement. As his journal reveals, his reaction to Le Corbusier's recent works was coloured by the ambivalence he felt on viewing the architect's earlier Parisian buildings in 1954 and 1955:

> It is with considerable nostalgia that one perceives for the first time the earliest works, some are deserted and the best stand like monuments dedicated to the way of life which specifically is dead and generally has never arrived (at least in Europe). They stand as reference to the formative days at the beginning of the century, the culture in which we now exist, though we hardly know why. The principles born in the 20s revolution have in no way been superseded and until we create our own theories or arrive at a new philosophy, it is better to understand our heritage than to try to produce in a void without direction.[145]

This is an apt expression of what has been called 'reflexive modernization', or that here might be termed 'reflexive modernism': in the face of new complexities, a sense of disenchantment with an older cultural formation as well as a sense that its presumptions had dissipated.[146] Stirling had to come to terms with this legacy, but he also had to make sense of Le Corbusier's more recent developments.

Stirling's first article, 'Garches to Jaoul: Le Corbusier as Domestic Architect in 1927 and 1953', appeared in *Architectural Review* in September 1955. The text was accompanied by fourteen of his own photographs (fig. 75), juxtaposing aspects of the villa at Garches and the Jaoul houses, then nearing completion in Paris: overall views, balconies, the relation between structural elements on the façades, and contrasts between materials and environmental devices (*brise-soleil* against concrete rainwater heads, for instance). But beyond the different properties of the buildings there were also photographic contrasts caused by the evident state of unfinish of the Jaoul houses: gaunt openings against shiny reflections in glass, cave-like vaults against transparent corners, rough against smooth. Above all, there were apparently incidental contrasts: the clean, well-maintained areas of Garches against the untidiness of the Jaoul building site with its propped ladders, piles of rubble, heaps of planks and lumber, hanging wires and barrels of water. In short, Stirling used his photographs to heighten differences between the machine aesthetic of the earlier house and the primitivism of the more recent ones. If there was a possibility that the Jaoul houses might themselves have internalised a dialogue between the industrial and the handmade,[147] this was outside the highly rhetorical structure of the essay.

How does the comparison with Garches work textually? The Jaoul houses, though unfinished, stand for the crystallisation of a new post-war development in Le Corbusier's approach to architecture. As bourgeois Parisian residences in Neuilly, the Jaoul houses were similar enough to offer a sensible point of comparison with Garches. But they were also vividly different. Between them, Garches and Jaoul represent extremes:

75   James Stirling, page of photographs from 'Garches to Jaoul', 1955.

the first representative of Colin Rowe's pristine neo-Palladianism, the second of a coarse *Art Brut* sensibility, then of some interest to the Independent Group;[148] 'the former, rational, urbane, programmatic, the latter, personal and anti-mechanistic'.[149] The smooth, white, rectilinear façade of Garches juxtaposed with the rough-edged, three-dimensional materiality of Neuilly, Garches's point structure and free plan against Jaoul's load-bearing brick walls and cellular plan.[150] Garches 'appears urban, sophisticated and essentially in keeping with "l'esprit parisien"', while the Jaoul houses 'seem primitive in character . . . out of tune with their Parisian environment'.[151] If Garches had received Rowe's endorsement as a building in dialogue with the Palladian tradition, then with Jaoul the dialogues were of a different, lower kind: with the regional and folkish, but possibly even with more atavistic experiences as expressed by the houses' grainy and sloppy material qualities. Yet, perversely, the Jaoul houses make the call for regionalist sensitivity absurd.[152] Built in the plush inner suburbs of Paris, they recall Provençal farmhouses and 'their pyramidal massing is reminiscent of traditional Indian architecture': 'it is perhaps disturbing to encounter the Jaoul houses within half a mile of the Champs Elysées'[153] and, it might be added, in a street full of stone and stucco neoclassical and art deco buildings. There is curiosity as well as fastidiousness in this comment. The contrast is so absurd – everything the Champs Elysées seems to stand for against an *Art Brut* paste put together by unskilled colonial labourers – that Stirling suspects some other agenda is at play.

Stirling found the same effects in Jaoul's interiors. 'The spatial effects,' he wrote, 'though exciting, are unexpected, encountered suddenly on turning a corner or glimpsed on passing a slit in the wall.' Yet this space does not flow; the double height of the living rooms 'appears as a dead area'. Contrastingly, Garches is a 'dynamic' space, by which Stirling meant that the house's limits could be apprehended at a glance, whereas Jaoul's space is 'static': it blocks larger views and breaks up smooth passage. And this stalling of the body and arresting of the eye is continued, Stirling argues, in the treatment of materials that are rich and varied in their 'surface impasto', including even the windows (which 'are no longer to be looked through but looked at') and their surrounds. While Garches's finishes are neutral, those in the Jaoul houses clamour and draw attention away from the contours and forms of the architecture: there are shutter-marked concrete, fair-faced brick, plastered walls, tiled floors, and, most significantly, the underside of the vaults are tiled and consequently 'cannot be expected to amplify "the magnificent play of light on form"'.[154] Reyner Banham noticed this emphasis on the surface and Stirling's use of the painterly word 'impasto' to describe it, linking it to Paolozzi's sculpture,[155] but he did not mention the complex visceral experiences of the building that so impressed and intrigued Stirling. Much of what Stirling saw in the Jaoul houses confirmed what he had already concluded about the crisis of a progressive industrial era.

The second of Stirling's articles on Le Corbusier's contemporary buildings, 'Ronchamp: Le Corbusier's Chapel and the Crisis of Rationalism' (1956), expands on these ideas while also taking them in new directions. Again Stirling adopts the same fascinated yet ambivalent and sometimes critical approach to his subject. The ambivalence had been expressed as bafflement in the Black Notebook:

> Most ephemeral, difficult to remember after departing, there is something about it (the idea in Corb's mind I think) which I have failed to grasp. With considerable on the spot study I feel it might eventually communicate something of great importance – what?[156]

Stirling's account of the building begins as a conventional description, outlining the distant view with 'the sweep of the roof, inverting the curve of the ground', the building achieving 'an expression of dramatic inevitability' like an encounter with Stonehenge or the dolmens in Brittany.[157] A sequence of five photographs supports this, demonstrating how, after the track from the village allowed only fragmented views, the chapel becomes suddenly apparent, looming above the visitor. But Stirling is quickly drawn to the building's surfaces, seeing these as responsible for its 'ethereal quality'.[158] The walls have an 'equivocal nature'; their whitewashed rendering gives them a weightlessness and an 'appearance of papier-mâché' that offsets the concrete of the roof. And this equivocation continues in the device of using the same wall surfaces inside the chapel.

Stirling seizes on those surface effects of the chapel that relate to the structure. 'Echoing the sag of the roof,' he writes, 'the concrete floor dips down to the altar-rail which appears to be a length of folded lead.'[159] The concrete altar blocks are 'cast to a marvellous precision', but the colours are troubling. There is a 'liturgical purple' on one wall, and the whitewash on the splayed reveals of the window openings returns to create three-inch frames on this same wall, reminding Stirling of 'the painted surrounds on houses around the Mediterranean coast'. Patches of green and yellow are placed either side of the main entrance as well as around the opening containing a statue of the Madonna that can pivot to face inside or outside. He notes of the north-east tower, painted red for its entire internal height, that it has 'the luminosity of "Dayglow"'.[160] Again, the sense of Stirling's instinctive fascination with something that his modernist instincts would otherwise dismiss is palpable here (all the more so, with hindsight, because of the importation of fluorescent colours into his work in the following decade). Stirling recognised the popular appeal of these and similar effects (including the chapel's acoustical properties), the sense that they might reach into a more elemental communal feeling than modernism had previously achieved.[161] Ronchamp's effects are 'sensational' and precisely because of this it has achieved 'easy acceptance by the local population', but when these emotions have subsided 'there is little to appeal to the intellect, and nothing to analyse or stimulate curiosity'.[162] Several of its features are deceits or what Stirling elsewhere had called 'imperfectionism'. Although 'it has the appearance of a solidifying object', the chapel's walls are not concrete but weight-bearing masonry. The shape of the walls was developed when it was thought that concrete would be sprayed onto wire meshing,[163] yet when the structural idea was changed this shape had been retained, filled in with masonry, rendered and whitewashed. Inside the building, Stirling points out, the west wall 'became so interrupted with openings' that a concrete frame was embedded in the masonry to reinforce the windows.

Instead of new materials and new techniques, Stirling argued, European modernists had turned recently to folk architecture and popular art for inspiration. Le Corbusier had led the way, frequently reproducing Mediterranean vernacular structures in his books. But where Jaoul's regionalism offered an aesthetic of contrariety, reacting against its context, Ronchamp's offered a practice of gathering and mixing. Stirling was drawn to the chapel's 'plastic incident' (fig. 76): the scattered openings on the walls splaying wilfully inwardly or outwardly, the mix of large stones and concrete in the walls of the outbuildings, and certain details like woodwork painted sky-blue and patterns decoratively applied to smooth renderings neither of which were based on 'formal, structural or aesthetic principle'.[164] He suggests that these vernacular sources are often undigested, that 'if folk architecture is to re-vitalise the movement, it will first be necessary to determine what it is that is modern in modern architecture'. Like Paolozzi, the Swiss architect has become a type of *bricoleur* or ragpicker: 'Le Corbusier's incredible powers of observation are lessening the necessity for invention, and his travels around the world have stockpiled his vocabulary with plastic elements and *objets trouvés* of considerable picturesqueness.'[165]

Again Stirling's fascination with this is apparent, his reflex of attraction in tension with his modernist instincts. The result is an ambiguity about whether the loss of 'the necessity for invention' might really be compensated for by a new aesthetic practice of sifting through cultural detritus, accumulating found objects, and splicing together the seemingly disparate lumber. Ronchamp is modern and it is archaic; it is natural and industrial; it evokes aircraft wings and shells; rather than an invention, a 'pure creation of the mind',[166] it is a machine for combining references, objects and experiences.

In its 'desire to deride the schematic basis of modern architecture'[167] and actually to turn design principles upside down, Ronchamp's complexity and contrariness makes it a mannerist building, writes Stirling using Rowe's terms. But rather than extending the

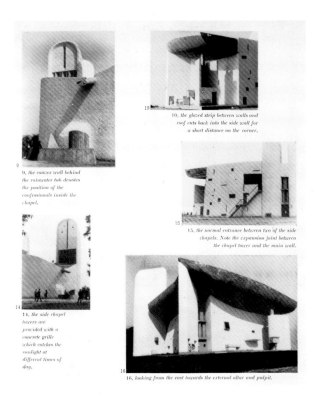

10, the glazed strip between walls and roof cuts back into the side wall for a short distance on the corner.

9, the convex wall behind the rainwater tub denotes the position of the confessionals inside the chapel.

15, the normal entrance between two of the side chapels. Note the expansion joint between the chapel tower and the main wall.

14, the side chapel towers are provided with a concrete grille which catches the sunlight at different times of day.

16, looking from the east towards the external altar and pulpit.

76   James Stirling, page of photographs from 'Ronchamp', 1956.

vocabulary of what has gone before, as a modernist or renaissance architect would do, it revels in a 'conscious imperfectionism'. It is 'a masterpiece of a unique but most personal order'. He summarises: 'the flight from the "academicism" of pre-war modern is questionable when it produces an architecture of the irrational.'[168] Yet this 'unsolved message' was culturally complex and alluring, not something easily wished away.

~

The *bricoleur* uses 'whatever is at hand'.[169] Whether or not they have been conceived for the task they are to be used for, these means are heterogeneous, left over, collected because they might come in handy, and changed or adapted if need be. Claude Lévi-Strauss, who through the 1950s was developing the idea that was to appear eventually in *La Pensée Sauvage* (1962), refers to the mytho-poetical nature of bricolage: the means or objects constitute a treasury; they already possess different meanings, 'transmitted in advance';[170] the repertoire can be permuted but freedom of manoeuvre is limited; and finally, new worlds are built from the fragments of shattered old worlds. These ideas about bricolage offer perspective on not only Stirling's view of Le Corbusier but his own thinking at this time. The comparison Lévi-Strauss makes between the *bricoleur* and the engineer, the type of maker who pushes at the limit of resources and questions rather than accepts the given, is particularly relevant to Stirling's distinction between 'art-architecture' and 'non-art architecture'. The *bricoleur*, unlike the engineer, 'does not subordinate each task to the availability of raw materials and tools conceived and procured for the purposes of the project'.[171] His tools are the 'contingent result of all the occasions there have been to renew or enrich the stock or to maintain it with the remains of previous constructions or destructions'.[172] The engineer works with concepts, Lévi-Strauss states, and the *bricoleur* with signs.[173] The engineer works without constraints, opening up new capacities; the *bricoleur* is retrospective, he interrogates, chooses between and redisposes his objects. Bricolage has been seen as 'critical language', or critical of language, in that it is opposed to one-to-one correspondence and the instrumentality of tools. But in a sense all languages and concepts borrow from what already exists.[174] If the engineer, as creator out of whole cloth,[175] is the *bricoleur*'s myth, then high modernism as a purely functional or rational architecture was the myth produced by late modernism.

Invoking bricolage later became standard in accounts of postmodernism. In Rowe and Koetter's *Collage City* (1978), or Silver and Jencks's *Adhocism* (1972), for example, bricolage was the emblematic panacea to the ills of modernism, much as for Manfredo Tafuri in 1974 it was a rewriting of modernism as an 'archaeology of the present'.[176] But to some extent the way those accounts used bricolage was already after the event by two decades. Bricolage might better be understood as a *post-war* strategy, as a poetics of the object in austerity rather than a critique of it under consumption.

'Junk, bunk and tomorrow' compasses, therefore, the new forms of aesthetic practice that interested Stirling in the early and mid-1950s – whether described as the 'as found', Eliotic modernism, Le Corbusier's bricolage, the 'imperfectionist' architects like Moretti, a new vernacular, the composite qualities of the baroque and the industrial, or the ghost-traces of undifferentiated visual material in Paolozzi. Fragmentary and immature as the productions associated with Stirling's 'junk, bunk and tomorrow' were, they cannot be reduced to a precursory state of postmodernism: they never simply posed arcadia against utopia, or made 'bricolage into myth', or froze architecture by simulating heterogeneity.[177] This is modernism recast as an open-ended or receptive project, recuperating the ugly and the ordinary as much as the durable and grand. It implies that there are many ways and many kinds of objects that can be adopted to negotiate with and intervene in the modern, as opposed to a modernism that was perceived as ossifying and becoming homogeneous as much in its forms as in its social visions and attitudes towards the past. Perhaps this was 'tomorrow' – looking backward while moving into the future.

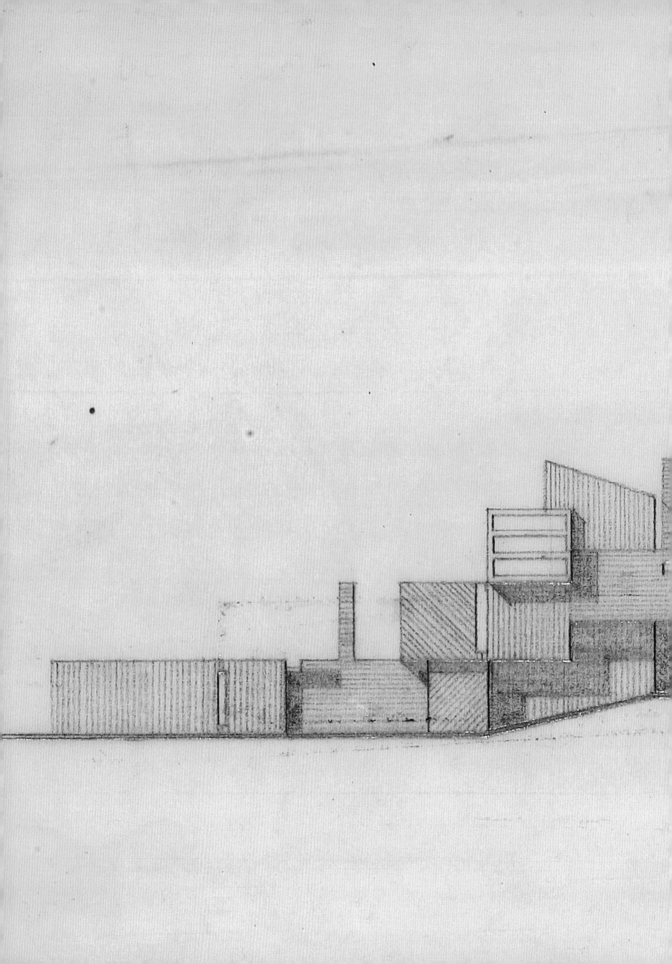

FOUR

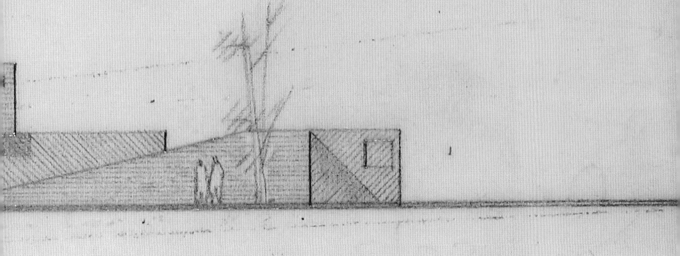

The Cube and the Pile-Up

The historical sense involves a perception, not only of the pastness of the past, but of its presence; the historical sense compels a man to write not merely with his own generation in his bones, but with a feeling that the whole of the literature of his own country has a simultaneous existence and composes a simultaneous order. This historical sense, which is a sense of the timeless as well as of the temporal and of the timeless and of the temporal together, is what makes a writer traditional. And it is at the same time what makes a writer most acutely conscious of his place in time, of his own contemporaneity.

(T. S. Eliot, 'Tradition and the Individual Talent', 1932)

Theories, competition entries, exhibition displays and hopeful designs for houses took Stirling only so far. So, too, did the work for Lyons Israel Ellis with its occasional opportunity to design a detail within one of their schemes. The royal road to architecture needed a commission that might be built, and suddenly late in 1955 it arrived. The group of flats at Ham Common proved too great a challenge for Stirling on his own to meet, so he invited James Gowan to leave his work at Lyons Israel Ellis and collaborate with him. The partnership that was formed early in 1956 lasted for another seven years, and although its output was relatively limited its impact on the architectural scene was enormous. It certainly launched Stirling's career as arguably the most important of post-war British architects, both nationally and internationally, although Gowan's was not to take off in the same way after the partnership dissolved. This chapter is concerned with the launch of that partnership and particularly with how design worked as a collaborative venture between the two architects. To do this it will analyse a number of housing projects, both built and unbuilt, dating from the first work of the partnership to the late 1950s.

The notoriously fractious relationship that developed between the partners was an important factor in their achievement. Mark Girouard has used the term 'creative tension' to describe this relationship, deriving it from an interview with Michael Wilford, who worked as an architectural assistant in the partnership's last years and later (in 1971) himself became Stirling's partner.[1] This formulation gains part of its currency from its relation to a colourful and discordant new architectural identity emerging at this time in contrast to the model of the anonymous public architect: a sometimes playful, sometimes edgy identity combining ideas about angry young men, Teddy boy architects and awkward, blunt provincials shaking up the big city. Stirling certainly played up to this image.[2] But 'creative tension' also bespeaks a particular dynamic within the partnership. In his biography of Stirling, Girouard used the term to label a photograph of Stirling and Gowan (fig. 77). Stirling leans easily to the side looking wryly towards the camera, while Gowan, absorbed and tense around the mouth, looks down and outwards to the right. Between the two is an evocative gap, measured out by a line of columns behind them. The contrast with a photograph reproduced later in the same book, of Stirling and Wilford sitting companionably across a table, seems to speak for itself.[3]

77   James Stirling and James Gowan, *c.*1956.

In analysing the partnership between Stirling and Gowan, however, we need to be wary of several aspects of 'creative tension'. Obviously, focusing on it might too easily gloss over such issues as design development, the apportioning of responsibilities for a building, and the roles of clients and planning authorities (critical in Britain after the 1932 and 1947 Town and Country Planning Acts). Moreover, 'creative tension' seems implicitly contrasted with a certain stereotype of a good partnership within architectural history, one in which a mercurial and inspirational partner is complemented by a practical and methodical one.[4] Against this model, Stirling and Gowan's 'creative tension' stands for a situation in which both partners make equal contributions to the creative side of the work but their attitudes, working rhythms or characters are ill-matched, and some of the creativity seemingly arises from the friction that results. The stereotypically balanced partnership, by implication, offers the corrective or norm against the creative but dysfunctional one, and it is this conventionally balanced partnership that is represented by Girouard's image of Stirling and Wilford. Too often in the commentary of historians and critics, some of the elements of the balanced partnership have been overlaid onto the Stirling and Gowan practice, and the loser has been Gowan. Stirling would be treated as the major designer, demoting

Gowan to a pragmatic problem-solver or details man at best, regarding 'Stirling & Gowan' as merely a corporate title, or even forgetting to mention Gowan at all.[5] The years from 1956 to 1963 became a vestibule opening onto the career of Britain's new Hawksmoor, in which anything deemed of value in the works produced in these years must be ascribed to Stirling. Such narratives in part reflect the needs of critics in close sympathy with the ambitions of Stirling's later career, and in part the tropes of architectural historians, particularly the need to find great masters or transcendent buildings whose subtle exegesis may reflect the historian's sensitivity but does not give enough credit either to the complexity of Stirling's career or to the actual dynamics of the collaboration with Gowan, let alone to the particular and broader contributions that Gowan made to the buildings produced during the partnership.

These problems have been augmented by Stirling's own retrospective editing of his career and management of his fame. The Leicester University Engineering building (1959–64) – to be discussed in Chapter Six – was the partnership's most famous work and the last to be fully designed within it. For Stirling, Leicester established the pattern of acclaim and criticism that marked his career from that moment onwards. For Gowan, however, its completion was the beginning of a much quieter career as an architect and teacher, one put into the shade by his ex-partner's greater fame. Stirling's trajectory was to be carefully publicised and stage-managed, with a particular slant given to the years of partnership with Gowan. In 1974, for example, Stirling exhibited drawings at the Heinz Gallery, London, with little acknowledgement of his erstwhile partner, elevating his own status further (or ironising it?) by using 'neat, brown antique British Museum lettering on cream mounts'.[6] Most importantly, in the early 1970s Stirling prepared a retrospective monograph of his work, employing Leon Krier over many months to help him redraw the early projects and presenting his work in the time-honoured format of Le Corbusier's *Oeuvre complète*.[7] *James Stirling: Buildings and Projects 1950–1974* (1975), or the 'Black Book' as it was quickly nicknamed, is demonstrably the result of an editing hand that plays fast and loose with the historical record, diminishing the importance of some buildings, redrawing early designs so they point more obviously forward to later work, sometimes emphasising unbuilt designs at the expense of actually erected buildings, and generally obscuring the contribution of Gowan to the work. Genius, it would seem, cannot abide a partner.

Finally, reconstructing the working practices of the partnership has also been made difficult as a result of Stirling's destructive folly in the early 1970s, when he threw away almost all preliminary sketches or conceptual drawings produced before and during the partnership, including those made by Gowan.[8] As a result there are few surviving drawings with the processes of composition or of dialogue between the partners made visible, although the exceptions here are the drawings for Leicester and, as we will see later in this chapter, a drawing for the Dodd house in Kensington. Such drawings only survived because Gowan gained possession of them.[9] This destruction of conceptual drawings may accord with a comment made by Colin Rowe that Stirling was 'determined to keep his architecture, or his conceptual struggles, very conspicuously private',[10] or it may be that the nature of Gowan's contribution to the partnership was deliberately or subconsciously obscured.

The argument in what follows is threefold. First, as already indicated, that in discussing a selection of early house projects, built and unbuilt, Gowan's contribution can be given more relief without implying any diminution of Stirling's overall achievement. Second, that rather than a generalised 'creative tension' there was a particular formal dynamic between the two architects that has not been previously recognised. This dynamic was founded upon an opposition between Stirling's tendency within the partnership to present bounded and balanced compositions based on box-like forms, and Gowan's preoccupation with picturesque groupings of various, sometimes disparate, parts. Third, and more speculatively, the chapter argues that it was the experience of collaboration itself, and specifically this formal dynamic, that enabled Stirling and Gowan to adopt what they called a 'multi-aesthetic' attitude, working through the modernism of their time and loosening its terms so that a reconsideration of other – sometimes older – styles and typologies might be brought back into play.

~

The partnership was formed around a practical problem and a confluence of interests, and the result was a group of flats that announced the arrival of the young architects on the architectural scene, linking them, despite their protests but to their great benefit, with the emerging New Brutalist tendency in British modernism.[11] The creative collaboration was forged out of the need to resolve contradictions between the developer's interests and the local town planners' legal responsibilities.

Late in 1955 Stirling was given a commission by Luke Manousso, a developer and the father of a student whom Stirling was helping with his final year work at the Architectural Association. The commission was to design several blocks of flats on a site at Ham Common in southwest London. Although this was Stirling's first independent work, he was unwisely cavalier about gaining the necessary planning permission. For the long, narrow site in the gardens of a large Georgian house (Langham House), he designed a total of thirty-two flats in two terrace-like blocks, the higher one with vertical windows.[12] The flats were laid out with gardens on either side, windows looking out over the boundaries of the site to east and west, and a long

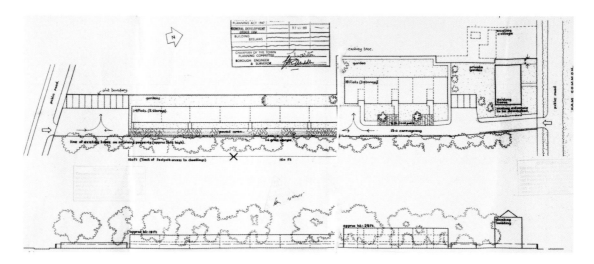

78   James Stirling, Ham Common Flats, November 1955, site layout.

paved area linking the two access roads at either end (fig. 78). However, the local planners rejected the scheme because not enough space was given for an access road of regulation width and the pavement was deemed inadequate for any emergency use by vehicles.[13] Stirling was now faced with a problem that he could not resolve. On the one hand, Manousso wanted a statutory service road running right through the site, so that the local council, rather than himself as the developer, would be responsible for services and the upkeep of public areas. On the other hand, day-lighting regulations demanded at most a sixty-degree angle from the top of the building to the edge of the site.[14] It seemed that the two-storey blocks had to be positioned in the narrow part of the site while, somehow, satisfying both requirements. The fit was simply too tight, and Stirling was caught in the trap of his first assumptions. Hasty but slight revisions were made, converting the paved area into a road, but again the plans were rejected.[15]

At the architectural office of Lyons Israel Ellis Stirling had become friendly with James Gowan, who as we have seen had been an assistant there since 1954. Both had Scottish ancestry, they had shared but independent interests in vernacular housing, castles and the industrial buildings of the nineteenth century, and they were both critical of the state of contemporary modernism. Stirling had bragged to Gowan about the Ham commission but was in some disarray at this second rejection.[16] Gowan encouraged him to keep going, and Stirling passed him the rejected scheme to look at. Evidently, Stirling had difficulty in moving beyond slight shifts and changes of emphasis in order to face the fundamental change his scheme needed if it was to proceed. He needed input from someone who could think very differently about how to arrange the required accommodation on the site. After a weekend of drawing, Gowan found a solution (fig. 79). He removed the access road running past the lower flats and reshaped them into two T-shaped layouts, each of which really consisted of two blocks placed at right-angles to each other and joined by a deep entrance hall. These were positioned in the narrow neck of the site, leaving a large garden area between them. As a result they could be serviced from either end so as to comply with refuse and fire regulations, instead of requiring a service road running the whole length of the site; and the lower ends of the buildings were now near the edges of the site, so resolving the day-lighting problem. This 'Scheme A' of January 1956 was submitted at almost the same time as another, final variation on the terraced idea, 'Scheme B', which had one terrace of houses and one of flats. Scheme B (for which drawings do not survive) was rejected, again because the street layout and access were considered unsatisfactory.[17] The layout made with Gowan's help, Scheme A, satisfied both the planners' and Manousso's concerns, and was given conditional planning permission in mid-January.[18]

The accepted scheme demonstrates the immediate chemistry between each partner's formal preoccupations and how from this a solution was crystallised to accommodate both the developer's needs and the local planners' constraints. Stirling had started with long blocks of flats and an approach that echoed the shape of the site, not dissimilar to the several previous attempts by other architects to design flats for this site.[19] Gowan had broken and reset one of these blocks into two more energetic compositions that looked back across the depth of the site. The forms of an only slightly modernised urbanism of terraces parallel to access roads had thus been remade into housing forms that, in their modest way, suggested a more fluid relation

79   Stirling and Gowan, Ham Common Flats, January 1956, site layout.

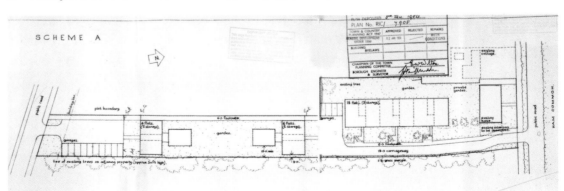

80   Eric Lyons and Partners, Parkleys Estate, Ham Common, 1954–56.

to the space of the site. A pattern had been established here that would run through all of Stirling and Gowan's early housing schemes. And on the basis of this solution, Stirling invited Gowan to join with him in formalising a partnership.

One of the architectural examples that undoubtedly influenced their thinking, even if only negatively, was the nearby Parkleys Estate (1954–56) recently completed by Eric Lyons and Partners (fig. 80). Manousso, in first approaching Stirling, clearly had the Parkleys Estate in mind as representing the kind of size, construction and price that he wanted for his own project.[20] Lyons had achieved a popular middle-class residential form in this and other suburban housing: laid out around cul-de-sacs, generously landscaped and faced with that variety of materials often called 'people's detailing', the Parkleys Estate also drew from the better examples of 1920s continental modernist social housing. Stirling and Gowan wanted something that was just as modern but more distinctive. Their flats set out from much the same ostensibly childless, middle-class world of privacy and individuality, looking out onto trees and gardens, but the architecture's materials and forms also attempted something a little less light-hearted and apparently complacent – to evoke the leaner, existentialist pleasures of integrity and austerity that had become shared values among the architect members of the Independent Group.

Working intensely, and complementing each other, within a month the new partners elaborated the scheme, meeting the local planners' conditions and working out all the major features of the flats that were to make such an impact on the contemporary architectural scene (fig. 81).[21] Footpaths were repositioned, setbacks articulated the previously sheer façades, the two identical but reversed two-storey blocks

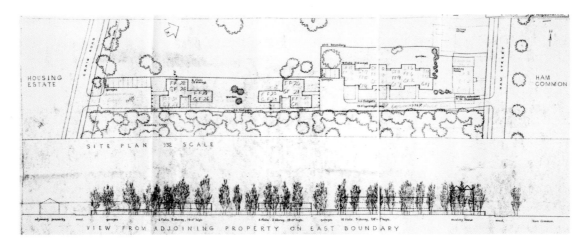

81   Stirling and Gowan, Ham Common Flats, February 1956, site layout.

were now laid out as tripartite interlocking compositions, and in the three-storey block the flats were staggered off a spine wall. Broadly speaking, although designs passed stepwise between the partners,[22] Stirling took more responsibility for the three-storey block, developing it into a Georgian version of Le Corbusier's Maisons Jaoul with inverted L-shaped windows derived perhaps from nineteenth-century warehouses, perhaps from high modernist examples (fig. 82).[23] The block's syncopated elevations, which make the living spaces of the flats project towards the road while the bedrooms recede relative to the garden, establish a dynamic contrast with the flat rear side of Langham House (fig. 83). Gowan designed the two lower blocks with strong contrasts between almost entirely blank brick walls beside the footpath, and setbacks of airy, entirely glazed walls exposing communal corridors and stairs. Woodwork was used as an external material equal to brick and concrete. Inside, games with light and gravity seem to be played in the suspended, concrete-walled upper corridors of the entrance halls (fig. 84). Although these lower blocks share the same handling of yellow brick and concrete components, they are far closer to the example of De Stijl (even the sense of contemplative domesticity in Gowan's thesis design) and quite distinct from the heavy structural dynamics and smaller scale wall articulations of the long terrace of flats (fig. 85).

The 'hostile attitude to the outside world'[24] of Le Corbusier's post-war manner and the radical spatial gestures of De Stijl houses were made over into an attempt to converse with the contexts of history and landscape. Already, in this first commission, Stirling and Gowan had established the temporal reference points that would overlap in the rest of their work: a tactile immediacy speaking of the

ABOVE 82   Stirling and
Gowan, Ham Common Flats,
1955–58, garden view of
three-storey flats.

RIGHT 83   Stirling and
Gowan, Ham Common Flats,
1955–58, three-storey flats with
Langham House.

LEFT 84 Stirling and Gowan, Ham Common Flats, 1955–58, corridor in two-storey flats.

BELOW 85 Stirling and Gowan, Ham Common Flats, 1955–58, two-storey flats.

86   Stirling and Gowan, Ham Common Flats, 1955–58, kitchen.

present; a conjuring up of the lost utopian, or 'programmatic', visions of the 1920s; and an ability to evoke deeper historical memories linked to the immediate built context, even if without resort to the picturesque *genius loci.*

In their living spaces the Ham flats oddly combine expansiveness of outlook and confinement of space, modernist lightness and 'primitive' stolidity. The tight spaces of the kitchens announce several interests (fig. 86): the plumbing is exposed in an 'as found' way below the sinks, while the cupboards and fittings are constructed – in a manner derived from De Stijl – of plainly separate pieces of joinery (even the vertical supports are made to appear as if they stop just short of the floor) painted gloss white or varnished to distinguish doors from support.[25] The central core for all the flats was the double-sided chimney pier (fig. 87). Here the contrast of the outer walls was brought to a pitch of elemental expression in the concrete mantelpieces, shelves and corbels set into their brick surrounds, a more brutish version of what Le Corbusier had created in his Maison de Weekend (1935).[26] As with some of the partners' other houses (the Isle of Wight house and the Dodd house, to be discussed later, for instance), these living rooms can seem over-tightly organised and the chimneys dominate the space despite their moderate size. But an interesting spatial dynamic was created: fluid yet somehow hieratic (the central hearth), alternatively flooded with light or tight and closeted. Certainly, the architects were concerned about how residents would live with their architecture, and they recognised 'the lack of an accepted form of taste and the divergence of visual outlook between specialist and layman'.[27] By contrast with the Parkleys Estate with its more neutral interiors and 'brisk fashion-forming publicity',[28] for instance, Ham Common risked seeming too cutting edge to attract purchasers, too inflexible in the character of its interiors. But the partners did not see it like this. They described the interiors at Ham as 'a middle course',[29] bringing the external character of the architecture into the interiors through the central core and kitchen fittings to encourage sympathetic decoration and furnishing without dominating the residents. But there was clearly a dilemma here. If the 'multi-variety of the occupiers' choices' would doubtless frustrate the desire of the architects to create a coherent design entity, should their design predict this by a 'bold arrangement of window members' to suppress discordant tastes in curtaining?[30]

The visual connections between Le Corbusier's Maisons Jaoul and Ham Common have been recognised ever since the flats were built. The most obvious similarities lie in the use of slender vertical and L-shaped windows, the cribbing of certain concrete details like gargoyles and projecting ventilation boxes, and the articulation of concrete components and brick infill (see fig. 75). But this handling also acts as a kind of commentary on the Paris houses. So, while brick and concrete are contrasted, concrete floor slabs exposed and

87   Stirling and Gowan, Ham Common Flats, 1955–58, living room.

formwork patterns retained, the more primitivising aspects of Jaoul's exteriors are ignored, even inverted (fig. 88). Where the timber shutter-boards at Jaoul had moulded the exposed concrete as coarsely roughcast and multidirectional, even if in a 'carefully contrived pattern' (fig. 89),[31] Ham's shutter-boarding seems by comparison much more neatly aligned. Jaoul's mortar appears slapped on in thick impasto and the concrete drips of the construction process have been left unscrubbed on the lower levels of brickwork, as if Le Corbusier wanted the record of making, of the labour of the construction site, to be retained in the finished house. At Ham, however, the two materials were kept carefully separate. Stirling even talked of using 'extreme gestures . . . to achieve visual clarity, such as the cutting away of the brick wall to expose the minimum building support, and the excessive use of concrete'.[32] Furthermore, the joints between bricks have their mortar considerably recessed so that the bricks appear dryly and neatly distinct from their fixing. This effect was achieved at Stirling's express instruction,[33] and was clearly calculated as diametrically different from Jaoul's effects. The mortar joint becomes a site of abstraction or removal, or at least a metaphor for these actions – the eradication of the signs of craft and the play of gravitational forces, leaving brick and wall as representative only of themselves.[34] This treatment makes the wall more like a pattern, unlike the Jaoul houses where 'the brickwork . . . is considered as a surface and not as a pattern.'[35] Thus, far from a record of reasoned and controlled construction, the cleaned wall and its pronounced bricks seem expressly conceived to draw attention to form and materials separated from their production.[36]

L E F T 88   Stirling and Gowan, Ham Common Flats, 1955–58, detail of exterior.

A B O V E 89   Le Corbusier, Maisons Jaoul, Paris, 1952–55.

From its onset the Stirling and Gowan collaboration was declared as one of equals, a shared working partnership with shared ideals. 'We were aiming for something similar at the beginning,' Gowan has explained, 'reacting against the older generation, setting up a critique of what might be done – a reaction against boredom, plainness and the mechanical nature of contemporary rationalism, of social rationalism and dainty well-produced things.'[37] But there were few good models for creative collaboration, and certainly none in the partners' previous work. Gowan's experience of Powell and Moya, for example, may have warned him of the problem of one partner not receiving enough credit for his work.[38] And Stirling had a distinctly low opinion of partners not involved in design. Lyons Israel Ellis was the shared experience and therefore key, if more for negative reasons. They operated rigid forms of collaboration, and they tended to see design as 'a luxury which you did at weekends or after hours'.[39] Although all three partners drew and they had an agreed practice for developing a design, the broader roles of the partners were quite fixed.[40] By the early 1950s Lawrence Israel, for instance, played the role of the pragmatic partner, 'the brick wall against which ideas were bounced';[41] Edward Lyons tended to work in romantic isolation; while Tom Ellis, the youngest of the three, was the conceptualist and innovator, the one who kept track of contemporary developments. As a partnership, then, Lyons Israel Ellis was more of a negative example of collaboration, and its rigid design methods and 'tyrannical' office practices were unappealing to both Stirling and Gowan,[42] even if other small but creative partnerships – like that between Alan Colquhoun and John Miller – would also spring out of the office. Other models of collaboration might have been intuited, such as that between Le Corbusier and his cousin Pierre Jeanneret. But although both Gowan and Stirling were steeped in the volumes of Le Corbusier's *Oeuvre complète*, not enough was known at this time about how the Corbusier–Jeanneret partnership actually worked for it to be seen as a model. (As it happens, it was far more like the stereotype of the good partnership outlined earlier rather than the partnership of equal creative forces that Stirling and Gowan had agreed on.)[43] In fact, there was no obvious model for the Stirling and Gowan partnership to emulate. Like other young architects starting out together, a shared outlook and complementary interests were more important than some established model of collaboration.

As part of the arrangement Gowan brought into the practice the house he had already designed for the family of his brother-in-law, a painter, on the Isle of Wight. This essay in neo-Palladian modernism might have taken its plan from the pages of Rudolf Wittkower's *Architectural Principles in the Age of Humanism* (1949), without the mediation of Colin Rowe and certainly predating any possible input from Stirling (fig. 90).[44] The site was just outside Cowes in a semi-rural suburb where the effect of its flat roof and stark window-to-wall relations was softened by its placement away from the road and neighbouring houses. The house as built was actually modified from the original designs because of interventions by the local planning authority, who disliked Gowan's proposed red

90 Stirling and Gowan, House in East Cowes, Isle of Wight, 1955–57.

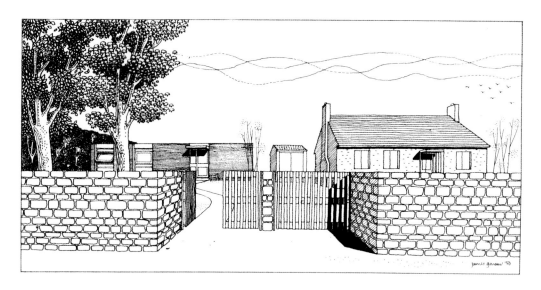

91   Stirling and Gowan, House in East Cowes, Isle of Wight, 1955–57, perspective by James Gowan.

bricks and suggested he add overhanging eaves to the roof.[45] But modifications were small (from red to buff bricks) given the original controversy the designs caused locally, and this must be attributed to Gowan's negotiations with the planning officer, not just by reasoning his design through in his correspondence but by sharing flattering references to classical proportions and to Aalto's use of brick.[46] The house can be seen as a kind of sympathetic critique of the suburban bungalow, accepting of its neighbours (as is made clear in Gowan's presentation drawings), harbouring its own secluded courtyard space so oriented that it looks into a small copse of trees, yet also exaggerating the depth of the site by setting the house back from the road (fig. 91).[47]

The house indicates some of the architectural interests that Gowan brought into the partnership. Its H-shaped plan contained two courtyards for the artist's young family, establishing a sense of measured disclosure in relation to the landscape and a clear separation of house functions (bedrooms and studio in one wing, living spaces in another, and kitchen and bathroom in the linking section) (fig. 92). Its cheapness resulted from disciplined, canny planning, a simple structure and a small range of components: all windows, for instance, are identical and wall surfaces are treated the same inside and out. It used mathematical proportions in plan and eleva-tion, based on five-foot-wide piers and a ten-foot grid, although the effect was grander in plan than in the rather pokey living spaces that resulted. The golden section determined window proportions and these windows were carried right up

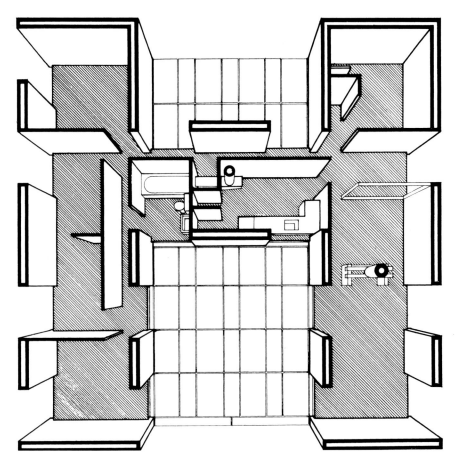

92   Stirling and Gowan, House in East Cowes, Isle of Wight, 1955–57, perspectival plan.

to the roof, stressing a vertical separation of window area from wall-as-pier and an abrupt transition from wall to roof, a formal device that would carry into several of the partnership's later works. The clarity of these proportions is a reminder that one reason for the impact of neo-Palladian modernism was as a reaction to the sense that modernist functionalism too easily produced ephemeral, contingent or merely pragmatic responses to a programme.[48] As Banham put it, neo-Palladianism 'offered a way out of the doldrums of routine-functionalist abdications'.[49] But as with the Smithsons' Hunstanton school, the house also emphasised the everyday as a measure of its integrity. Epitomising the frank revelation of materials, the kitchen sink's plumbing was prominently exposed, its pipe placed exactly central to the window in explicit display of 'as-found' industrial materials. Similarly, the fireplace located cen-

93   Stirling and Gowan, House in East Cowes, Isle of Wight, 1955–57, living room.

trally in the living room was dominated by an exposed flue constructed out of precast concrete drainpipes and standing on a simple concrete lintel over the stove (fig. 93). Here were both plain measures and plain objects.

With the flats at Ham Common and the house on the Isle of Wight mostly finished, the partners turned to the problem of how to devise a way of designing together – or, at least, so their later statements suggest.[50] The so-called house studies were the result: a series of drawings of small houses supposedly undertaken to devise a working method in the newly formed partnership. But there is reason to be sceptical about the notion that these house studies represent an experiment in the sharing and developing of ideas.[51] The house studies were not some free-standing exercise but actually the preliminary work for a specific commission, the Expandable House. Later on they became separated from that commission in retrospective accounts by the ex-partners, accounts that exploited the lack of resemblance between the final version and the earlier studies. Less like mountaineers roped together, Stirling and Gowan had actually set out on different trails, one later than the other. Produced under pressure and to a commission, the house studies that survive were all done by Gowan, with his characteristic notations and graphic style, despite their frequent later reproduction in publications devoted only to Stirling.

In the spring of 1957 Michael Middleton, the editor of *House & Garden* magazine, asked the partners to produce designs for an expandable house 'for young marrieds whose ambition outruns their bank balance'.[52] Stirling knew Middleton through his friends Michael and Cynthia Wickham, who worked as photographer and journalist, respectively, on the magazine.[53] It was one of a series of occasional commissions to young architects that included, for instance, the 'House of Ideas' in September–October 1956, repeated in June 1957.[54] With its appeal across gender and amateur–professional divides, *House & Garden* was one of those organs that helped modernism infiltrate British society on a wider front than before the war, domesticating it, making it a style in the service of modernisation and part of the environment for mass consumption, straightening the bright wrappers of the 'aesthetics of plenty' with the lingering good conscience of the 'age of austerity'. In the mid-1950s a shift occurred within the magazine. For some time it had published occasional articles on houses by the likes of Peter Womersley, Casson & Conder and Ernö Goldfinger, but now this became a more consistent current. One catalyst was the arrival as architectural editor of Joyce Lowrie from the AA, and with her she brought her young architect friends and contacts (David Gray, Kit Evans, Neave Brown), and thus a direct link to the home-grown avant-garde.[55] The House of Ideas, for instance, was one of a series of projects explaining modernist approaches in simple and practical terms. But, importantly, much of the magazine's old eclecticism remained.

With the deadline for the expandable house a month away, Gowan, working over the weekends, produced the first tranche of design ideas.[56] A prodigious set of drawings resulted, of which four of the most worked-up groups were shown to Stirling. It is these that have often since been reproduced (figs 94–97). In these studies the houses are envisaged as picturesque concatenations of varied volumes: some forms bridge over and straddle other forms or are stacked up as incrementally projecting masses; monopitch roofs hint both at vernacular sources and at abstract, centrifugal forces; core functions are held in a wing-nut volume that dodges in and out of other forms or are buried in a pile-up of rooms; ramps are thrust out or line up alongside the house. The house studies are made of suggestive fragments and condensed allusions, once functionally expressive volumes simplified and abstracted so as to lose any original logic. Gowan later wrote that the studies were concerned with showing 'how a family might develop from a modest beginning; a small domestic core con-

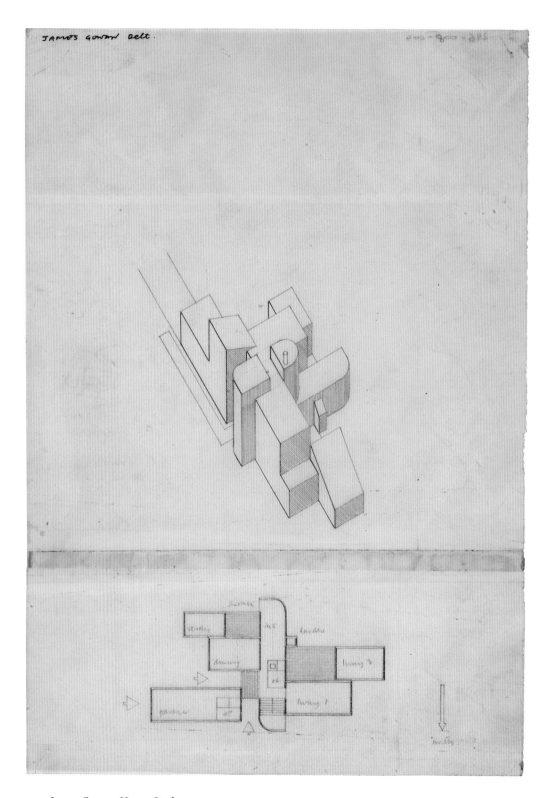

94   James Gowan, House Study, 1957.

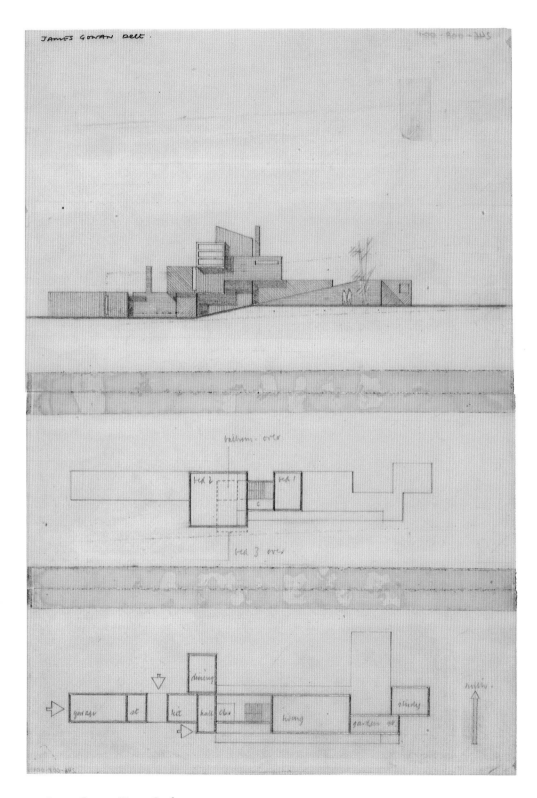

95   James Gowan, House Study, 1957.

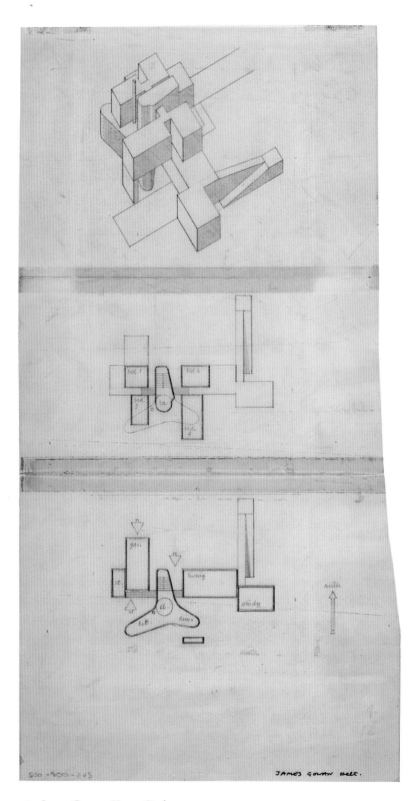

96   James Gowan, House Study, 1957.

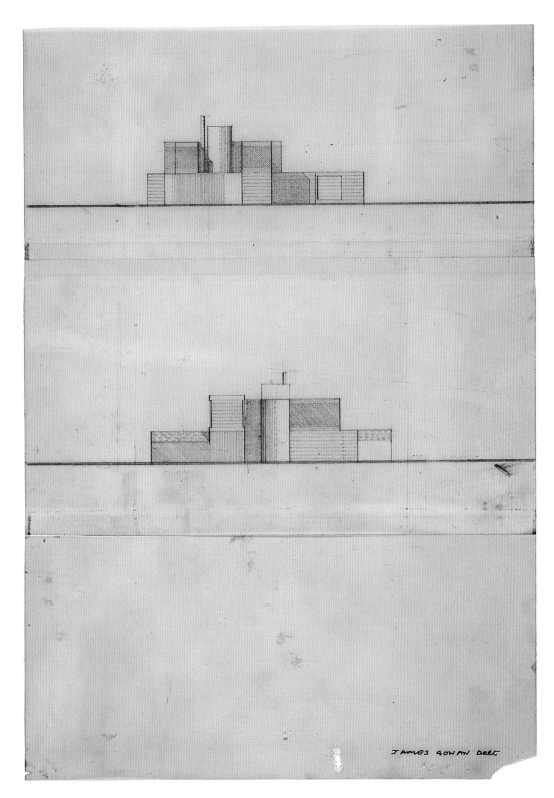

JAMES GOWAN Delt

97   James Gowan, House Study, 1957.

taining kitchen, bathroom and stairway. Future additions were shunted on to this with much energy and dramatic effect and there was a relaxed attitude towards the use of a mish-mash of materials.'[57] Thus, in graphic terms, rather than throwing a unifying veneer over his volumes, Gowan's differently angled and differently spaced lines, with areas coloured red and yellow, further emphasised the separateness of volumes, presenting the houses as amalgams of different materials, loose alliances of pronouncedly discrete units.[58] The articulation of surfaces in these house studies implies that walls were to be treated not as load-bearing but as applied, non-volumetric surface material, and this had important implications for Stirling and Gowan's later work. With their diversified masses, their additive, ad hoc planning and their 'dynamic asymmetry',[59] the House Studies can thus be seen as departing radically from the modernist obsession with the cube and its dematerialisation.[60]

Some clarity is required about what might be meant by the term 'picturesque' in characterising Gowan's house studies. Out of the term's full range of uses in the post-war period, three meanings are of particular relevance here. One is 'picturesque modernism', as advocated by the *Architectural Review* as a regionalist version of modernism for Britain.[61] It involved the placement of modernist volumes for visual effect, evoking surprise and disclosure according to a *genius loci*, with the traditions of British landscape theory and the 'functional tradition' behind it. Associated with figures like Pevsner and the modernist mainstream, this understanding held little interest for Stirling and Gowan, even when it could be linked with some of Le Corbusier's work.[62] A second and more specific sense was the notion of a functional picturesque based on pragmatic reasoning. This was found in mid-nineteenth-century composition according to Colin Rowe,[63] and attempted by Stirling himself in several projects before his partnership with Gowan. As shown in Chapter Three, in his unbuilt Woolton house (1954) and village housing project (1955), Stirling had adopted vernacular forms and given their asymmetrical disposition a functionalist rationale. But the formal contribution of Gowan to the partnership, as described earlier, constitutes a distinct third meaning or practice of the picturesque (though the word itself would not have been used by Gowan to describe his approach and indeed both partners used it more often negatively than positively). Without implying that all of Gowan's contributions had this approach, it can certainly be found in the works discussed in this chapter. Overt vernacular forms were not necessary to this version of the picturesque, and its functionalism was more playful than dogmatic. Instead, it combined an assertive relation to the situational context, a treatment of the complex as an additive combination with distinct, almost collage elements (as Gowan had found in Alexander 'Greek' Thomson's work), and the use of surface details underlining the difference between the constituent parts. Perhaps unexpectedly, the approach echoes Wittkower's description of Palladio's 'crystalline conception of architecture': 'He cannot think in terms of evolution, but envisages ready-made units which . . . may also be extended or contracted.'[64]

Yet Stirling cleaved to the cube; for him, Gowan's ideas were too loosely picturesque and spontaneous. With *House & Garden*'s deadline looming, in an example of collaboration by concession, it was Stirling's idea that was settled on and developed. Stirling had been thinking in terms of a simpler exercise: drawing from the centralised geometry and standardised construction of his so-called Stiff Dom-ino housing of 1951, taking the idea of the core containing the house's basic functions from Gowan's studies, attaching a multifunctional room, and building all the main structural walls at the first stage (fig. 98). The expandable house in this incarnation was an experiment in adaptable modular housing for middle-class families, and it was envisaged as either a mass-produced solution to a national problem or something for individual clients using traditional methods and materials. The problem as defined by the architects was that the size of contemporary houses 'did not allow for the growth and change which form the pattern of family life'. Suburban semi-detached houses – too large for a newly married couple, too small when the family grew, and once more too large when the children left home – were simply obsolete in relation to the contemporary need for flexibility. The requirement, solved by Stirling's design concept, was 'to build a house which can be added to in stages, which will appear an architectural entity at each step, and which is capable all its life of 100% efficiency'.[65] Expansion would be achieved through adding quadrants of the same shape and size, with prefabricated roof units – which would be clamped between the core and the structural walls as the family grew – using the pinwheel circling movement that was to be developed in Stirling and Gowan's later works.[66] When it reached maximum size, the block was completed and with it the nuclear family. As the children grew up and left home, partition walls could be moved and the quadrants could be successively given over to a new growing family.

A number of expandable house designs were produced at this time, as residences capable of planned extension briefly seemed an appropriate response to rising affluence, both working and middle class.[67] The expandable dwelling was therefore a specific response within the larger fields of prefabricated housing and 'clip-on' architecture.[68] Among this subfield of expandable designs we may contrast Stirling and Gowan's design with the extendable bungalow that *Ideal Home*, *House & Garden*'s rival, had published in 1954 (fig. 99). In this small, brick bungalow *Ideal Home*'s notion of expandability is seen as determinedly handcrafted, and certainly pre-consumer culture: it implies a picturesque, dynastic and gradual expansion that

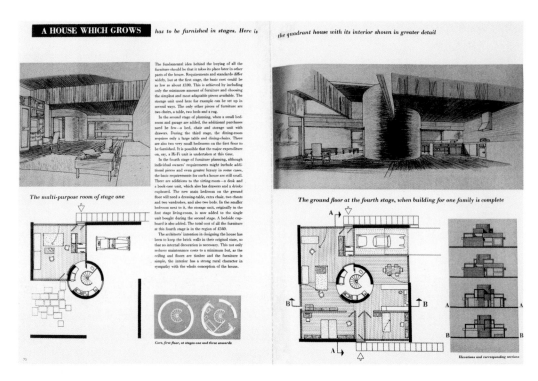

98   Stirling and Gowan, Expandable House, 1957.

serves the growing family's needs. Its young married couple, we may imagine, crave roots and are attached to the site, whereas *House & Garden*'s expandable house residents – true devotees of the consumer society – desire generational mobility and speed of transition. So, for instance, the claimed rural character of the expandable house would function mainly as a prompt to greater affluence.[69] Effectively, it was a minimal dwelling only for those at a stage before affluence. Another contrast is with Lionel Schein's widely publicised House of Tomorrow or *maison tout en plastique* (1956), a project again sponsored by a magazine (in this case, *Elle*) and shown at the Paris Ideal Home exhibition in 1956 as a prototype for mass production (fig. 100). Schein's design took much more cognizance of the techniques of mass production than Stirling and Gowan's: its moulded plastic components were to be prefabricated and assembled on site. But the absence of any reference to class here is particularly telling by comparison with the expandable house's complex and knowing play on its inhabitants' class position.

Drawings of the first stage of the expandable house, perhaps inadvertently, show a dwelling that appears more exposed and ad hoc than part of a phased development.

ABOVE 99 Extendable Bungalow, 1954, architect unknown, as published in *Ideal Home.*

RIGHT 100 Lionel Schein, House of Tomorrow, 1956.

But as the house develops, units are wrapped protectively around the central core, a car is acquired and the family is transformed from wandering indigents to people at leisure, enjoying a sun-shaded terrace (fig. 101). Their domestic life seems modestly furnished, as befits disciplined middle-class consumers, and the images try not to overprescribe their accoutrements: a television is visible in an alcove, white goods are discretely tucked away, but a book lies ostentatiously open on a bare table. In other images accompanying the plans, however, the family members are lined up, certainly ironically, as isotypes or visualised sociology,[70] the statistical units of post-war municipal rehousing propaganda. These are certainly not, therefore, the independent, leisured and informed consumers that *House & Garden* normally presented as the mirror image of its readers, but icons of the politics of housing need (fig. 102). Class battles are glimpsed, then, beyond the pages of *House & Garden.* Rights to

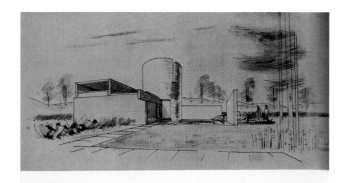

A HOUSE WHICH GROWS

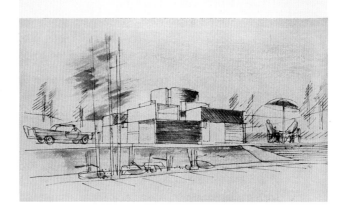

101   Stirling and Gowan, Expandable House, 1957.

leisure, resentments over expanded consumption, working-class couples forced to live with their parents, even the spectre of eviction – all these shade the aspirations of the nuclear family.

If architecture represents models or precepts for living, then Gowan's House Studies imagined the family unit as a loose confederation, each member having a distinct character but tied to a common purpose: they represent the extended or the picturesque family. In the final expandable house, however, the house conceives the family as a functional group that expands in a reproductively disciplined manner, with identical units simply added to form a whole that had already been imagined at its outset. What is represented here is not so much an embodiment of the economics of a consumer culture as an image of what it might mean to *live* as a con-

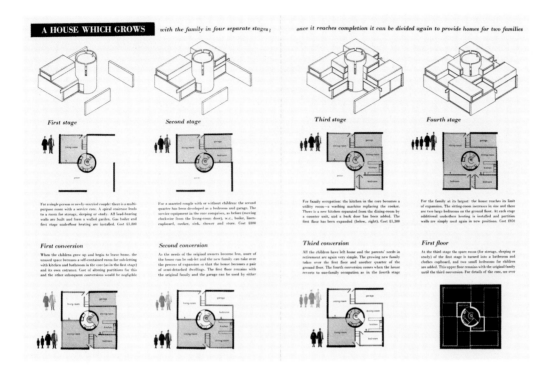

102 Stirling and Gowan, Expandable House, 1957.

sumer; after all, the consumer society of the 1950s was still less an economic fact than an aspiration, a willed identity. The house is expandable, not expendable; the life of the nuclear family is embodied or commodified here, not that of the building.[71] The play blocks of Gowan's house studies are abstruse and characterful; their fragmentary syntax is capable of inventive combination or of picturesque agglutination. The building blocks of the final expandable house, however, are purposeful and homogeneous things, modular parallels to the isolated nuclear family that was emerging at the time, particularly among the professional classes.[72]

∼

There were failed collaborations within the partnership, where one or the other partner would shear off and distance himself from the work. A house at Whiteleaf in the Chilterns was among these. Once more what was saved for posterity from this stands for something very different from what actually happened. Stirling initially took responsibility for this commission, gained from M. S. Kissa, a wealthy clothing

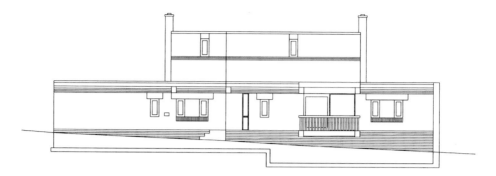

103   Stirling and Gowan, Kissa House (large house, first design), Buckinghamshire, June 1956, redrawn elevation.

manufacturer and friend of Luke Manousso, the partnership's client at Ham Common.[73]

The first designs, in June 1956, were for two houses because Kissa wanted to sub-divide the extensive plot. The larger house, which was never published, was envisaged as a long, flat-roofed block with two one-storey wings either side of it, the whole arranged down the sloping site so that it would not intrude on views from surrounding amenities, and containing a sequence of garage, dining area, living area and terrace (fig. 103). The smaller house, which was published,[74] was conceived as two closely joined cubes (like the house in north London, discussed in Chapter Three) housing an interior notable for its skewed spaces – a kind of diagonalised free plan (fig. 104). Both designs show bands of ceramic brick of different widths and in four colours (red, dark green, dark blue and light blue) inset into a yellow brick wall. The colouring is actually even more complicated than this suggests because the banding changes with each wall surface while a single vestigial brick marks a band that does not continue round a corner (fig. 105). Precast beams spanned the internal spaces and projected beyond the outer walls, and red brick chimneys were attached to the sides of the houses, towering over and emphasising the flat roofs. The local planning officer, however, rejected these polychromatic designs, probably because the colours and the flat roofs were seen as out of keeping with the character of the locality.[75]

Stirling now dissuaded his clients from building the second smaller house on the site,[76] and argued for a three-storey house with split levels, ignoring the fact that Kissa's wife had mobility problems and wanted a single-storey house.[77] It was Gowan who developed this second design in September 1956, with Stirling working largely on the elevations (notably close in style to the drawings of the Jaoul houses that Le Corbusier had published in his *Oeuvre complète*).[78] Once again, as at Ham Common,

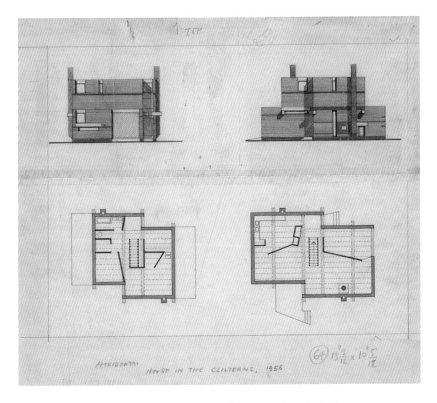

104   Stirling and Gowan, Kissa House (smaller house, first design),
Buckinghamshire, June 1956, elevations and plans.

Gowan broke open and rethought Stirling's more rectilinear scheme. Having abandoned the extraordinary, High Victorian colours of the first scheme, the asymmetrical
composition and prismatic volumes of the second scheme brought a dynamic De Stijl
effect,[79] with the house conceived as nearly autonomous cubic units spinning off from
a central stair (fig. 106). The site was a grand escarpment looking down onto an
extensive plain, and Gowan's signed perspective shows how the house would echo the
landscape as well as exaggerate its spiralling steepness further by a line of steps cutting
down one slope.[80] Gowan's scheme presented, therefore, an entirely different conception of the house's relation to its landscape, using the diagonal of steps to establish
and dramatise the movement of syncopated cubes above, and presenting different
stepped silhouettes to all four directions. Yet even though local brick was envisaged
and the house was now placed lower down the slope, this design too was refused
planning permission as 'detrimental to the needs of the locality',[81] probably because
it was now deemed to be overly visible from the nearby golf and cricket clubs.

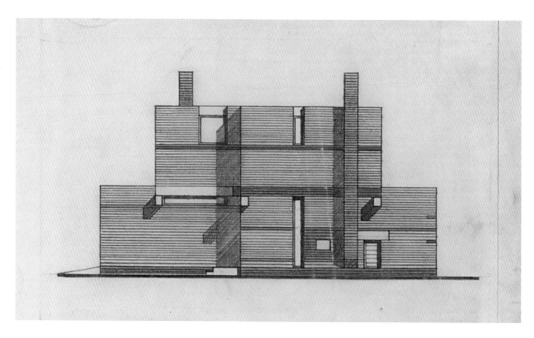

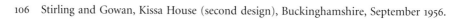

105 Stirling and Gowan, Kissa House (smaller house, first design), Buckinghamshire, June 1956, detail of fig. 104.

106 Stirling and Gowan, Kissa House (second design), Buckinghamshire, September 1956.

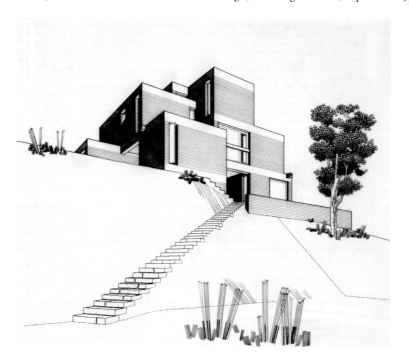

107   Stirling and Gowan, Kissa House, Buckinghamshire, 1956–57, side elevation during construction.

This was how the Kissa house seemed to have been left. Neither three years later, when designs were published, nor in 1975, when Stirling published the project again in the Black Book, was there any sign that a house had actually been built.[82] In fact, however, with Gowan disenchanted but with Manousso determined to produce a house for his friend, Stirling had persisted with the commission and developed a third design, which actually got built (fig. 107). Instead of looking for a compromise with or development from Gowan's scheme, he returned to the long two-storey affair of the first design, stripped it of its polychromy, used local red brick, and topped the whole with a conventional pantiled roof.[83] With this Stirling finally gained planning permission, but the various compromises produced a house that managed to be both banal and quixotic in terms of modernist architectural culture: in Gowan's words, a 'railway crash thing', barely distinguished from stock developers' housing by certain characteristic details.[84] Only in these details – the way the windows seem to run into the eaves, and the blue colouring mixed into the mortar at basement level (reminiscent of the blue bands at the bottom of the first scheme) – would the provenance be indicated here. Indeed, it is the abandonment of almost everything that marked out the first two designs while continuing with the demanded compromises that may distinguish the house almost despite itself. The utter pragmatism of Stirling's approach – in getting the house built while preserving for posterity only the radical earlier schemes – marks a point where modernism could be treated as an empty sign for avant-garde status, forms without content except as publicity, while the house as built was wiped from the record.[85]

It needs saying, however, that there was a difficult line to judge here: to build something close to developers' housing, yet to retain credentials as a serious architect and, more importantly, to have something interesting to say with the idiom. Clearly, Gowan's house in Stevenage (discussed in Chapter Two) veered on the wrong side of this line: it was pragmatic and virtually indistinguishable from what surrounded it. The Smithsons, however, had stayed just the right, interesting side of this line in their Sugden house (1955–56) that also deployed some of the speculative builders' clichés of the time. The Sugden house, it has been suggested, reworked that speculative housing through different window forms and spatial layout, injecting something fresh into the idiom.[86] Stirling and Gowan, too, in their unbuilt Sunninghill Housing had also stayed the right side of this line and published their designs despite the fact they came nowhere near building them (fig. 108).[87] Stirling in particular had been for some years frustrated by local planners' refusal of his designs, as was seen with

108   Stirling and Gowan, Sunninghill Housing, Berkshire, c.1959, elevations and plans.

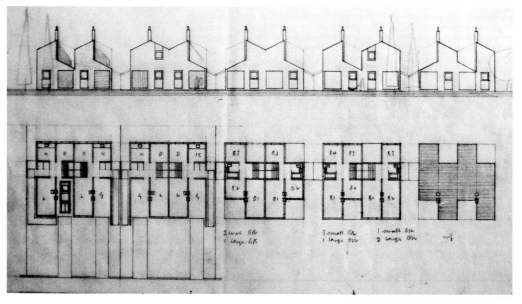

his north London house. He was dismayed by the mismatch between his modernist desire to design critically, especially within an environment he disliked, and the often narrowly context-led rationale that guided planning decisions. So why publish Sunninghill and not the actually built Kissa house; what made Sunninghill acceptable? One answer perhaps is that Sunninghill could be understood as a form of the 'as found', where the Kissa house could not. To allow the backs of Victorian houses to inspire the design of a row of speculative suburban semis was to find some other rationale for their appearance than merely the expression of consumerist identity. Here, in equally commonplace housing of a century before – the historical distance was crucial – might be found 'an honest expression of the sectional organization of the house'.[88] Something about integrity was now present, something about the designer's eye, even perhaps the probity of the inhabitant.

~

One of the most enticing schemes of this early period in the partnership, and one about which little is known, is the design for a group of three houses for the Mavrolean family in Hyde Park Gate, Knightsbridge (1956–57). Taken out of the context of the regionally and locally attuned designs of this time, this scheme might easily seem a portent of the classical end of postmodernism rather than the continuation of a West End historicism disregardful of modernism (fig. 109). It is certainly far from Miesian exemplars of modernist luxury, but that it was to be luxurious there can be no doubt. The client, Basil Mavrolean, was a member of an extended family of Greek shipping tycoons, and he probably commissioned Stirling and Gowan through Luke Manousso. Mavrolean owned a prime piece of central London real estate, just south of Hyde Park in a street where Sir Winston Churchill lived across the road and Jacob Epstein was a neighbour. Here he proposed to build three family homes, one for himself and the others for his two sons.[89]

The suitably grand model for Stirling and Gowan's layout was the French *hôtel*, that urban palace-type in which buildings are organised around a walled courtyard. Like most *hôtels*, the Mavrolean scheme was entered from a gate let into a high wall, with gardens placed to the rear of the site. Its three free-standing houses were laid out almost identically, with the father's house in the middle, and each house dominated by a large entrance hall rising the full height of the building and lit by a skylight. Stirling, who took the lead with the design,[90] responded to the client's preference for Georgian architecture by drawing up restrained elevations punctured by vertical and slit windows and topped by low-pitched roofs.[91] Horizontal windows were mostly placed on the edges of the site or high up, in abrupt conjunctions with

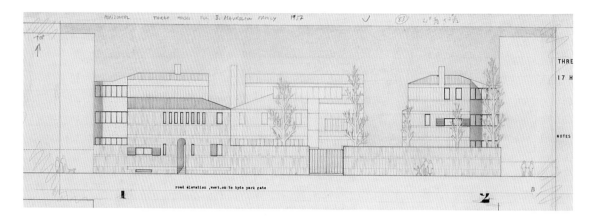

109   Stirling and Gowan, Mavrolean Houses, Knightsbridge, 1956–57, elevations.

the roofs. All external walls were to be covered by white marble revetment cut to half the size of the basic window unit, and there were to be bronze window frames and shutters as well as copper roofs. One can only imagine how these marble surfaces would have looked if realised, especially their contrast with the lines of exposed concrete floor slabs. One drawing, lovingly coloured in by Stirling probably many years after the design,[92] shows a palette of pinks and oranges gently warming the cold marble and lifted by the green copper roof above. The buildings appear like smooth graph paper, an impression enhanced by the continuous surface shared by the house nearest the street and the wall. This is cut into by a round-arched entrance and short flight of steps, evoking the Mediterranean more than Georgian London. By using the *hôtel* type, however, the scheme was entirely unlike its neighbouring terraced mansion houses and flats. Even more importantly, its low densities ran foul of the planning authorities.[93]

The Mavrolean design demonstrates how far Stirling and Gowan were prepared to go in modulating their work to a sense of historical context (even if, as here, very generalised) or the clients' wishes. How the interiors might have looked can only be guessed from the plans, but the emphasis on strongly demarcated circulation and reception spaces as well as the ranges of vertical windows would surely have resulted in highly formal spatial sequences geared to promenade and display. Some of the Mavrolean elements seem to be replayed in a nearby terraced house in Kensington (1957–60), gained interestingly enough from clients, a Mr and Mrs E. Dodd, who had seen the architects' work in *House & Garden*.[94] But now – perhaps because of the small scale of the commission, perhaps because it was actually built – the results are more 'schizophrenic', to use one of Stirling's favoured words at this time.

For the Dodd house Stirling and Gowan at first took a 1920s modernist approach, though a knowingly playful one. The site was tiny: a trapezium of leftover ground between tall Victorian terraces, nineteen feet wide at the front and extending only thirty-four feet back. Into this, the architects at first proposed to drop a little demonstration of twentieth-century abstraction. Their early design is shown in one of the few surviving examples of a conceptual drawing by them, one even more valuable because it clearly manifests the stepwise dialogue that often occurred between the partners when developing a design (fig. 110).

This approach was forced on them by circumstances. In the first year of the partnership's work they could live off the money paid for the Ham flats, but after that both were compelled to teach part-time: so Gowan worked at the Architectural Association from 1958 to 1960 and Stirling at Regent Street Polytechnic from 1958 and then at Yale from 1959.[95] To deal with their different teaching schedules in the early partnership years, one partner usually left his design on the drawing board for the other partner to develop; for only one day a week were they likely to be in the office at the same time.

In the case of the Dodd design the sheet has two elevations which each show a small house sketched with the same limited range of elements. According to Gowan his design, which is at the top, was done first and Stirling's response to this is below. Gowan's drawing seems most concerned with using a staggered composition of concrete lintels and lines of brick courses to suggest a spiralling dynamic around the centralised brick chimney, and the shifts of recession and projection, particularly at the sides, subtly reinforce this. The whole façade echoes the spirit of the stepped volumes that were planned internally at this stage (inspired, it seems, by an erroneous belief that the site itself was on split levels).[96] Stirling's response is to move Gowan's elements so that the framing qualities of the house are reasserted against what in Gowan's drawing threatens to disintegrate. Lintels are now drawn across the whole façade as continuous floor levels and the chimney shifted so it marks the golden section (and is closer to its final position). Where Gowan's dynamic tends to work vertically and in depth, Stirling's is aligned horizontally, parallel with the line of movement along the street.

In miniature this dialogue between the partners exemplifies the qualities described earlier in relation to the Ham flats, the Kissa house and the house studies that led to the Expandable House. It is striking, for instance, that the second Kissa design is like an expansive version of the interior planning of the early Dodd designs, and, like Gowan's drawing, its asymmetries and dynamic volumes were inspired by Dutch modernism of the 1920s. Gowan's Dodd drawing is a kind of picturesque play on illusion, movement and surprise, whereas Stirling develops the qualities of the dema-

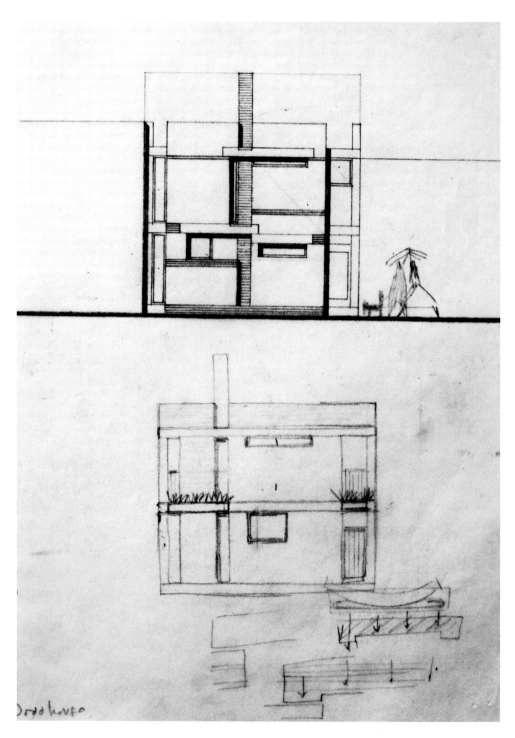

110   Stirling and Gowan, Dodd House, 1957, sketches of elevations.

terialised cube if now in a flatter, Mondrian-like manner.[97] Where they agree is in an exposure of materials and structure but not, it seems, according to some rhetoric of rationalism; instead, bands and columns of brick as well as concrete lintels are extended for aesthetic or scenographic effect.

However, when the planning authorities rejected the street elevation of this early scheme as out of keeping with the stucco and brick nineteenth-century terraces nearby, the architects redesigned the project and built it with an entirely different frontage.[98] What emerged was not the playful modernist call to order of the early designs, whether of a neo-Palladian or picturesque form, and instead a stranger and in its way much more challenging creation (fig. 111). This, treated now in a kind of stark Regency style on the outside, was not published in Stirling's later account of his career, his Black Book. The façade was now in stucco with inscribed lines suggesting masonry courses and windows simply set into this. The neo-Victorian rear elevation used red brick copings, a facing of yellow London stock bricks, a shallow curved course of red brick, and a curved and chamfered concrete lintel –

111   Stirling and Gowan, Dodd House, Kensington, 1957–60.

LEFT 112   Stirling and Gowan, Dodd House, Kensington, 1957, rear elevation.

ABOVE 113   Stirling and Gowan, Dodd House, Kensington, 1957, upstairs landing.

glorying in what Gowan called 'inaccessible splendours which would never be gazed upon' (fig. 112).[99] In the courtyard an 'as found' concrete sewage pipe was used for fuel storage.[100] Sandwiched between the contrasting façades, 'virtually oppressed by its surroundings',[101] the interior disregarded the outside, but not now through the spiralling space and oblique internal views suggested by the first design. Like the houses that André Wogenscky and Jaap Bakema had designed for themselves, and that Stirling had admired in his Black Notebook, there was a deliberate discrepancy or 'schizophrenia' between inside and out. The plan was changed by moving the stair to the side, aiming at flexible, interlinked rather than stepped spaces. Interior effects were created by plastering the inner faces of the external walls, boarding the floors and ceilings, and creating boarded interior walls whose patterns make a joinery equivalent of the shaded patterns in Gowan's house studies.[102] There were also 'secret' doors (similarly boarded and set flush), timber and glass screens, glass doors that folded back on themselves, a kitchen with the now-familiar 'as found' exposed plumbing, and a planked, spoke-like, and top-lit spiral stair with a teasingly minimal, looping rail (fig. 113). This 'ship's-cabin aesthetic', in which every wooden element has its independent identity preserved, did not, however, dominate every aspect of the interior.[103] The living room, for instance, was centred on a very simple stove and free-standing flue, like the Isle of Wight house (fig. 114).[104] The interior

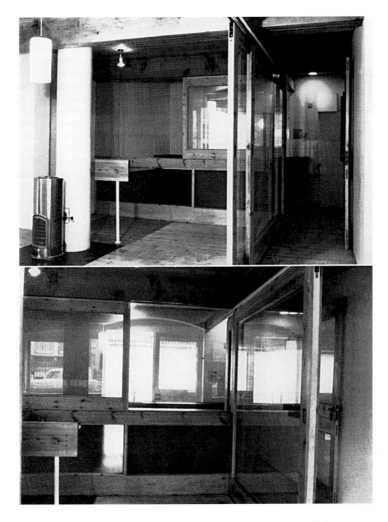

114   Stirling and Gowan, Dodd House, Kensington, 1957–60, living room
with stove.

exploited transparency, reflection and the flexibility of screen-walls to allow both
open plan spaces and contained, functionally specific rooms. In a sense it was a
kind of answer in miniature to the planning dichotomy that had worried Stirling
ever since his thesis design.

The Dodd house was hardly manifesto-like; certainly not by comparison, for
instance, with the Smithsons' house in Soho (1953) for a similar urban site (fig. 115).
Far from being the 'take it or leave it' simplicity and brutal material aesthetic of the
Smithsons' house, where domestic space and workshop become collapsed together as

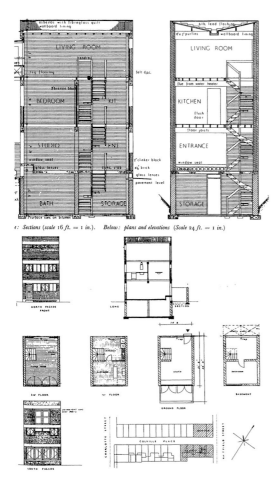

e : Sections (scale 16 ft. = 1 in.).   Below : plans and elevations (Scale 24 ft. = 1 in.)

115   Alison and Peter Smithson, Soho House, 1953, plans, elevations and sections.

the same equalised and direct attitude towards life, Stirling and Gowan's house is more about illusion, hidden spaces and heightened variety. Again, this sense of internal fantasy contrasted with strait-laced external formality is pointed up by one of the architects' own photographs where the house is seen head on and a male figure (Stirling himself?) peers into the front window, his amoebic shadow falling away to the left (fig. 116). Effectively, Stirling and Gowan had exploited the planners' decision and accommodated the house skin-deep with its neighbours, so that unexpected and dissonant contrasts could be created between interior and exterior effects.

~

This account of the early house schemes indicates some of the formal dynamics of the earlier years of the Stirling and Gowan partnership. It is often assumed, even by some of the partnership's assistants, that Stirling originated most of the projects.[105] Gowan undoubtedly made the first design studies for the expandable house, he probably initiated the Dodd house design, and the Isle of Wight house was entirely his work. (In addition, as will be shown in later chapters, he made the first designs for the steel mills in south Wales, Camberwell Assembly Hall, Churchill College, Cambridge and the Leicester University Engineering building.)

The Dodd and Mavrolean houses indicate a tendency that runs through all of Stirling and Gowan's house projects after Ham Common. This is a fundamentally distinct attitude to what it means to be neo-avant-garde, to be distanced both from modernist first generation heroics and from contemporary institutionalised versions of modernism. However, to an old 1920s avant-gardist like Arthur Korn – a German émigré architect, ex-member of the Novembergruppe and Der Ring, and the author of the first survey of the partnership's work in 1959 – Stirling and Gowan represented the return of his youthful ideals. He praised their uncompromising approach and the sense of 'unlimited possibilities' that linked them, without qualification, to continental modernists of the 1920s and 1930s.[106] And this was useful to the young architects even if they felt their relation to these sources to be more ironic, often critical, and certainly discontinuous. For Stirling and Gowan the very distance in time from the historical avant-garde allowed them to become active producers and consumers of styles, to see them as relative rather than as a matter of faith. Both architects' Beaux-Arts training was founded on an eclectic attitude to style. But importantly, this lesson was allied to what Stirling had taken from Le Corbusier's late works, specifically the Maisons Jaoul, which baffled him but left him with a sense that architectural development need no longer be tied to technological advance or one line of stylistic development.[107] Gowan had also learnt this more negatively through his encounter with the narrow Bauhaus modernism at Kingston School of Architecture and his disaffection with Stevenage's architecture.

116   Stirling and Gowan, Dodd House, Kensington, 1957–60.

Around about the same time in the late 1950s both Stirling and Gowan came to call their flexible attitude to style a 'multi-aesthetic' approach or 'the style for the job', the second a better-known formulation because of Reyner Banham's appropriation of it.[108] In other words, this was an approach to style that went beyond typology, that arose from the specific functions of the brief and was implicitly superordinate to issues of personal or collective style. It aimed, in Gowan's words, to 'intensify the architectural expression by making self-evident what the building was'.[109] The partners often spoke about their buildings as bespoke responses to the specifics of the brief, the site and the planning authority, rejecting any notion they had an exemplary status or application to universal issues.[110] Related to this, the 'multi-aesthetic' also responded to Stirling and Gowan's understanding of the complexity of the post-industrial culture they worked in, of its different paces of change, different consumption habits and different tastes and fashions. The full implications of this may only have been barely grasped at the time, but they were certainly controversial.[111] More importantly, the 'multi-aesthetic' opened up an appropriative attitude to the past – of irony, quotation, collage – and a darting, playful, defiantly complicating attitude to the concerns of the present.

FIVE

The Uses of Nostalgia

To a visitor they are understandably depressing, these massed proletarian areas; street after regular street of shoddily uniform houses intersected by a dark pattern of ginnels and snickets (alley-ways) and courts, without greenness or the blueness of sky. . . . But to the insider, these are small worlds, each as homogeneous and well-defined as a village. . . . It is because for all ages such a life can have a peculiarly gripping wholeness, that after twenty-five it can be difficult for a working-class person either to move into another kind of area or even into another area of the same kind.

(Richard Hoggart, *The Uses of Literacy*, 1958)

Many of the yards are packed with clothes hanging on the line, prams, sheds, boxes of geraniums and pansies, hutches for rabbits and guinea-pigs, lofts for pigeons, and pens for fowls. The only difference between the houses is the colour of the curtains and doorsteps which the wives redden or whiten when they wash down the pavement in front of their doors in the morning. Dilapidated but cosy, damp but friendly, in the eyes of most Bethnal Greeners these cottages *are* the place, much more so than the huge blocks of tenement buildings standing guard, like dark fortresses, over the little houses. On the warm summer evening of the interview, children were playing hop-scotch or 'he' in the roadway while their parents, when not watching the television, were at their open windows. Some of the older people were sitting in upright chairs on the pavement, just in front of their doors, or in the passages leading through to the sculleries, chatting with each other and watching the children at play.

(Michael Young and Peter Willmott, *Family and Kinship in East London*, 1957)

In the 1950s and 1960s the blitzed areas of Britain's cities and the post-war slum clearance schemes offered great opportunities and great threats. Drawn to this issue, sociologists Michael Young and Peter Willmott studied the effect of the newest of social institutions, the housing estate, upon one of the oldest, the family. Although Richard Hoggart was more concerned with the impact of the mass media on working-class culture, he too recognised that the environment for that culture was at stake. The new architecture of British public housing in the 1950s and 1960s had much to do with this situation. In its mainstream and its avant-garde productions, architecture was meant to embody change more than signalling continuity. In particular, it was tasked with solving the problems of reconstruction and carrying through the agenda of the welfare state. By contrast, in their housing scheme at Preston and in other buildings for social and community purposes in south London (at Putney, Blackheath and Camberwell), Stirling and Gowan's architecture became finely attuned to the 'peculiarly gripping wholeness' of these 'small worlds', to the importance of 'watching . . . children at play', and to the contradictions of wanting both change and continuity.

The housing scheme at Preston (1957–61), the main focus of this chapter, has been relatively neglected in accounts of Stirling and Gowan's architecture. Considering it at some length at the very least helps to make the received story of the practice's development, usually seen as culminating in the Leicester University Engineering building (1959–64), to be discussed in Chapter Six, less linear and more properly complex. Two important resources were brought to the work at Preston: the architects' interest in regional aspects of the 'functional tradition' and, overlapping with this, a new open-mindedness about explicit reconnection with premodernist urban and architectural traditions, especially the despised Victorian city. Strikingly, then, and controversially at the time, the Preston scheme challenged modernist orthodoxy about historical development, architectural abstraction and technological progress, and in this it is part of that broader post-industrial attitude characteristic of the architects' work. The chapter gathers its various strands together around the issue of nostalgia, as it was used negatively in reviewing the scheme and positively by the architects in promoting it. Instead of a jackdaw-like and often ironic attitude towards a fragmented, premodernist and strictly architectural past – later characteristic of postmodernism – the positive use of nostalgia enabled the architects to reconsider the possibilities, both forward- and backward-looking, of a place-specific, historically and communally minded architecture in post-war Britain. Similar themes can be found in the other buildings discussed here, and as a whole they offered ways of engaging the welfare state with the industrial city, ways that were quite distinct from other contemporary architectural responses.

Victorianism can be understood as an aspect of the modernist regionalism that interested many architects in the 1950s. For Stirling the obvious sources for British urban regionalism were the 'unselfconscious and usually anonymous' warehouses and other industrial buildings, especially from Liverpool and the industrial north where he had grown up, and these epitomised the 'infinite idiosyncrasies of locality'.[1] Victorian architecture offered other positive examples. Although Stirling disliked 'the ugliness of the stylistic merry-go-round', he preferred the form taken by Victorian expansion on the edges of cities, with its 'social and constructional innovation in low density housing', to modern suburbs.[2] Brick became almost ubiquitous in his and Gowan's projects at this time, and Stirling cited the Victorian 'knowledge in detailing structural brickwork' as a specific inspiration.[3]

Given the sympathy for things Victorian in their writing, it might seem strange if Stirling and Gowan's architecture did not also reflect Victorian traits. Indeed, there is evidence of more than just the concession that their buildings might 'look a bit Victorian',[4] and even a use of literal Victorianisms in certain buildings and projects that have been neglected or edited by the historical record. Three examples from the previous chapter are worth mentioning again. In the Dodd house in Kensington, as well as the Regency front the rear wall could easily be mistaken for the reuse of a Victorian remnant; but in fact its arched windows, brick polychromy and chamfered concrete were entirely new.[5] In another example, their proposed semi-detached houses at Sunninghill, Stirling and Gowan were inspired by the 'architecture of the "Backs"', the rear view of nineteenth-century terraces, to design an asymmetrical syncopation of gable ends for the *front* of their scheme. These backs revealed the terraces' 'true organisation', showing clearly the different levels and unequal sizes of rooms and how the outhouses defined the property walls, an observation contemporary with the Preston housing and, as will be shown, clearly having a relation to that scheme.[6] Lastly, for the Kissa house in the Chilterns the architects proposed to articulate their buff-coloured brick elevations with courses of coloured brick like the constructional polychromy beloved by High Victorian architects. The examples may indicate a tentative reaching for an alternative vocabulary, but all these forms and details would be used in the Preston scheme.

While the Ham Common flats reworked the window details of nineteenth-century industrial buildings, and respected the scale and materials of their Georgian context, like the other early projects the flats stayed at a level of historical abstraction consonant with modernism. This meant, for example, that despite the protestations of the architects, the flats could be used as an example of the New Brutalism by Reyner Banham.[7] By contrast, the regionalist elements in the infill housing at Preston were joined to a level of historical and even anthropological specificity that tipped the project into controversial waters and also resigned it to a near oblivion (meaning that no defence could be offered against its almost total demolition in the 1990s).[8] In common with Preston, all three of the London projects to be discussed in this chapter had a social agenda, and all three might be considered as representations of the idea of community. Furthermore, all three were defined either by their relation with the surrounding Victorian city or by the affiliations they made with Victorian architecture.

~

The housing scheme in the Avenham area of Preston (1957–61), consisting of sixty-two units of accommodation in a group of three- and four-storey terraces and some housing for old people, can be seen as the culmination of the various built and unbuilt projects of the mid-1950s, and it was certainly Stirling and Gowan's largest project to date. Together with two eleven-storey tower blocks by Lyons Israel Ellis, who had passed on the job of designing the lower development, Stirling and Gowan's buildings were part of the first phase of Preston Borough Council's slum clearance project close to the heart of the town.[9] Until clearance started in 1955 the area was occupied by a set of parallel bye-law streets, the typical

117   Victorian terrace housing in Brunswick Street, Preston, c.1954.

products of Victorian public health legislation and the work of private builders. These streets were filled with early Victorian terraces, many of which had pubs and mission halls at their ends (fig. 117). Behind the terraces were narrow paved yards congested with outhouses for coal storage and lavatories.[10]

At Preston, therefore, Stirling and Gowan had in place all the components and conditions for a reassessment of the Victorian past through a serious engagement with the forms of the local housing and a presumption of the continuity of working-class community. Adopting urban elements of the Victorian city, they arranged their buildings as two three-storey terraces and one four-storey block of flats, placed around three sides of the large island site, with a separate group of two-storey houses and flats for old people (fig. 118).[11] By locating units suitable for the nuclear family close to other forms of accommodation, the proximate extended family was also recognised.[12] Through reversing one of the three-storey terraces, the architects managed to present three different faces to the surrounding streets, both deferring to and playfully reshaping the bye-law vernacular. These terraces had one-bedroom flats on the ground floor and two-storey maisonettes above. They were planned *ad quadratum* and given unremarkable conventional interiors. The maisonettes were entered via a shared deck that was raised above the yards of the flats and bridged between the maisonettes and their individual 'outhouses'.

Such decks were essential to the way that architects of the recently named New Brutalist tendency, like the Smithsons, attempted to preserve old patterns of street

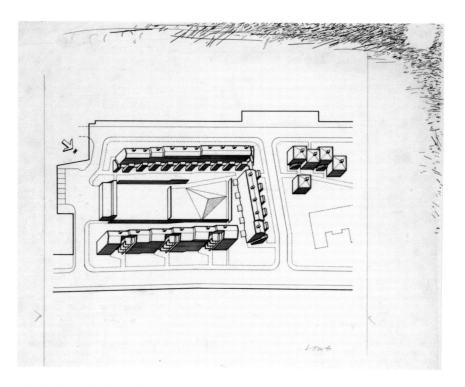

118   Stirling and Gowan, Preston Housing, 1957–61, bird's-eye view of the site.

life within modernist mass housing developments without the historicist revival of the streets themselves.[13] But where the streets in the Smithsons' Golden Lane housing (1952) were effectively one-sided, wide access decks (rather than the internal streets of Le Corbusier's *Unités*), Preston's were more terrace-like, open to the sky and yet easily accessible from the ground. This might be seen as a counter to the tendency of 'streets-in-the-air' to stifle any full street life through their overly linear, mono-functional qualities. Furthermore, the Smithsons' Golden Lane failed to match its 'streets-in-the-air' with anything equivalent to those private backyards essential to terraced housing.[14] At Preston a little more was attempted. Just as the deck stood in for, or 'maintained the spirit of' the street or back alley, so the outhouses suggested the 'spirit' of the coal-shed (or even a decommissioned outside lavatory), that ubiquitous feature of the backyards.[15]

Formally the mini-towers created by these outhouses, accented by long strips of wood acting as louvres on their window slits, gave the terraces a distinctive and non-regional stepped back form. This expressed what Stirling, echoing the picturesque effects of his earlier Woolton house and village housing, was to call 'the articulation

and identification of the scale of accommodation of which a building is made up'
(fig. 119).[16] The outhouses, together with
the castellation of the roofline suggested
by the inset windows of the top floor, also
lent the whole terrace a somewhat defensive effect (an idea to be given even more
prominence in the architects' Blackheath
old people's home and their Churchill
College competition entry). At the ends
of the housing blocks, below the side elevations with their hint of warehouse walls,
strongly defined ramps and bridges gave
access to the decks and provided angular
sculptural elements at three corners of
the site, but particularly at the west corner
where two ramps were built. In one statement the architects emphasised that the
openness and visibility of the access spaces
was made 'so that the movement and

119   Stirling and Gowan, Preston Housing,
1957–61, view of three-storey terraces.

meeting of people can be seen and enjoyed by everyone'.[17] These ramps, then, were
intended as the most striking stage for this play of urban theatrics.

   Although the four-storey block of flats was the largest element of the scheme, it
was also the most self-effacing (fig. 120). It presented its inset entrances and its access
stairways on its outward-facing side, and here the details were mostly abruptly
modern, with awkward junctures between wood, concrete and brick components.[18]
Both long sides of the block were broken up with staggered groups of windows,
their unevenness justified by the need to step down on the sloping site. Less a Victorian terrace in inspiration, this was more reminiscent of those warehouses that
Stirling had admired and illustrated in his 1957 essay on regionalism: 'the outside
appearance of these buildings', Stirling had written then, 'is an efficient expression
of their specific function whereas today they may be appreciated picturesquely and
possibly utilised arbitrarily.'[19] Less industrial in derivation were the timber and glass
balconies and gallery fronts used for the access stairways and which, in the three-
storey blocks, screened the small yards of the ground-floor flats. These balconies
were almost absurdly high, as if expressing a child's sense of scale: clearly a foretaste
of the chunky, over-scaled parapets at Leicester and in much of Stirling's later work.
The large courtyard behind the blocks was reminiscent of similar areas in Lubetkin

120   Stirling and Gowan, Preston Housing, 1957–61, view of four-storey flats.

and Tecton's housing estates; areas essentially for play were given hints of some more profound purpose, with a low grassed pyramid (hiding contractors' debris) and lengths of wall that suggest, perhaps, the backyard perimeters left behind by the terraces.[20] In an 'as found' appropriation, sewage block-traps were turned on their sides, placed on the walls of the outhouses and used as rainwater spouts (fig. 121). Like the drain cover used in the Dodd house, such devices are opportunistic bits of making-do, with no pretension to some larger significance.

The five small blocks of old people's housing were placed over the road from the reconstituted terraces (fig. 122). Four of these were positioned in an informal row, the fifth slightly detached from them. External stairs were placed in the re-entrant spaces created by the informal grouping, their angular sheer brick walls marking their family resemblance to the ramps of the terraces. In one of the most telling devices in these otherwise four-square volumes, 'an architectural joke on the modern movement', the entrances to the lower flats were cut through the external staircases.[21] The buildings were given

121 A and B   Stirling and Gowan, Preston Housing, 1957–61, rainwater spouts.

pyramidal roofs while the walls were articulated with exposed concrete lintels and lines of blue engineering brick at the levels of the floors and roof-slab. The Victorian effect was extended to the chamfered edges of the lintels.[22] In one unfamiliar device the roofs stopped short, allowing the walls to extend upwards as parapets and giving the buildings a starker effect, like Victorian faces with modern hairstyling.

Almost cheek-by-jowl with Victorian terraces, Stirling and Gowan's scheme used other details from these buildings: splayed setbacks, for example, copings made of bricks set on edge, and bull-nosed bricks used for window sills. Bricks were chosen partly to cut costs, but they also had the effect of making the familiar strange. These semi-engineering bricks have sharply defined edges and a hard semi-reflective surface. Normally used for industrial buildings, Stirling particularly wanted them for their 'out of context' effect.[23] They

122   Stirling and Gowan, Preston Housing, 1957–61, old people's flats.

too, therefore, had an 'as found' aspect to them. They were everyday objects – local, off the shelf, cheap – whose qualities, normally taken for granted, were to be newly appreciated.

For avant-garde architects in the 1950s to use the kind of bricks that were associated closely with Victorian housing or industrial buildings was in itself provocative. Bricks were usually seen as a dismal building material, the enemy of light and space.[24] But the Preston bricks do not tell their age easily; their surfaces refuse the patina of wear and tear. They do not, in other words, evoke the negative or 'bad everyday' connotations of bricks so common in nineteenth- and early twentieth-century Britain: bricks signifying repetitive labour, the desolate and the unpleasant, 'a wilderness of dirty bricks'.[25] But neither, however, are they easily associated with the 'good everyday', as bricks often were in a different nineteenth-century tradition where the appearance of bricks was seen to embody the positive valence of ordinary actions.[26] By contrast, the sheer surfaces and reflective effects of Stirling and Gowan's bricks seem, in part, to provide a distancing of the otherwise familiar qualities of the Victorian terrace, a way of putting the latter in parenthesis or in quotation marks. In this way the effect, if for different ends, continues the emphasis on the distinct, patterned qualities of the bricks at Ham. This results at Preston in buildings that everywhere stress their planarity and hardness, echoing qualities in the city around them. Everywhere they are precise in their profiles or silhouettes, a precision that derives from emphasising the thinness and tautness of the medium, giving the resultant walls a curious weightlessness.[27] This is the beginning of that 'prismatic style of hard shiny surfaces' that became an admired feature of Stirling's later work,[28] but also of the solemn and carefully calibrated planes of brick that characterised Gowan's.

Whatever affiliations its details made, the suggestion that the reconstructed Victorian terrace could be renovated was made within a larger context of rupture with the nineteenth-century street pattern. The advantages of natural surveillance in the street and the learnt limits to propinquity – so closely identified with the terraces – were inevitably fragile: as much form-specific as socially specific qualities. The reality was that, however much the Preston scheme evoked the Victorian terrace, it was built within a new set of limits and assumptions, including new bye-laws insisting upon seventy feet between frontages.[29] It was a publicly owned rather than commercially driven development, an estate centred on an empty play space rather than a shared channel of movement, an island of attempted continuity within a public space eviscerated through de-industrialisation. So, the penetrability of the ends of these terraces into and out of the yard, the restricted public use of street decks, and the ambiguous ownership of proximate public spaces created from converting terraced streets into a perimeter block of housing, all implied new behavioural codes or disciplines to be learned. In other words, Stirling and Gowan's scheme was not content to leave tradition and community merely on the level of representation but displaced them into an urban form that was, hopefully, more resistant to the dislocations of modernity even as it aped or was compelled to use several of its forms. In getting away from Stevenage and Saint-Dié, Preston sought to reanimate other urban models and figures: a consultation of the industrial *genius loci*, an attempt to express separate dwelling functions, and a merging of the forms of the terrace and the perimeter block.

～

To understand the Preston scheme better requires an insight into how the architects intended it to be understood and how contemporaries reacted to it. For their intentions, as well as the published statements used already there are a number of photographs made by Stirling soon after the buildings became inhabited; these were sent to the architectural press by the architects and used by some journals when reviewing the work.[30] Not simple statements of intention, rather these are an attempt to canalise or at least modify responses to the scheme. Among the photographs is a striking

123   Preston, 1961. Photograph by James Stirling (?).

view of a group of Victorian industrial buildings in Preston, possibly indicating local affiliations with the architects' approach, though probably photographed after the scheme was completed (fig. 123).[31] In most other contemporary contexts this subject would provide an opportunity for images of smoggy air, mouldering brick, and hard, mean figures: as, for example, in the documentary films of Paul Rotha or Bill Brandt's photographs of desolate northern townscapes. In Stirling's photograph, however, the figures carry no emotional burden and the attention is on the buildings. Although these are of variable heights, they cluster together to form a densely articu-lated huddle, all angled gables, sheer walls of brick in pointillist grey and white, and dramatically contrastive shadows created by a raking light from the side. The whole is unified by the flattening effect of a deep-focus lens and some sly framing that lines one edge with a lamp post and fills one corner with a bulgy black car. When it appeared in *Architectural Design*, it was captioned: 'the character of the city is tough, dark and complex', identifying those qualities with which Stirling and Gowan wanted the new scheme to be associated.[32] The photograph, of course, portrays a rather different image of Preston than the mid-nineteenth-century terraces that were the more immediate context of the new housing – it is an image of working environs rather than residence – and by doing so it offers formal precedent for a looser and more varied group of cubic shapes, giving licence for the wilful placing of windows and for the abrupt termination of planes in the final scheme.

If this was the preferred image of Preston itself, Stirling's photographs of the finished project tended to emphasise seemingly ad hoc encounters between residents and buildings. Although architectural photography showing buildings actually as used or populated was still extremely unusual at this time, the obvious precedents for Stirling's work were Roger Mayne's images of Park Hill, Sheffield, that had appeared in *Architectural Design* only a few months previously in September 1961 (fig. 124).[33] These works, as well as Nigel Henderson's and Humphrey Spender's related imagery,[34] are clearly behind Stirling's photographs, especially in their evocation of a world of blurred movements and suggestive shadows, of the randomness of human association and out-of-doors play. In one of Stirling's photographs, two groups of children are seen sitting on the angled parapets of the ramps at the western corner, a particularly important part of the scheme for the architects (fig. 125).[35] The photograph is cleanly composed, balancing heightened figurative and abstract elements. The new scheme appears as large flat slices of wall that are enlivened, even ornamented, by the children and the strong shapes of their shadows, labile body images entirely at one with the sun-reflective sheets of brick. The past is manifested by a small cluster of chimneys that appears discreetly just behind some of the children to the right, their television

124   Park Hill, Sheffield, 1961. Photograph by Roger Mayne.

125   Children on ramps of Preston Housing, 1961. Photograph by James Stirling.

aerials indicating modern accretions. We look at the children as they gather on the walls like birds on a line, entirely at home in their environment. Importantly, as with other photographs by Stirling, the children actively engage in a highly tactile, bodily relation with the buildings. A photograph like this, looking upwards at planes of wall and sky, seems to deny perspective; instead of a suppression of the other senses in favour of rationalised sight, the photograph wants to mediate our physical relation to the buildings through the bodies of the children.

126   Children running
past three-storey terrace
at Preston Housing, 1961.
Photograph by
James Stirling.

In another photograph children again provide the signs of human life, this time caught running past a three-storey block, which once more is cut abstractly by the edges of the image (fig. 126). They could be an illustration for the famous descriptions of children playing in Young and Willmott's book.[36] A wedge of black shadow at the bottom again denies perspective. Here the old is even more ethereal – a fuzzy shadow of a chimney – while the children and their shadows are even more like biomorphic hieroglyphs for life. In a third image the photograph is divided into two halves by the beginning of one of the street decks (fig. 127). Two children improvise play on this level and two more sit on the brick parapet of a ramp in the lower half. Seen through the glass of the street deck rail or by the strong back lighting that silhouettes them, the children's bodies are now cut across, fragmented and rendered partly two-dimensional. In the immediate foreground the 'open', 'penetrable' architecture of modernist aesthetics is epitomised by the street deck, but seen through this, like temporal layers, are the new-built lintels and brick polychromy of one of the old people's houses, and then further back the familiar shapes of a Victorian terrace. The boy to the lower right characterises the physical engagement with the

127   Children on bridge of Preston Housing, 1961. Photograph by James Stirling.

architecture: he sits casually astride the parapet while his head and arms perfectly span the change of levels between lintel and window in the old people's home behind. Almost as interesting as these images, though, is one that was not published (fig. 128). Here a middle-aged couple stand on the first-floor walkway looking straight back at the camera. Their rigidity alliterates almost too well with the architectural features around them: they, like their surrounds, are rectilinear, slightly off-centre but slotted into place as elements in a pattern pushed flatly against the picture plane.

128   Middle-aged couple on three-storey terrace of
Preston Housing, 1961. Photograph by James Stirling.

Knowing one's place, stoicism, even architectural imprisonment: none of these were
desired associations.

Most of Stirling's published images,
however, are populated by children, and
this implies a double association: with an
optimistic future of adulthood to be, as
well as with a remembered past of childhood that was. Although the second of
these is not an association one finds in
Mayne or Henderson's street photography,
where children are more often used to
suggest deep 'tribal' meanings, including
the semiotics of street gestures and figural
inscriptions, it is an association that seems
legitimated by part of the quotation that
Stirling and Gowan chose to accompany
their own statement on the scheme. In this
quotation Somerset Maugham reports Charlie Chaplin remembering his childhood:
'To him the streets of southern London are the scene of frolic, gaiety and extravagant
adventure.'[37]

What these photographs by Stirling make clear is that the Victorian past is not
rendered an accidental element of the urban environment, nor are the new buildings
juxtaposed with Victorian terraces in the form of a surreal encounter. Unlike Stirling's
later buildings, where such encounters with the past were often rendered either
surreal or highly ironic, at Preston the encounter is both generational and generative.[38] It seems intended to say something about continuities across epochs as well
as to produce new syntheses. The past and the present are sometimes layered, sometimes intermingled. Where we have come from, the photographs suggest, is always
a presence in where we are going.

~

Stirling and Gowan's published statements on the Preston housing demonstrate their
commitment to transferring the spatial anthropology of working-class life into the
new scheme.[39] A particular current of sociology, led by the work of Michael Young
and Peter Willmott, was arguing at this time for a re-evaluation of the spaces of
working-class areas, especially for their intricate contribution to forms of social life.

Regarded by some as backward-looking, nevertheless such sociology contributed directly to the work of young Team 10 members and CIAM apostates like Alison and Peter Smithson, with whom Stirling had plenty of contact during this period.[40] The Smithsons' thinking is well known: the abstract functional zoning of modernism should give way to the promotion of identity and community using comprehensible anthropological concepts of human spatial association. Streets and houses, districts and cities, were all right after all.

Although their buildings seem more replete with historical forms and references than the Smithsons would ever allow, Stirling and Gowan's attitude to the pre-existing social realities of Preston follows some of this Team 10 thinking. Citing recent research by the anthropological survey group Mass Observation,[41] the architects believed 'that the most remarkable aspect of worktown over the last two decades is its great unchange, particularly in the habit and character of its people – despite greater affluence'.[42] The latter was a mere matter of 'gadgets'.[43] Echoing Willmott and Young, they argued that the 'neighbourliness and communal vitality' fostered by the Victorian city meant that there had to be equivalents to the 'alley, yard, street terraces', maintaining their 'spirit' if not actually reconstructing them.[44] 'The alleys and pavements were just big enough for their purpose,' the architects wrote, 'and they were crowded and vital places, in contrast to the oversized roads, pavements and building setbacks in the New Towns.'[45] Yet what was actually happening in the Avenham area of Preston, as in other areas of British cities at this time, was wholesale slum clearance involving not only the demolition of Victorian bye-law terraces and the transfer of private property into public hands through compulsory purchase, but also the erasure of old street patterns and the creation of a new road system aimed often at creating isolated pockets or estates of housing and flats.[46] What Stirling and Gowan could do in the face of this to assert the 'great unchange' was bound to be peripheral. Furthermore, there is even in Stirling and Gowan's buildings some ambivalence towards the existing spatial forms of community, despite the obvious links of motif and material. They seem to be seeking to renovate those forms rather than reinstating them.[47] On one level, renovation can be seen in the transplanting of the bye-law street into the raised, usually single-sided deck typical of New Brutalism. On another level, it can also be seen in the way the main blocks seem lifted above as well as withdrawn from the surrounding streets: not quite courtyard block, not quite terrace, but isolated and unable to reconnect with the terraces. Meanwhile, over the road, the old people's housing is staggered informally but awkwardly, seemingly unsure whether it belongs to a village or to the new street lines. It is as if the architects wanted to have some elevated, more archetypal sense of place while also retaining a strong link with the familiar environmental forms of the area.

In these ways Stirling and Gowan's scheme was riven through with (mostly) unintended paradoxes and contradictions. Its rhetoric was of a repairing of a rupture with the past, yet it had only come about because of that rupture. It seemed to preach the reassuring verities of traditional housing scale, yet it was conceived by Preston Borough Council, and knowingly entered into by the architects when they took on responsibility for the lower buildings from Lyons Israel Ellis, as merely the soft, low-rise end of a 'mixed development' that also included eleven-storey tower blocks; in other words, it was only able to be low-rise because of high-rises nearby.[48] It elevated the supposed transfer of the coal bunker into a modern scheme as a matter of respecting custom, while it denied its increasingly affluent residents the backyards or private gardens of their previous houses.[49] Finally, it celebrated the benefits of neighbourly propinquity while subjecting expected notions of front and rear to a radical reversal.[50]

These complex and unresolved qualities at Preston bear witness to a shifting of ground beneath the practice of modernist architecture; its very irreconcilability with the past produces a heterogeneous if rifted architecture. The estate's traditional and social realist features point in one direction, while its top-down welfarism and modernist disjunction point in another. How was it possible to preserve a social world yet also to accommodate it to modernity?

~

Contemporary accounts identified the Preston scheme directly with other representations of working-class life. One such was *Saturday Night and Sunday Morning*, Alan Sillitoe's 1958 novel of working-class life in the northern industrial city, a model study of frustration with the limitations of that life and of the allure of affluence as an escape from it. Many critics regarded the Avenham estate as a similar hemming in, re-enacting a similarly brutal determinism. In part these remarks may reflect a London-centric and largely middle-class profession reacting against the idea of the north as an alternative (rather than antithesis) to their versions of modernity.[51] For a commentator on *Architectural Design*, the buildings were too reminiscent of the sites of Victorian labour: 'although preserving the intimate quality of the slums is possibly better than sterile suburbia, must the executed theory be so forbidding? . . . the mill was the daily drudgery from which worktown escaped, not the idiom they returned to, nor the "vital spirit of the alley". This seems like grinding them in.'[52] The *Housing Review* questioned what appeared to be 'an unnecessary perpetuation of the grim background of living in industrial towns'.[53] When the scheme won the 1963 Good Housing Competition, the *Daily Mail* reported that it had caused uproar among architects for being 'deliberately designed . . . to look like slums'.[54] A few years later Nikolaus Pevsner, who had warned against a 'return to historicism' in 1961, commented tartly that '[Stirling and Gowan's] terraces . . . are evidently an attempt at reverting to the mood of the Victorian vernacular. It is curious that some people should have moved on recently to a nostalgia for the grimmer aspects of Victorian architecture.'[55] Even the Italian journal *Casabella* pushed Preston's post-industrial nostalgia further by including comparative images of a Victorian terraced street and a painting by L. S. Lowry, doyen of the glum northern scene.[56]

Reyner Banham's review of the Preston housing is the most interesting precisely because it is the most ambivalent. It was made from a position closer to Stirling and Gowan's, though Banham shared with Pevsner a rejection of any hint of stylistic revivalism and had recently described the Italian Neo-Liberty style as 'infantile regression'.[57] Certainly, Preston was likely to raise the issue of how it related to the broader trend in post-war European architecture (especially in Scandinavia, Italy and Eastern Europe) of a return to pre-modern housing types. In Europe this trend went by the terms 'Neo-Realism' or 'Socialist Realism': attempts, under varying political regimes, to react against modernism and assert continuity with forms of dwelling or community disrupted or destroyed by the war.[58] Some considered there was a British version of this, to be found in the 'New Empiricism' fostered by the *Architectural Review* and in that wing of the LCC Architect's Department responsible for the Alton East estate in Roehampton, and typified by shallow-pitched roofs and the 'people's detailing' of tile-hung, weatherboarded or pebble-dashed façades, if not by historical revivalism.

Like his friend Stirling, Banham was a second generation critic of established forms of modernism, particularly damning of the older generation's picturesque modernism. Nevertheless, there is a sense in his review of Banham trying to suspend normal critical judgement, of making superfine distinctions in the face of what could easily seem like a betrayal of any kind of modernism, 'heroic' or not. In Banham's view, the image of close-knit working-class life implied by Stirling and Gowan's buildings was not of the same ilk as the 'sentimental Hoggartry' which believed that working-class virtues were the product of intimate physical propinquity; it was not a simple recidivism, a desire to turn the clock back.[59] Like the Smithsons, and Team 10, Stirling and Gowan had rejected what Banham called the 'architectural charity' of modernism, its philanthropic pretensions, and had come to regard working-class culture as inherently valuable. Banham identified the key components in this move as, first, the rediscovery of the vernacular through Le Corbusier, then a revaluing of English regional materials and a reawakening to the life of working-class streets as Mayne and Henderson had pictured them. But what worried Banham in the Preston scheme was that, unlike the Smithsons, who had taken the function of the street but placed it within an utterly different architectural form, there was a danger in Stirling and Gowan's work of 'socialist formalism or working-class scene-painting'.[60] Banham pointed to the 'slackly wilful' effect of the placing of windows on the four-storey block of flats, but he approved of the outhouses and the street decks in the other two blocks: 'these two terraces have the air of a vernacular tradition craftily re-assessed in terms of a society in transition.'[61] Most intriguing and problematic were the old people's homes. Here 'the whole effect is so Victorian that they could almost be re-named Bessemer Cottages,' and because the building-forms were so close to actual Victorian types, 'everything fits together with an unforced logic.'[62] Yet this too made Banham uneasy. As the rest of the scheme had shown that working-class community could be evoked with new spatial forms (the street deck), what was the meaning of these apparently retardataire houses; what was their 'intended social content'?[63] There was a real contradiction here. Were the architects serving a durable and unchanging working-class life, or was this a form of revivalism, providing 'an architecture that forces the working class into the role of picturesque peasantry'?[64] Banham's own judgement seems apparent by the end of the article: though the Preston scheme may provide 'a functional and visual setting for much that is valuable in proletarian culture *at the moment* . . . [it] may leave a developing working class lumbered with an unsuitable functional environment twenty affluent years from now.'[65] Here the difference between Banham's 'second machine age' and Stirling and Gowan's more ambivalent post-industrialism seems laid bare.

∼

In these responses, including Banham's more equivocal review, Stirling and Gowan stood accused not just of a failure to develop but of a deliberate recidivism. The Preston scheme was not understood as nostalgia for utopia, the brandishing of fragments of an older modernism that was more often found in the work of the neo-avant-garde.[66] Instead, Stirling and Gowan were accused of nostalgia for perhaps the worst of all pasts at that time, the Victorian age. It seemed odd, even perverse, in these immediate post-war decades with their blitzed and slum-cleared wastelands, and certainly untypical of the architectural profession, to savour such a past in the heart of the city. After all, for nearly three decades since at least the early 1930s, and arguably since the start of the Garden City movement, progressive British architects and planners, abetted by documentary filmmakers and photographers, had berated what they regarded as the typical features of the Victorian city. The worst subject of their ire and their campaigning for new planning laws was the bye-law street, but invectives were also directed at inner-city pollution, lack of green spaces, and the absence of zoned planning: all offended against an aesthetics of hygienic and thera-peutic order.[67]

Modernism had been narrated by Nikolaus Pevsner as a movement initiated by 'pioneers' finding their way out of the Victorian jungle of style through new tech-nologies and new materials and then later, once the movement was established, moderating a functional rationalism with the more familiar aesthetics of the pictur-esque.[68] The Victorian city, therefore, acted as the 'Other' to modernism's enlightened city of towers and open spaces; it provided confirmation by contrast with the mod-ernisation of the post-war period. Although the Festival of Britain had sparked a revived interest in Victorian design, this was very far from the Victorian slums, the vistas of mouldering brick, and the catastrophes of Victorian industrialism that populated modernist nightmares. But there were other, confusing factors here. For those of an avant-garde disposition, liking Victorian architecture at this time was to risk association with the soft or picturesque wing of modernism, or with fogeys and revivalists of an older generation like John Betjeman and Osbert Lancaster.[69] But liking what was deemed as the deliberately ugly and violently clashing contrasts between the medieval and the industrial, as could be found in High Victorians like William Butterfield, was an accepted part of the world of New Brutalist references and could be seen as a more extreme form of the picturesque.[70] Among all these factions, however, there was hardly any attempt to reappreciate the harder, slummier aspects of the Victorian city – exactly what Stirling and Gowan called its 'tough, dark and complex qualities'.[71]

The partners had anticipated the objections to Preston; indeed, the idea that their scheme was nostalgic was one they themselves took up and turned to positive effect in promoting the scheme's virtues. This is one of those examples of what could be called a principle of contrariness in their architecture that continued in Stirling's later work. Contrariness here involves the transgression of accepted tenets – in this case modernism's revulsion for nostalgia and its desire to consign the Victorian slum to oblivion – so that they could come into productive tension with their opposites.[72] Together with their project description, plans and photographs, Stirling and Gowan also sent the press the quotation from Somerset Maugham that has already been mentioned but is now worth quoting in full. Maugham is writing about Charlie Chaplin:

I have a notion that he suffers from a nostalgia of the slums. The celebrity he enjoys, his wealth, imprison him in a way of life in which he finds only constraint. I think he looks back to the freedom of his struggling youth, with its poverty and bitter privation, with a longing which knows it can never be satisfied. To him the streets of southern London are the scene of frolic, gaiety and extravagant adventure. They have to him a reality which the well-kept avenues, bordered with trim houses, in which live the rich, can never possess. I can imagine him going into his own house and wondering what on earth he is doing in this strange man's dwelling. I suspect the only home he can ever look upon as such is a second-floor back in the Kennington Road. One night I walked with him in Los Angeles and presently our steps took us into the poorest quarter of the city. There were sordid tenement houses and the shabby, gaudy shops in which are sold the various goods that the poor buy from day to day. His face lit up and a buoyant tone came into his voice as he exclaimed: 'This is the real life, isn't it? All the rest is just sham'.[73]

Taking into account that Chaplin may have been playing up a particular role for Maugham's sake, there is little doubt that the prominence given to this account in presenting the new scheme at Preston is meant to extol a *nostalgie de la boue*.[74] Chaplin displays the classic symptoms of the disease of homesickness. Derived from the Greek *nostos*, or return, and *algos*, or suffering, nostalgia is a modern term denoting the melancholy and pain, often treated as a medical condition in the eighteenth and nineteenth centuries, caused by an unappeased impulse to go back, to return home.[75] It is about two different times and is usually felt on the other side of some event or long period of time from what it yearns for – most typically, as with Chaplin, the places and experiences of one's childhood – and it acts through a narrative reconstruction of that supposedly more authentic past. However, it is often, as with Stirling and Gowan's reviewers, used negatively to imply that the feeling is at least only a sentimental one and at worst a morbid overidentification with the past. In either case, it involves escape from the present into an idealised and distorted past, particularly a vicarious, overly rosy idea of the bygone times of other people.

This negative view of nostalgia was deeply inscribed in modernist architectural thinking. Nostalgia was a synonym for the distortion of history, a sign of backward-looking and anti-progressive sentiment, and something irrational and therefore irrelevant to strictly architectural thinking. Furthermore, although memory – likewise denied by modernism – may have returned as an approved concept and one often used for ironic ends since the onset of postmodernism, nostalgia remains a term of derision.[76] Ignoring the overlap between the two concepts, it would seem as if memory is admitted into critical theory because it conjures up the meta-historical, offering resistance to both official history and modernist amnesia, while nostalgia is seen as lacking any galvanising powers. Yet as Chaplin's statement reminds us, the experience of exile and the feeling of nostalgia were important features of modernist expression in other art forms and often seen as fundamental to the dislocating effects of the modern world, as the word's modern provenance indicates.[77] To identify loss borne by the exiled or displaced subject, the stresses of modernity on the individual sensorium, was the motivation of much modernist art.

All this makes it even more interesting that Stirling and Gowan should have presented the Preston scheme under the banner of nostalgia. They very precisely summoned up the heresy of nostalgia, partly as an act of provocative contrariness – enabling the return of what modernism had repressed – and partly as a declaration of independence from contemporary architectural mores. Nostalgia for them was neither a negative concept nor merely a symptom of the rejection of modernity; it signalled an engagement with the past and offered some critical purchase on the present,[78] as much a 'cultural practice [as] a given content'.[79] It was perfectly compatible with defamiliarising devices which recalled the known but at the same time made it strange, remaking nostalgia's traditional links with the uncanny.[80] Most tellingly, and unlike the referential use of the past in some of Stirling's later works, the Preston scheme did not offer the past as an isolated fragment, nor was it merely contextualist, resuscitating some form of social realism.

What makes Chaplin's nostalgia different from one that denies the present is not just that the past seems more real than the 'sham' of present wealth; it is also that poverty and wealth coexist and can be found in the same city as part of lived experience rather than vicarious reconstruction: one is the critique of the other. These feelings are identified closely with buildings: the 'well-kept avenues' and 'trim houses' of the rich, as opposed to the 'sordid tenement houses' and 'shabby, gaudy shops' of the poor. Chaplin's own trim home can only seem not homely enough, a 'strange man's dwelling', under the power of nostalgia. The trimness and strangeness of this home are easily read, in the new context of post-war architectural discourse, as a way of indicating modernism. Similarly, and even more provocatively, the term 'sham' is turned inside out from what had become a common modernist adjective for the Victorian past and instead now indicates the modern itself. Nostalgia may also have had personal, Chaplinesque meaning for Stirling. His birth in a Glasgow tenement (even if only on a short visit to grandparents) followed by his upbringing in middle-class Liverpool suburbs offered fertile soil for a detached, knowing *nostalgie de la boue* and one from which Stirling clearly drew later in his career.[81] While he saw himself, according to Colin Rowe and others, as a 'provincial hero', he was also 'never completely at ease' in London.[82]

The significance of nostalgia, then, depends on where you stand. The architect's agency as reinterpreted by modernism was to intervene, to defamiliarise, to act *on* the city. Patently, though, nostalgia could be more manifold than architectural modernists believed; it could reflect actual displacements and assert continuities which otherwise the ever spinning wheels of progress merely fix as constant repetition, or the ever forward-moving impulse of modern architecture seeks to dispel by vanquishing anxiety about the future. Nostalgia particularly seems to accompany seismic change; it is that loss felt as a corollary of large-scale development, crisis, the uprooting caused by disaster. Perhaps surprisingly, through its anxieties about the future or disaffection with the present, nostalgia can offer criticism while acknowledging change. It can preserve histories, offer analeptic counter-narratives and figures of difference despite the commodification of the past. Because it revalues elements of a despised past, making parochial or personal misfortunes publicly meaningful, nostalgia can question myths of progress and offer the perspective of users, the victims or the powerless.[83]

Preston was an attempt to bracket off modernist architects' usual aspiration to master change, and to represent change instead from another position. In this sense, a critical or positive nostalgia is close to the work of contemporary social theorists like Richard Hoggart or Michael Young and Peter Willmott, all of whom stressed that the changes they described had been made within living memory and that their books were inspired by the fear that something of great distinction, based upon an identification between community and place, might be lost to a new 'faceless' culture.[84] The question is whether Stirling and Gowan's work offered a critical perspective and a form of resistance to modernisation, or whether, as many of its critics felt, it was a betrayal of the present and its potential for the sake of a familiar but limited past. The Preston scheme sought, as suggested earlier, to renovate a still active memory. It indicated displacement – but, emphatically, not disappearance – through its materials and its references to industrial buildings, while also reconfiguring shared spaces (street, alley, yard) within the new terms of a public housing estate.

~

Preston was not alone in Stirling and Gowan's work. Other commissions also focused their attention on the public sector, the idea of community and the presence of the Victorian city, and with equally tight price limits.[85] In 1958 a commission to design a small assembly hall for a primary school in Brunswick Park, Camberwell, resulted in Stirling and Gowan's first educational building (fig. 129). The design can be understood in one sense as the built progeny of the expandable house, translating that design's expanding quadrants into three monopitch roofs housing the assembly spaces and turning around a quartered plot whose fourth quarter was filled with a flat-roofed service area. (As the next chapter will show, the motif can also be found

129   Stirling and Gowan, Assembly Hall, Brunswick Park School, Camberwell, 1958–61.

in the library for the Churchill College design, which is contemporary with Camberwell.) Here again it was Gowan who started the design, this time because when the commission came in autumn 1958 Stirling was away teaching at Yale.[86] Gowan took the quadrants and combined them with the idea of sheltering the building behind earthen banks so that it would hug the ground on the large site (fig. 130). For these raised banks Gowan found sources not just in medieval castles but also in Frank Lloyd Wright's later houses.[87] His first designs show that initially the bank or glacis was not thought of as cupping the whole building and only three of the quadrants were used; in addition, the pentroofs were lower pitched, there were three colours of brick (yellow, red and blue), and the kitchen – signalled by the flue – was more integrated with the assembly hall function.[88] There were other variations on this early design, the most striking of which envisaged an angular moat as well as a glacis.[89] From Yale Stirling responded by increasing the height of the roofs. Later, he also added embellishments like the Victorian detail of the coping trim on the walls, while Gowan refined the windows. A further collaborator in this instance was the engineer Frank Newby, who sorted out the structure for the roof. Finally, after the

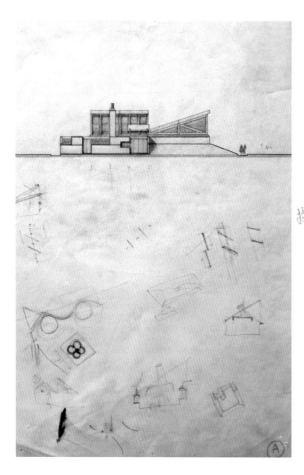

130   Stirling and Gowan, Assembly Hall, Brunswick Park School, Camberwell, 1958–61, drawing of early design, elevation.

clients expressed reservations about not having low-level views out onto the grassed surrounds, Gowan added windows cut into the banks (fig. 131).[90]

What resulted from this redesigning and dialogue with other parties was a building whose presence belies its modest size. Indeed, tightly contrasting sensations are triggered by several aspects of the assembly hall. While entering it is like retreating to a bunker, once inside the spaces are filled with light from three directions. While the embankments half bury the building as if prepared to repel some attack, the windows rise generously – if vulnerably – above them. And while the proportions of the hall's forms are determinedly distinct from its surroundings, even 'heroic' in a modernist way, it offers low-lying windows and other details at the scale of the children who are its predominant users. It was the effect of the high windows that interested Gowan most in his publicity photographs, using his daughters and their friends to populate the hall (fig. 132). Gowan's sprite-like figures appropriate the space as their own, taking playful measure of its volumes, their gawkiness offsetting the light angling into and around its vaulting roofs. Like Stirling's photographs of Preston, hints of Victorianism are played off against the animation of moving children.

But unlike Preston, the assembly hall is strikingly different from its surroundings.[91] It was located on a cleared bombsite large enough for possible future expansion once temporary prefabricated housing was removed.[92] The structure is boldly declared and daringly simple: four reinforced concrete beams spanning from the outer walls onto a central column define a cruciform structure; timber trusses then span from these beams to support the roof. The hall rises above a four-sided mound and lifts three banks of studio windows to three different sides of its site, pinning a fourth side

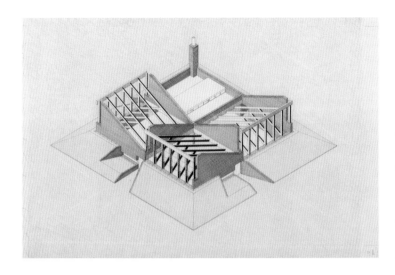

133   Stirling and Gowan, Assembly Hall, Brunswick Park School, Camberwell, 1958–61.

with a chimney flue rising almost sheer from a corner. In a foretaste of the daring glazing that would soon flood Stirling and Gowan's designs, the studio windows step outwards slightly as they rise. It is notable that when Stirling illustrated the hall in his Black Book he airbrushed all surrounding buildings out of his main image, showing the building totally isolated (fig. 133). Without any sense of scale, it could be some oddly angular modern castle set on its mound with a flue for a keep. Its colour, predominantly light buff bricks but with some red brick trim, also underlines this sense of difference from its surroundings, as if the Queen Anne style school neighbouring it belonged to an entirely separate institution.

What meaning can be found in this sense of isolation and difference? One reviewer understood the building as '[drawing] the earth close to it to try to hide from its depressing neighbours' and saw the surrounding area as 'grim . . . a compression of buildings in every conceivable style'.[93] The architects would have agreed. They saw the environment as irredeemably chaotic and overcrowded; a new building here could not try to bind this together or make contextual allusions. Instead, they wanted 'an island of open space and green lawns'.[94] The engulfing banks, in this way of seeing things, were a solution that 'if taken to its impractical extreme would have entailed burying the new building'.⁹⁵ But unlike Preston, no comprehensive redevelopment was happening here; the feeling of embattled difference was an immediately local one. The point was to create a sense of both enclosure and potential. There was no need to defend the continuity of a community in the face of change.

The Putney children's home and the Blackheath old people's home were each seen as essentially the work of one partner – Putney by Gowan and Blackheath by Stirling.⁹⁶ The commissions came from the LCC, from whom the partners had already received the Camberwell commission. As they arrived at the same time, it seemed best to divide responsibilities.⁹⁷ The Putney children's home (1960–64) was arranged across the full length of a deep site (figs 134–35). Almost necessarily this evokes the site for the Ham Common flats and that for Le Corbusier's Maisons Jaoul, and like both of those precedents the home has its access road placed at the edge of the site, and screens or protects its private open areas from the main street by arrang-

134   Stirling and Gowan, Children's Home, Frogmore, Putney, 1960–64, axonometric.

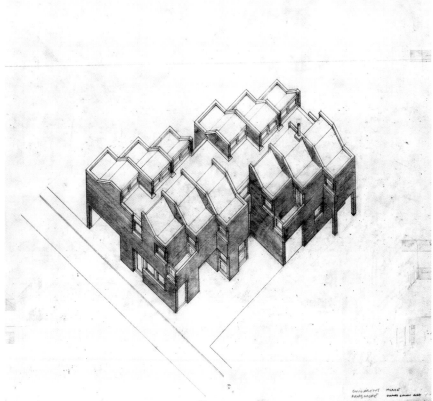
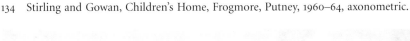

135 Stirling and Gowan, Children's Home, Frogmore, Putney, 1960–64.

ing one of its buildings across the mouth of the site (in Ham this function was performed by the already existing Georgian house). But almost every other aspect of the planning is new. The home consists of two low-rise buildings, each housing seventeen children, whose planning is based on nine-foot bays. Because of their staggered set-back form, each structure has the appearance of a collection of small buildings. The structure nearest to the road abuts it only in the north-western corner of the site and then steps back away from it, sheltering its entrance – which is almost exactly central to this end of the site – after two setbacks and turning almost all of its first-floor bedroom windows at right angles to the street. Service rooms were grouped to create a barrier zone on the street side, with communal rooms on the garden side. Behind this building, in the middle of the site, are a group of four differentiated play areas, and then at the rear of the site is placed the second building. This is almost identical in plan to the first but now turned clockwise through ninety degrees. The informality of elevations achieved by this planning has some similarities with what the partners were attempting in their Sunninghill housing and in the staff housing for the Churchill College competition (see Chapter Six). But the Preston scheme is also a presence here, most obviously in the smooth red facing bricks, so different from the yellow stock London bricks of the neighbouring buildings.[98] There are also lines of coping bricks and the regular angles of pentroofs, but little hint of the overtly Victorian detailing of Preston.

For the children's home Gowan has talked about wanting to bring the scale down to counteract the size of the commission (for seventeen children),[99] and Stirling about exaggerating its sense of family. Not only would the carers act like mum and dad, the home's scale would be kept small to encourage a sense of family unity and the architecture would be a 'caricature of the domestic house', even like a doll's house.[100] This may be why the house is scaled differently from its surroundings; certainly, the home was divided into two buildings to reduce its scale.[101] The stepped back form and the open porches were no doubt intended to create a sense of layers of protection and privacy as well as a sense of belonging. The bedrooms were articulated as the most important parts of the building – 'children playing in the gardens are able to identify with their own particular room'[102] – much as the accommodation entities were signalled at Ham and Preston. If there is a suggestion of the terrace, then this is broken and turned so that a distinct kind of community is promoted, one with traces of the past but also discontinuous with it. The symbolism of this aspect of the imagery is, perhaps, almost too explicit. It literalises discontinuity in order to escape an overly institutional feel to the home, but at the same time could be accused of making the children's social position too distinct, too recognisable.[103]

The Perrygrove old people's home in Blackheath (1960–64) is a long building, stepped in profile, which has been turned back around itself in forty-five-degree angles to make a hollow polygon (fig. 136).[104] The long corridor within the building is also bent, as if the 'driving axle' of the corridor in the Sheffield University competition entry has lost its thrust and now gained a meandering character instead, shifting in width as it changes angles and realising the potential of the corridor-led design that Stirling had felt when writing about his Poole scheme in 1951 (fig. 137). The corridor is made more intimate and less institutional by the fact that it avoids long vistas and allows for seated areas in its wider parts: 'no timorous soul need ever feel the victim of perspective at Blackheath'.[105] Bedrooms for the sixty-two residents are located off the corridor on all three levels, their regular shapes and sizes (dictated by LCC guidelines)[106] compensated for in the curving plan by irregularly shaped store-rooms. Like Putney and Preston, these interiors – whether for cost reasons or because the architects wanted to avoid the problems of Ham – are left 'undesigned', mere shells for the tastes of their inhabitants.[107]

Closer in programme to Putney than Preston, where the old people's home takes these schemes to an extreme is in its even more overtly defensive imagery of community. Blackheath is a kind of castle, defending its residents from unwanted atten-

136   Stirling and Gowan, Perrygrove Old People's Home, Blackheath, 1960–64.

tion but also giving them plenty of light and many intimate spaces. The institution itself – a local authority-run home – is symbolised in a way that combines informality, enclosure and defence. Over all this presides the matron, provided with an office adjoining the entrance hall and a flat above. Privacy was again an important consideration, especially given the high council flats nearby – hence the sheltered garden/courtyard in the middle of the building that has lower sides on the south and west to enable sun to penetrate (fig. 138). The peripheral walls are all structural, and, unusually for the partners, there is no differentiation in external treatment between bedrooms and other accommodation. The walls speak of their load-bearing nature through the articulation of the buttress-like piers, each getting thinner as it rises, each step or stage marked by two courses of angled coping stones. Great attention was paid in the drawings to the relation between continuous stretcher courses, coping bricks, stretcher

137   Stirling and Gowan, Perrygrove Old People's Home, Blackheath, 1960–64, plan of upper floor.

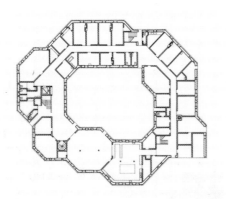

plinths and bonding details.[108] As Stirling explained, 'why use modern building techniques when ancient hand-making methods of construction are still the cheapest and easiest to build in the twentieth century?'[109] This appearance was calculatedly Victorian, less the bye-law street than the 'functional tradition' of industrial buildings,[110] but with a hint of battlements at the roofline. Lacking bye-law discipline, as well as a courtyard building's usual conformity to its surrounds, the home stands as an isolated redoubt. One building that might have been in Stirling's mind here was the sailors' home in Liverpool (John Cunningham, 1846–49) (fig. 139), which had a four-square but distinctly castle-like exterior, and inside harboured its residents in galleries around an internal court.[111] And like the sailors' home, Perrygrove manages to combine an image of security with extensively glazed inner walls. Where it takes its informality further is in its roofline, particularly the stepped sequence down to the entrance. The imagery is much more gentle than it might suggest in other hands: a kind of modern Gothick folly with a social purpose.

~

Surprisingly, given its scale, the Preston housing has not figured very significantly in accounts of Stirling's architectural development or even of his period of collaboration with Gowan. Indeed, the area of their work discussed in this chapter has been neglected except, as in the case of the Camberwell assembly hall, to find precedents for aspects

138   Stirling and Gowan, Perrygrove Old People's Home, Blackheath, 1960–64, courtyard.

139   John Cunningham, Sailors' Home, Liverpool, 1846–49.

of the Leicester University Engineering building. Gowan himself has said recently that Preston 'put both of them off the Victorian thing'.[112] Stirling did not mention Preston in his 1965 account of his work or in his Gold Medal acceptance speech in 1980; it is entirely absent from Mark Girouard's biography of the architect and from Robert Maxwell's monograph,[113] and when it is present in other accounts it has played a minor role in their narratives, regarded half-damningly as 'the most insular and vernacular [scheme] to come from the partnership'.[114] However, it is possible to understand Preston not as a cul-de-sac or as a route merely sketched out in Stirling and Gowan's work and later marginalised by retrospective accounts, but rather as the first example in post-war British architecture of an attempt to sit across a gap between modernism and previous architectural forms – indeed, to treat the contrast or contrariness as one of dialectical possibilities, of contradiction enabling a new formulation.

In this light we might return to nostalgia and the Odysseus myth. In relation to the notion of nostalgia as a betrayal of the present, Chaplin's story is a kind of warning that has links with the Greek myth of Odysseus, trapped on Calypso's island and living a life of leisure and perpetual youth, or even the related myth of the lotus-eaters, blithely neglecting all memory of home in their pursuit of present pleasures. Odysseus's nostalgia is a necessary pull to his duties, which are the only cure for his pain. Just as for Chaplin, it is 'real life' that is missing from Odysseus's travels and his frolicsome existence with Calypso. Unlike Chaplin, however, his conscience overwhelms his life of delights and drives him home. As Milan Kundera has written, 'rather than ardent exploration of the unknown (adventure), [Odysseus] chose the apotheosis of the known (return). Rather than the infinite (for adventure never intends to finish), he chose the finite (for the return is a reconciliation with the finitude of life).'[115]

But this is where the myth may lose its relevance. What is real life and what is frolic in the Preston scenario? What are duties and what is leisure there? Who or what is Penelope and who or what Calypso? Earlier Stirling and Gowan's avowed nostalgia was seen as a positive – even critical – stance, not tinged by despair or loss but activated by an ideal of renovation. Perhaps, then, what Preston stands for, and to some extent the other buildings discussed here, is not a choice between an always progressing modernity and an always finished past, nor even (or at least not yet) the 'interleaved historicity of many-times at once' characteristic of a later postmodern-ism,[116] but instead a vision of coexistent and heterogeneous temporalities.[117]

SIX

The Mechanical Hobgoblin

It is a fault of the Anglo-Saxon mind, that it is too *nice*. That is, I believe, incontestable: it has incessantly been pointed out by horrid foreigners, as well as by Anglo-Saxons themselves. . . . The *prettiness* has not been rooted out, only overlaid. There has, as a fact, been no external agency powerful enough to accomplish any such radical operation. . . . But to return to the robustest artist: the intellect athletically enjoys itself in the midst of matter, and is not afraid of objective things because it has the power to model them and compose a world of its own out of objective substance.

(Wyndham Lewis, *Men Without Art*, 1934)

Ah, the harbour bells of Cambridge! Whose fountains in moonlight and closed courts and cloisters, whose enduring beauty in its virtuous remote self-assurance, seemed part, less of the loud mosaic of one's stupid life there, though maintained perhaps by the countless deceitful memories of such lives, than the strange dream of some old monk, eight hundred years dead, whose forbidding house, reared upon piles and stakes driven into the marshy ground, had once shone like a beacon out of the mysterious silence, and solitude of the fens. A dream jealously guarded . . .

(Malcolm Lowry, *Under the Volcano*, 1947)

The Leicester University Engineering building is a great, awkward monument left by the ebb tide of modernism (fig. 140). It is also a building that still seems unfathomed in what it offered for the future. Leicester made the partners' reputation in architectural circles beyond Britain, and further university buildings in the mid- and late 1960s were to cement Stirling's international status. Before Leicester there were two other designs for university buildings, both unbuilt yet sketching out dramatic new departures in the partners' work. The larger context for these projects was the successive waves of government-sanctioned university expansion, from the Butler Act of 1944 onwards, including reports specifically on the provision of student residences.[1] This activity encouraged new thinking about the relation between higher education and society at large as well as dozens of high-profile commissions for architects. Universities, then, were the making of the partnership just as they were the 'institutional archetypes' of this period.[2]

140   Stirling and Gowan, Leicester University Engineering Building, 1959–64. Photograph by Richard Einzig.

The key figure in offering the partners these university projects was Sir Leslie Martin, whom Stirling had met during the days of the Independent Group.[3] Martin was a patrician modernist of the second generation who had achieved great behind-the-scenes influence by the late 1950s through his work for government bodies and his activity on advisory boards and competition juries. Martin looked benevolently upon a number of young architects, passing them commissions that had come his own way or recommending they be invited for closed competitions.[4] All three of the schemes discussed in this chapter had Martin's charity behind them, and all arrived in less than a year. Although his own architecture was more sober than theirs and more part of the modernist mainstream stemming from Gropius, it had taken on some of Aalto's interest in materials and regionalism. Martin would certainly have seen Stirling and Gowan's work in the architectural press and may even have understood their much-publicised Ham Common flats as the romantic equivalent to his own more measured brick idiom.

Initially, it might seem there was nothing particularly new in how Stirling and Gowan thought about universities. If their designs and buildings were visually startling, they sat easily within already defined university building types: the college quadrangle, the student dormitory, and the combined science department and laboratory. There is no evidence of the 'total institution', where students would be separated entirely from the world in unabashedly contemporary campuses, which was the ideal of the new universities of the 1960s and their architects.[5] If Stirling's Sheffield University competition design of 1953 indicated in any way how the partnership would approach its university work, then it was as a fully engaged part of an already existing complex, an attitude in which the overtly functional aspects of the design dynamically related to the immediate physical conditions of its surroundings. This engagement might be sympathetic, it might be contrary and even critical; it either treated the actually existing as complex and layered, not wanting to wish it away, or sought to bring the functions of the institution to bear meaningfully upon its situation.

~

Churchill College is the most enticing yet in many ways the most enigmatic of Stirling and Gowan's unbuilt schemes, suggesting a vista of new possibilities. The project, to design Cambridge University's first new post-war college, was directly a result of the perceived need to train more scientists. Inevitably Leslie Martin, who was already the college's architectural advisor, acted as one of the assessors, recommending competitors and establishing the terms of the brief. In January 1959 twenty-one practices were invited to enter a limited competition for this new college campus on a suburban

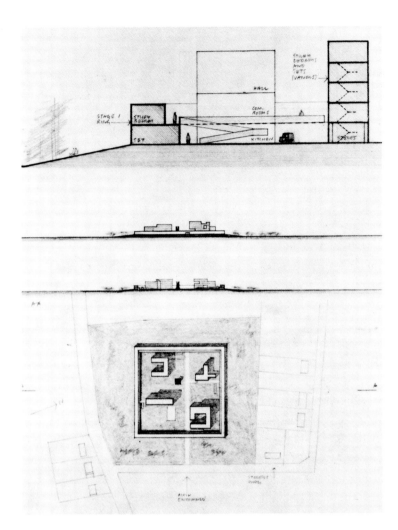

141 Stirling and Gowan, Churchill College, Cambridge, 1959, conceptual design for first stage of competition. Drawing by James Gowan.

field to the north of Cambridge.[6] It was to be a modern design for 600 students and dons, built in four separate stages, and retaining the courtyard as a valid collegiate form.[7] Until that date this was the most ambitious post-war university expansion scheme, and the invited architects represented a cross-section of the current state of modernism, from well-established practices like Ernö Goldfinger and Frederick Gibberd to still emerging ones like the Smithsons and Stirling and Gowan.

Little is known about the design the partnership entered for the first stage of the competition, though it must have been an outline scheme with plans at a small scale. All that survives is a conceptual drawing by James Gowan (fig. 141).[8] Marked with Gowan's annotations,[9] the drawing shows him thinking through many of the features that were to make the partnership's Churchill College design one of the most memorable architectural images of its period: from the high 'Roman' wall set on a raised turf bank and containing ramparts above student rooms that marks out a large square court for the college, to the free-standing college buildings whose complex silhouettes project above the wall to suggest a walled town from outside. Seemingly, both the site's windswept exposure and the suburban houses that overlooked it were being defended against here. The vastness of this site, and the problem of giving shape to a college in a suburban location, also suggested a strong geometric form.[10] But Gowan energised the square-walled compound with an asymmetrical entrance axis, placed buildings of very different shapes up against the edges of the implied quarters and, in the section at the top of the drawing, suggested ways of linking the outer cloister walls with these inner buildings at first-floor level. The drawing also shows Gowan thinking through some of the more playful aspects of the scheme. A small black monument, for instance, was placed near the centre of the compound as if to offset the idiosyncratic and informal effects of the other inner buildings. This oddly battlemented stump actually refers to Churchill's famous two-fingered salute. In effect, the traditional college quadrangle was subjected to an only partly veiled satire here, the deliberately over-emphatic outer wall licensing the play of shape and placement within it. In their report on this first scheme, Gowan and Stirling noted that the character of the undergraduate rooms and sets would be 'signified by the broken silhouette of roof terraces' containing a miscellany of double-height studios, and described how their scheme would use 'close juxtaposition of smooth and rough finishes' such as through 'a contrast of large areas of smooth white stone and smaller areas of grooved patterned concrete'.[11] Broken, picturesque outlines, combined with the contrasts of material that Gowan had exploited as early as the House Studies, were the means by which a more light-hearted, perhaps wilder, vision of undergraduate life than the 'boring old Cambridge sets' was to be projected.[12]

Another design for the first phase, by Fry Drew Drake and Lasdun, might also be considered here. Designed by Denys Lasdun, the concept at first seems diametrically opposite to Stirling and Gowan's. The college is planned as a cruciform configuration with four main buildings arranged pinwheel fashion around four linear courtyards (fig. 142). Dormitories with stepped sections are evident, but the variety of forms suggests an interlinked megastructure. Again, though, a strong statement of diagrammatic rigour responding to the suburban shapelessness of the site was then softened by devices like varying the roofline with student penthouses, or the contrast between the formal east front and the more casual fronts facing in other directions. But the fundamental difference with Stirling and Gowan's approach was that Lasdun's cross was only really visible in plan whereas their court was always evident: his was a

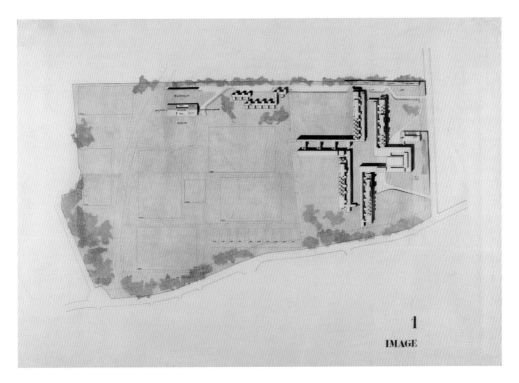

142   Fry Drew Drake and Lasdun, Churchill College, Cambridge, 1959, site plan of design for first stage of competition.

concept that might be reused for very different later commissions; theirs was a typology strongly tied to the Cambridge college tradition but both enlarged and rigidified by the new site.

In April 1959 the partners heard they had succeeded where Lasdun and even their old employers, Lyons Israel Ellis, had failed. They were listed as one of the four final competitors, together with Howell Killick and Partridge, Chamberlain Powell and Bon, and Sheppard Robson and Partners. A number of voluntary assistants were grafted in – mostly friends of the architects like Kit Evans, David Gray and Neave Brown – to help cope with the demanding roster of drawings.[13]

The development of the Churchill College design between first and second stage proposals shows that creative dynamic of cube versus picturesque grouping which, as Chapter Four argued, runs through many of the partnership's designs. Consequently, if the final project for the second stage of the competition can be described in Colin Rowe's terms as 'Churchillian' in the sense of 'intransigent and very memorable',[14] this was partly because Stirling, in particular, had pulled it back towards his

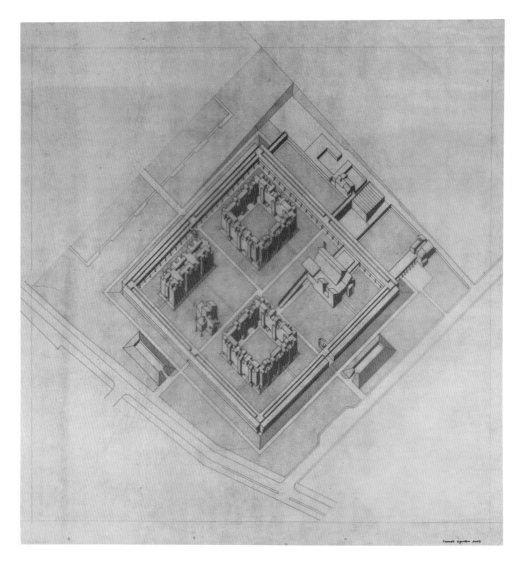

143   Stirling and Gowan, Churchill College, Cambridge, 1959, design for second stage of competition, axonometric.

fundamentals; the progress of this design therefore echoed the development from the house studies to the expandable house.

Stirling played a stronger role in the submission for the second stage of the competition in June 1959 (fig. 143). The finalists were now asked to provide more developed schemes worked out on twelve large-scale sheets. Stirling's revisions were partly motivated by a new injunction to conceive of the schemes specifically as memorials to Winston Churchill.[15] Monumentality would be assured by the four-square podium, but the new scheme underlined and formalised this in several ways, introducing 'further dominating elements'.[16] It emphasised axiality by placing the entrance centrally and used paths to divide up the internal space into four equal parts like a Roman camp, their quadrant nature now underlined, if anything, by joggling the paths at the central meeting point (fig. 144). Without the two-fingered folly of the first design, however, this meeting point was now a mere void. Beyond the courtyard, the main axis was taken through the playing grounds, passing double-rowed rectangles of trees on its way. The roof of the cloister became a virtual exercise circuit, half a mile in length yet reached by only two stairs. The free-standing buildings – library, dining and common rooms, and three dormitories – were placed within each of the quadrants, and the typology of the college quadrangle restored by reiterating it in the heart of the two square internal residential buildings, much as the same family of forms was evident in the inset corners of wall and residences. Stirling explained the articulation of these dormitories: 'These rooms and sets were treated as a series of related and interlocking blocks of space evolved as additions to a basic cell; and like building blocks they could be lapped, butted, and interlocked in various combinations.'[17] By contrast, the rooms in the outer wall were arranged horizontally and access was gained from a cloister. The internal buildings were now entirely isolated from the outer wall and given uniform step-backs at roof level, calming the previously more irregular skyline.

All the skittishness that characterised the first design was now condensed into the little library (fig. 145). Close kin to Gowan's house studies, the library played with a set of angular motifs (splayed piers, pentroofs and outlying stairs) and graphically contrasting materials (especially ribbed concrete and stone revetment) like a thumbnail of the architects' motifs. Some of these elements were part of the dining and common room building, the only inner building connected with the outer wall, whose roofscape also reiterated the dramatic structures of the Camberwell assembly

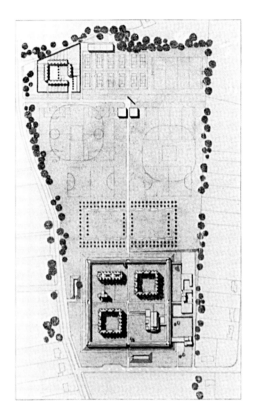

144   Stirling and Gowan, Churchill College, Cambridge, 1959, design for second stage of competition, site plan.

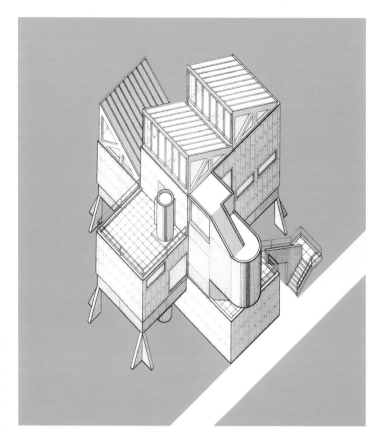

145   Stirling and
Gowan, Library for
Churchill College,
Cambridge, 1959,
design for second
stage of competition.

hall. Just outside the court wall, a master's lodge and senior tutor's house adopted the vernacular elements of Stirling's Woolton house. A compound of married quarters was positioned to the west beyond the main college buildings.[18] Less defensive than the rest of the college, these quarters were designed as a combination of Preston's terraced courtyard layout and Ham's stepped elevations. But the effect of positioning the staff buildings outside the great court was to emphasise student life as the hub of the college. Apart from the library, the whole design was given a heavier, more sombrely fortified and medieval air, more like the castles and walled towns that Stirling illustrated together with the scheme in the same year than the traditional college courtyard.[19] But the source that makes most obvious the idea that the second design was in some sense an architectural portrait of Churchill was his ancestral home, Blenheim Palace. Stirling illustrated the main front of this baroque house together with elevations and sections of the college design in an article published the same year (fig. 146).[20] Blenheim's front appears like a mirror of the college eleva-

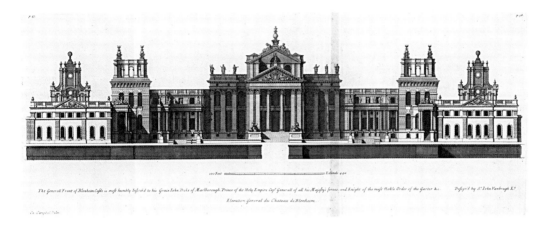

The Generall Front of Blenheim Castle is most humbly Inscrib'd to his Grace John Duke of Marlborough, Prince of the Holy Empire Cap: Generall of all his Majestys forces, and Knight of the most Noble Order of the Garter &c.   *Design'd by S.r John Vanbrugh K.r*

Elevation General du Chateau de Blenheim

146   Blenheim Palace, Woodstock. Oxfordshire. From Colen Campbell, *Vitruvius Britannicus*, 1715.

tions seen from beyond the outer wall: dauntlessly four-square and facing out at the world, with relentless horizontals lower down and a broken roofline above. Placed on an empty plain, this exterior-facing aspect of Blenheim is as significant as the type of the largely interior-oriented Cambridge college.

If there are familiar historicising aspects to the Churchill design, these also contain its most jarring effects. Its inescapable axiality ran counter to the prevailing dogma about college organisation,[21] and its quartered form was far more geometrically rational than the usually ad hoc and accretive layouts of such colleges. Furthermore, instead of integrating non-dormitory functions into the circuit of the quadrangle, they were isolated in the four quarters of its court. Then, finally, the college courtyard itself was made into a vast compound, far bigger than the closeted medieval court: three times that of Trinity Great Court, for instance.[22] Unlike the multitude of court-yards that characterised many other competition entries, here the courtyard and all it implied of the medievalism of donnish life received inflated, almost over-exagger-ated respect.[23] This was the 'historical solution' which the architects had looked for, and its response to the 'dilemma' of unchanging function ('if the function has not changed why should a new college building look different from an old one?')[24] was to overplay, to exaggerate, to generate heightened thrills from the conventional forms of college life. All this, it seems, was too much for the assessors, whose meeting in July 1959 was chaired by Churchill himself. They found the overall concept 'impres-sive' but criticised its accommodation as uncollegiate and its costing as dubious.[25] Instead, they settled for the tame brutalism and pretty layout of Sheppard Robson and Partners' design, a truer 'Blenheim of the welfare state'.[26]

~

Perhaps encouraged by the progress they had made in the Churchill College competition, Leslie Martin also recommended Stirling and Gowan for work at Selwyn College, Cambridge, late in June 1959. The college was not entirely committed to new buildings even from the beginning, but nevertheless the architects were asked to develop a design for a new dormitory of forty-eight apartments and a junior common room, and then a little later to present plans for expansion across the college grounds.[27] The college had decided that the site for the new dormitory should be a gap in its main quadrangle of late nineteenth-century buildings, but the partners argued instead that a better place was the garden beyond the quad, facing the college but set well back from the gap so as not to spoil the view into the garden.[28] They presented several other possibilities to the dons, probably intended to highlight the virtues of the scheme they most favoured.[29] Each scheme responded differently to the potential of this gap and the relation between the quad and its raised courtyard, a linking flight of steps, and the informal garden. In one design the junior common room was absorbed into a rectangular block placed squarely facing the quad. In another a longer block was turned to act as an extension of the north wing of the quad, leaving the gap clear. And in a third scheme the block was placed deeper into the garden, and the junior common room was separated as a free-standing building close to the existing north wing.

These schemes were evidently much less well developed than the architects' favoured design,[30] one that seems impishly daring, lighter yet somehow more inevitable (fig. 147). Here the third scheme's placement of buildings was adopted, but the basic idea of the dormitory dramatically changed. This was now imagined as a gently curving wall of glazed and irregularly faceted bedrooms lifted onto a raised bank. Unlike Churchill College's dormitories, the provision here fitted exactly with the Niblett Report's recent recommendations on student residences – small numbers of rooms on a staircase plan clustered around common rooms – though its community of students was much smaller than Niblett's ideal of between 120 and 150.[31] The glass would be opaque and perhaps in different colours, to enhance the privacy of the residents.[32] The building's rear had a very different kind of elevation, largely brick and windowless and punctuated by three sets of service towers containing staircases, bathrooms and utility rooms. The junior common room maintained its place as a pavilion beside the edge of the quad, and was notably simple in plan – a rectangular volume raised to a double-height square at one end, glazed on the ground floor, sheer brick above.

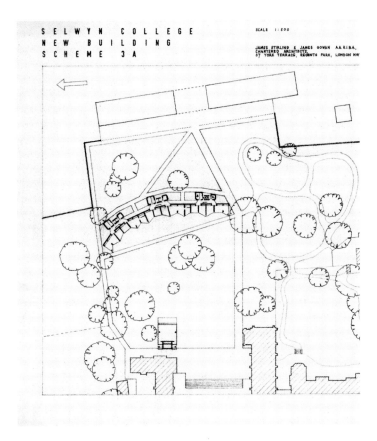

S E L W Y N   C O L L E G E
N E W   B U I L D I N G
S C H E M E   3 A

SCALE 1:500

JAMES STIRLING & JAMES GOWAN A.A.R.I.B.A.,
CHARTERED ARCHITECTS,
37 YORK TERRACE, REGENTS PARK, LONDON NW

147   Stirling and Gowan, Selwyn College, Cambridge, 1959, site plan
with new dormitory block and junior common room.

Although sharing Churchill College's concept of a wall-like student dormitory as well as its sensitivity to site, this Selwyn design was also quite radically different, a difference inspired by a reaction to the internal context or disposition of the college rather than Churchill's response to its suburban site. Even if internal to the college itself, the Selwyn dormitory was equally a piece of urban thinking, now conceived as an extension and enhancement of an existing architectural entity. The architects described how they attempted to 'retain, and even accentuate, the special character of the gap. . . . More stress is laid on the change in level here between the existing court and the gardens beyond, by making a broad flight of steps with a terrace.'[33] Emphasising the character of the garden required a relaxation in the formalities of the existing buildings.[34] This was expressed by the responsive qualities of the glass

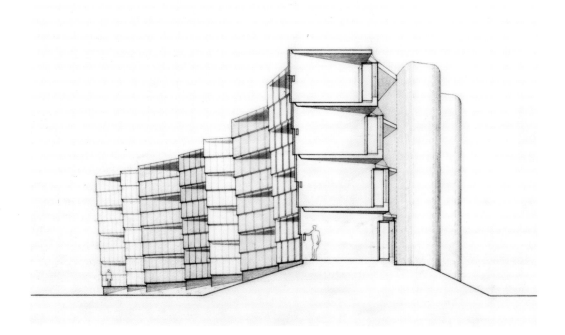

148   Stirling and Gowan, Selwyn College, Cambridge, 1959, section of dormitory.

membrane itself: college members, Stirling noted, 'would have seen reflected in the glass a shattered cubist image of the trees in the garden' (fig. 148).[35] The court would look onto the new building and the new rooms would look back into the court, the relationship mediated by the position of the junior common room. The curved wall of building would contain the view from the courtyard while also directing it towards areas planned for further development.

In this favoured Selwyn dormitory scheme, it was Gowan who developed the basic form as a combination of distinctly shaped entities, much as the house studies had been developed in the previous year. Two towers, differently sized in plan, were attached to a staircase block. The rooms were set in front and provided with a faceted elevation, and this schema was then repeated three times to make the block. Stirling, thinking perhaps more of the Camberwell assembly hall, raised the block on its grass bank and designed the section so that its windows were staggered outwards as it rose.[36] The beauty of these devices was in enabling the dormitory to respond to the raised quadrangle while screening the college from the university's new faculty of arts building (designed by Casson and Conder) then rising to the east of the site.[37]

Stirling also bent the whole façade so that it responded to the garden's irregular layout, embracing the view from the gap and reclining gently in its bosky environs. This is one of those moments where the dynamic between the two architects had come to a point of formal balance.

There are several possible sources for the rich confluence of ideas distilled so effectively in this Selwyn scheme. Louis Kahn had been developing his concept of the differentiation of buildings into served and servant spaces through the 1950s, a project in parallel with Stirling's own critique of the modernist free plan. Kahn's ideas were apparent in two buildings that Stirling knew from his teaching at Yale: the Yale University Art Gallery as well as the Richards Medical Research building, then being erected in Philadelphia (fig. 149).[38] In the latter the separation of laboratories from taller service towers has the same clarity of conception as the Selwyn design. Alvar Aalto's Baker House for MIT (1947–48), which Stirling had seen during his 1948 visit, provided typological precedent for a student dormitory adopting a snaking plan. There was also the

149   Louis Kahn, Richards Medical Research Building, Philadelphia, 1957–65.

Smithsons' terraced house scheme of 1955, which projected a curved arena of backward tilting terraced houses, the shape conceived as more of a sun scoop than a response to any specific site.[39] Selwyn's tilting, stepped and faceted façades have more than a hint of the courtyard of Oriel Chambers or warehouses in Liverpool, as well as several apartment building designs by Le Corbusier,[40] although here the irregular facets express the different sizes of the rooms within. Finally, there is the floor to ceiling glazing. Given Stirling's expressed disdain for curtain walls,[41] this is perhaps surprising, but Stirling had only attacked their indiscriminate enveloping of a variety of internal functions. The immediate source at Selwyn was probably the Maison de Verre (Chareau and Bijvoet, 1932) and its glazed walls, which Stirling had visited on a trip to Paris in the summer of 1959.[42] And yet the Selwyn design has a resolved simplicity about it that distinguishes it from these sources.

In spring 1960 the college dons, perhaps intrigued by Stirling and Gowan's understanding of the college site as a whole, also asked the architects to suggest schemes for further college development.[43] Only one of these was ever published by the archi-

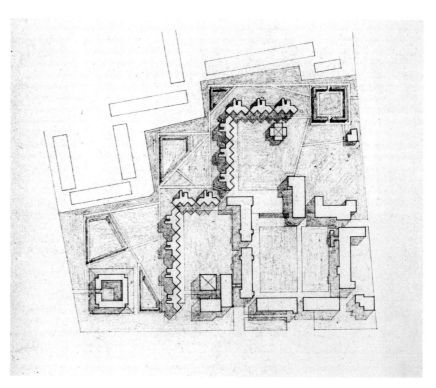

150 Stirling and
Gowan, Selwyn College
Master Plan, 1960.

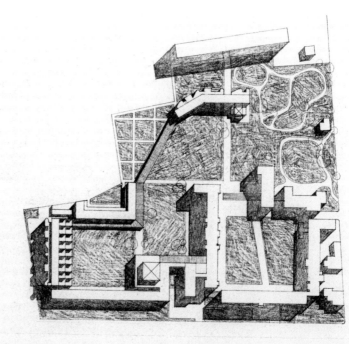

151 Stirling and Gowan,
Selwyn College Master
Plan, 1960.

tects,[44] but like the dormitory there were actually several alternative ideas sketched out, and it is likely they too were intended more to point the dons towards the architects' favoured scheme than to provide viable alternatives.[45] The schemes proposed a number of master plans, each one placing the greater part of the development to the north of the college but swinging round to connect with the proposed dormitory in the east, and each consisting of a group of loosely related buildings. One of the plans developed an S-shaped space twisting out of the existing quad yet stiffened by long rectangular blocks. Another proposed a rival quad to the north, also defined by long blocks. A third suggested an array of twelve small dormitories, each saw-toothed in plan and with 'servant' functions at the rear, lined up to define a new quad and to regularise the garden; these were augmented by an enigmatically fortified building, along Churchillian lines (fig. 150). The more serious schemes were those in which two new quads were suggested to the north (fig. 151). These were first defined by a variety of building shapes, which were then linked by colonnades to the dormitory building, attempting to get the best of the informal garden and more formally framed courtyard-like spaces.[46] As the architects wrote, '[the new building] should be the start of a terrace or wall directing the flow of space and people out of the existing court by way of the gap, through an irregular garden area and into successively more formal spaces and courts.'[47]

The only scheme published later by the architects appears, then, as something they dreamt up afterwards (fig. 152).[48] In this scheme they extended the arc of the proposed dormitory into a sinuous curve of buildings in the northern part of the college garden, defining the new extension less as quads than as flowing, framed extensions to the garden. The longest building was a double curved version of the dormitory building, but there was also a virtual replica of it filling a large gap between buildings on the northernmost part of the site. Apart from its consistency of treatment, the appeal of this scheme was that it left the old quad alone and retained the garden, pushing all the expansion to the edges of the college while lending those edges definition and continuity. The side effect of this line of growth, and one clearly intended,[49] was to reimagine the old gap not as an absence but instead as the focus for the whole college. A new flight of steps with terraces above and below would establish the auditorium-like character of this space, with the new junior common rooms now central to the site. A kind of subversion has taken place, emphasising openness and flow and shifting the spatial fulcrum of college life onto the students. Albeit with very different means, the same reorientation had also been attempted in the Churchill design.

Although none of these designs was developed very far, it is quite likely that the other schemes were never published simply because they were not favoured by the

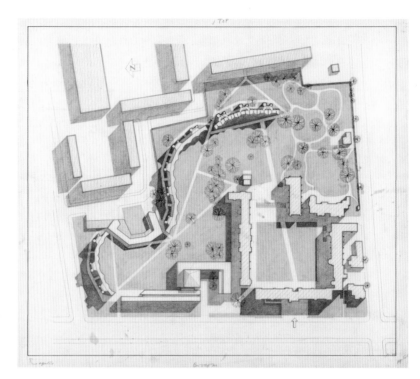

152 Stirling and
Gowan, Selwyn College
Master Plan, 1960,
published scheme.

architects; certainly, there was no particular preference expressed by the college. Any
warmth from the dons towards the architects' dormitory seems to have rapidly cooled
at the same time. They disliked the invasion of a glass-faced alien, let alone any other
incomer.[50] Any remaining interest froze over when Stirling 'pulled out his box of slides
and gave them a talk. . . . he showed them Wright's Johnson Wax building.'[51] This was
not how the dons envisaged their neo-Tudor surrounds. The only trace today of
Stirling and Gowan's efforts is in the old courtyard: once a sunken lawn, this was raised
at their suggestion to make it visible from their never-built dormitory.[52] More importantly, the Selwyn designs were the first promise of a new kind of glass architecture,
faceted and translucent yet responsive to its surroundings.

~

The partners were appointed as architects for a new engineering building at Leicester
University in July 1959, while designs for Selwyn were still being formulated but just
after the declaration of the Churchill result.[53] Again, Leslie Martin was their benefac-
tor: he acted as consultant architect at the university, he had devised its master plan,

and he was to attend many of the same building committees at which the partners presented their designs. The architects met Edward Parkes, the newly appointed head of engineering, early in August, receiving a brief from him a few weeks later. Parkes listed his requirements on a single sheet of paper: ground-level laboratories of 20,000 square feet, assorted high-level laboratories of 12,500 square feet, twenty-five offices and two lecture theatres, all to service a student population of 200. Each of these was accompanied by several desiderata, such as 'aspect to Victoria Park' for the staff offices, 'holes in floor' for the heat lab, or 'water tank at 100 feet head' for the hydraulics lab.[54] Also, at some time early on, the university requested that if concrete was used it should mostly be covered.[55]

On the basis of these rather bare notes, the architects began to rough out and adjust the volumes that would accommodate the brief, 'programming the hierarchies'.[56] They rapidly developed three alternative sketch designs that were presented in late August. Although they do not survive, each was a volumetric exercise exploring the relationship between the site and the brief.[57] One of these was probably the 'narrow block of single-banked offices at the front, sheds at the back'.[58] But the preferred design provided access all around it while satisfying the space requirements by building vertically.[59]

In November 1959 the architects presented sketches and a model that established the essential configuration of the design. A large rectangular workshop with electrical and aerodynamic laboratories was placed at the rear of the site, and in front a ninety-foot tower block was lifted above two lecture theatres and an entrance hall.[60] A photograph of a model that no longer survives is the earliest image of the project and may show the scheme at the time of this first presentation to the university (fig. 153). Evidently, although a distinction between offices and laboratories or workshops is in place, there is not such a sharp distinction as would soon emerge. Strongly articulated lecture theatres provide a base for a squat tower with a wedge of podium further down. The shed's modular grid is emphasised and there are a number of different box-like volumes placed on it, each presumably housing the specialised laboratories. There is no attempt yet to dynamically exploit the

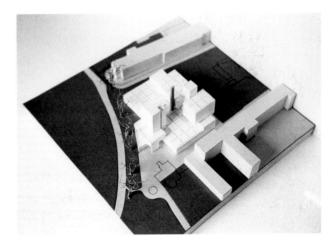

153   Stirling and Gowan, Leicester University Engineering Building, early model, 1959.

triangular site with matching diagonal forms, and the scheme is laid out so that it appears to continue the grid suggested by the existing buildings around it.

This November 1959 design opened a series of reiterations and negotiations, principally between the architects and Parkes though with the university's building committee watching over all. Parkes's contribution to the authorship of the building from the beginning was crucial. He applauded the use of the cramped site and admired the exterior, but he had critical comments about the location of certain labs and stores and, as will be discussed later, about the symbolism of the chimneys.[61] By mid-December revised drawings and a new model were completed for a second scheme, responding to Parkes's comments.[62] But Parkes found that this second scheme reduced the amenity he enjoyed in the first scheme: the views over the park from the offices of the first scheme's tower were lost in favour of south and west windows.[63] He also disliked using the two awkward triangles of land on the edges of the site for buildings; one area at least should be left as grass 'and not give the (truer) impression that we are bursting at the seams'.[64] Parkes's interventions were, then, not just towards utilitarian ends; he had a strong sense of the appropriate image he wanted his building to present to the world. Stirling met with Parkes at Stanford University in late December 1959 and discussed further revisions with him: 'we seem to be agreed', Parkes reported, 'that although the new scheme solves the workshop and certain other problems, it is architecturally inferior to the original.'[65] In particular, he was keen that the tower be returned to its position in the first scheme, and as this was written direct to the building committee in forceful terms, it seems likely that he was voicing a view he shared with the architects.[66] In March 1960 a third scheme was presented that dealt with all of Parkes's suggestions except for his problems with the columns that held up the projecting labs on the rear or west side of the building and blocked easy vehicular access.[67] Subject to the provision of an 'alternative cantilever scheme', the clients approved the design.[68]

Within five months of their appointment, Stirling and Gowan had worked out all the major features of the building. The basic organisation was of a low-lying shed, fronted on one side by a cluster of towers. The main towers were linked and served by three shafts containing lifts and staircase. Circulation at ground level was divided in two: one for human use between towers and workshop, the other for the transportation of machines at the rear of the workshop. The format had several relevant precedents: the Victorian railway hotel that fronted those iron and glass sheds admired by the partners; factory complexes wherein a building housing reception and offices provided the street façade in front of a factory shed, a type for which the architects had some credibility from Gowan's experience designing factory prototypes at Stevenage;[69] and more specifically Frank Lloyd Wright's Johnson Wax building at Racine, Wisconsin, whose brick podiums, tiled interior and glazed and banded tower would offer tantalising echoes to many later admirers of the Leicester building. A more immediate if then obscure source was a fourth-year Architectural Association student project by Edward Reynolds, who was known to both Gowan and Stirling (fig. 154). This 1957–58 design, for a warehouse in Bristol, had a shed covered with a glazed steel network and a shuffled stack of expressionist towers on one side.[70]

From the clients' view the further revisions that cropped up were relatively minor. When the University Grants Committee and the City Council added their approval by May, for instance, several small issues were raised concerning the position of stairs, the size of the periodicals room, and the entrance to and arrangements within the small lecture theatre.[71] The first set of working drawings were finished in September 1960, clearance of existing buildings started that December, and building work began in February of the following year.[72] In the meantime, Stirling and Gowan's office had grown to cater for the extra work of this, their largest project. In August 1960 Michael Wilford was employed full time to develop the working drawings and help organise a building team with others who had already worked for the architects like David Walsby, Quinlan Terry and Malcolm Higgs, with Kit Evans and Julian Harrap doing occasional work.[73]

There was never a hard-and-fast division between what the two partners worked on. The conglomerate nature of the design allowed an occasional division of labour, as when in the spring of 1960 Stirling was detailing the tower complex and Gowan the workshop. But this was only brief, and both partners worked flexibly across the whole scheme.[74] Looking at the evolution of these designs shows how Stirling and Gowan accepted the conglomerate nature of Parkes's original brief from the beginning and then elaborated on it, responding to the new requirements that Parkes produced in a series of designs that developed greater differentiation and honing of parts. Piecing this together is, however, a tentative matter as very few contemporary conceptual drawings survive and fewer still are dated. The earliest drawing, dated 25 February 1960,[75] shows that the workshops had achieved their broad disposition with

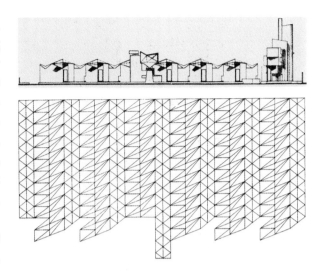

154   Edward Reynolds, Warehouse in Bristol, 1957–58, Architectural Association fourth-year student project.

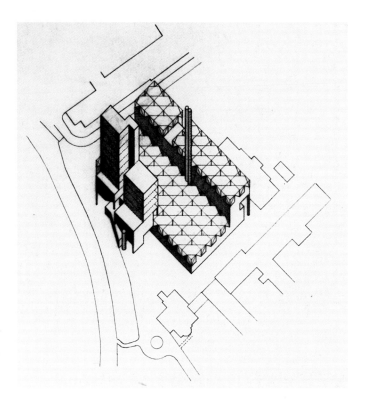

155   Stirling and Gowan,
Leicester University
Engineering Building,
axonometric dated
25 February 1960.

diagonal north lighting and higher specialised workshops at the back (fig. 155). However, the two towers, each perched on a different lecture theatre, stand unrelated and reversed from their eventual arrangement, with an odd L-shaped plane placed against the lower tower. A revealing detail is the as yet vestigial podium that is canted and dodges under and between the two towers, closely reminiscent of similar volumes in the House Studies. The idea of the building as a collection of separately characterised volumes, reflecting the different activities housed within them, is now clearly established.

A sheet of drawings, probably from March 1960, shows the architects devising alternative approaches to affixing stair and lift shafts to the two towers, and working through the structural role of the large lecture theatre using careful axonometric drawings as well as sketchier perspectives to test the effects (fig. 156).[76] The May 1960 scheme, approved by all the key parties, is preserved in an axonometric drawing (fig. 157).[77] Here many details of the tower complex have been resolved except for the glazing between the two towers. The lecture theatres are in place and their structural relationships worked out. The podium still lacks the eloquence it would later achieve,

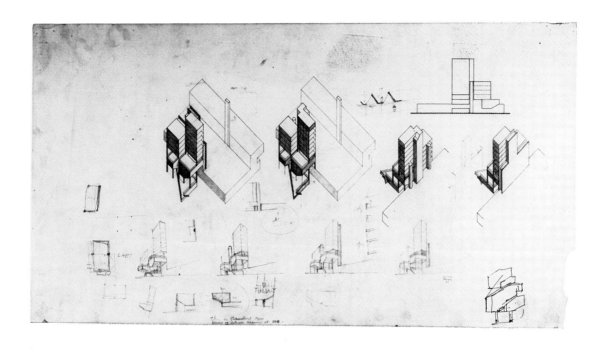

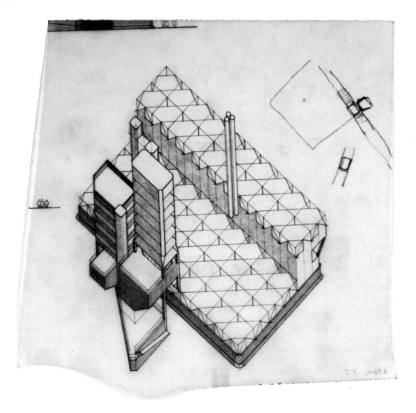

ABOVE 156 Stirling and Gowan, Leicester University Engineering Building, sheet of various drawings probably March 1960.

LEFT 157 Stirling and Gowan, Leicester University Engineering Building, axonometric and sketch dated May 1960.

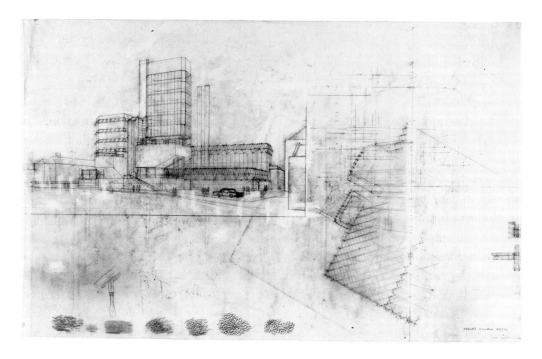

158   Stirling and Gowan, Leicester University Engineering Building, perspective and plan, probably spring 1961.

and the workshop roof is north facing and has a kind of space frame with top chords, but the rear of the workshop already has its propped struts. The axonometric shows how the tower complex's details have been worked out; some corners are angled and others shorn off so that, with the thrust of the podium, a lively diagonal dialogue chatters across the building. A ramp has now appeared, transferred as it were from the house studies and adding zing to the podium to which it is affixed, momentarily, on its inner side.

A drawing from nearly a year later shows almost all these important details resolved: the research laboratory tower with its banded windows now with their prismatic, triangular profile (angled so as to exclude drafts), the administration tower with its smaller patent glass panels, and the workshop roof newly supplied with its boxed ends that express the diagonal ridges as they meet the edges of the roof (fig. 158).[78] While the basic disposition was settled by early 1960, the refinements and subtle accommodations were evolved more gradually. Some – like the abandonment of the top chords on the workshop roof for trusses and the idea of the diamond-shaped boxes – were worked out by midsummer 1960, but others (like the single flue) were not resolved until very late in the process.[79] It had moved from a design of sensible arrangements to one of both unexpected delicacies and surprising logic. Here and elsewhere the flexibility of this process is manifested in the fact that all of the designs were done in pencil, and ink was only resorted to in the presentation drawings.[80]

The five various larger functions of the project were given their most appropriate forms and diversified structural supports, and then, as it were, fitted together like the 'pile-up' that Gowan had admired as a student or the bricolage approach that had fascinated Stirling at Ronchamp. Each part retained its volumetric integrity, each was logically positioned (giving the offices a view and keeping them away from the noisy workshops, for example), and each came into a different relation with the central circulatory core to which it could appear in parallel or plugged in, or from which it was suspended. The approach is consistent with similar thinking in the expandable house and in the second version of the Kissa house, and in all cases it seems to derive from an ultimately De Stijl or neoplasticist dynamic of abstract, weightless volumes and spiralling or pinwheel movements around a vertical hub.[81] At the same time, Leicester's irregular volumes and ad hoc juxtapositions – its chamfering of corners, angling of ramps and formalising of entrance – relate to function in ways quite alien to De Stijl's platonic abstractions. This is connected to Stirling and Gowan's fondness for axonometric drawings, seen in several Leicester designs as well as in previous projects.

As well as a means of synthesising different views (plans and elevations) while retaining true dimensions, the axonometric was closely identified with modernism.[82] Used by De Stijl, Bauhaus and constructivist architects, the axonometric seemed the ideal way of stilling and capturing the new space-time, a spatial awareness intrinsic to modern experience. Axonometric drawings played an increasingly important role as a mode of drawing within the partnership.[83] But unlike most previous examples where the axonometric was used as a presentation drawing, at Leicester axonometric drawings were used very early in the design process. Obviously, in part this was to communicate with the clients but also, one suspects, to envisage how to contain and somehow discipline the various elements, very different from the estranging or utopian optic that is associated with 1920s axonometric drawings. Unlike perspectives, axonometrics also isolate the building, denying its picturesque potential, presenting it as autonomous, and even – with up-view axonometrics – as an impossible floating object. With their increasing use by Stirling in the 1960s and 1970s to publicise his buildings, it was easy to imagine the actual buildings as more independent of their contexts than they actually were, a point which will be returned to later.

There may be some answer in the approach at Leicester to what Robert Maxwell called 'the dilemma of functionalism in an affluent society'.[84] Stirling and Gowan

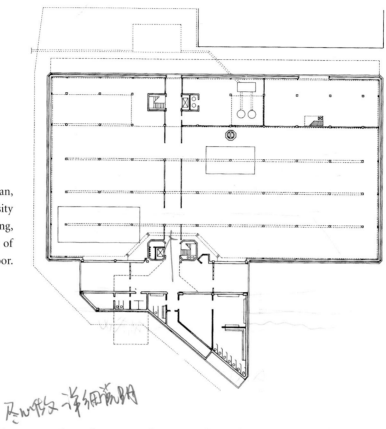

159   Stirling and Gowan,
Leicester University
Engineering Building,
1959–64, plan of
ground floor.

were elaborating their forms or choosing them from a range of sources and adapting them to fit the specifics of the job. There was never to be a glass curtain wall covering all; even the two towers are quite distinct, differentiated as much by the squatness of one and the elegance of the other as by the difference in glazing: one with angled windows and underside louvres to create cross ventilation, the other with a grid of more Georgian proportions (see fig. 140). And in between these towers was one of those pregnant negative spaces Stirling had come to admire in the vertical slots that often divided Moretti's façade compositions.

Having established this conglomerate composition, these forms remained legible and distinct as other functions and lesser services were fitted in. So, for instance, the main entrances and the foyer between them would appear merely inadvertent spaces in the gap or 'natural shaft' leftover by the meeting of the conjoined elements around them (fig. 159).[85] Somehow, as if by ad hoc means – like the concrete pillars that support the office tower but also frame the entrance – the dignity of entrance and reception is still clearly established. This is done matter-of-factly, like the railway bunkers that Gowan admired in north London, giant structures on legs that allow

160   Le Corbusier, Maison
locative à Algers, 1933.

trains to pass between their slender supports.[86] But the almost prehensile qualities
of these pillars as they meet the tower, as well as the fine chamfering of the tower's
haunches, hint at that Victorianism in Stirling and Gowan's work discussed previously in relation to the Preston housing. It is known that Stirling admired the work
of William Butterfield and even that of Frank Furness in Philadelphia,[87] each a distinctive purveyor of faceted and juxtaposed planes of brickwork. Yet Leicester never
suggests a literal historical revivalism. And so a balancing, if previously unconsidered,
source for these chamfered and prehensile effects is the model for a tower in Algiers
illustrated in Le Corbusier's *Oeuvre complète 1929–1934* (fig. 160).[88] Cantilevered out
from its hill, one corner of the tower is sheared off while its weight rests on three
slim pillars. It seems like an exemplification of Stirling's 1950 admonishment of
towers that 'plunge into the ground like a spear',[89] and like many similar instances – particularly in Le Corbusier's work – a criticised effect stayed in the mind, and its

elegant delicacy and denial of weight was then, contrarily, adopted.[90] But, as well, the chamfering of Leicester's highest tower is part of a repetition of diagonals that picks up on both the triangular site itself as well as the dominant diagonal patterning across the building – the ridges of the workshop roof. These diagonals, together with the redness of the bricks and tiles, are the architectural glue that links the various parts of the complex.

The workshop's dazzling prismatic roof was partly fortuitous. It came out of the need to use the cramped site to the full while also providing the workshop with north-facing lights so that a more constant, moderate light would illuminate the work

161   Stirling and Gowan, Leicester University Engineering Building, 1959–64, workshop interior.

spaces and their machinery. This requirement must have emerged as the design developed,[91] by which time the space requirements demanded that almost all the site be covered, and so it was impossible 'to twist the building to the conventional north–south relationship that you got in a factory roof'.[92] The architects therefore turned their ridge lights at a forty-five -degree diagonal to the workshop space below, a move that seemed arbitrary to some critics but one that resulted in crisply pleated, crystalline effects, especially where the meeting of angled ridges with the vertical wall was expressed by diamond-fronted boxes (fig. 162).[93] The workshop was designed on the basis of a ten-foot module governing both plan and section. Its interior was geared towards flexibility, with temporary walls, raised workshops at the rear of the site to allow machines to be lifted in, and the floor paved with movable slabs enabling machines to be fitted or replaced easily (fig. 161). As Parkes put it, 'I hadn't got the slightest idea of what engineering would look like in ten years' time.'[94])

A telling example of the design's evolution occurs with the lecture theatres, an example that is especially important in the light of later claims about the building (fig. 163). In Parkes's brief they were simply a small and a large lecture theatre with raked floors. In the final designs they take clearly differentiated and dynamic forms: each is cantilevered out as a separate volume beneath a tower but at ninety degrees to each other, so that while one suggests a thrust into the campus, the other bolsters the building line parallel to the park. Many writers have seen a constructivist precedent for these lecture theatres in Konstantin Melnikov's Rusakov Workers' Club in Moscow (1928) (fig. 164). However, the question of how Stirling and Gowan might have seen Melnikov's design is not easily resolved.[95] Furthermore, the theatres' arrangement at Leicester is signifi-

162   Stirling and Gowan, Leicester University Engineering Building, 1959–64, construction
photograph, *c.*1962.

163   Stirling and Gowan, Leicester University Engineering Building, 1959–64.

164   Konstantin Melnikov, Rusakov Workers'
Club, Moscow, 1928. From Vittorio de Feo,
URSS architettura 1917–1936, 1963.

cantly different in form and effect from Melnikov's. The latter's theatres fan out over the entrance to the building, forming an honorific canopy to the 'new man' of Soviet dreams, gesturally relating the club to the wider city as – in Melnikov's words – a 'volley aimed at the future'.[96] Leicester's theatres have none of this rhetoric. While one of them certainly acts as a canopy (and the other, smaller lecture theatre has canopy-like effects), this function is expressed not as a political gesture towards the outside world but rather as part of the building's formal extrapolation, an ulterior logic of concatenation and interpenetration, reversing the terms of lightness and heaviness and contrasting canopied entrance (under the large theatre) and canopied blank wall (under the small theatre). Also, the prominence of the lecture theatres in the overall appearance of the building seems to derive from Stirling's earlier work as well as Gowan's house studies. Stirling had made a point in both his thesis community centre design (see fig. 17) and his Poole College design (see figs 39–40) of allowing the distinctive wedge shapes of lecture theatres to be glimpsed through glazed walls, and in his organic chemistry laboratory design (1949) the lecture hall became a free-standing sculpture outside the main building (see fig. 7). In the Sheffield University design this was taken further with the repeated shapes of grouped lecture theatres forming a frieze-like pattern in the very middle of the elevation (see fig. 42). So already the supposedly functional or 'as found' lecture theatre shape was given a starring role.

In the early model and drawings for Leicester the theatres are clearly developed from the Sheffield configuration. In the drawing dated 25 February 1960, for example (see fig. 155),[97] the theatres project as separate volumes, but they are parallel and back onto each other in the Sheffield manner. The theatres' further development was led by the idea of them acting as modest porticoes for the main entrances as much as dynamic volumes energising the building's relation to the park by – in the manner of the house studies – setting up a pinwheel movement that evokes the first model's rectilinear disposition. In the final result, therefore, the 'activity of emptiness'[98] of Sheffield's repeated blank walls is moved away from, and instead the theatres are given fully three-dimensional and differentiated roles, cubist rather than constructiv complex spatial and representational effects, even Morettian in their sense of enigmatic moulded solids. Yet although they are now turned at ninety degrees to each other, this contrast was already intimated in the way the two theatres projected at different distances from the towers above them in the earlier designs. There is no evidence to show that Melnikov was in the architects' thoughts as they designed Leicester; instead, all the evidence suggests the connection was made after the building's completion. If Melnikov was an influence, it was at best a confirmation of a tendency already in the partners' work rather than a distinct revelation. The arrangement of the theatres was 'not an image imposed on the building but a happening,'[99] arrived at through the design evolution.

Honing the structural relationship of these lecture theatres to the rest of the building depended on collaboration with a second major figure, Frank Newby, the consultant engineer working for F. J. Samuely and Partners.[100] Newby was unusually sympathetic to the architects and pragmatic with his advice. He had already met Stirling through his own involvement in Independent Group circles; indeed, his wife had helped Stirling with his *Architectural Review* articles.[101] It was Newby's calculations that enabled the daring cantilever of the main lecture theatre, which, because it was stabilised by the tower above it, could do away with supports on the park side. Newby devised a means to transfer the paired corner columns of the office tower, via shaved-off joints, to four slender columns above the lecture theatre, each of which was then joined by a star beam under the tower. He also helped Gowan to come up with the final exhilarating form of the workshop roof.[102] But although he is often given credit for replacing vertical columns with diagonal struts at the rear of the workshop, this change, for functional and aesthetic reasons, was made more at the instigation of Edward Parkes with Newby working out its engineering solution (fig. 165).[103]

What the architects had arrived at was, in Gowan's words, the 'style for the job', an exterior determined by all the different needs of the building's functional programme, much as had long been called for by modernist theorists. The difference was that this was a style calculated for a particular set of tasks rather than assuming functionalism to be the prerogative of one particular set of forms; in other words, this was closer to the 'functional style' than functionalism as a style. Rather than, say, the ubiquitous office block then nearing completion for Oxford University's engi-

165   Stirling and Gowan, Leicester University Engineering Building, 1959–64, rear of workshop.

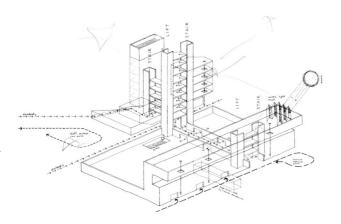

166   Stirling and Gowan, Leicester University Engineering Building, 1959–64, diagram of circulation routes etc.

neering building,[104] Leicester – from the moment that the analogy with offices and factory was made – was almost excessively expressive of its clients' needs, both housing and representing them in the different forms of the building. In this it was an answer to what had worried Stirling in modernism's machine aesthetic; its machine likeness was not the same as the functional logic of real machine elements.[105] Almost simultaneously Banham had also criticised the superficial imitation of the machine in modernism: its use was 'too orderly', too much of an aesthetic vision.[106] Banham greeted Leicester thus: 'the character emerges with stunning force from the bones of the structure and the functions it shelters.'[107] Appropriating Gowan's phrase 'style for the job', Banham contrasted Leicester with Preston, where he claimed the character arose subjectively 'on the basis of arbitrary sociological decisions'.

At some points Leicester's design process even seems satirical in the excessive way that some functions were determined. A diagram routinised all the circulation routes and human and machine separations, showing the movements of machines into and out of the building as a conveyor belt of functions (fig. 166).[108] Another example – surely unnecessary – was a 'density graph' plotting quantities of human movement upwards through the building, resulting in a 'tapering pyramid' justifying the diminution of landing spaces as the building rose.[109] Just as Stirling often empha-sised his deferral to the specialist knowledge of his clients,[110] so in these diagrams it is as if some alibi was being found in techno-scientific authority. (And inevitably there is bathos in the contrast, within the archives, with later diagrams showing water penetration through louvres or the adhesive failure of tiles.)[111]

One aspect of this 'style for the job' was the glazing of the office tower (see fig. 140). The changes here included, in spring 1961, substituting patent glazing for the originally intended plate glass.[112] Patent glazing was normally used for industrial purposes. It is cheap glass with light aluminium bars cut to fit on site, and with simple details of bolts and flashing. Gowan had argued for the change to patent glazing both because of costs and because he wanted this industrial look to be applied more consistently across the whole building, rather than leaving the office tower out because of some sense of typological decorum.[113] Taken 'as found' and wrapped over many volumes 'like polythene',[114] the tower's glazing certainly played down the differences between it and the workshop; in other words, although functional difference is expressed volumetrically, patent glazing has a symbolic role in denying hierarchical difference. Work with machines, experimental work, desk work and teaching all had their distinct places, but there was no priority among them, so the manner of glazing implied.

Leicester's use of brick continues aspects of both Preston and Ham. Brick always seems to carry weight, yet at Leicester its coursed gravity, in common with the tiles that cover much of the concrete, often veils or screens the actual elements that carry the building's mass. The tiles are used as cladding and applied regardless of surface to walls, to the underside of the lecture theatres and to floors, with details like guttering and drains developed from standard catalogue types. Bricks, tiles and patent glass are, then, treated in the same way, as cheap off-the-peg products carefully adapted to fit Leicester's particular needs. *agreed with text?*

Commentators have rightly focused on the relation between surface and volume as one of Leicester's most significant formal attributes. Peter Eisenman's important article, 'Real and English: The Destruction of the Box I', published in 1974,[115] recognised the eclectic assemblage of sources and the way this started from 'an essentially multi-volumetric composition', arguing that the building 'takes the compositional attitude of Constructivism, rather than its vocabulary and brings it into some sort of dialectic with the concept of the vertical plane in Le Corbusier'. Eisenman proposed that the polemical intention behind this was based on 'distorting the form of the iconic structure', not to critique the cube through some dematerialisation of it – which had long been a standard modernist routine – but to erode the very *conception* of shape in favour of some deep syntactic structure.[116] In his article also published in 1974, Manfredo Tafuri saw this as characteristic of Stirling's approach, working 'salvage operations' on fragments, creating a 'montage of architectural materials . . . extenuation of forms . . . controlled bricolage', leading to a 'renunciation of clear narrative' in favour of 'a succession of "events"'. This was essentially a linguistic process, according to Tafuri, 'reducing the architectural object to a syntax in transformation', deforming the architectural language but never completely shattering it.[117]

But this approach, as discussed earlier in this book, was brought into the partnership by Gowan and was already characteristic of the partnership's work. As a reminder, in a sketch for one of the house studies of 1957 (fig. 167) are seen not only the distinc-

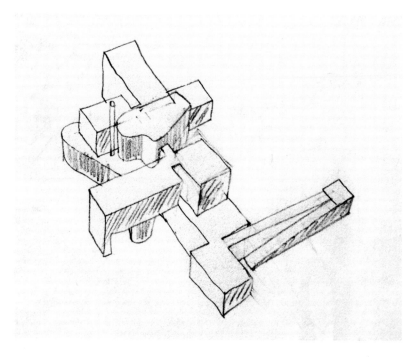

167   James Gowan, House Studies sketch, 1957.

tive extruded ramps of the partnership's Preston housing and the jaunty volumes and
outer ramp of the little library designed for the second stage of the Churchill College
competition, but also the piling up of heterogeneous components that were to make
Leicester famous: a podium that serves both as platform to and as visual link between
a range of disparate solids; a ramp that angles out from the main body; an entrance
framed by the supports of an upper unit; and the pinwheel effect of forms of similar
shape radiating out from a solid body.[118] This repurposing of objects was at Leicester
given visual unity by an approach similar to the alchemical operation Paolozzi had
worked in his recent sculpture, where disparate objects – machine parts, toys,
debris – were imprinted in wax and then cast in a unifying bronze that retained their
original shapes.[119] A practice related in its effects, if not its processes, was also emerging in the work of another sculptor, Anthony Caro, whose assembled girders, metal
sheets and piping were unified with coats of brightly coloured paint.

   These architectural and sculptural practices exemplify a working through of the
materials of industrialisation, treating them as detached from their origins and purposes. Industry is regarded not as a model for modernism as it had been earlier in
the century, but rather – much as Ulrich Beck has described 'reflexive modernisa-

tion' – as something to be dis-embedded and then re-embedded,[120] taking objects out of their exhausted normal contexts and resetting them so that new purposes and meanings might emerge.

∼

One of the few comments made by Edward Parkes on the symbolic dimension of the architects' work came in response to the first designs in November 1959. Although pleased with the exterior, he was bothered by what he called 'an aesthetic and political' issue:

> I do not like the two free chimneys. They seem to me out of harmony with the rest of the design. Perhaps to you they symbolise engineering, but free-standing chimneys are not a common feature of modern engineering works, and I particularly wish to avoid giving the rest of the university the idea that the "dark satanic mills" have come amongst them.[121]

Whether or not the architects intended the association detected by Parkes, and it seems likely they mentioned it in discussion with him, the point relates to the concern they shared with Parkes about the marginal position of engineering, physically and symbolically, in relation to the rest of the university. The line to adopt was a delicate one, and the chimneys issue reveals this. Where for Parkes the image simply had to be indubitably modern, for the architects it also had to be markedly different from the particular forms of the modern already adopted at Leicester University. As it turned out, they were persuaded by Parkes and only had one chimney, capping this with exposed draught tubes to leave no doubt over its contemporaneity.

The chimneys signal some larger issues. One was how Stirling and Gowan might actually have designed a building with industrial purposes. In fact, there is only one example of this from the practice's work, an unbuilt design for cladding a steel mill in Margam, South Wales, dating from 1958–59 (fig. 168).[122] The project here was to design corrugated steel panels as cladding for the existing structure. The surviving drawings and photographs of a model show an immensely long elevation articulated by a grid of panels, each with differently angled corrugations. The panels are occasionally angled out to provide light or are interrupted by grills. Entrances are simple, revealing stoutly rounded forms and slender pillars. The design is highly formal and abstract, its graphic articulations reminiscent of the house studies but divorced from any volumetric discipline. What we can gather from this design is that here, in the only commission to come their way that actually had industry as its subject,[123] the architects made no attempt at a bald statement of industrial production. It is unclear

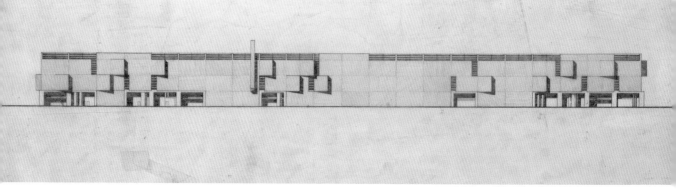

168   Stirling and Gowan, Steel Mills for Margam, South Wales, 1958–59, elevation.

if the panels were 'as found' objects, but there was certainly no representation of either industry's unveiled powers or its conventional associations.[124] Industrial romanticism was confined within the partnership to evoking industrial structures in non-industrial buildings.

Another issue is the image of engineering beyond Leicester. A crisis was perceived at this time in the relation between the arts and sciences in Britain, a relation or non-relation that seemed to bear upon Britain's declining industrial and economic fortune. C. P. Snow, the novelist and scientist (who was actually brought up in Leicester), argued this most famously in his 'Two Cultures' thesis.[125] Snow identified a chasm of mutual incomprehension between the arts and sciences and an anti-scientific attitude in the dominant traditional or literary culture. Already primed by the Independent Group's fascination with interactions between technology and culture, Stirling was certainly aware of the debate provoked by Snow's thesis, and he referred to Snow several times in lectures.[126] For others, the problem identified by Snow was joined with concerns about the post-war supply of graduates for industry, especially engineers.[127] These concerns were not allayed by the government's plans for university expansion, particularly its undervaluing of technical education.[128] Donald Cardwell, for instance, argued in 1957 that if there was a drive to expand science, then insufficient attention was paid to engineering.[129] Engineering was, therefore, a particular focus of concern about British decline. The worry was that it had neither the prestige nor the funding to play its desired role.

This ambivalence about engineering, and the belated investment in it,[130] was physically exemplified in the results of Leicester's own efforts in the late 1950s to upgrade itself from a university college to full university status (finally achieved in 1957).

Crucial to this was campus architecture. Leslie Martin was appointed in 1956 to advise on Leicester's expansion, and his master plan set out the very image of a rationally planned campus centred on an elevated and soberly disposed precinct, set on a ridge but low in profile and linking old and new parts of the campus.[131] Indiscernible at ground level, or indeed at any level except in the plan itself, Martin laid out his design to trace a slow, circumferential movement around the pivot of the science lecture theatre (figs 169–70). Around this terrace, low-lying, flat-roofed and yellow brick buildings, designed either by Martin himself or by other dutifully drilled architects, mirrored the idea of an abstractly disposed set of academic departments: physics, chemistry, geology, biological sciences and so on.

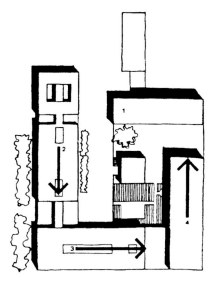

169   Leslie Martin, Master Plan for Leicester University, c.1956.

But engineering found no place in Martin's scheme, even though the possibility of a building for it had been discussed as early as March 1957.[132] It was not considered a priority, and a site was only belatedly found for it on the periphery of the campus. This was not even a site within the university grounds; it was occupied at that time by a Victorian establishment, the Lancaster Boys School. Described by Gowan as 'uninspiring' and by Stirling as 'bloody awful',[133] the peripheral and leftover nature of this site figured strongly in their minds (even as they played down its attractive park-side setting). Stirling, for example, talked about the advantage of 'not having to fit in with the general appearance of the campus' because of the site.[134] Revealingly, the university did not even consider the approaches to the building until 1962.[135] And, although Martin was instrumental in the appointment of Stirling and Gowan, everything that his master plan represented was to be upended, even implicitly subverted by their building: in Rowe's words, it was a 'breach of institutional decorum'.[136] This certainly explains Martin's later ambivalence about the engineering building: its *parti* was too assertive, its massing too monumental.[137]

170   Leicester University, view of main campus laid out according to Leslie Martin's Master Plan.

15   engineering
building
not whole
uni

Where Martin's plan attempted to capture the corporate life of a university in the form of a secularised, modernist monastery, the engineering building was set apart from this, pointing to the industrial city as its more relevant framework. Where Martin's plan was axial and symmetrical and earthbound, a thing of terraces and courts around rectangular masses, the engineering building was angular, tall and gravity defying, a conglomeration of individually shaped volumes making little concession to forging an architectural ensemble around it.[138] This is to suggest not that the partners' approach was narrowly focused on the immediate context, but rather that Leicester's recent architectural history was an integral part of their many calculations. Spectacular and alluring in itself, the engineering building remains a separate thing; its gestures towards the park (the prow of the podium) or lines of approach from the rest of the campus (the entrance framed by concrete pillars) tend to dramatise its own isolation.[139]

~

Returning to those two chimneys mentioned earlier, what Parkes saw in them was an image of engineering he felt was already held by the university as well as more widely in the general culture. While Stirling and Gowan probably had less of a stake in the chimneys' symbolic properties, they were certainly of a piece with their desire to shape a building which embodied a radically different view of engineering from that implied by its absence from the Martin master plan, one that would take up the banner of marginality in order to define a positive alternative, even an architectural critique of the kind of academia being brought about nearby. Martin's plan envisaged a series of nested disciplines, subservient to the larger order of the university. Engineering, however, would be dis-embedded from that idea and re-embedded as a discipline dedicated to finding or inventing new possibilities.[140] In other words, engineering would be a real community of scholars, something like the 'organised community' that Snow saw in the discipline,[141] brandishing the power to transform the understanding and use of base matter. It would be housed in a bespoke building unconstrained by Martin's gentlemanly conception of a university's architectural form and instead defined by a functionalism pushed to its extreme expressive limits, with different forms given to distinct functions necessarily breaking out of any merely architectural box. The engineering building could be said, then, to instantiate a new idea of modernity, the product not of simple or 'classical modernisation' – equated with Martin's plan – but of the 'reflexive modernisation' of a newly emerging post-industrial society.[142]

Stirling at just this time defended the use of 'certain extreme gestures . . . to achieve visual clarity', and called this 'a hierarchy of architectonic expression . . . clarifying the volumetric composition (organizational pattern), the social significance of spaces (accommodation), and perhaps to a lesser extent an explanation of the structural support'.[143] The geometric complexities of the glass skin between the two towers was a lesson in itself (fig. 171), solving a complex problem not abstractly, nor by reference to precedents (although it is reminiscent of the window façades of certain Liverpool or Manchester warehouses), nor in an overly exquisite way, but first through Wilford's probing axonometric studies – thinking through the angle and shape of each faceted section of glass – and then through an analogous process of ad hoc detailing developed on site in the construction process itself.[144] The exhilarating cascade of glass results from an 'imperfectionist' acceptance of the ad hoc, a crafted compromise revealing anti-Aristotelian beauties. The materials may be industrial, but their handling has something artisanal about it: a unique solution for this job at this time.

171   Stirling and Gowan, Leicester University Engineering Building, 1959–64, glass cascade.

In accord, therefore, with the clients' own discipline, the building was shaped into the specific forms that best suited its multiple purposes. A group of details tells of this attention to local incidents. The corners of the workshop block nearest to the tower complex are treated as junctures of folded planes and contrasting materials (fig. 172). A deep recess separates the walls of brick forming the workshop podium from the collar or ring beam of concrete. While the concrete visually moderates between glass above and brick below, the recess denies any structural continuity between the three materials. The milky-white plyglass, seeming to house cubic solids, reflective but not transparent, has an ambiguous weight. The corner where the two walls meet is marked by a chamfered edge, and this is carried down through to the bricks on end, canted to express the weighty substance of the brick wall where it joins the ground.

172   Stirling and Gowan, Leicester University Engineering Building, 1959–64, corner detail.

Above the recess, however, the concrete is shaped with a re-entrant angle, and then the line of the corner is taken up and back through the arris of a glass prism set between the two diamond-shaped ends of the roof. The outward thrust of the corner prow thus, as we look above it, first undergoes a retreat, and then disappears between the roof ridges.

The idea of giving material form to a community was the architects'. It did not appear in the brief, although a reciprocity of interests emerged as the design developed.[145] There is a less specific sense of community here, too, that is contributory to the feeling of being 'intensely alive' that the building generates.[146] The most obvious manifestation of this is the corridor that ploughs between workshop and tower complex, with large-scaled entrance fore and aft and the building's informal social spaces in and around it (fig. 173 and see fig. 159). This complexly articulated meeting point might be seen as the join or transition zone between the paper products and knowledge-disseminating functions of the tower and the engineering gear and knowledge-generating function of the workshop. But the community was also mirrored by a community of forms, of subliminally anthropomorphic shapes and empathetic spaces, inviting constant discovery in their oddities and changefulness, and offering generous views and physical engagements with multiple aspects of the building. The complex silhouette partakes of this. Seen from the park, the building seems to adopt the pose of a crouching archer or coiled

173   Stirling and Gowan, Leicester University Engineering Building, 1959–64.

discobolus, with one knee on the ground and a cloak laid out behind; contrariwise, it might be seen as a 'mechanical hobgoblin' (fig. 174).[147] Leicester triggers such fanciful associations and descriptions:

> the sumps in the floor for the virgins and the corpses of machinery to move in and out. The red-brown wedges sticking out and sticking in, the hollow wedges. The squatting towers and the great water tank hovering above, and the lovely cock-eyed, wide-eyed glass boxes, the first real hall of mirrors, on the outside. And the polygonal obelisk on the wavy, glassy sea-roof.[148]

The wit and craftiness of the building thus express and augment the community's complexity, and they are one result of the architects' lack of interest in an aesthetic of structural 'honesty'. To put this differently, because the building's surfaces and volumes display such unconcern with expressing load-bearing work – instead they have value as 'metaphorical substance'[149] – then a gamut of ways of representing or relating to the building's programme are licensed. A moral prohibition has been breached, and the effects go further than contradictions and ambiguities in the 'archetypal "stuff" of architecture'.[150] Almost everywhere one looks there are exam-

174   Stirling and Gowan, Leicester University Engineering Building, 1959–64.

ples of this. Thus, the snorkel on the podium announces the basest of human functions, the toilets otherwise hidden away in the unwindowed wedge below (fig. 175).[151]
Three 'secret' doors (doors flush with and made from the same materials as their
surrounds, as had appeared previously inside such buildings as the Dodd house) are
located around the building's outer wall (see fig. 163).[152] Covered by thin brick tiles,
these doors maintain the continuity of the brick skin but also hint at hidden machi-
nations. Another case is the overscaled parapet on the podium – a detail that occurs
in many of Stirling's later buildings. Covered with tiles and resting on thin metal
supports, this manages to be bench and rail at the same time as well as a feature
that reads strongly against the larger solids around it, partly perhaps because it is
treated as two long rectangular volumes that stop short of each other above the
angled corner. The glazed spiral stair that leads to the rear of the large lecture theatre
is, as many have pointed out, reminiscent of Peter Ellis's Cook Street offices in
Liverpool (see fig. 25), but it is also a flaunting of the theatre's cantilever: a faceted
stocky column, transparent, holding nothing up just where we might expect a
support (see fig. 140). Moving around the building is to discover unexpected spaces:
a grotto of angled red walls, for instance, is suggested below the protective awning
of the small lecture theatre (see fig. 163). The play with scale was also found in the
wonderfully proportioned office tower, actually much smaller and narrower than

175   Stirling and Gowan, Leicester University Engineering Building, 1959–64.

176   Stirling and Gowan, Leicester University Engineering Building, 1959–64, upper-floor landing.

the perspective recession that its patent glazing grid suggested before it was changed to double glazing more recently (to become 'like a string vest on a Modigliani').[153] The intimacy of spaces in this tower, particularly in the periodicals room, comes as a surprise: the room is small yet spans the full depth of the tower, benefiting from glazing on all three sides. Most wittily, the human members of this community are housed below the water tank, a secondary effect of the need to place the tank high up but an effect that might warn them from regressing into a self-regarding technocracy.

These effects are found almost everywhere. The site may be cramped but that is never the feeling inside: in the glazed waiting room that leads off the podium and where we gain a sense of the integrated promenade of ramp, stair and roof garden, translated from Corbusian villa to Midlands campus; in the foyer, open at both ends and with views across and upwards into other parts of the building; and in spaces that echo the foyer's effects, like the landing outside the large lecture theatre where we look up at a suspended corridor like the entrance spaces at Ham Common, across at various bands of glazing and the faceted angles of the roof/wall that cascades down in front of the stair tower (fig. 176), then back to views down over the lobby and across to the workshop roof. By contrast, inside the lecture theatres themselves the sense of constructed masses is abandoned in favour of rounded corners and shaped benches, each part of which is carefully articulated through slightly chamfered corners or gently curved hollows as a discrete piece of joinery or padded backrest (fig. 177). It is a building that enables extraordinary access, both for light let through the glazing and for views across and out of it. Among the most exhilarating aspects of this are the views first across and then down onto the rest of the building as one ascends the stair tower. At first the glazed rhomboid ends of the workshop roof loom up against the tower block, close angled presences like geometrically bug-eyed monsters. Then, as one ascends, the roof becomes a coursed landscape or some regularly glinting sea (fig. 178).

The colour too, which at first seems sober and disciplined, a monotone of red brick and tile, turns out to be more subtle and complex. There is the close encounter with silver metal piping and grey concrete in the stairwells (fig. 179), and elsewhere

177   Stirling and Gowan, Leicester University Engineering Building, 1959–64, benches in lecture theatre.

178   Stirling and Gowan, Leicester University Engineering Building, 1959–64.

chocolate-brown lift doors, fleshy-pink handrails, dark blue rails and doors in the workshop, and pillar box red lecture doors.[154] The neo-arctic landscape of the workshop roof is now less bleached than the 'cubist detergent' that Banham saw there,[155] and the light within has a diffused, gelid quality. Ironically, given that the architects rejected English glass because of its green tint,[156] as the plyglass has aged so its milky whiteness has become augmented by a range of tints: soft yellows, hints of turquoise, green washes and the most delicate pinks. These tiles and bricks – that we know to be ferrous, hard and angular – are also a skin unexpectedly conjuring up the warmest of sensual and womblike associations; sometimes as if we are inside a body looking out, sometimes as if we look back at another body, sometimes both at once. So

179   Stirling and Gowan, Leicester University Engineering Building, 1959–64, staircase.

colour is disciplined and sober, and yet insidiously evocative; it can make industrial and historical associations, yet also intimate a fleshy if mechanically enhanced body. If the red brick and tile skin seems alien to the campus, we have only to look at one of the building's immediate neighbours, College House, to see a contrary point to it (fig. 180). College House, which appears in plan or outline in many of the preliminary drawings, is a free-standing late Victorian building, predominantly of buff brick walls but with red brick trim around its windows. The same proportions of colour, now inverted, are seen in its big neighbour, where red is the dominant wall colour but a buff concrete 'trim' plays a minor role.

180   Stirling and Gowan, Leicester University Engineering Building, 1959–64.

~

To understand Leicester as evoking a community and, as part of that, presenting a roster of differences with the contemporary development of the surrounding university is to see in it also the crystallisation of many of the themes that have been discussed in Stirling and Gowan's work. Equally, there is its position in regard to its historical moment. Some writers have noticed the way it alludes to the neighbouring city,[157] an essentially Victorian, light industrial town of red brick and tile, and Stirling certainly played this up in his Black Book where a high view across the workshop roof towards terraces in the distance is titled 'Roof Landscape' (fig. 181).[158] It clearly does not relate to its city in Preston's manner: historical evocations are far more abstracted, the building's off-the-peg materials are unequivocally of the mid-twentieth century, and – despite some concessions to its immediate surroundings – the building has a monumental quality about it, a sense of defiant separateness that denies any nostalgic relation to the past. Nevertheless, there are parallels to the generic industrial city's repetition of brick terraces and glass roofs and even perhaps to its great places of work, the docks, railway stations and warehouses which are conjured up as much by the engineering building's glazing as by its stilt legs, gantry-like window cleaning mechanisms and prominent lifting tackle. Despite the modernist references discussed earlier in this chapter, the building's primary affiliations seem equally to be with the nineteenth century because that was still the defining state of the contemporary urban landscape, from which modernism offered only aloofness, disdain or utopian escape. In this sense Stirling and Gowan's realist approach to matters like function and building materials, as well as their dexterity in transforming them, is distinct from any technological positivism. Rather, it is an assertion of what could be made out of what exists in the urban vernacular. Engineering is also an act of contriving. The building is a reminder of what might be brought about by, engineered out of, a post-industrial state.

181   Stirling and Gowan, Leicester University Engineering Building, 1959–64, 'Roof Landscape'.

SEVEN

Aftermath

'By dint of constructing,' he put it with a smile, 'I truly believe that I have constructed myself.'

(Paul Valéry, *Eupalinos, or The Architect*, 1921)

This double movement is a profound one: architecture is always dream and function, expression of a utopia and instrument of a convenience.

(Roland Barthes, 'The Eiffel Tower', 1964)

The partnership's end had become inevitable. The ideal of close cooperation was tested by Stirling's teaching commitments at Yale, first in 1959 and then in most succeeding years.[1] As the need to take on more assistants on commissions multiplied, so the intensity of the partnership's early dynamic was dissipated.[2] Things somehow held together through the early challenges of Leicester and the sheer intensity of its creative elaboration. Elsewhere, however, a pragmatic division of responsibilities took over and often became a dividing wall, with schemes going ahead without joint agreement between the partners. In some accounts the crisis came with Stirling's dislike of Gowan's design for a house in Hampstead, and possibly too Stirling's impatience with an early alternative design that Gowan had produced for the Cambridge History Faculty building, a project that came into the practice in the spring of 1963. In other accounts Gowan had finally become disenchanted with what he saw as Stirling's concern with his own reputation and his sins of omission in properly acknowledging Gowan's role.[3]

Dissolution was formalised on 11 November 1963. While both partners continued to complete Leicester, two existing commissions were divided between them: Stirling got the Perrygrove old people's home and Gowan the children's home in Putney, completed under the partnership's name. Other commissions were allocated to a single partner and appeared under his name alone. Stirling acquired the Cambridge History Faculty, a block of flats in Camden, and an eventually lost commission for the *New Statesman*'s offices in Holborn.[4] Gowan retained commissions for housing at Creek Road and Trafalgar Road in Greenwich, a block of flats in Edgware (not built), warehouses in Dalston, and the Schreiber house in Hampstead.[5]

If the balance of its formal preoccupations was shattered, nevertheless the partnership's lessons ramified through the work of the now separated architects. A selection of this work up to 1970, treated in more summary form, is the main material for this concluding chapter. Gowan established a strong if limited formal agenda based on the typological problems of housing and light industrial structures, guided with the former by the idea that relatively simple exteriors could house interiors of great variety and elaboration. He was intrigued now by the 'restrained lineage' of the Georgian city and its 'declaration [of] . . . shared common cultural values'.[6] By implication, industry and commerce would be disciplined within the restraints of an older urban decorum. Stirling, who had a wider range of commissions, first tried to work through Leicester's example, then diverged into buildings of intricate articulation that adopted either industrial building methods or strong industrial imagery. But by the end of the decade, as this concluding chapter suggests, the dialogue between industry and modernism, so critical to the partnership, had taken on a different character for both architects.

~

We must return to Leicester and its legacy to see the way ahead. The building had not been short of admiring reviews by influential critics. It was acclaimed for breaking away from a safe, formulaic modernism,[7] and doing so with 'wit, sophistication, sense and bloodymindedness'.[8] It was not only the most distinctive British building since the war, but one that suddenly shifted the terms on which British architecture was regarded within the international architectural scene; the experiments and polemics of the young British avant-garde had produced their most resonant monument. But the more negative responses are also revealing because they usually hinged around the same aspects that were praised. Nikolaus Pevsner, famously, was so bothered by the spectre of expressionism in what he called this 'post-modern' style that he completely misremembered the building's materials and colour as 'exposed concrete [and] . . . blue engineering bricks'. Sensing the snook cocked at the master plan by the new building – Leslie Martin's bricky version of Bauhaus modernism was one of his favoured contemporary brands – Pevsner accused the architects of aggressive 'expressional' and formal decisions, refusing for instance to see the functional point of the diagonal ridge lights over the workshop.[9]

Another criticism was made separately by Peter Smithson and Kenneth Frampton. This was that the building was so closely specified for its brief that it offered no wider cultural use; if it was epochal it was not exemplary. Smithson saw its 'bloody gothic profile' as part of a set of essentially personal, artistic decisions in the design of the building arrived at irrespective of the 'larger environmental situation' (by which he meant the state of architecture in contemporary society). He regretted that its ad hoc design, its lack of archetypal principles based on searching out the 'deepest roots in a situation', meant it could never be seen as part of a larger totality and its influence would be found only in superficial copying of it as a 'formal prototype', an infection of stylistic influence or mere emulation.[10] The criticism, then, was essentially of a lack of responsibility to the future, a failure to respond to the potential of university buildings as 'institutional archetypes of our age'.[11] Put without the same negative judgement, as many aspects of Stirling and Gowan's architecture attest, this is precisely the crux on which the post-industrial turns.

Frampton, who otherwise praised the building, voiced his criticism only slightly differently. A building acclaimed as major is automatically seen as a source of general principles or a system whose syntax allows it to be accessed by the general culture. Within such a building distortions of form for programmatic reasons can be legitimated. But Leicester lacked the 'rational discipline' that would enable it to be understood in this way.[12] Frampton saw Leicester as caught somewhere between such precedents as Le Corbusier's earlier modernism and the constructivists, on the one hand, and Frank Lloyd Wright on the other. The most interesting aspect of this argument was how Frampton related it to ideas about technology. In 1920s modernism rational systems allowed both programmatic distortion and the admission of 'non-aesthetic standard elements', thus relating the work to the 'technological capacity of the whole society'. In Wright's work, however, all such distortions and other elements were contained within a 'closed individual aesthetic'. Leicester's innovation, but implicitly its failure too, was its attempt to 'reconcile the essential conflict existing between two distinct cultures of the environment'. Interestingly, Stirling himself had made a similar distinction in his journal around 1954: the task, as he saw it, was to draw together the two paths of 'art-architecture' and 'non-art architecture', and the one who could combine these tendencies would be 'the greatest architect of them all'.[13] The argument made earlier in this book is that it was precisely what Frampton called 'the technological capacity of the whole society' that was in crisis in 1950s Britain, and that to turn to specific or even 'expressional' solutions to this in terms of one building – as at Leicester – was a more realistic response to such a changing situation than to assume the architect's privilege of insight into the archetypal, to accede to an idea of the inherent good of welfare state modernism, or to pretend to a sunnily positive and in its own way nostalgic view of technological development. And this position continued to direct the separated architects' work for the next few years.

A comparison with a slightly younger architect's reaction to the same situation is revealing. In Cedric Price's Potteries Thinkbelt (1964–65) a new vision of a university

182   Cedric Price, Potteries Thinkbelt, 1964–65, perspective drawing on photograph.

as a 'High-Tech think tank' was sketched out,[14] one in which a system of movement and assemblage that exploited the old industries of railways and engineering would install a flexible campus in the heart of an area of industrial blight (fig. 182). Price's vision has become almost routinely turned to in recent years to castigate the more architectural, designed solutions of his contemporaries.[15] But although it used a rhetoric of freedom founded in notions of indeterminacy and the 'recasting of obsolete systems of production',[16] the Potteries Thinkbelt was what Stirling had earlier castigated as a 'one idea' scheme.[17] The only new thinking it was engaged with in the universities was cybernetics and game theory, employed as a solution to all problems. It was a vision ideally suited for an administrative view of universities as a set of systems, of calculated inputs and predicted outputs. The architect was a space provider, the lecturer or student a space occupier; the qualities of space were irrelevant and the contribution of architecture to its environment still less so. Like Price's Fun Palace, as well as the best-known product of his influence, the Beaubourg Centre, the Potteries Thinkbelt pretended to place all emphasis on architecture as frame, leaving architecture's content as a void. This was a position alien to both Stirling and Gowan, for whom the attempt to shape and make sense of institutions in the present – whether it was the nature of housing or the specific character of a university – was paramount.

Gowan's work after 1963 may lack the more obvious complexity of Stirling's as well as its protean qualities, but it was far more consistent in its developing concerns. If the Schreiber house was one of the causes of the break up with Stirling, then we might expect it to show Gowan's architectural disposition at its most personal. Fin-

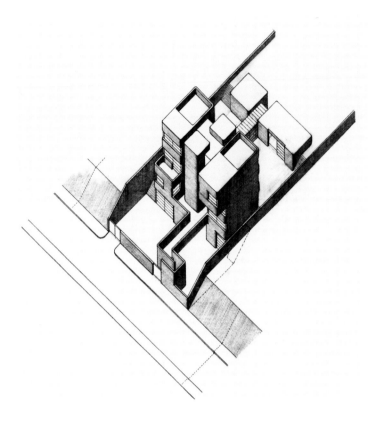

183   James Gowan,
Schreiber House study, 1963,
axonometric.

ished in 1965, the client was the furniture manufacturer Chaim Schreiber. While the house continues several themes that had developed within the partnership, it also looks back to Gowan's work before Stirling. The first designs were tight, cubist articulations of privacy and outlook (fig. 183). But the house as built was more serene and aloof. There are the same alternating bands of brick and windows, with the latter breaking into the roofline as in the Blackheath old people's home, and the same lifting onto a plinth as in many previous partnership works (fig. 184). But now the castle-like impunity of the exterior belies the luxury of the interiors. Even though Schreiber made his money in the lower end of the furniture market, the internal fittings are flatteringly precise and expensively bespoke; if any are 'as found', they are a de luxe version of that aesthetic. Located on the edge of Hampstead Heath, the house rebukes its neighbours in certain obvious ways: it ignores their gables and its dark blue brick spites their oranges and browns.[18] Although it is rigorously abstract, it recalls the verticality of those Georgian terraces Gowan had come to admire. Yet by breaking its volumes into expressive units, it also sets up a counterpoint with its parkside location. The cutting into of the perimeter wall, followed by a suddenly

184   James Gowan, Schreiber House, Hampstead, London 1963–65.

turning stair, creates a sense of urbane privacy. From there the house's disposition, laid out on a three-foot grid (as are the windows and brick piers between them), becomes apparent as the entrance axis is then cut by a cross axis through the full length of the house. This neo-Palladian formality is reminiscent of the house on the Isle of Wight, but with flexibility now provided by double doors enabling the spaces to flow into one another when required. A semi-detached stair tower – a vestige of the 'servant' towers in Leicester – encourages a greater sense of the separation of floor levels, suggesting a formality of domestic ritual that marries with the Georgian proportions of the windows seen from within.[19]

The Creek Road (1964–67) and Trafalgar Road (1966–68) housing estates in Greenwich came into the partnership originally because the partners were on the LCC panel of architects. In Gowan's handling they update and correct the position the partners had reached at Preston. Creek Road was the simpler and smaller of the two: a terrace of two linked blocks of maisonettes in a serrated plan, providing a kind of front or screen to one of those inter-war neo-Georgian estates that can be found all over London (fig. 185). Trafalgar Road was designed as a group of four blocks around a courtyard but with one block facing as a terrace onto the road (figs 186–87). The language in both estates was now more like the bricky urbanistic Dutch proto-

185   James Gowan, Creek Road Housing, Greenwich, London, 1964–67.

modernism of Dudok than that of De Stijl, while the geometric corrugations of their plans are reminiscent of Gowan's designs for the Edinburgh Medical School of some twenty years before. In fact, the housing model now was also related to the Edinburgh design; it was the screening, enclosing qualities of Georgian terraces with their ability to combine small units into large-scale compositions that were evoked.[20] Where the elevations of the three-storey blocks at Preston gave a sense of stepped volumes, at Trafalgar Road the blocks suggest a giant order in the rhythm of projecting and recessed bays. The original severity of this to the outside world (now softened by mature trees) was a side-effect of the privacy it achieved for residents: windows were moved away from the front plane, entrances were set within cloistered passages, and access galleries were shielded by bridging volumes. The rearmost of Trafalgar's blocks makes a remarkably cubist configuration while retaining the disciplines of the terrace,

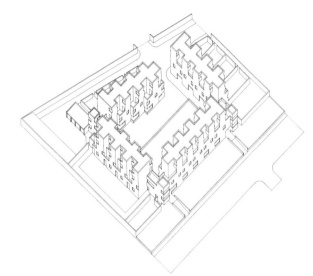

LEFT 186   James Gowan, Trafalgar Road Housing, Greenwich, London, 1966–68, axonometric.

ABOVE 187   James Gowan, Trafalgar Road Housing, Greenwich, London, 1966–68.

its volumes stepping back to line the diagonal edge of the site. Tied into the existing street patterns, both estates tried to avoid the abrupt truncations of private space and overly proximate relations of family units found in Preston.

~

Frampton's and Smithson's concern about the exemplary nature of Leicester was borne out by what immediately followed in Stirling's career. His next few buildings – in Cambridge and Oxford especially – repeat aspects of Leicester's appearance as if to demonstrate that the critics were wrong and that it could indeed provide principles. These are red brick, tile and glass buildings, faceted and complex elaborations of the stylistic signature of industrial materials, Victorian allusions and, by the 1960s, self-proclaimed constructivist forms established at Leicester. But there was also something newly aggressive about the relation of these buildings to their contexts and their typologies, and in this respect they broke away from the 'style for the job' approach of Stirling's work with Gowan,[21] while also proving problematic in their construction and maintenance.[22] The replication of Leicester as brand might be understood, on one level, as Stirling's attempt to establish a clear architectural continuity and to claim it as a signature style for himself or perhaps, on another level, as a lessening of the intense relation Leicester had made with the modernist tradition.[23] Another new element was the more self-contained nature of these buildings. Where Leicester's functional expressiveness led to an urbanistic complexity, one making connections with many aspects of its surroundings even when it intervened in them, these later so-called 'red buildings' folded their elements around a central core. They were imagined almost as fragments of the old sacred precinct of modernism: 'vest-pocket utopias',[24] highly specified and assertive interventions. While the Cambridge and Oxford buildings, in particular, were treated as objects of singular isolation, they were also ambiguous monuments that evoked both the now heroicised modernism of the first generation and also the pioneering structures of the Industrial Revolution. If Gowan was right to point to the way the replication of Leicester's vocabulary betrayed its 'style for the job',[25] at the same time the inward-turning nature of these buildings and their concern with giving spatial form to the idea of their institutions as communities brought an even more focused anthropological element into Stirling's work.

The Cambridge History Faculty (1963–68) presents the contrasts of authorial style versus 'style for the job', and of evoked historical precedents versus cutting edge technologies, most starkly (fig. 188).[26] The concept here – to unite academic accommodation and library in one encompassing volume – was developed early in the

188   James Stirling, Cambridge University History Faculty, 1963–68.

design process, and its forms had a strong typological relevance.[27] Essentially, it is a sliced quarter of a panopticon roofed with a slope of glass and backed by an L-shaped configuration of academic offices and teaching rooms, the whole symmetrical when seen from a diagonal axis. But the concept was partly undermined when the clients had their site reduced by half, compelling Stirling to turn his plan anticlockwise through ninety degrees to fit.[28] The entrance now faced west and, more compromisingly, the greenhouse roof was turned south-east. Leicester's circulation towers reappear at Cambridge as well as the attenuation of circulation space as the building rises, although with a profile more reminiscent of Antonio Sant'Elia's unrealised futurist schemes. Leicester's patent glazing also reappears, but now, with its facets, double-glazing and Venetian blinds, it is less a transparent skin and more a vitreous wall. The greenhouse roof and side walls of repeated glazing elements, as well as the profiled expanses of brick, inevitably evoke the Victorian monuments of Stirling's early days: Liverpool's Lime Street Station, the office buildings of Peter Ellis, and the sheer end elevations of Victorian brick terraces.[29] Also relevant for Stirling was the entirely glazed rear elevation of York House, Manchester, which he had photographed (see fig. 72).[30] These are surely still the primary reference points for the building rather than the more opportune, post hoc links made with the recently opened American Space Center headquarters at Cape Canaveral.

Stirling regarded Cambridge's reading room as a space of criss-crossing visual interests (fig. 189).[31] Apart from the panoptic view from the central librarian's post across the reading room and down the radiating book stacks, the readers themselves could relieve their book-weary eyes by looking up at the light effects of the first, frosted layer of glass in the roof above. From the upper corridors with their bays designed purely for viewing purposes, passing students and staff could look down onto the reading room as well as through clear glass panels into the mechanics of the roof.[32] This intersecting and focused pattern of sightlines – enabling looking for pleasure, for relief and for surveillance – was a 'perception field'[33] encouraging allegiance to the idea of an integrated community. Effectively then, rather than the more conventional idea of honouring the institution through the building's entrance and its foyer, which in this case are both relatively small and marginalised (one might say the pretensions of their customary expectations are deflated),[34] Cambridge History Faculty centres community onto a space that combines both the storage of knowledge and the act of reading. In doing this it breaches another propriety by cladding the building with industrial patent glazing. The roof may be like that of a Victorian greenhouse but, just as redolently (and offensively for some), it is also a realisation of a dream of early twentieth-century glass architecture – that a crystalline structure might house a community's signal institutions.[35]

189   James Stirling, Cambridge University History Faculty, 1963–68, reading room.

The Florey building for Queen's College (commissioned 1964, built 1968–70), sited just outside Oxford's collegiate heart, responded to its riverside environs and to recent architectural examples (fig. 190).[36] Basil Spence had finished the Erasmus building, a dormitory for Queen's College, Cambridge, in 1961 on a very similar site and had turned the L-shaped rear of his building to the River Cam. Spence presented a similar, if more distanced, target to what Martin had stood for at Leicester. Where Spence's building was a rectilinear exercise in the now old lessons of the Pavillon Suisse, the Florey building reversed almost every one of Spence's premises while dealing with an almost identical commission. Another relevant example, if for a different type of building, was the scheme Le Corbusier had designed for a museum on the banks of the Seine (1935), which created a three-sided courtyard backed on two sides by blocks stepped back and supported on single- and double-height *pilotis*.[37] But unlike both Spence and Le Corbusier, Stirling sought from early in his design process a form that could articulate student life in a

190   James Stirling, Florey Building, Oxford, 1964–70.

manner that was both more informal and more theatrical, responding to the river with something of the drama and flexibility (and some of the details) that he had observed back in 1948 in Aalto's just-completed Baker House along the banks of yet another river (the Charles just outside Boston).[38]

The Florey is an irregular, open polygon with its five levels of stepped back student residences grouped around a raised pavement facing the river Cherwell. It develops what was implied in the Blackheath old people's home, folding the glazed volume of the Selwyn design so that it now formed a kind of amphitheatre (fig. 191). A-frame struts lift the building off the ground like some animated chair, raising the glazed dormitory rooms towards the light but also opening up a cloister beneath. Cloister and amphitheatre establish the terms of shelter and display, privacy and prospect, between which the experience of the Florey is balanced. Reversing the visual dynamics of Cambridge's library, community is now defined by a shared physical focus that

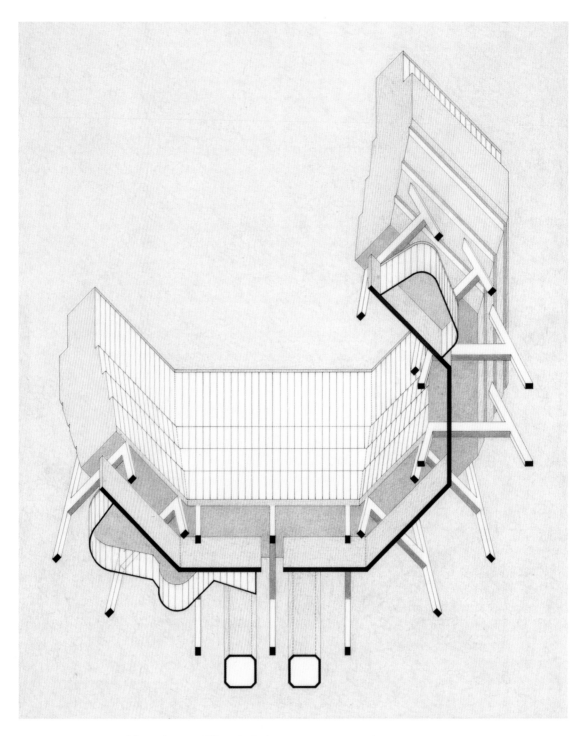

191   James Stirling, Florey Building, Oxford, 1964–70, axonometric.

accepted the risk of 'outraged privacy' (the dormitory rooms looking across at one another) as part
of what is due to the institution.[39] Leicester's
example is mined not just for the materials but
also for certain devices: the service towers that
now also suggest a gate-like function,[40] the ramp
that was to have provided equal access into the
residence from the riverside, and an oversized rail
or parapet, now awkwardly angled to bridge
between platform and lower level. A flue in the
centre of the courtyard reworks the funnel at
Leicester, or even the periscope in Le Corbusier's
Beistegui apartment. And here, just as the focus
of Leicester's plinth was to serve banal but necessary bodily functions, the flue guided by its
weather vane swivels to direct cooking smells
from the kitchen below away from the bedrooms
above. The building seems to require a new kind
of resident, a cadre of student industrialists for
whom the industrial is not so much a realm of

192   James Stirling, Dorman Long
Headquarters, Middlesbrough, 1965, model.

possibilities as an ambiguous condition of life, mock-heroic and exhibitionist, in
teasing association with the vestigial elements of a cultural past.[41]

There were other currents in Stirling's work at this time apart from these university buildings.[42] Of particular relevance is the most machine-like of his designs, for
the unbuilt Dorman Long headquarters in Middlesbrough (1965) (fig. 192). Stirling
was taken by the sublime or 'satanic' qualities of a site 'positioned at the end of the
steel mills and surrounded by the symbols of heavy industry – slag mountains,
cooling towers, flaming chimneys'.[43] Here, the extruded structure of the early Honan
competition design was given entirely new significance, perhaps betraying the influence of Cedric Price's work. But unlike Price, Stirling's turn to a wholly industrial
appearance matched the nature of the project. The main fourteen-storey structure
was presented as an exoskeleton in front of a glazed façade, with the lower storeys
splayed on the front to take in the greater movements of human traffic at lower
levels. Stirling's aesthetic interest in this structure is clear from the sculptural attention given to the exoskeleton and its arbitrary formal solutions; the I-beams appear
to rest gently on other girders, like Anthony Caro's gravity-defying welded sculpture.
The basic arrangement of a potentially extendable block, glazed on one side and with
service towers on the other side, follows the format established at Selwyn College.

What is new here is the way the building is projected as an advertisement for the client through both the demonstration of their product on the exoskeleton and the sign proclaiming 'Dorman Long' that extends vertically from a smaller ancillary building.

By contrast, with the Andrew Melville Hall at St Andrews University (1964–69) Stirling found that the logic of a prefabricated system assembled on site was an apt way also of expressing the repeated individual bedrooms within the vessel of the residence as a whole (fig. 193). It is this that gives the building its sense of anthropological rightness,[44] that the contrasting experiences of atomistic study and shared dormitory life had found their appropriate and yet also most suggestive expression. Presented with a rangy escarpment site, the two residential blocks cascade down the slope and then reach towards the sea like promontories or ships at dock. Students enter the complex from the high side of the site, a relaxed composition of linking bridge and the simple blank back wall of the main building. From there they descend past communal rooms before they arrive at wide promenade decks, another variation on 'streets-in-the-air' if without their reconstitutive social programme,[45] faced along their entire length by windows of patent glazing. At certain points, marked by big

193   James Stirling, Andrew Melville Hall, St Andrews University, 1964–69.

194   James Stirling, Runcorn Housing, 1967–73.

porthole windows on their inner wall, the decks give access via stairs to more private internal corridors above and below that lead along the length of the blocks to the study-bedrooms with their own individual views onto the sea. Different spaces, distances, shapes and light effects thus mark out a diversity of relations between student and institution. Like the Florey and Cambridge, the building harbours an open space at its centre, but the problematic relations at the Florey between privacy and publicity, the individual and the institution, are now minimised. The walls relate simply to the turfed slope, downplaying the drama of the natural amphitheatre.

Stirling's own 'correction' of Preston came with a two-phase housing estate at Runcorn in Cheshire. Here he also returned to a vision of eighteenth-century urban housing, or at least a vestige of this tradition (fig. 194). Commissioned in 1967 and built in 1968–73 and 1974–78, the housing was organised in the first phase as five-storey blocks of houses, maisonettes and flats laid out in squares and a crescent, linked by a raised walkway to the shopping centre. The imagery of machine production and technology was strong, from the glass-reinforced polyester panels to the circuitboard-like grid, to the heating ducts that span the roads in the later two- to three-storey development. Like Gowan, Stirling achieved a giant order by placing staircase towers as a kind of colonnade in front of his larger blocks, linking with flats on the fifth storey.[46] But where Gowan's flats continue to mature, Runcorn was pulled down in the 1990s, barely twenty years after completion, the victim of a combination of its own design problems – its walkways, unpopular materials and scarcity of gardens – and a lack of commitment from the Development Corporation in maintaining it.[47] Far from convincingly correcting Preston, then, it represents the exemplary case for the counter-principles that Leon Krier, one of the assistants on the project, developed in the 1970s: it was an estate isolated from existing towns, designed in the last flush of cheap oil and seemingly without heed either for what its tenants might want or for its own longevity. It was also the last of Stirling's housing projects to be built.

~

Something new had undoubtedly entered Stirling's work before the Runcorn housing was finished, and whatever the reason – Leon Krier's entry into his office in the late 1960s,[48] the continuing and well-publicised problems of the Florey and Cambridge History buildings – this marked a shift in Stirling's work. Two unbuilt projects, both sited in the middle of towns – the Derby civic centre (1970) and the arts centre at St Andrews University (1971) – are the manifesto pieces of this new manner.[49] Both were projects of public utility, with the arts centre the first of Stirling's many designs for art galleries in the next phase of his career. At Derby an amphitheatre ringed by a shopping arcade was punctuated by a repositioned eighteenth-century façade now tilted to supply a proscenium (fig. 195). At St Andrews curved glazed walls were to link three existing buildings and provide a new outdoor space, both close-packed and formal, with changing images projected onto the building (fig. 196). The attri-

195   James Stirling, Derby Civic Centre, 1970, drawing.

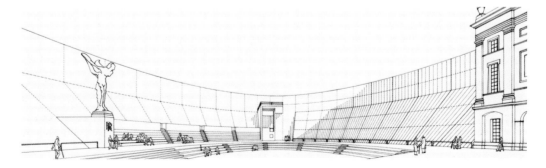

196   James Stirling,
St Andrews Arts Centre,
1971, model.

butes of place which had been intermittently powerful up to this point (in Sheffield and Preston, for instance) now became a consistently prime motivation, shifting the focus from the internalised space of community in the mid-1960s works to the urban surrounds treated as an 'outdoor room' in which the new addition is just one element.[50] It is for this reason that figure-ground maps of the urban context appeared with both projects when they were published in the Black Book, showing the projects as acts of patching and embellishing the city, either additions to an already dense palimpsest of fragments or attempts, as at Derby, to return a sense of civic order to a town seriously damaged by post-war reconstruction. In part inspired by Stirling's work, the approach was elaborated theoretically a little later by Colin Rowe and Fred Koetter in their postmodernist manifesto, *Collage City* (1978).[51] For Stirling it represented the final push away from Saint-Dié and Newton Aycliffe, the achievement of an urban complexity to match the complexity of any individual project.

Yet just as the historical references became more explicit in these projects, so the intensity of the engagement with the idea and continuity of industry lessened. For Rowe, certainly, the allure of an old aristocratic culture was always greater than any interest in the fate of an industrial civilisation, and occasionally this affected Stirling too.[52] Whatever the attractions of a collaged city, and they are many, there are also disturbing aspects to it. The book, as Anthony Vidler has pointed out, is 'permeated with a sense of defeat' as if modernism no longer had any role in harnessing modernisation in the modern city.[53] Cities, in Rowe and Koetter's view, were to be developed and animated by dense juxtapositions of past forms and modernist images, an 'argument between type and context' exemplary of a humanist philosophy.[54] But on closer examination technology and the modern had barely a peripheral role in collage city; the thick palimpsest of the past gave little space to them. We are allowed to curate the city as a museum, to demonstrate that we love its perplexities and fragments, but we must give up not just on a 'truly modern' contribution to it but, more importantly, the sense that we have any right to significant agency within it. As Bruno Latour has characterised it, '"No future": this is the slogan added to the moderns' motto "No past".'[55] History, accordingly, tends to bypass collage city and find other, less fastidious parts of the world on which to wreak its lessons. Stirling's approach, however, remained more responsive to popular culture and modern technology than Rowe and Koetter's, attempting to balance consumerist excitements with spaces of public encounter.

Some of these considerations, if with different implications, can also be found in more obscure projects by each of the ex-partners. In these examples the multi-aesthetic was reimagined as a kit of parts or as a structural core to which rooms might be added. After his housing in Trafalgar Road was finished, Gowan suggested an elaboration of the project that would take it even further from the model established at Preston. The stark bricky volumes of the scheme might be modified and enlivened by the tenants using what he called a 'personalization kit': 'perhaps with the architect's guidance but not necessarily so' (fig. 197).[56] In part Gowan was motivated by his own dissatisfaction with the colour and quality of the brick that had been assigned to him, but more

197   James Gowan, 'Personalization Kit' for Trafalgar Road, Greenwich, London, 1968.

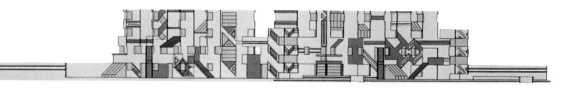

importantly he wanted to imagine how the estate as a 'communion of tenants' might enable personal expression within the collective.[57] Once the tenants could purchase their flats and administer the estate communally, they could also enliven it by choosing from a number of clip-on parts – screens, trellises, conservatories, balcony covers and lean-to stairs – in theory adding colour and pattern as well as more bespoke convenience and individuality to the façades.[58]

Stirling's elaboration of low-cost eclecticism came when, in 1969, he was invited to enter a limited competition for mass housing in Lima, Peru. Deserving to be better known, the idea of this Peruvian government and United Nations-sponsored competition was to experiment in

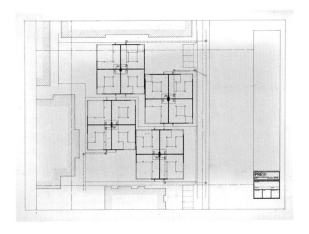

198   James Stirling, Lima Housing, Peru, 1969, plans.

dwelling use and building technology in order to satisfy the housing needs of the Peruvian poor.[59] Stirling's response was to remake the expandable house as a kind of systematised version of the *barriada*, those do-it-yourself and often illegal settlements. Arranged in groups of four-house units around a patio courtyard, the Lima housing's structure of precast concrete walls and columns was designed to be built in a first stage by a state contractor (fig. 198). In the second, self-build stage, the frame around the patio could be filled according to the wishes of the residents, allowing anything from small terraces, to groups of cell-like rooms served by single-loaded corridors, to large L-shaped rooms or whole open-plan floors, and including workshops and garages as needed. This flexibility also allowed for any form of individual expression in windows and walls: Krier's drawings for Stirling indicate, for example, ogee, pointed, round-arched and Palladian windows, and walls made of any locally available material (fig. 199). Eventually, an extensive development by Peruvian and international architects was built, including three of these clusters of four-house units by Stirling.[60] Over the years, the residents of Stirling's scheme did not reach the flights of historical fancy envisaged in Krier's drawings, but nevertheless Stirling's project does seem to have encouraged far more self-build additions than the other schemes.[61]

In his Lima housing Stirling transcribed and rerouted the expandable house from consumer-oriented housing for the nuclear family to mass housing for the extended family, and produced it in a society whose spending power was closer to that of austerity Britain of the 1950s than the 'affluent society' of the 1960s. And in Gowan's

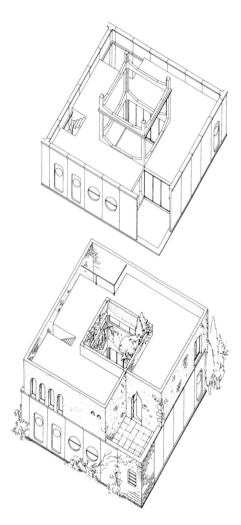

Trafalgar Road 'personalization kit' the benighted council tenants of modernist welfarism were reimagined as active consumer-tenants, their responsibility rewarded with the power to reshape their environs. There are suggestions in both projects of a critical practice of postmodernism, one in which the sovereign skills and tastes of the architect might cede ground to the rights and tastes of the inhabitant, the supposedly distracted user of architecture. Yet Lima and Trafalgar Road had little impact or influence; the realisation of one was barely registered (even Stirling's Black Book published no images of the project as built), while the other was little more than a private whim.

Stirling rarely practised the 'façadism' of which many postmodernists of the 1980s could be accused. His ventures into postmodernism were mostly tempered by strong urbanistic, typological and spatial concerns, beyond the scope of this present book. But if there is a single scheme that marks the nature of the change, it is the unbuilt design for the Siemens AG headquarters (1969) (fig. 200).

While Dorman Long had erected stark signs in a barren landscape, Siemens makes a familiar street out of a factory. In both projects industry and industrialisation are things to be conjured up, made representable, by the architectural imagery. But Siemens also takes this in another direction. This is not a building but a giant complex spreading across the landscape with mechanomorphic and Arcadian references. Ten six-storey towers contain spaces for computer research and development with workshops behind and a boulevard in front. Krier's

199   James Stirling, Lima Housing, Peru, 1969. Drawing c.1974 by Leon Krier.

perspective offers a memorable image, his graphic elisions and flat aquamarine sky bringing out the strain of industrial romanticism in Stirling's work. Work and leisure, production and the good life, seem in alluring if uneasy balance. Relaxed industrialists, clad in thirties suits, spill out onto the boulevard. Harboured under a pink colonnade they seem unaware of the stocky towers above them, blankly panelled and fitted with revolving sunscreens. These towers make for brilliant images, alternately gargantuan classical fragments or massively indifferent machine parts. If this is a

200   James Stirling, Siemens AG Headquarters, Munich, 1969. Drawing *c.*1974 by Leon Krier.

work place as plugged-in mainframe, it is also an attempt to give familiar forms of civilised urbanity in eighteenth-century terms to the industrial complex, the vista petering out in a double line of poplars but implying infinite extension – part-Poussin, part-Ballard. This is a programme not so distant from Leicester, with offices in front and workshops behind. But now new dreams and metaphors offer work as a form of play.

~

At the heart of their work Stirling and Gowan accepted a truth about architecture that many of their contemporaries rejected – that architecture is a material thing *and* a representation. It belongs in the world; it is made of its matter and must abide by its laws, yet it also displays an attitude towards the world. What could this entail, their work seemed to ask, in post-war Britain, in a place of ruins and exhaustion yet also of hope and exhilaration, where the tectonic plates of culture and society were suddenly shifting? Even with the vagaries of clients and commissions, it seemed that form-giving could make some sense of this. It seemed one could be pragmatic about means and realistic about ends, yet also imaginative about possibilities.

One of the arguments of this book has been that the sense of uncertainty about industrial progress, partly because it led to an aesthetic redemption of industry's forms, was generative for Stirling and Gowan. And this redemption or reuse implied not so much a disregard of other concerns as a foregrounding of the multiplicity of meanings, sensual responses and range of experiences attributable to industry and its creations.[62] That some of their imagery was confident, even aggressively so, is plain to see, and so too their handling of technology. But this had to be achieved by questioning the commonplaces of the machine aesthetic. It was the clash and mingling of modernism and this post-industrial mindset that gave Stirling and Gowan's work its particular potency. The complex and intriguing qualities of their work almost always derived from its ability to hold these in creative tension. The 'late modernism' of their contemporaries rarely achieved this. Where the post-industrial became of issue to other architects – like Cedric Price or even high-tech architects like Richard Rogers and Norman Foster, all notably younger than Stirling and Gowan – it was treated as something that had already happened, the realisation of which could help move architecture into new realms of expression. And for Stirling and Gowan, once the after-effects of this intense encounter between the modernist and the post-industrial had been worked through in the mid- and late 1960s in works that followed the end of the partnership, then their work became absorbed in a wider international phenomenon.

The postmodernism of the 1970s and 1980s carried plenty of baggage with it. Brought up to regard modernism as the defining and inevitable architecture of their epoch – of its 'moral rightness'[63] whatever its problems – neither Gowan nor Stirling would ever allow their work to be called postmodernist.[64] In Stirling's case this became particularly strained as his work was willingly used within the manifesto events and publications of the new architectural order.[65] For both architects postmodernism was something to be cagey about. It could easily be seen merely as a parade of styles detached from their historical motivations; of knowing, often condescending references to mass popular culture; of the reduction of the architecturally sensuous to scenography, and the loss of typological 'thickness' of effect in favour of merely semantic connotation. By contrast, Stirling and Gowan had operated within an expanded conception of modernism; it was not enough to treat it as the *lingua franca* of their culture, the common or orthodox mode of working – not just because the culture was too complex to be evened out by sheer will, but because complexity itself was to be valued above purity. Modernism had to lose any belief in a Great Divide between high and low cultures; it had to be made to relate to its own history and prehistory if it was to take better measure of its moment. Part of the partnership's energy, then, was to do with an appropriative attitude to modernism, often rediscovering marginalised elements within it; part of it was to understand the cultural wealth of industry and its creations over and above polarised conceptions of it as either obsolescent or inherently progressive. Both architects contributed to this enterprise, generating its energy from their distinct yet usually complementary architectural characters.

What has been described as the post-industrial architecture of the Stirling and Gowan practice was always concerned to root architecture within the layered temporalities of its moment. Leicester University Engineering building marked the culmination of the fascination with industrialism. The aesthetics of bricolage and the pile-up had been transmuted, reconciling the expressive articulation of functions through consistencies of form and materials. Perhaps the architects' own terms 'multi-aesthetic' and 'style for the job' seem partial or contingent, less rallying cries than ways of explaining practice. But there is an obdurate persistence to the post-industrial theme through the partnership work and much of the post-partnership work of the 1960s. With the dissipation of the strength of this theme around 1970 came also an abandonment of any idea – representational or actual – of architecture keeping in some kind of dialogue with the forces of production, making them culturally resonant. There is a sense that the newly emerging 'cultural dominant' of postmodernism was far less consciously related to the 'logic of late capitalism' than the post-industrialism of a previous era.[66] Nostalgia, ruins and decline had powerful meaning in post-war Britain; they were not the flimsy ciphers, the mere effects of the 'fragment' and the 'nostalgesque', that their later espousal by postmodernism made them out to be,[67] but nor were they detached from the ongoing developments of industry. There are reminders and lessons here for architecture today. The partnership work had many imitators, fans and detractors, but if there is an example of any longevity then it is to do with its disabused probing of the matter at hand and the resourcefulness and eloquence of its aesthetic intelligence.

Notes

INTRODUCTION

1   Robin Evans, *The Projective Cast: Architecture and its Three Geometries*, Cambridge, Mass.: MIT Press, 1995, p. 70.

2   A good guide to these currents in post-war architecture is Sarah Williams Goldhagen, 'Coda: Reconceptualizing the Modern', in Sarah Williams Goldhagen and Réjean Legault (eds), *Anxious Modernisms: Experimentation in Postwar Architectural Culture*, Cambridge, Mass.: MIT Press, 2000, pp. 301–23.

3   Demetri Porphyrios, *Sources of Modern Eclecticism: Studies on Alvar Aalto*, London: Academy Editions, 1982, p. 58.

4   Peter Eisenman, 'Real and English: The Destruction of the Box I', *Oppositions*, 4, October 1974, p. 7.

5   Especially noteworthy in bringing Gowan's contribution back into focus are the following: Ellis Woodman, *Modernity and Reinvention: The Architecture of James Gowan*, London: Black Dog, 2008; John McKean, *Leicester University Engineering Building: James Stirling and James Gowan*, London: Phaidon, 1994; and the chapter on Leicester University Engineering building in Peter Blundell Jones and Eamonn Canniff, *Modern Architecture Through Case Studies 1945–1990*, London: Architectural Press, 2007. However, the need to find a unique architectural creator, thus to neglect Gowan, is persistent: see, for instance, most of the articles in the special issue of *Oase*, 79, 2009.

6   Gowan refused to be interviewed by Girouard, perhaps because he feared that the biographical mode would not accept his own co-creation of the partnership work: Mark Girouard, *Big Jim: The Life and Work of James Stirling*, London: Pimlico, 2000, p. xvi.

7   Most especially the exhibition *Notes from the Archive: James Frazer Stirling* on display during 2010 to 2012 at the Yale Center for British Art, New Haven, Tate Britain, the Staatsgalerie, Stuttgart, and the Canadian Centre for Architecture, Montreal. Also the accompanying catalogue: Anthony Vidler, *James Frazer Stirling: Notes from the Archive*, Montreal, New Haven and London: CCA, YCBA and Yale University Press, 2010.

8   They are supplemented by Peter Arnell and Ted Bickford (eds), *James Stirling: Buildings and Projects*, New York: Rizzoli, 1984.

9   Girouard, *Big Jim*, pp. 186–97.

10 On 'operative criticism' see Manfredo Tafuri, *Theories and History of Architecture*, London: Granada, 1980, pp. 141–70.

11 This view is associated with two very different wings of political theory: on the one hand, the neo-conservative theorists of 'post-industrial society' of the 1970s and since, and, on the other, the more recent theorists of 'Empire' as a globalised condition which, aided by information technologies, promises new forms of sovereignty. See Daniel Bell, *Coming of Post-Industrial Society*, New York: Basic Books, 1973; Michael Hardt and Antonio Negri, *Empire*, Cambridge, Mass. and London: Harvard University Press, 2000.

12 See, for instance, Paolo Portoghesi, *Postmodern: The Architecture of the Postindustrial Society*, New York: Rizzoli, 1983, pp. 11, 72–77.

13 David Kynaston, *Austerity Britain 1945–51*, London: Bloomsbury, 2007, 398–99; David Edgerton, *Science, Technology and the British Industrial 'Decline', 1870–1970*, Cambridge:

Cambridge University Press, 1996, p. 4; Sean Glynn and Alan Booth, *Modern Britain: An Economic and Social History*, London: Routledge, 1996, p. 257.

14 Tony Judt, *Postwar: A History of Europe since 1945*, London: Pimlico, 2007, p. 162.

15 Donald Cardwell, *The Organisation of Science in England*, Melbourne: Heinemann, 1957; C. P. Snow, *The Two Cultures: And a Second Look*, Cambridge: Cambridge University Press, 1964; Corelli Barnett, *The Audit of War: The Illusion and Reality of Britain as a Great Nation*, London: Macmillan, 1986; Martin J. Weiner, *English Culture and the Decline of the Industrial Spirit 1850–1980*, Harmondsworth: Penguin, 1985.

16 Nikolaus Pevsner was one who was blind to the change: Paul Crossley, 'Introduction', in Peter Draper (ed.), *Reassessing Nikolaus Pevsner*, London: Ashgate, 2004, p. 18.

17 Norbert Wiener had found 'the keynote of the second industrial revolution' in new forms of automatisation: Norbert Wiener, *The Human Use of Human Beings: Cybernetics and Society*, Garden City, New York: Doubleday Anchor, 1950, p. 150.

18 Reyner Banham, *Theory and Design in the First Machine Age*, London: Architectural Press, 1960, p. 12.

19 Banham, *Theory and Design*, pp. 9–10. Banham's analysis and periodisation are similar to Ernest Mandel's, even if for Mandel the mid-twentieth century revolution in technology is the third in a sequence (the other two being in the mid-nineteenth century and at the turn of the century): Frederic Jameson, 'Postmodernism, or the Cultural Logic of Late Capitalism', *New Left Review*, 146, July–August 1984, p. 78. As has also been argued by Mike Davis, Mandel's periodisation is better suited to the post-war condition (as described here) than in Jameson's use of it to provide economic context for his theory of a postmodernism dating from around the 1970s onwards: Mike Davis, 'Urban Renaissance and the Spirit of Post-

modernism', *New Left Review*, 151, May–June 1985, pp. 107–8.

20 Ulrich Beck, *Risk Society: Towards a New Modernity*, London: Sage, 1992, p. 10.

21 The classic statement of the renewal of this in the post-war period is Banham's *Theory and Design*, p. 329: 'The architect who proposes to run with technology knows now that he will be in fast company, and that, in order to keep up, he may have to emulate the Futurists and discard his whole load, including the cultural garments by which he is recognised as an architect.'

22 Beck, *Risk Society*, p. 10. The difference in time may be accounted for by the earlier onset of deindustrialisation in Britain, compared to the continental Europe that is Beck's reference point. On post-war Italy see Andrew Leach, 'Continuity in Rupture: Post-Modern Architecture before Architectural Postmodernism', in Mark Crinson and Claire Zimmerman (eds), *Neo-avant-garde and Postmodern: Post-War Architecture in Britain and Beyond*, New Haven and London: Yale University Press, 2010.

23 Ulrich Beck, 'The Reinvention of Politics: Towards a Theory of Reflexive Modernization', in Ulrich Beck, Anthony Giddens and Scott Lash, *Reflexive Modernization: Politics, Tradition and Aesthetics in the Modern Social Order*, Cambridge: Polity, 1994, p. 23.

24 'The more modern a society becomes, the more unintended consequences it produces, and as these become known and acknowledged, they call the foundations of industrial modernization into question': Ulrich Beck, *Democracy without Enemies*, trans. Mark Ritter, Cambridge: Polity, 1998, p. 90.

25 Beck, *Risk Society*, p. 11. See also Beck, Giddens and Lash, *Reflexive Modernization*. For Beck on Koolhaas see his essay, 'The Open City: Architecture in Reflexive Modernity', in Beck, *Democracy*, especially p. 117. On first and second modernity see Ulrich Beck and Johannes Willms, *Conversations*

with Ulrich Beck, Cambridge: Polity, 2004, pp. 27–33.

26 Civil building remained under wartime controls until as late as November 1954.

27 My own university recently demolished its mathematics tower (Scherrer and Hicks, 1968), a homage to the Leicester University Engineering building, as if this was a required part of the university's international, twenty-first-century ambitions.

1 FORMULAS, FREE PLANS AND A PIRANESIAN CITY

1 James Stirling, 'An Architect's Approach to Architecture', *RIBAJ*, 72, May 1965, p. 231.

2 'In the schools at the time, the rightness of modern as against past styles was not even debated; the overpowering logic of modern architecture was completely accepted and the pioneering stage was over': James Stirling, 'Influence of Corb on Me Now and When a Student', in Mark Crinson (ed.), *James Stirling: Unpublished Early Writings on Architecture*, London: Routledge, 2009, pp. 74–75.

3 Stirling, 'An Architect's Approach', p. 231.

4 Mark Girouard, *Big Jim: The Life and Work of James Stirling*, London: Pimlico, 2000.

5 Stirling quoted ibid., p. 13.

6 Ibid., p. 26.

7 And this despite training many of the leading members of the second generation of modernists such as Maxwell Fry, William Holford, and Stirrat and Percy Johnson-Marshall.

8 Robert Maxwell, correspondence with the author, 5 September 2008. This perhaps was more of a perceived fustiness in Velarde's person than a real one in his buildings – he managed to combine modernist simplicity with early Christian planning in many of his church designs.

9 Gordon Cherry and Leith Penny, *Holford: A Study in Architecture, Planning and Civic Design*, London and New York: Mansell, 1990, p. 135.

10 Two of Stirling's fellow students have attested to his strong impact: Robert Maxwell, interview with the author, 8 December 2006; Robin Dunn, interview with the author, 26 June 2007. It was probably Eden who took Stirling on a group visit to Bath in 1947: Girouard, *Big Jim*, p. 37.

11 University of Liverpool Archives, S.3173.

12 James Stirling, lecture notes, undated but probably *c*.1959: CCA DR2007:0083.

13 *Architects' Journal*, 100, 6 July 1944, p. 100.

14 Robert Maxwell, correspondence with the author, 5 September 2008.

15 Boleslaw Szmidt (ed.), *The Polish School of Architecture 1942–1945*, Liverpool: University of Liverpool, 1945, p. v; Roman Soltynski, *Glimpses of Polish Architecture*, London: Standard Art Book, *c*.1944, pp. 7, 38.

16 Colin Rowe, 'James Stirling: A Highly Personal and Very Disjointed Memoir', in Peter Arnell and Ted Bickford (eds), *James Stirling: Buildings and Projects*, New York: Rizzoli, 1984, p. 13.

17 Interview with Christopher Owtram, Mark Girouard Collection.

18 Robert Maxwell, interview with the author, 8 December 2006.

19 Lady Stirling Collection.

20 *Prospectus of the Liverpool School of Architecture 1945–46*, Liverpool: University of Liverpool, 1945, p. 4.

21 Ibid.

22 Ibid.

23 Colin Rowe, review of Talbot Hamlin, *Forms and Functions of Twentieth Century Architecture*, in *Art Bulletin*, 35, June 1953, p. 170.

24 Ibid., p. 172.

25 See also Reyner Banham's summary of Gaudet's theory in his *Theory and Design in the First Machine Age*, London: Architectural Press, 1960, pp. 14–22.

26 Rowe, review, p. 170.

27 Ibid.

28 Ibid., p. 172.

29 James Stirling, 'Beaux-Arts Reflections', *Architectural Design*, 48, 1978, p. 88.

30 James Stirling, 'Architectural Aims and Influences', *RIBAJ*, 87, September 1980, p. 36.

31 University of Liverpool Archives, S.3625, S.3632.

32 Stirling, 'Architectural Aims', p. 36.

33 University of Liverpool Archives, S.3639.

34 It gained the best mark for this project, with 200 out of a possible 250 marks: University of Liverpool Archives, S.3173.

35 These were being published in the architectural press from 1947 onwards: Andrew Saint, *Towards a Social Architecture: The Role of School Building in Post-War England*, New Haven and London: Yale University Press, 1987, p. 257, n. 75.

36 This was awarded a mark of 175 out of 250: University of Liverpool Archives, S.3173.

37 Another drawing in the CCA – AP140.S1.SS1. D11.P1.2 – shows two courtyard façades for the fashion house as well as what appear to be alternative elevation treatments for the two outer (south and east) façades. These use juxtaposed grids of different scales while still having the same hectic variety in the elevations.

38 This gained a mark of only 80 out of a possible 200 marks: University of Liverpool Archives, S.3173.

39 Lionel Budden, 'The Liverpool School of Architecture', *The Liverpolitan*, 16:11, November 1951, p. 10.

40 Stirling, 'Beaux-Arts', p. 88.

41 Girouard, *Big Jim*, p. 46.

42 Jennifer Kron, 'To Further the Advancement of Learning: A History of the Harvey S. Firestone Memorial Library', http://etcweb.princeton.edu/CampusWWW/Studentdocs/Firestone.html (accessed 14 October 2008).

43 This and the following quotations in this paragraph are all from a letter Stirling wrote to 'Robin, Al, Pat etc', *c.* 18 September 1948, Mark Girouard Collection.

44 Dominic Sandbrook, *Never Had It So Good: A History of Britain from Suez to the Beatles*, London: Abacus, 2006, p. 135.

45 As Girouard has pointed out, the George Washington Bridge was also admired by Le Corbusier in the book that Stirling had acquired just before leaving for New York, *When the Cathedrals Were White*: Girouard, *Big Jim*, p. 45. See also Colin Rowe, 'Eulogy: Jim Stirling', *As I Was Saying: Recollections and Miscellaneous Essays*, 3 vols, Cambridge, Mass.: MIT Press, 1996, vol. 3, p. 344.

46 Stirling letter to 'Robin, Al, Pat etc', *c.* 18 September 1948, Mark Girouard Collection.

47 John Jacobus, 'Introduction', in James Stirling, *James Stirling: Buildings and Projects 1950–1974*, London: Thames and Hudson, 1975, p. 15. Stirling later (around 1990) claimed also to have visited San Francisco, Los Angeles and Chicago during his stay: James Stirling, 'Statement', in David Robbins (ed.), *The Independent Group: Postwar Britain and the Aesthetics of Plenty*, Cambridge, Mass.: MIT Press, 1990, p. 195. There is, however, no evidence of this and it is quite possible – from Stirling's claim to have visited the Eames house, which wasn't finished until late 1949 – that in his memory he was transposing two visits.

48 University of Liverpool Archives, S.3173. Other fourth-year projects included a restaurant façade and a setting for *The Shape of Things to Come*: University of Liverpool Archives, S.3645.

49 Colin Rowe, 'The Mathematics of the Ideal Villa: Palladio and Le Corbusier Compared', *Architectural Review*, 101, March 1947, pp. 101–4.

50 The links between Liverpool students and Wittkower would be worth exploring in their own right. Bob Maxwell met him as part of his research for his 1948–49 thesis on a new Warburg Institute. Sam Stevens and Robin Dunn were two other students who knew Wittkower personally: Robin Dunn, interview with the author, 26 June 2007.

51 On this see also Anthony Vidler, *Histories of the Immediate Present: Inventing Architec-*

tural Modernism, Cambridge, Mass.: MIT Press, 2008, pp. 62–63.

52 See Irena Murray and Julian Osley (eds), *Le Corbusier and Britain: An Anthology*, London: Routledge, 2008.

53 Rowe, 'Mathematics', p. 104.

54 Ibid.

55 Colin Rowe, 'Mannerism and Modern Architecture', *Architectural Review*, 107, May 1950, pp. 289–300.

56 Ibid., p. 290.

57 The journal kept by Stirling in the mid-1950s makes it clear that he had read the article: James Stirling, 'Black Notebook', in Crinson (ed.), *James Stirling*, p. 38.

58 Rowe, review, p. 170.

59 Ibid., p. 171.

60 Ibid., p. 173.

61 Ibid.

62 Ibid., p. 174.

63 Robert Maxwell, interview with the author, 8 December 2006.

64 Robert Maxwell, 'James Stirling: Writings', in Robert Maxwell (ed.), *James Stirling: Writings on Architecture*, Milan: Skira, 1998, pp. 8–9.

65 Robert Maxwell, *James Stirling Michael Wilford*, Basel: Birkhäuser, 1998, p. 7.

66 Stirling, 'Architectural Aims', p. 36.

67 Maxwell (ed.), 'James Stirling: Writings', p. 9.

68 Stirling to 'Robin, Al, Pat etc', *c.* 18 September 1948, Mark Girouard Collection.

69 Rowe, 'Mannerism', pp. 290–91.

70 Rowe, 'James Stirling', p. 12.

71 Robert Maxwell, correspondence with the author, 5 September 2008. Contrast this with the case of Gordon Stephenson in the 1930s. Stephenson worked in Le Corbusier's office between 1930 and 1932 and when he came to teach at Liverpool in the mid-1930s certainly encouraged his students to work in a Corbusian manner: Gordon Stephenson, *On a Human Scale: A Life in Civic Design*, South Fremantle: Fremantle Arts Centre, 1992, pp. 29–44.

72 Both F. R. S. Yorke and Richard Sheppard were promoting modernism in the early 1940s: Robin Dunn, correspondence with the author, 22 September 2008.

73 Robin Dunn, correspondence with the author, 22 September 2008.

74 Stirling, 'Influence of Corb', p. 75.

75 Robert Maxwell, interview with the author, 8 December 2006.

76 Stirling, 'Influence of Corb', p. 75.

77 Ibid.

78 Rowe, 'James Stirling', p. 16.

79 Liverpool School of Architecture thesis titles, University of Liverpool Archives.

80 David Thistlewood, 'Modernism with Ancestry', *Architects' Journal*, 141, 11 May 1995, p. 64.

81 F. J. Osborn and A. Whittick, *The New Towns: The Answer to Megalopolis*, Cambridge, MA.: MIT Press, 1963, p. 279.

82 Eden's approach can be seen in the series of articles he published on 'The English Tradition in the Countryside', *Architectural Review*, 77, March, April and May 1935, pp. 87–94, 142–52 and 193–202.

83 James Stirling, Thesis, University of Liverpool, 1950, p. 34: CCA DR2000:0042:002:003:001–007.

84 Whether he actually visited France during work on his thesis is open to some doubt. He may have visited Paris in the summer of 1947, and he certainly visited Paris and the south of France in the summer of 1950, but this would have been after his thesis was submitted: Girouard, *Big Jim*, pp. 38, 47.

85 These visits and readings are listed in Stirling, Thesis, pp. 34, 72.

86 Ibid., p. 11.

87 Ibid., p. 7.

88 Ibid., p. 24.

89 Two such drawings are reproduced in Anthony Vidler, *James Frazer Stirling: Notes from the Archive*, Montreal, New Haven and London: CCA, YCBA and Yale University Press, 2010, p. 48.

90 Le Corbusier, *Towards a New Architecture*, trans. F. Etchells, London: John Rodker, 1931, p. 43.

91 Stirling, Thesis, p. 22.

92 Ibid., p. 29.

93 Ibid., p. 46.

94 CCA DR2000:0042:002:004:001–014.

95 By the late 1950s Stirling was dismissing this kind of 'formalised patterning of elevations' as 'one of the clichés of our time': Stirling, 'Influence of Corb', p. 76.

96 Rowe saw more of Mies's library and administration building at Illinois Institute of Technology and Charles Eames in these elevations than Le Corbusier: Rowe, 'James Stirling', p. 19.

97 CCA DR2000:0042:002:006–009.

98 Stirling, Thesis, pp. 21–22.

99 See Vidler, *James Frazer Stirling*, pp. 67–68.

100 Stirling, 'An Architect's Approach', p. 231.

101 Ibid.

102 Rowe, 'Mannerism', p. 297.

103 See John Allan, *Berthold Lubetkin: Architecture and the Tradition of Progress*, London: RIBA, 1992, pp. 449–520.

104 *Prospectus of the Liverpool School*, p. 4. The Diploma was certainly no bar to future success. Another architect who only received a Diploma was Percy Johnson-Marshall, one of the major architect-planners of the post-war scene.

105 University of Liverpool Archives, S.3173.

106 Ibid.

107 Typed sheet titled 'Aesthetics of Structural Form' dated 1950 – this is Stirling's 'thesis statement': CCA DRCON2000:0027:003:001–007.

108 Robert Maxwell, interview with the author, 8 December 2006. Reilly had encouraged students to study Liverpool's neoclassical civic buildings, but it is unclear how much this continued in the post-war years.

109 'Play around docks', he wrote in some lecture notes from 1959–60: James Stirling, 'Notes for a Lecture', in Crinson (ed.), *James Stirling*, p. 59. Later he commented, 'A lot of my

visits with my father involved playing around the dockland. . . . my friends and I would play around [the Albert Dock]': *James Stirling*, video directed by Michael Blackwood, Michael Blackwood Productions, 1987. The latter is also the source of the 'magical places . . . huge objects' quotation.

110 Stirling, 'Notes for a Lecture', p. 69. In the same notes he also compared it to 'New York '80s – Joyce's Dublin': Ibid.

111 Murray Fraser and Joe Kerr, *Architecture and the 'Special Relationship': The American Influence on Post-War British Architecture*, London and New York: Routledge, 2008, pp. 72–73.

112 Quoted in Lionel Esher, *A Broken Wave: The Rebuilding of England 1940–1980*, Harmondsworth: Penguin, 1981, p. 223.

113 Francis E. Hyde, *Liverpool and the Mersey: An Economic History of a Port 1700–1970*, Newton Abbot: David & Charles, 1971, p. 160.

114 Liverpool Public Relations Office, *Liverpool Builds 1945–65*, Liverpool: City and County Borough of Liverpool, 1967, p. 17.

115 Hyde, *Liverpool*, p. 197.

116 Rowe, 'James Stirling', p. 10.

117 Ibid.

118 Stirling, 'Black Notebook', p. 56.

119 Stirling's views, written in the mid-1950s, were ambivalent (ibid.): 'this area remains intact but may shortly be pulled down to make way for neo-Edwardiana, which is filling the bombed site on the old street pattern, thus the crime which arrested the development of the style is carrying on today – to our personal shame.' The real regret here seems to be not allowing modern buildings (the development of the 'St Louis style' as he saw it) but preferring 'neo-Edwardiana'.

120 Ibid.

121 Permit from the Mersey Docks and Harbour Board dated 9 June 1961: CCA DR2006:0022: Stirling I–II.

122 CCA DR2000:042:027:683.

123   CCA DR2000:042:002:006.

124   Stirling later acquired two copies of Quentin Hughes's *Seaport* (1964), which describes Liverpool's architecture in just these terms.

125   I am grateful to Joseph Sharples for information on the buildings in all three of these photographs.

126   Several of these images were later reproduced in Stirling's 1957 article on 'Regionalism and Modern Architecture' and probably used in many lectures: James Stirling, 'Regionalism and Modern Architecture', *Architects' Year Book 8*, London: Elek Books, 1957, p. 64. Another image of the Harrington Street building appears in James Stirling, '"The Functional Tradition" and Expression', *Perspecta*, 6, 1959, p. 90.

127   CCA DR2006:0022, DR2000:042:027:683. Also, undated slides in Lady Stirling Collection.

128   He noted in his journal around 1954, 'buried in Wallasey cemetery left £70,000 when he died. These are the only buildings he put up? Otherwise he has a patent recorder invented or patented? A type of lift (Paternoster?). Invented a pistol type. Is this the first building to get away from considerations of composition, elements, principal motives? More information on Peter Ellis – he committed suicide (as a result of not being able to clean the windows of Oriel Chambers!). He was a pupil of Paxton': Stirling, 'Black Notebook', p. 56.

129   Joseph Sharples, *Liverpool*, New Haven and London: Yale University Press, 2004, p. 171.

130   Stirling, 'Architectural Aims', p. 36.

131   'I think it is without doubt that a certain number of students at Liverpool during the late forties and very early fifties did feel themselves to be, in some quite important way, avant garde; and I believe that I myself probably did have something to do with crystallising this position': Colin Rowe, quoted in Jacobus, 'Introduction', p. 14.

2   THIRD GENERATION

1   James Gowan, interview with the author, 4 September 2006. See also Sir Philip Powell, '"No visible means of support": Skylon and the South Bank', in Elain Harwood and Alan Powers (eds), *Festival of Britain*, Twentieth Century Architecture 5, London: Twentieth Century Society, 2001, pp. 83–86.

2   John Summerson, 'Introduction', in Arts Council, *'45–55: Ten Years of British Architecture*, London: Arts Council, 1955, p. 6.

3   Nicholas Bullock, *Building the Post-War World: Modern Architecture and Reconstruction in Britain*, London: Routledge, 2002, p. 281.

4   Summerson, 'Introduction', p. 5.

5   See John Summerson, 'South Bank Postscript', *New Statesman and Nation*, 42, 6 October 1951, pp. 363–64.

6   For more on the characteristics of this third generation see Philip Drew, *Third Generation: The Changing Meaning of Architecture*, London: Pall Mall Press, 1972.

7   James Stirling, 'An Architect's Approach to Architecture', *RIBAJ*, 72, May 1965, p. 231. 'Festivalia' became a term of abuse for Stirling. He used it to disparage certain details in Le Corbusier's chapel at Ronchamp, for instance: James Stirling, 'Ronchamp: Le Corbusier's Chapel and the Crisis of Rationalism', *Architectural Review*, 119, March 1956, p. 156.

8   Colin Rowe, 'James Stirling: A Highly Personal and Very Disjointed Memoir', in Peter Arnell and Ted Bickford (eds), *James Stirling: Buildings and Projects*, New York: Rizzoli, 1984, p. 16.

9   Reyner Banham, 'The Style: "Flimsy . . . Effeminate"?', in Mary Banham and Bevis Hillier (eds), *A Tonic to the Nation: The Festival of Britain 1951*, London: Thames and Hudson, 1976, pp. 190–98.

10   Colin St John Wilson, 'The Vertical City', *The Observer*, 17 February 1952, reprinted in Irena Murray and Julian Osley (eds), *Le Corbusier*

and *Britain: An Anthology*, London: Rout-ledge, 2008, pp. 170–72.

11 James Gowan, interview with the author, 4 September 2006.

12 Alan Powers, 'The Expression of Levity', in Harwood and Powers (eds), *Festival of Britain*, pp. 49–56.

13 James Gowan, interview with the author, 4 September 2006.

14 James Gowan, interview with the author, 30 October 2008.

15 Alan Powers, 'Edwardian Architectural Education: A Study of Three Schools of Architecture', *Architectural Association Files*, January 1984, pp. 56–59; Robert Proctor, 'Tradition and Evolution: Glasgow School of Architecture under Eugène Bourdon', in Ray McKenzie (ed.), *The Flower and the Green Leaf: Glasgow School of Architecture in the Time of Charles Rennie Mackintosh*, Edinburgh: Luath Press, 2009, pp. 80–94.

16 Ellis Woodman, *Modernity and Reinvention: The Architecture of James Gowan*, London: Black Dog, 2008, p. 168.

17 In fact, this shared arrangement had existed ever since the establishment of the school in 1903.

18 Proctor, 'Tradition and Evolution', p. 87. However, see also Proctor's comments on the destination of most Glasgow students: ibid., p. 91.

19 James Gowan, *Style and Configuration*, London: Academy Editions, 1994, p. 8. There had long been a suspicion that the Glasgow Institute of Architects only wanted 'a system for training cheap labour to run the local offices': correspondence of 18 and 19 May 1934 in Papers of Joint Committee on the Glasgow School of Architecture, Strathclyde University Archives.

20 Woodman, *Modernity*, p. 168. Gowan's marks show that he particularly excelled in architectural history and in design projects: Glasgow School of Art, student records. But the school was not as entirely sealed off from modernism as later memories would indi-

cate. J. M. Richards lectured there in 1941 on 'Modern Architecture and the Future', and occasional studio subjects picked up on contemporary interests such as pithead baths: see Report of the Governors for the Session 1940–41, and *Glasgow School Art Calendar 1942–1943*, both in the Glasgow School of Art Archives and Collections.

21 James Gowan, interview with the author, 30 October 2008.

22 *Glasgow School of Art Calendar 1940–1941*, Glasgow School of Art Archives and Collections.

23 Gowan, *Style*, p. 62.

24 James Gowan, 'Post War', *RIBAJ*, 72, October 1965, p. 499. Stirling had written, 'end of a war is always the start of something, we returned from war as students to the schools of architecture. The cities were bombed and devastated, from now on everything could only get better': James Stirling, 'Influence of Corb on Me Now and When a Student', in Mark Crinson (ed.), *James Stirling: Unpublished Early Writings on Architecture*, London: Routledge, 2009, p. 74.

25 Gowan, 'Post War', p. 499.

26 Ibid.

27 Ibid.

28 Ibid.

29 Ibid.

30 Gowan, *Style*, p. 40.

31 Ibid., p. 8.

32 Charles Reilly even compared Kingston's break with the past with his own reform of Liverpool four decades before into a Beaux-Arts school: *Architect and Building News*, 198, 25 July 1947, p. 67. Gowan was recommended to go there by an assistant in the office of Brian O'Rorke, where he was then working, who spoke dismissively of the AA's post-war chaos: James Gowan, interview with the author, 30 October 2008.

33 James Gowan, interview with the author, 30 October 2008.

34 Ibid.

35 Ibid.

36 James Gowan, interview with the author, 4 September 2006.

37 Neither partner had served in the armed forces, which may have helped with their immediate post-war success.

38 Woodman, *Modernity*, p. 169.

39 James Gowan, interview with the author, 9 February 2010.

40 James Gowan, interview with the author, 4 September 2006 and 9 February 2010.

41 Woodman, *Modernity*, p. 171.

42 Quoted in Stan Allen and Hal Foster, 'A Conversation with Kenneth Frampton', *October*, 106, Fall 2003, p. 48.

43 Woodman, *Modernity*, p. 171.

44 'A Report on the Designs for a Medical School', *Architects' Journal*, 113, 15 February 1951, pp. 208–9. Also mentioned in this review is an entry in an anglicised Corbusian mode by a partnership including Robert Maxwell, Douglas Stephens and Alan Colquhoun.

45 The first stage of Stirling's Runcorn New Town Housing (1967–76), for instance.

46 *Architects' Journal*, 114, 6 December 1951, pp. 673–82.

47 The only image that survives of this scheme is the one reproduced in Arthur Korn, 'The Work of James Stirling and James Gowan', *Architect and Building News*, 215, 7 January 1959, p. 9. In this article Gowan's Poole design is reproduced on the same page as Stirling's entry for the Sheffield University competition, with no indication that both schemes were produced before the partnership was formed, each with different partners.

48 *James Stirling*, video directed by Michael Blackwood, Michael Blackwood Productions, 1987.

49 RIBA Archives, TyJ/6/5. The school had previously been part of the AA.

50 Jacqueline Tyrwhitt, 'School of Planning: An Account of its History, Aims and Objectives and Proposals for Future Development', RIBA Archives, TyJ/6/2.

51 Lecture notes, probably from late 1950s: CCA DR2007:0083.

52 'Conversation between Alvin Boyarsky, James Stirling, Alan Forsyth and David Gray', in Alan Forsyth and David Gray (eds), *Lyons Israel Ellis Gray: Buildings and Projects 1932–1983*, London: Architectural Association, 1988, p. 204. He was listed on the register of members of the APRR in 1952: RIBA Archives, TyJ/6/7.

53 Stirling, 'An Architect's Approach', p. 231.

54 It may have been inspired by the hexagonal pattern of housing of the Gröndal Estate near Stockholm (Backström and Reinius, 1944–45), a neo-realist scheme well known at that time in Britain and one of the sources for the so-called 'New Empiricism' that Stirling would soon join other young modernists in opposing.

55 CCA DR2000:0042:001:005.

56 Lecture notes, probably from late 1950s: CCA DR2007:0083.

57 Robin Dunn, interview with the author, 26 June 2007.

58 Sarah Menin and Stephen Kite, *An Architecture of Invitation: Colin St John Wilson*, London: Ashgate, 2005, pp. 32–34.

59 For a later rationalisation of this see 'Stirling Stuff: Conversation with Sunand Prasad and Satish Grover' (1987), in Robert Maxwell (ed.), *James Stirling: Writings on Architecture*, Milan: Skira, 1998, p. 234.

60 Bullock, *Building the Post-War World*, particularly chapter 11; John Gold, *The Practice of Modernism: Modern Architects and Urban Transformation, 1954–1972*, London: Routledge, 2007, particularly chapter 3.

61 See Stephen Kite, '"Softs" and "Hards": Colin St John Wilson and the Contested Visions of 1950s London', in Mark Crinson and Claire Zimmerman (eds), *Neo-avant-garde and Postmodern: Postwar Architecture in Britain and Beyond*, New Haven and London: Yale University Press, 2010.

62 'Mainstream modernism' is Reyner Banham's term: Reyner Banham, *The New Bru-

talism: Ethic or Aesthetic?, London: Architectural Press, 1966, p. 41.

63 John Baker, correspondence with Claire Zimmerman, 31 July 2007.

64 'South Africa Travel Centre', *Architectural Design*, 22, March 1952, pp. 82–87; 'South Africa Travel Centre, Piccadilly', *Architectural Review*, February 1951, pp. 108–9.

65 Lim Chong Keat, correspondence with the author, 1 August 2007.

66 CCA DR2000:007:002:001–002.

67 John Baker, correspondence with Claire Zimmerman, 31 July 2007.

68 There have, for instance, been suggestions that Stirling helped detail the practice's building for Sheffield Technical College, a commission it was given on the back of its successful entry to the Sheffield University competition. Design for this project did not start until 1954, by which time Stirling had already left the practice. However, Stirling listed 'Sheffield Technical College, first stage and workshops' on the curriculum vitae he provided for Leicester University in 1959: Leicester University Archives, EST/BUI/ ENG/13/5.

69 This was at the time of his APRR course, contradicting his later statement that it was *after* the course that he 'did a series of competitions': Stirling, 'An Architect's Approach', p. 231.

70 CCA DR2000:0042:008:005.

71 Ibid.

72 Stirling, 'An Architect's Approach', p. 231.

73 For instance, from notes for a lecture given probably in 1959, 'Very specific Cubist type space – for millionaires' houses. Uneconomical in terms of £s per square foot. Will not persist in housing': Stirling 'Influence of Corb', p. 75.

74 These may be there to help give what Stirling hoped would be a 'technical' appearance, rather than the appearance of a university or school: CCA DR2000:0042:008:005.

75 Ibid.

76 Tony Judt, *Postwar: A History of Europe Since 1945*, London: Pimlico, 2007, p. 162. For a typical editorial on how this affected the building industry see *Architect and Building News*, 203, 8 January 1953, p. 2.

77 The seminal articulation of this was Siegfried Giedion's *Space, Time and Architecture: The Growth of a New Tradition*, Cambridge Mass.: Harvard University Press, 1941.

78 Stirling also found justification for this in the modernists themselves, 'Corb never has implied an advanced technology or even change': Stirling, 'Influence of Corb', p. 75. This will be explored further in the next chapter.

79 Sheffield University Administrative Archives, Sheffield University Competition, Box 2, Dr Lodge file.

80 *Architects' Journal*, 118, 26 November 1953, p. 652; Sheffield University Administrative Archives, Sheffield University Competition, Box 4, Building Committee Minutes.

81 James Stirling to Le Corbusier, 18 June 1955; Le Corbusier to James Stirling, 22 June 1955: Fondation Le Corbusier, Paris. Le Corbusier refused.

82 Stirling's notes on a draft of Colin Rowe's introductory text for the Arnell and Bickford edited *James Stirling: Buildings and Projects*: CCA DRCON2000:0027:720. There is a puzzle concerning Cordingley's involvement. Prospective competitors were asked during the competition period whether they would be entering, and Cordingley indicated that it was 'unlikely' that he would. When Stirling submitted his entry, there was no mention of Cordingley in it, and he certified, as all competitors were required to, that his drawings were his own: Sheffield University Administrative Archives, Sheffield University Competition, Box 4.

83 James Stirling, 'Black Notebook', in Crinson (ed.), *James Stirling*, p. 25.

84 Report on Sheffield entry: CCA DRCON 2000:0027:720.

85   Stirling, 'Black Notebook', p. 24. There are, of course, many possible sources for this link to St Mark's but perhaps the most pertinent in terms of a modernist re-evaluation of the Piazza San Marco is the reported discussion at the session 'Discussion on Italian Piazzas' at CIAM 8 in 1951: see J. Tyrwhitt, J. L. Sert and E. N. Rogers (eds), *The Heart of the City: Towards the Humanisation of Urban Life*, New York: Pelligrini and Cudahy, 1952. Vidler has also pointed to Ralph Tubbs's 'Heart of the City' plan from his *Living in Cities* (Harmondsworth: Penguin, 1942): Anthony Vidler, *James Frazer Stirling: Notes from the Archive*, Montreal, New Haven and London: CCA, YCBA and Yale University Press, 2010, pp. 87 and 91.

86   Stirling, 'Black Notebook', p. 25.

87   Ibid.

88   Ibid.

89   Ibid., p. 35. He continues, 'although Seaton Delaval and Archer's Westminster church have burnt out innards and damaged exteriors, they are such dominating and powerful designs that they are today still two of the most magnificent buildings.' This was written around 1953–54.

90   Although Colin Rowe described the Shef-field design as 'an exceptional urbanistic statement of which the implications are still not yet resumed', and he recognised a preoccupation with 'the idea of Piazza San Marco': Rowe, 'James Stirling', pp. 13, 25.

91   Bullock has remarked on Stirling's '"take it or leave it" comments on the . . . "aggressive" forms of the building': Bullock, *Building the Post-War World*, p. 122. However, these comments were written some twenty years later and for a very different audience: James Stirling, *James Stirling: Buildings and Projects 1950–1974*, London: Thames and Hudson, 1975, p. 28. Colin Rowe suggested that 'such a piece is inherently incapable of enclosing space. . . . a *Zeilenbau* piece is inherently insular and . . . for this reason, it can never serve to discriminate spatial realms

of different value': Rowe, 'James Stirling', p. 25. However, the Arts and Administration block would have extended right from the line of the main street to another street at the far north end of the campus – it was more like a terrace or boundary wall than an insular *Zeilenbau*.

92   For a manifesto statement of this see J. M. Richards, Nikolaus Pevsner, Osbert Lancaster and Hubert de Cronin Hastings, 'Editorial', *Architectural Review*, 101, January 1947, p. 36.

93   Another possible source is the repeated blank balcony walls in the GAMMA housing blocks known as the *cité verticale*, shown at CIAM in 1953, and of which – as Chapter Three will show – Stirling was almost certainly aware.

94   This has also recently been suggested by James Gowan: Woodman, *Modernity*, p. 202.

95   Examples of neo-Palladian plans include the Smithsons' entry for the Coventry Cathedral competition (1951) and John Voelcker's designs for electrical engineering stations. For the latter see Banham, *The New Brutalism*, p. 15.

96   Colin Rowe, 'Mannerism and Modern Architecture', *Architectural Review*, 107, May 1950, pp. 290–91.

97   Ibid., p. 292.

98   Ibid., p. 290.

99   Ibid., p. 299.

100   Stirling, 'Influence of Corb', p. 77.

101   CCA DR2000:0042:010:003:001–002.

102   Angelo Dell'Aquila, 'Soccorso agli Inglesi', *Spazio*, 2, August 1950, p. 90.

103   Mark Girouard, *Big Jim: The Life and Work of James Stirling*, London: Pimlico, 2000, p. 73; Robin Dunn, interview with the author, 26 June 2007. Reyner Banham had recently published on Moretti's architecture: Reyner Banham, 'Casa Del Girasole: Rationalism and Eclecticism in Italian Architecture', *Architectural Review*, 113, February 1953, pp. 73–77. Paul Manousso, another friend of

Stirling's, had met Moretti: interview with Paul Manousso, Mark Girouard Gollection.

104   Luigi Moretti, 'Strutture e sequenze di spazi', *Spazio*, 7, December 1952–April 1953, pp. 9–20.

105   Stirling, 'An Architect's Approach', p. 231.

106   Ibid.

107   Ibid., p. 232.

108   Another example of this was Stirling's tendency in later lectures to pair an image of the Art and Administration building with a picture of a section through a cylinder: see, for instance, 'Jim the Great', *Casabella*, 399, 1975, p. 22.

109   There is a sketch for this drawing which has been claimed as contemporary with the competition. I see no evidence for this; indeed, it seems more likely to be a sketch for the Krier drawing: Vidler, *James Frazer Stirling*, p. 88.

110   For the winning designs see *Architects' Journal*, 118, 10 December 1953, pp. 718–24.

111   James Stirling, letter to secretary of Sheffield University Competition, 14 September 1953: Sheffield University Administrative Archives, Sheffield University Competition, Box 3, Competition Correspondence.

112   This is clear from the letter of 14 September: ibid.

113   Sheffield University Administrative Archives, Sheffield University Competition, Box 4, Building Committee Minutes.

114   Secretary of the Sheffield University Competition, letter to James Stirling, 23 September 1953: Sheffield University Administrative Archives, Sheffield University Competition, Box 3, Competition Correspondence.

115   James Gowan, interview with the author, 30 October 2008.

116   Alan Colquhoun, 'A Note on the Office of Lyons Israel Ellis', in Forsyth and Gray (eds), *Lyons Israel Ellis*, p. 93.

117   David Gray, 'Lyons Israel Ellis: Three Partners', in Forsyth and Gray (eds), *Lyons Israel Ellis*, p. 48.

118   John Miller, quoted in Forsyth and Gray (eds), *Lyons Israel Ellis*, p. 107.

119   Alan Colquhoun, quoted in Forsyth and Gray (eds), *Lyons Israel Ellis*, p. 108.

120   This and the preceding points on design are drawn from Neave Brown, 'Lyons Israel Lyons Israel Ellis Lyons Israel Ellis Gray' in Forsyth and Gray (eds), *Lyons Israel Ellis*, pp. 11–12.

121   Neave Brown, quoted in Forsyth and Gray (eds), *Lyons Israel Ellis*, p. 107. Stirling described a similar process in his own work at the time: 'Valuation of the functional and sociological importance of the various elements. Conception arising from a partly intuitive perception of the plastic potentialities inherent in the accommodation (and circulation). Intellectual selection of elements into a hierarchy striving to an architectural integration expressing a series of inventions': Stirling, 'Black Notebook', p. 28.

122   See *Architectural Design*, 29, January 1959, pp. 22–23.

123   Brown, 'Lyons Israel Lyons', p. 12.

124   James Gowan, interview with the author, 30 October 2008. See also Girouard, *Big Jim*, p. 87. Tom Ellis's son has written, 'I remember Jim and my father coming home for dinner and afterwards the two of them excitedly poring over the latest volume of Corb's *Oeuvre complète* analysing the plans and sections like Talmudic scholars': John Ellis, correspondence with author, 14 May 2009.

125   'Conversation between Alvin Boyarsky, James Stirling, Alan Forsyth and David Gray', in Forsyth and Gray (eds); *Lyons Israel Ellis*, p. 204.

126   Colin Rowe, 'The Mathematics of the Ideal Villa: Palladio and Le Corbusier Compared', *Architectural Review*, 101, March 1947, p. 104.

127   Robert Maxwell, correspondence with the author, 3 February 2008; drawing in CCA 140–0415. According to Maxwell it was he who recommended Stirling to Creed and

Stirling produced the design over two weeks of evening work.

128   It was Robert Maxwell who made these alterations, simplifying the one- and two-bed flats so that they read as one episode: Robert Maxwell, correspondence with the author, 3 February 2008.

129   For a discussion of the early impact of the *Unité* on public housing in Britain see Bullock, *Building the Post-War World*, pp. 102–6.

3   JUNK, BUNK AND TOMORROW

1   He was a subscriber between 1944 and 1949: Lady Stirling Collection.

2   Mark Girouard, *Big Jim: The Life and Work of James Stirling*, London: Pimlico, 2000; Jeremy Lewis, *Cyril Connolly: A Life*, London: Pimlico, 1998.

3   'Frequently I awake in the morning and wonder how is it that I can be an architect and an Englishman at the same time, particularly a modern architect. Since the crystallisation of the modern movement around about 1920, Britain has not produced one single masterpiece and it must be practically the only European country which has not produced a "great man" or a single building': James Stirling, 'Black Notebook', in Mark Crinson (ed.), *James Stirling: Early Unpublished Writings on Architecture*, London: Routledge, 2009, p. 34.

4   James Stirling, 'Regionalism and Modern Architecture', *Architects' Year Book 8*, London: Paul Elek, 1957, p. 62.

5   Ibid.

6   Ibid.

7   The term 'une architecture autre' was used in 1955 by Reyner Banham with these connections in mind: Reyner Banham, 'The New Brutalism', *Architectural Review*, 118, December 1955, pp. 355–61.

8   Manfredo Tafuri, 'L'Architecture dans le Boudoir: The Language of Criticism and the Criticism of Language', *Oppositions*, 3, 1974,

republished in K. Michael Hays (ed.), *Architecture Theory since 1968*, Cambridge, Mass.: MIT Press, 2000, p. 149.

9   Harold Bloom, *The Anxiety of Influence: A Theory of Poetry*, New York: Oxford University Press, 1973.

10   Stirling, 'Black Notebook', p. 18.

11   Ibid., p. 19.

12   Published in Alison and Peter Smithson, *The Charged Void: Architecture*, New York: Monacelli, 2001, p. 108.

13   Stirling, 'Black Notebook', p. 21.

14   Ibid.

15   Ibid.

16   Ibid.

17   Ibid.

18   Ibid., p. 22.

19   Ibid.

20   'Usually manifesting itself as a structural system or circulation effect. This approach would be legitimate where the accommodation was actually only one element, or one element dominating a number of minors ie Smithsons' Coventry Cathedral (structural), Entwistle Crystal Palace (circulation)': ibid., p. 26.

21   Ibid., pp. 22–23.

22   Ibid., p. 31.

23   See Nigel Whiteley, *Reyner Banham: Historian of the Immediate Future*, Cambridge, Mass.: MIT Press, 2002, p. 39

24   Stirling, 'Black Notebook', p. 33.

25   Ibid., p. 37.

26   Ibid.

27   Ibid., p. 38. There may be some echo here of Ruskin's admiration of 'imperfection' in gothic architecture: 'imperfection is in some sort essential to all that we know of life. It is the sign of life in a mortal body, that is to say, of a state of progress and change. . . . in all things that live there are certain irregularities and deficiencies which are not only signs of life, but sources of beauty': John Ruskin, *Stones of Venice* (1851–53), vol. 2, chapter 6, 'The Nature of Gothic', paragraph XXV.

28 Colin Rowe, 'Mannerism and Modern Architecture', *Architectural Review*, 107, May 1950, p. 292.

29 He absorbed these into an account of Moretti's architecture that emphasised its rationalist disciplines and strict control of eclectic elements within a modernist framework: Reyner Banham, 'Casa del Girasole', *Architectural Review*, 113, February 1953, pp. 73–79.

30 Peter Smithson, 'Architect's Own House in Rotterdam, Van den Broek and Bakema', *Architectural Design*, 24, August 1954, p. 228.

31 Stirling, 'Black Notebook', p. 38.

32 James Stirling, 'Ronchamp: Le Corbusier's Chapel and the Crisis of Rationalism', *Architectural Review*, 119, March 1956, p. 160.

33 Girouard, *Big Jim*, p. 77.

34 Mark Girouard, interview with the author, 18 January 2008.

35 Stirling, 'Black Notebook', p. 30.

36 CCA 140–0660.

37 Peter Bürger, *Theory of the Avant-Garde*, Minneapolis: University of Minnesota Press, 1984. See also Hal Foster, *The Return of the Real*, Cambridge, Mass.: MIT Press, 1998, pp. 8–12; Mark Crinson and Claire Zimmerman (eds), *Neo-avant-garde and Postmodern: Postwar Architecture in Britain and Beyond*, New Haven and London: Yale University Press, 2010.

38 See, for instance, John Summerson, 'Introduction', in Arts Council, *'45–55: Ten Years of British Architecture*, London: Arts Council, 1955, p. 10.

39 On the Independent Group see especially Anne Massey, *The Independent Group: Modernism and Mass Culture in Britain, 1945–1959*, Manchester: Manchester University Press, 1995; and David Robbins (ed.), *The Independent Group: Postwar Britain and the Aesthetics of Plenty*, Cambridge, Mass.: MIT Press, 1990.

40 Mary Banham, interview with Mark Girouard: Mark Girouard Collection.

41 Banham quoted in Whiteley, *Reyner Banham*, p. 11.

42 Girouard, *Big Jim*, pp. 50–63, 72.

43 This was in a statement made around 1990: Robbins (ed.), *The Independent Group*, p. 195.

44 Sarah Menin and Stephen Kite, *An Architecture of Invitation: Colin St John Wilson*, London: Ashgate, 2005, p. 35.

45 See Whiteley, *Reyner Banham*, pp. 98–101; Massey, *The Independent Group*, pp. 77–78.

46 John McHale had a fellowship at Yale in 1955. See also Whiteley, *Reyner Banham*, p. 99.

47 Robbins (ed.), *The Independent Group*, pp. 193, 195.

48 Reyner Banham, *Theory and Design in the First Machine Age*, London: Architectural Press, 1960, p. 9.

49 Ibid., pp. 329–30.

50 Ibid.

51 David Mellor, 'A "Glorious Techniculture" in Nineteen-Fifties Britain: The Many Cultural Contexts of the Independent Group', in Robbins (ed.), *The Independent Group*, pp. 229–36.

52 The term 'immaterial labour' has more recent coinage. It is defined as 'labour that produces an immaterial good, such as a service, a cultural product, knowledge, or communication': Michael Hardt and Antonio Negri, *Empire*, Cambridge, Mass. and London: Harvard University Press, 2000, p. 290.

53 Banham, *Theory*, pp. 9–10.

54 Ibid., p. 12.

55 Whiteley, *Reyner Banham*, p. 94.

56 The clients were Hugh and Sue Forsythe and designs are dated October 1955: CCA DR 2000:011:001:001–002 and CCA DR2000:011: 002:001–006.

57 James Stirling, 'A Personal View of the Present Situation', *Architectural Design*, 28, June 1958, p. 233.

58 James Stirling, 'House near Liverpool', *Architectural Design*, 26, July 1956, p. 241.

59   Stirling, 'Black Notebook', pp. 38–41. Like other young avant-gardists, Stirling affected to despise the Scandinavian modernism that was so popular at this time. Yet his brief comments on Danish buildings reveal a different perspective. At their heart, in their treatment of ground and roof, he asserted, contemporary Danish houses were still traditional. And this was no bad thing; in fact what interested him here had repercussions for his own work. Changes of floor levels and exposed timber trusses often echoed each other in Danish houses, by implication offering the flexibility of space and appearance of greater scale that could be found in some of Stirling's neo-vernacular designs at this time.

60   This living space was the subject of one of Leon Krier's elegant mid-1970s drawings in which both its height and length were exaggerated: James Stirling, *James Stirling: Buildings and Projects 1950–1974*, London: Thames and Hudson, 1975, p. 32.

61   Stirling, 'House near Liverpool', p. 241.

62   Stirling, 'Regionalism', p. 62.

63   Stirling said that in the early 1950s he received six commissions for private houses from friends, four of which were 'rejected as being aesthetically substandard', though whether this was by the client or a planning authority is not known: Unpublished lecture notes *c.*1960, CCA DR2007:0083; James Stirling, 'An Architect's Approach to Architecture', *RIBAJ*, 72, May 1965, p. 232. Whether or not the total number is exaggerated, only the Woolton and North London house projects are recorded. From this period dates Stirling's resentment towards the planning authorities: see, for instance, Stirling, 'A Personal View of the Present Situation', p. 233.

64   This often happened in later lectures: see, for instance, James Stirling, '"The Functional Tradition" and Expression', *Perspecta*, 6, 1959, pp. 90–91; and 'Jim the Great', *Casabella*, 399, 1975, p. 22.

65   Unpublished lecture notes *c.*1960, CCA DR2007:0083.

66   According to Theo Crosby, it was one of the schemes 'submitted to the CIRPAC meeting at La Sarraz in September 1955': Theo Crosby, 'Contributions to CIAM 10', *Architects' Year Book 7*, London: Paul Elek, 1956, p. 39.

67   The British participants were the Smithsons, Voelcker, Stirling, Wilson and Carter, Drake and Lasdun, and Peter Ahrends, although neither Stirling's grid nor that of Wilson and Carter was mentioned in CIAM's official list: Eric Mumford, *The CIAM Discourse on Urbanism, 1928–1960*, Cambridge, Mass.: MIT Press, 2002, p. 335, n. 183.

68   Kenneth Frampton, interview with Mark Girouard: Mark Girouard Collection. 'Smithson presented these projects as if they were from something like the Smithsons' studio, that is what I heard. Anyway, I resented [how] a kind of common attitude was suddenly turned into personal ideologies and from that time I rather fell out with Smithson': James Stirling, unpublished lecture, Delft, 1977: Library of Delft University of Technology.

69   For discussion of this theory and its development within Team 10 see Mumford, *The CIAM Discourse*, pp. 239–43; Max Risselada and Dirk van den Heuvel, *Team 10 1953–81: In Search of a Utopia of the Present*, Rotterdam: NAi, 2005, p. 53.

70   This was a narrower interpretation of 'cluster' than Team 10 had envisaged: see Francis Strauven, *Aldo Van Eyck: The Shape of Relativity*, Amsterdam: Architectura & Natura, 1998, pp. 270–71.

71   Like the Woolton house, the village housing also seems to have drawn upon Stirling's awareness of contemporary Danish buildings: there is, for instance, the use of clerestory type windows in the wall space between two levels of lean-to roofs. There was also the example of Le Corbusier's 'Maisons Murondins', a scheme that appeared in the *Oeuvre complète 1938–1946* (2nd edn, 1950).

The Murondins – meaning wall and logs – were for simple farms and rural youth clubs imagined as linear rows of buildings constructed either side of a party wall with clerestory windows set between the differently pitched roofs.

72 Again, this was a feature shared with Le Corbusier's Murondins project: see Le Corbusier, *Les Maisons Murondins*, Paris and Clermont-Ferrand: E. Chiron, 1942.

73 James Stirling, 'Village', *Architectural Design*, 25, September 1955, p. 287.

74 This did not stop several critics from accusing Stirling's scheme of 'sentiment': Strauven, *Aldo Van Eyck*, pp. 67, 268. Indeed, the idea of a 'dwelling archetype' and 'organic solutions' were common translations of the 'scale of association' approach: see Crosby, 'Contributions to CIAM 10', p. 33.

75 Reyner Banham, 'School at Hunstanton. Norfolk', *Architectural Review*, 116, December 1954, p. 153.

76 Ibid.

77 Banham, 'New Brutalism', p. 361.

78 See Whiteley, *Reyner Banham*, pp. 126–27, 130.

79 N. Henderson, R. S. Jenkins, E. Paolozzi, and A. and P. Smithson, 'Documents 53', in Claude Lichtenstein and Thomas Schregenberger (eds), *As Found: The Discovery of the Ordinary*, Baden: Lars Müller, 2001, p. 39.

80 Alison and Peter Smithson, 'The "As Found" and the "Found"', in Robbins (ed.), *The Independent Group*, p. 201.

81 Ibid.

82 Stirling, 'Regionalism', p. 62.

83 Nicholas Bullock, *Building the Post-War World: Modern Architecture and Reconstruction in Britain*, London: Routledge, 2002, p. 116.

84 David Robbins, 'The Independent Group: Forerunners of Postmodernism?', in Robbins (ed.), *The Independent Group*, p. 243.

85 Statement by James Stirling, in Robbins (ed.), *The Independent Group*, p. 195. The reason for this doubt is that Stirling was in

the States in 1948 (his statement in the Robbins book wrongly says '1949'), there is no evidence that he visited the West Coast on that occasion, and the Eames house was not finished until late 1949: *Arts & Architecture*, 66, December 1949, pp. 26–39. There are, however, slides by Stirling of the Eames house that seem to date from the mid- or late 1950s: Lady Stirling Collection.

86 Reyner Banham, 'Klarheit, Ehrlichkeit, Einfachkeit . . . and Wit Too!: The Case Study Houses in the World's Eyes', in Elizabeth A. T. Smith (ed.), *Blueprints for Modern Living: History and Legacy of the Case Study Houses*, Cambridge, Mass.: MIT Press, 1986, p. 186. Frank Newby had written about the use of factory components in the work of Charles and Ray Eames, but not about any collage aesthetic in this work: Frank Newby, 'The Work of Charles Eames', *Architectural Design*, 24, February 1954, p. 31–35.

87 James Stirling, 'Packaged Deal and Prefabrication', *Design*, 123, March 1959, p. 28.

88 Ibid., p. 30.

89 Massey points out that the show was not the entire responsibility of the Independent Group and only twelve of the thirty-six participants were members: Massey, *The Independent Group*, p. 97; see also Robbins (ed.), *The Independent Group*, pp. 52, 135.

90 Massey, *The Independent Group*, p. 98.

91 Although one review included a photograph of the work it did not mention it: *Architecture and Building*, September 1956, p. 331.

92 D'Arcy Wentworth Thompson, *On Growth and Form*, 2nd edn, Cambridge: Cambridge University Press, 1942, vol. 1, pp. 361–62, vol. 2, pp. 483–88, 556–59, 599–600.

93 Robbins (ed.), *The Independent Group*, p. 143.

94 Statement accompanying Group Eight work: Whitechapel Art Gallery, *This is Tomorrow*, London: Whitechapel Art Gallery, 1956, unpaginated.

95 Ibid. This is from part of the statement left out of the reprinted version in Robert

Maxwell (ed.), *James Stirling: Writings on Architecture*, Milan: Skira, 1998, p. 265.

96   Whitechapel, *This is Tomorrow*.

97   Sandy Wilson later suggested that Stirling didn't grasp the significance of the exhibition, and Stirling himself later wrote that he was 'a bit casual and tongue in cheek about the project': Girouard, *Big Jim*, pp. 85–86.

98   Le Corbusier, *Towards a New Architecture*, trans. Frederick Etchells, London: John Rodker, 1931, p. 81.

99   This was specifically denied by both Stirling and Pine: Robbins (ed.), *The Independent Group*, p. 143.

100   Banham's two reviews did not even mention Group Eight: *Architects' Journal*, 124, 16 August 1956, p. 63; *Architectural Review*, 124, September 1956, p. 187.

101   This was a distinction made in contemporary reviews: Robbins (ed.), *The Independent Group*, p. 135.

102   Rowe included a set of diagrams showing 'harmonic decomposition of the Ø rectangle from Matila Ghyka's *The Geometry of Art and Life* (1946)': Colin Rowe, 'The Mathematics of the Ideal Villa: Palladio and Le Corbusier Compared', *Architectural Review*, 101, March 1947, p. 104. The proportions marked on elevations of the Core and Crosswall house bear a distinct resemblance to some of these diagrams.

103   Peter Arnell and Ted Bickford (eds), *James Stirling: Buildings and Projects*, New York: Rizzoli, 1984, p. 33.

104   Both of these projects are a little mysterious. No contemporary or even near-contemporary published record of either the Core and Crosswall house or the Stiff Dom-ino housing exists. Drawings for the former include two small sheets with elevations and plans that in drawing style may belong to the 1950s: CCA DR2000:005:001:001–002, CCA DR2000:005:002:001–006. Drawings for the Stiff Dom-ino housing all seem to have been made after the 1950s (CCA DR2000:006:001:001–003), although there

are photographs that may be earlier: CCA AP140.S2.SS1.D3.P2.1/P2.2/P2.3/P2.4.

105   Institute of Contemporary Arts, *Tomorrow's Furniture*, 1952. There is also a cabinet from this period: neo-plasticist in design, made of plywood, and painted black, grey and red. This is in the collection of the Victoria and Albert Museum: V&A W.6–2004.

106   H. Bayer, W. Gropius and I. Gropius (eds), *Bauhaus 1919–1928*, New York: Museum of Modern Art, 1938, p. 215.

107   For an illustration see Massey, *The Independent Group*, p. 40.

108   The site was apparently bordered by inter-war semi-detached houses, and the planning application was rejected because the design was deemed to be out of keeping with the area: Arthur Korn, 'The Work of James Stirling and James Gowan', *Architect and Building News*, 215, 7 January 1959, p. 12. This free-standing house was for a site in Mill Hill, north London, for a client known as 'A. Lothain and family' and drawings are dated August 1955. It was envisaged also as repeatable in a terrace form elsewhere.: CCA DR2000:009:001:001–002, DR 2000:009:-002:001–003. It was reworked as a 'proposed house type for St John's Wood' (also north London) a little later: CCA DR2000:027:-009:003, CCA DR2000:020:001:001–002.

109   Stirling, 'Regionalism', p. 62.

110   *Architectural Review* (special issue on 'The Functional Tradition'), 122, July 1957, p. 21.

111   Ibid., p. 5. The special issue was also published as a book: J. M. Richards (ed.), *The Functional Tradition in Early Industrial Buildings*, London: Architectural Press, 1958. Previous articles on aspects of this tradition had been appearing in the journal since 1938: John Piper, 'The Nautical Style', *Architectural Review*, 83, January 1938, pp. 1–14; there was also the special issue on 'The Functional Tradition', *Architectural Review*, 108, January 1950, pp. 2–66, and the issue on canals, *Architectural Review*, 106, July 1949, pp. 1–64.

112 *Architectural Review*, 122, July 1957, p. 7.

113 Ibid., p. 5.

114 Stirling, 'Regionalism', p. 65.

115 Stirling, '"The Functional Tradition"', p. 89.

116 CCA DR2006:0022.

117 CCA DR2006:0022; CCA DR2006:0022:001 VIII; CCA DRCON2000:0027:683.

118 Stirling, 'Black Notebook', p. 35.

119 The phrase is from Ben Highmore, 'Hopscotch Modernism: On Everyday Life and the Blurring of Art and Social Sciences', *Modernist Cultures*, 2:1, Summer 2006, p. 74.

120 *James Stirling*, Video directed by Michael Blackwood, Michael Blackwood Productions, 1987.

121 James Stirling, 'Architectural Aims and Influences', *RIBAJ*, 87, September 1980, p. 36.

122 Stirling, 'Black Notebook', p. 35.

123 This is probably the colliery that Stirling reportedly 'raved about' in the late 1940s: Girouard, *Big Jim*, p. 38.

124 Alyson Cooper, 'Natural and Artificial Lighting in the Manchester Textile Warehouse', in Clare Hartwell and Terry Wyke (eds), *Making Manchester: Aspects of the History of Architecture in the City and Region Since 1800*, Manchester: Lancashire and Cheshire Antiquarian Society, 2007, pp. 64–65. The building was demolished in 1973.

125 Particularly apt, in the light of what has been said about Stirling's Sheffield design and his interest in colliery buildings, are Banham's comments on the Smithsons' Sheffield design. This was, he wrote, an expression of 'aformalism' like the paintings of Burri or Pollock, in which the blocks 'stand about the site with the same graceless memorability as Martello towers or pit-head gear': Banham, 'The New Brutalism', p. 361.

126 Stirling, 'Regionalism', pp. 62–65.

127 Ibid., p. 65.

128 W. R. Lethaby, *Form in Civilisation* (1922) as quoted ibid., p. 65. This self-critique is unusual in Stirling's writing and may be an effect of trying to adopt a Rowe-like writing manner: 'The number of book references in this article is considerable, and indeed one of our vices is an over-literary approach to Architecture. . . . The influence of the camera must also have affected our observation': ibid., p. 68.

129 Ibid., pp. 65–68.

130 Stirling is actually quoting the novelist John Wain: ibid., p. 68.

131 Anthony Vidler, *Histories of the Immediate Present: Inventing Architectural Modernism*, Cambridge, Mass.: MIT Press, 2008, p. 216, n. 54.

132 Girouard, *Big Jim*, p. 97. Stirling later commissioned Paolozzi to create a hanging for the Leicester Engineering building, and from the late 1960s he collected the sculptor's prints.

133 Eduardo Paolozzi, 'Notes from a Lecture at the Institute of Contemporary Arts, 1958', *Uppercase*, 1, 1958, unpaginated, as quoted in Fiona Pearson, *Paolozzi*, Edinburgh: National Galleries of Scotland, 1999, p. 32.

134 Edouard Roditi, *Dialogues on Art*, London: Secker & Warburg, 1960, p. 164. In this interview Roditi makes comparisons between Paolozzi's aesthetic practice and urban and architectural objects, suggesting first that Paolozzi's work would look best in a 'deserted square in the heart of a disastrously bombed city', then that Paolozzi's studio itself – made from a row of three salvaged and converted cottages – was like 'the aesthetics of *objets trouvés* as they are daily and unconsciously applied in the fields of real estate and building': ibid., pp. 166–67.

135 Ibid.

136 Ibid., p. 159.

137 Paolozzi, 'Notes from a Lecture'.

138 Lawrence Alloway, 'Eduardo Paolozzi', *Architectural Design*, 26, April 1956, p. 133.

139 Ibid.

140 Stirling, 'Black Notebook', p. 55.

141 This was an 'illustrated report' on Le Corbusier's chapel at Ronchamp. It was held at the ICA and the other speakers were Hitch-

cock and Peter Smithson: Walker Art Gallery, Liverpool, and Building Centre, London, *Le Corbusier*, Liverpool and London, 1958, p. 90. This does not seem to have been an event sponsored by the Independent Group: Massey, *Independent Group*, pp. 142–44. For a fuller account of Stirling's engagement with Le Corbusier see my article, '*L'Architecte Anglais*: Stirling and Le Corbusier', in Crinson (ed.), *James Stirling*.

142   Printed brochure inserted into Stirling's copy of Walker Art Gallery, *Le Corbusier*. Lady Stirling Collection.

143   Colin Rowe, 'Le Corbusier: Utopian Architect', *The Listener*, 12 February 1959, pp. 289–91. This includes a short account of a discussion in the programme that Stirling took part in – 'Le Corbusier and the Future of Architecture'.

144   It has even been suggested that Rowe co-wrote Stirling's articles, although there is absolutely no evidence for this: Thomas Muirhead, review of Robert Maxwell (ed.), *Stirling: Writings on Architecture* in *Journal of Architecture*, 3, Winter 1998, pp. 377–78.

145   Stirling, 'Black Notebook', p. 53.

146   Ulrich Beck and Johannes Willms, *Conversations with Ulrich Beck*, Cambridge: Polity, 2004, p. 29.

147   Caroline Maniaque, *Le Corbusier et les Maisons Jaoul*, Paris: Picard, 2005, p. 117.

148   Banham, 'The New Brutalism'.

149   James Stirling, 'Garches to Jaoul: Le Corbusier as Domestic Architect in 1927 and 1953', *Architectural Review*, 118, September 1955, p. 145.

150   And as he put it in the Black Notebook, 'the spaces are unexpected, unrelated, they are encountered suddenly as one turns a corner': Stirling, 'Black Notebook', p. 51.

151   Stirling, 'Garches to Jaoul', p. 146.

152   A historian might point to the earlier manifestation of some of these traits in the Weekend House (1934–35), which, according to Kenneth Frampton, was a 'conscious move away from modernization and its faith

in the inevitable benevolence of modern technology': Kenneth Frampton, *Studies in Tectonic Culture*, Cambridge, Mass.: MIT Press, 1995, p. 345.

153   Stirling, 'Garches to Jaoul', p. 146.

154   Ibid. p. 148.

155   Reyner Banham, *The New Brutalism: Ethic or Aesthetic?*, London: Architectural Press, 1966, p. 85.

156   Stirling, 'Black Notebook', p. 57.

157   Stirling, 'Ronchamp', p. 156.

158   Ibid.

159   Ibid.

160   Ibid.

161   'Le Corbusier could be tied in with popular culture': James Stirling, 'Statement', in Robbins (ed.), *The Independent Group*, p. 195.

162   Stirling, 'Ronchamp', p. 161.

163   Stirling's source for this was probably the *Oeuvre complète 1946–1952*.

164   Stirling, 'Ronchamp', p. 161.

165   Ibid.

166   Le Corbusier, *Towards a New Architecture*, p. 5.

167   Stirling, 'Ronchamp', p. 161.

168   Ibid., p. 160.

169   Claude Lévi-Strauss, *The Savage Mind*, trans. John and Doreen Weightman, London: Weidenfeld and Nicolson, 1966, p. 17.

170   Ibid., p. 20.

171   Ibid., p. 17.

172   Ibid.

173   Ibid., p. 20.

174   Jacques Derrida, *Writing and Difference*, trans. Alan Bass, London and New York: Routledge, 1978, p. 360.

175   Ibid.

176   Tafuri, 'L'Architecture', p. 149. Colin Rowe and Fred Koetter in their book *Collage City* urged the architect to recognise himself as a *bricoleur* and advocated a 'politics of bricolage' as an alternative to 'scientific' urban planning: Colin Rowe and Fred Koetter, *Collage City*, Cambridge, Mass.: MIT Press, 1978, pp. 102–5. In their 1972 book, *Adhocism*,

Nathan Silver and Charles Jencks presented the *bricoleur* as a kind of patron saint for postmodernists. At the same time, in 1972 Alan Colquhoun in his 'Historicism and the Limits of Semiology' insisted that the *bricoleur*'s act of recombination itself was always invested with values and ideological effects: reprinted in Alan Colquhoun, *Essays in Architectural Criticism: Modern Architecture and Historical Change*, Cambridge, Mass.: MIT Press, 1981.

177　Robin Evans, *The Projective Cast: Architecture and its Three Geometries*, Cambridge, Mass.: MIT Press, 1995, pp. 75, 78; Alan Colquhoun, 'From Bricolage to Myth, or How to Put Humpty-Dumpty Together Again', *Oppositions*, 12, Spring 1978.

4　THE CUBE AND THE PILE-UP

1　'The tension was creative': Michael Wilford quoted in Mark Girouard, *Big Jim: The Life and Work of James Stirling*, London: Pimlico, 2000, p. 107.

2　To give one example – 'Ernesto Rogers referred in an article to Stirling and Gowan as the "teddy boys of English architecture", to which Stirling responded by sending Ernesto a neatly-packed, rusty cut-throat razor': Malcolm Higgs, 'James "Bad Boy" Stirling: The Early Years', unpublished lecture given to the Twentieth Century Society, 27 November 2003.

3　Substantiating its importance, this later photograph also appears as the final image in James Stirling, Michael Wilford and Associates, *James Stirling Michael Wilford and Associates: Buildings and Projects 1975–1992*, London: Thames and Hudson, 1994, p. 308.

4　For further discussion of this see Michael J. Lewis, review of *The Chicago Auditorium Building: Adler and Sullivan's Architecture and the City* by Joseph M. Siry, and *The Chicago Tribune Competition: Skyscraper Design and Cultural Change in the 1920s* by

Katherine Solomonson, in *Art Bulletin*, 87, September 2005, pp. 546–48.

5　To take a few influential examples, in Colin Rowe's important article, 'The Blenheim of the Welfare State', Rowe successively erases Gowan from the work. He starts out with 'Stirling and Gowan', which later becomes 'Stirling and his partner', and finally 'Stirling's scheme': Colin Rowe, 'The Blenheim of the Welfare State' (1959), *As I Was Saying: Recollections and Miscellaneous Essays*, 3 vols, Cambridge, Mass. and London: MIT Press, 1996, vol. 1, pp. 143–52. Rowe also paid Gowan scant notice in an important introductory essay: Colin Rowe, 'Introduction', in Peter Arnell and Ted Bickford (eds), *James Stirling: Buildings and Projects*, New York: Rizzoli, 1984, pp. 10–27. In Alvin Boyarsky's article, 'Stirling "Dimostrationi"', although much of the article is about the Leicester University Engineering building, Gowan's name goes completely unmentioned: *Architectural Design*, 38, October 1968, pp. 454–55. And, in a typical later survey, William Curtis completely forgets Gowan in his discussion of Leicester: *Modern Architecture since 1900*, Oxford: Phaidon, 1996, p. 534. The tendency has been to look at Stirling's later buildings and assume that, because certain formal traits appear in them, he must have been responsible for the same formal traits in buildings produced during the partnership with Gowan.

6　*Architects' Journal*, 159, 1 May 1974, p. 930.

7　Girouard, *Big Jim*, pp. 186–87 and 192–95.

8　Ibid., pp. 188 and 194–95. Stirling explained this to Gowan as necessary because of the 'lack of storage space': James Gowan, interview with the author, 4 January 2006. The implication in Leon Krier's account is that Stirling was simply unaware of, or uninterested in, their value: Girouard, *Big Jim*, p. 188.

9　Many of the original drawings for Leicester are now in the possession of the Deutsches Architektur Museum, Frankfurt (hereafter

DAM). The Kensington drawing is in James Gowan's possession.

10   Colin Rowe, 'Eulogy: James Stirling', in Rowe, *As I Was Saying*, vol. 3, p. 346. This may complement Malcolm Higgs's observation that designs seemed to arrive fully formed in the office, although his view may have been affected by his position as an architectural assistant not privy to the design process: Malcolm Higgs, interview with the author, 31 October 2005.

11   See James Stirling and James Gowan, 'Afterthoughts on the Flats at Ham Common', *Architecture and Building*, 34, May 1979, pp. 166–69. On Ham as brutalist see Reyner Banham, *The New Brutalism: Ethic or Aesthetic*, London: Architectural Press, 1966, pp. 87–89.

12   Stirling thought he could get these past the local planner and then change them: James Gowan, interview with the author, 4 January 2006.

13   Planning Office, London Borough of Richmond upon Thames (hereafter LBR), microfilmed drawings dated 3 November 1955, permission refused 2 December 1955. Permission was decided by the local planner and his Town Planning Committee. In the case of the house on the Isle of Wight, discussed later, the planner was backed by an Architects' Panel.

14   James Gowan, interviews with the author, 4 January 2006 and 30 June 2006.

15   LBR, microfilmed drawings dated 3 December 1955; permission refused 15 December 1955.

16   It is possible that he was also stressed by the extra work; he had been making site visits to Ham during time he was supposed to be giving to his work at Lyons Israel Ellis and, according to Gowan, the strain was showing: James Gowan, interview with the author, 4 January 2006.

17   LBR, permission applied for 1 January 1956, and refused 30 January 1956.

18   LBR, microfilmed drawings dated 3 January 1956; conditional permission granted 12 January 1956.

19   LBR, planning applications dated 4 April 1955, 19 May 1955, 6 June 1955, 7 June 1955 and 17 June 1955. In overall layout, Stirling's early schemes were similar to those previously submitted by the architect Alexander Flinder on 7 June 1955.

20   James Stirling, 'An Architect's Approach to Architecture', *RIBAJ*, 72, May 1965, p. 233. For critical reaction comparing the two projects see Reyner Banham, 'Plucky Jims', *New Statesman*, 19 July 1958, pp. 83–84.

21   LBR, microfilmed drawings dated 7 February 1956; permission given without conditions 16 February 1956.

22   'One did a bit, the other did a bit; the first developed that, the second took it on': James Gowan quoted in John McKean, *Leicester University Engineering Building*, London: Phaidon, 1994, p. 18.

23   For instance, Bijvoet and Duiker's Nirwana Flats in The Hague (1928–30). Stirling pointed to Liverpool warehouses as the inspiration: James Stirling, '"The Functional Tradition" and Expression', *Perspecta*, 6, 1959, p. 90.

24   Kenneth Frampton, *Modern Architecture: A Critical History*, London: Thames and Hudson, 1985, p. 225.

25   The partners' interest in furniture, announced here, would continue later in their careers: with Stirling this was through his collecting activities and the design work of his wife, Mary (Shand) Stirling; with Gowan through a number of commissions for the furniture manufacturer Chaim Schreiber.

26   Photographs of the interior of the Maison de Weekend were available in the *Oeuvre complète 1934–1938*, Zurich: Girsberger, 1945.

27   Stirling and Gowan, 'Afterthoughts', p. 166.

28   Ibid.

29   Ibid., p. 167.

30   Ibid., p. 168.

31 James Stirling, 'From Garches to Jaoul', *Architectural Review*, 118, September 1955, p. 146.

32 Kit Evans, 'Eight Questions to Stirling and Gowan', *Polygon*, 5, 1960, republished in Mark Crinson ed., *James Stirling: Early Unpublished Writings on Architecture*, London: Routledge, 2009, p. 79.

33 Gowan has recounted that he actually found Stirling demonstrating the point to the builders, making the joints deeper by gouging them out with a stick, contrary to Gowan's own concern that their load-bearing capacity might be lessened: James Gowan, interview with the author, 30 March 2007.

34 My argument here is similar to an observation by Peter Eisenman about Leicester University Engineering building: Peter Eisenman, 'Real and English: The Destruction of the Box I', *Oppositions*, 4, October 1974, p. 10. The important difference is that while Eisenman saw this as a critical challenge or assault on modernism in general, I see it as an attempt to position the building between late modernist primitivism and the production calculus of contemporary public housing.

35 Stirling, 'From Garches', p. 150.

36 An extension to the flats was planned a little later consisting of a four-storey block more loosely articulated in its variety of heights and setbacks than the 'terrace' of flats already built and with spiral stairs inside: CCA DR2000:027:021:002; Arthur Korn, 'The Work of James Stirling and James Gowan', *Architect and Building News*, 215, 7 January 1959, p. 13.

37 James Gowan, interview with the author, 4 January 2006. Stirling may well have wanted to present the image of Gowan as the workhorse partner, the practical man in the background with Stirling as the performer and extrovert: Girouard, *Big Jim*, p. 89.

38 'Jacko [Moya] sacrificed quite a lot. The tremendous talent that he had never actually shone through. In the system that they had, Philip [Powell] just accepted anything that Jacko designed and then went on to build it, at speed': Ellis Woodman, *Modernity and Reinvention: The Architecture of James Gowan*, London: Black Dog, 2008, p. 170.

39 Alan Forsyth and David Gray (eds), *Lyons Israel Ellis Gray: Buildings and Projects 1932–1983*. London: Architectural Association, 1988, p. 107.

40 Ibid., pp. 11–12 and 48.

41 David Gray, interview with the author, 17 October 2005.

42 James Gowan, interview with the author, 4 January 2006. Stirling spoke of planning as 'never very marvellous during the time I was there' and of how he 'never saw a concept drawing': Forsyth and Gray (eds), *Lyons Israel Ellis*, pp. 204–5.

43 'Le Corbusier seems to have concentrated his efforts into dealing with clients and designing; Pierre Jeanneret supplied the anchor of common sense and supervised contractors': William J. R. Curtis, *Le Corbusier: Ideas and Forms*, London: Phaidon, 1986, p. 81. Although the principals of the office were Le Corbusier and Pierre Jeanneret, it was actually called 'L'Atelier Le Corbusier'.

44 Finished designs were submitted to the local planning officer by 15 January 1956: microfiche copies of plans and drawings, Planning Office, Newport Council, Isle of Wight. Gowan was still listed under his Stevenage address at the time of this submission: Deutsches Architektur Museum, 246–007–001–006. Modifications to the original design continued into the early months of the partnership with Stirling, but there is no sign of Stirling's involvement in the correspondence with the planning authority. Despite Gowan's authorship of the design, it was always accepted by the partners that it would be presented as part of the partnership's output, though Stirling may have been pushing at the limits of this understanding when,

twenty years later, a plan of the Isle of Wight house was used in his 1977 revisions to the Nolli plan of Rome: see Stirling, Wilford and Associates, *Buildings and Projects*, pp. 45–47. For a house with an almost identical plan see R. Towning Hill and Partners' winning design for the House for the Professional Man: *House & Garden*, 11, January 1956, pp. 44–45.

45 County Planning Officer to Gowan, 20 March 1956, and Gowan to County Planning Officer, 25 March 1956: Planning Office, Newport Council, Isle of Wight.

46 Gowan to County Planning Officer, 4 March 1956 and 16 August 1956: Planning Office, Newport Council, Isle of Wight.

47 The house's vastly changed present condition – with pitched roof, new windows and refaced walls – shows, in a sense, how the suburbs have reclaimed it.

48 For a review appreciating just these aspects of the building see J. M. Richards, 'Criticism', *Architects' Journal*, 128, 24 July 1958, pp. 119–22. For a leading critic like Richards to review this small and fairly remote building was a notable feather in the cap of the young partnership.

49 Reyner Banham, 'The New Brutalism', *Architectural Review*, December 1955, pp. 358–61.

50 According to Gowan the studies that ensued 'were undertaken to devise a working method in the then newly formed partnership': *James Gowan*, ed. David Dunster, Architectural Monographs 3, London: Academy Editions, 1978, p. 55. 'We agreed the free right to share drawings, to take one from the other's boards and carry on with it. And we developed a rule as to how we'd end an argument. It would be decided by what suits the building': Gowan in McKean, *Leicester*, p. 15. 'These were a series of academic exercises undertaken when the Stirling/Gowan partnership was formed, in order to establish a working method': James Stirling, *James Stirling: Buildings and Projects 1950–1974*, London: Thames and Hudson, 1975, p. 42.

51 See McKean, *Leicester*, p. 15. Gowan has said that his later published statements on the house studies 'were meant to emphasise joint working in the context of Stirling's later disavowal of the partnership': James Gowan, interview with the author, 7 July 2006.

52 *House & Garden*, 12, April 1957, p. 67.

53 Girouard, *Big Jim*, 93.

54 For a fuller discussion of *House & Garden* as a context for the Expandable House see my essay, '"A House Which Grows": Stirling and Gowan, the Smithsons and Consumer Society', in Mark Crinson and Claire Zimmerman (eds), *Neo-avant-garde and Postmodern: Postwar Architecture in Britain and Beyond*, New Haven and London: Yale University Press, 2010.

55 Cynthia Manners (née Wickham), correspondence with the author, 11 December 2007.

56 This account of the process of designing the house studies and Expandable House is based on James Gowan, interview with the author, 4 January 2006.

57 James Gowan, *Style and Configuration*, London: Academy Editions, 1994, p. 62.

58 This device of differently shaded units, with their hard, engraved line effect, was taken up in the 1958 scheme for steel mills in Wales, using cladding as a means of articulating but also binding together the extremely long frontage. It can also be seen in many of the early drawings for Leicester, and it may have had some role in the corduroy concrete patterns of the prefabricated units in Stirling's student housing for St Andrews University (1964).

59 James Gowan, interview with the author, 7 July 2006.

60 Particularly as described by Colin Rowe in 'Mannerism and Modern Architecture', *Architectural Review*, 107, May 1950, p. 297.

61 See Reyner Banham, 'Revenge of the Pictur-esque', in John Summerson (ed.), *Concerning Architecture*, London: Allen Lane, 1968.

62 The key work here being Le Corbusier's Villas La Roche and Jeanneret: for Stirling's criticism of the picturesque effects of these linked villas see Stirling, 'Black Notebook', in Crinson (ed.), *James Stirling*, p. 43.

63 Colin Rowe, 'Character and Composition; Or Some Vicissitudes of Architectural Vocabulary in the Nineteenth Century', written in 1953–54 but first published in *Oppositions*, 2, 1974.

64 Rudolf Wittkower, *Architectural Principles in the Age of Humanism* (1949), London: Academy Editions, 1973, p. 75. If there is a historical precedent for this approach in the picturesque movement itself, it might be found in Thomas Hope's remodelling of Deepdene (1818–23).

65 *House & Garden*, April 1957, p. 67.

66 Not only the School Assembly Hall, Camberwell (1958), but also the design for the Nordrhein Westfalia Museum, Dusseldorf (1975), and even the Neue Staatsgalerie, Stuttgart (1977–83).

67 Apart from the two examples discussed here it's worth mentioning Utzon and Møgel-wang's courtyard house for Skåne (1953), which Stirling and Gowan may well have known through its publication in *Architects' Year Book 6*, London: Elek, 1955, pp. 80–82.

68 For the latter see Reyner Banham, 'A Clip-on Architecture', *Architectural Design*, 35, November 1965, pp. 534–35.

69 'The interior has a strong rural character in sympathy with the whole conception of the house': *House & Garden*, April 1957, p. 70.

70 See Iain Boyd Whyte (ed.), *Man-Made Future: Planning, Education and Design in Mid-Twentieth-Century Britain*, London: Routledge, 2007, p. 31. Both Stirling and Gowan had experience of this kind of propaganda: Stirling through the APRR, Gowan through his work at Stevenage.

71 Compare this with Banham's position, in which taking on expendability was essential if modernism was to keep step with contemporary technology: Reyner Banham, 'Vehicles of Desire', *Art*, 1, September 1955, republished in Clocktower Gallery, *Modern Dreams: The Rise and Fall of Pop* (Cambridge, Mass. and London: MIT Press, 1988), pp. 65–69.

72 See Arthur Marwick, *British Society since 1945*, Harmondsworth: Penguin, 1982, p. 65.

73 Manousso played a strong role in seeing this house through to completion, and he also commissioned Stirling and Gowan to produce a site layout for a housing estate in Baddow near Maidenhead, again in 1956: James Gowan, interview with the author, 30 June 2006. This importance of Manousso to the fledgling practice adjusts Girouard's statement that Manousso only employed Stirling and Gowan for the Ham Common flats: Girouard, *Big Jim*, p. 90.

74 Korn, 'Work', p. 19.

75 Building Control Service, Wycombe District Council (hereafter WDC), letter from planning officer to Stirling and Gowan, 3 August 1956.

76 WDC, letter from Stirling to local planning officer, 14 September 1956.

77 Gowan comments, 'Confronted with this dominating architect and the dominating Manousso, Kissa behaved as if everyone was doing him a favour.' Gowan also recounts a similar affair when Leslie Martin passed on a commission for a house in Cambridge for another disabled client. Stirling was sacked after two weeks, specifically because of his insistence on split levels and slow ramps: James Gowan, interview with the author, 4 January 2006.

78 Le Corbusier, *Oeuvre complète 1946–1952*, Zurich: Girsberger, 1953.

79 This second design is dated 13 September 1956: CCA DR2000:0042:027:002:001–005. De Stijl architecture would have been famil-

iar to Stirling and Gowan from a number of sources including the *De Stijl* journal itself, as well as H. L. C. Jaffe's *De Stijl 1917–1927*, Amsterdam: Meulenhoff, 1956.

80 DAM, 246–006–003.

81 WDC, microfilmed drawings dated 13 September 1956, application made 25 September 1956, application refused 5 October 1956. Both James Gowan and the present owners of the house have said that a local architect who lived in his architect-designed house nearby and who disliked Stirling and Gowan's proposals played a role in these successive refusals.

82 Korn, 'Work', pp. 19–21. Interestingly, Korn's article set the pattern for later representations of this scheme, only publishing the smaller house from the first scheme, and the second scheme. In his Black Book, Stirling simply wrote that '[it] was rejected by the local planning authority': Stirling, *Buildings and Projects*, p. 8. In the same book Stirling also published the smaller house design from the first scheme, again with no indication of the sequence of designs or any mention of a house being built: ibid., p. 43.

83 WDC, microfilmed drawings signed 29 November 1956, application for approval dated 19 December 1956, approval granted 11 January 1957.

84 James Gowan, interview with the author, 4 January 2006.

85 There are negatives of views of the house as nearly finished, but although these were kept in Stirling's possession they seem never to have been printed and were certainly never published by him: CCA DR2006:0022:001 VIII.

86 Sarah Williams Goldhagen, 'Freedom's Domiciles: Three Projects by Alison and Peter Smithson', in Sarah Williams Goldhagen and Réjean Legault (eds), *Anxious Modernisms: Experimentation in Postwar Architectural Culture*, Cambridge, Mass. and London: MIT Press, 2000, p. 76. Goldhagen

claims this encouraged the inhabitants into a 'radical re-evaluation of themselves'.

87 Korn, 'Work', p. 22. The Sunninghill housing has a precedent also in the Smithsons' close housing project, shown together with Stirling's village housing project at CIAM Dubrovnik in 1956.

88 Korn, 'Work', p. 22.

89 For papers concerning these schemes see London Borough of Kensington and Chelsea, planning records for 17 Hyde Park Gate. Manousso was clearly acting as middleman for some of the period 1956–57. Manousso's son, Paul Manousso, has also recalled that his father introduced Stirling to Mavrolean as well as Kissa: interview with Paul Manousso, Mark Girouard Collection.

90 James Gowan, interview with the author, 6 July 2007.

91 Stirling, *James Stirling*, p. 44.

92 CCA DR2000:019:001, DR2000:019:002:001–008. The drawing seems original, but the colouring may have been added for the exhibition of Stirling's drawings at the Heinz Gallery in 1974, as it is now mounted similarly to other drawings shown then and the colouring is not evident in the version published in 1959: see Korn, 'Work', p. 14.

93 The houses would have had a density of 24 persons per acre, while the County of London Plan stipulated a density of 200. Epstein, whose studio adjoined the site, took a close interest in the various schemes. Ernö Goldfinger made proposals in May 1958. Finally, in the spring of 1959, the Mavrolean residences having already been abandoned, it was decided to build the block of flats which still stands on the site: London Borough of Kensington and Chelsea, planning records for 17 Hyde Park Gate.

94 CCA DR2007:0083, unpublished lecture notes.

95 It has often been mistakenly reported that Stirling taught at the Architectural Association: see, for instance, Anthony Vidler, *James*

Frazer Stirling: Notes from the Archive, Montreal, New Haven and London: CCA, YCBA and Yale University Press, 2010, pp. 21, 100, 103. Stirling gave help to Paul Manousso when the latter was a student at the AA; he also occasionally lectured there and was invited onto crits, but he was never appointed as a tutor.

96 This is evident from the section drawings published in Korn, 'Work', p. 23.

97 It is relevant to remember here that Colin Rowe described De Stijl as absolutely opposed in its compositional approach to Gaudet and the Beaux-Arts. 'De Stijl advanced what was called "peripheric" composition, developed not toward a central focus but toward the extremities of the canvas or wall plane, and involving, in a building, not a gravitational but a levitational scheme': Colin Rowe, review of Talbot Hamlin, *Forms and Functions of Twentieth Century Architecture*, in *Art Bulletin*, 35, June 1953, p. 172.

98 Stirling later seems to have tried to disavow the external design as 'too literal . . . not entirely successful': unpublished lecture notes, kept in Black Notebook, Lady Stirling Collection. One contemporary account suggests that the designs were rejected twice, once for the internal layout and then for the elevation, before they were accepted: *Architect and Building News*, 20 July 1960, p. 79. Approval was complicated because it had to be obtained from both the local authority and the surveyor for the estate that owned the land.

99 Gowan, *Style and Configuration*, p. 62.

100 James Gowan, interview with the author, 6 July 2007.

101 Korn, 'Work', p. 23.

102 These patterns of wooden boarding were also used on a small and obscure project in 1959 for a school kitchen in Eltham, south London. In some unpublished lecture notes Stirling mentioned 'LCC kitchen – Churchill consolation – minor work': CCA

DR2007:0083. Gowan has confirmed that the work consisted of designing a servery and a larger hatch for an existing building, a commission that came to them from having their names on the LCC small works list: James Gowan, interview with the author, 22 February 2008. Photographic negatives of the finished kitchen exist in CCA DR2006:0022:001 VIII.

103 'Ship's-cabin aesthetic' is the term given at the time. The *Architectural Review* suggested that the Dodd house 'takes this trend about as far as it can go': *Architectural Review*, 127, March 1960, p. 191.

104 According to Gowan, 'If you design too much you leave your client with a museum': 'The Architect Answers', *The Tatler*, 4 April 1962, p. 32. Publicity photos of the interior contrast the ship's-cabin effect with the exotic promise of a leopard skin rug provided by the architects: 'House in Kensington', *Daily Telegraph*, 19 January 1960, p. 9.

105 See, for instance, Michael Wilford's statement in Girouard, *Big Jim*, p. 247. Assistants like Michael Wilford, however, were only involved in the later period of the partnership, and most – though not Wilford – were only part-time.

106 Korn, 'Work', p. 8.

107 Stirling, 'From Garches', pp. 145–51.

108 For 'multi-aesthetic' see James Stirling, 'A Personal View of the Present Situation', *Architectural Design*, 28, June 1958, p. 233; James Gowan, 'Curriculum', *Architectural Review*, 126, December 1959, p. 316. For 'the style for the job' see Reyner Banham, 'The Style for the Job', *New Statesman*, 67, 14 February 1964, p. 261.

109 Woodman, *Modernity*, p. 188.

110 See, for instance, 'Eight Questions to Stirling and Gowan', originally published in *Polygon*, 5, 1960, 10–21, and Stirling's 'Royaumont Talk' originally given to the 1962 Team 10 meeting. Both of these are republished in Crinson (ed.), *James Stirling*.

111 Gowan has recently alluded to this in relation to his 1959 'Curriculum' article – 'The AA School head Michael Pattrick tried to stop the publication but *AR* went ahead. Nikolaus Pevsner wanted to initiate a printed discussion with me but I declined': James Gowan, correspondence with the author, 14 June 2005.

5   THE USES OF NOSTALGIA

1   James Stirling, 'Regionalism and Modern Architecture', *Architects' Year Book 8*, London: Elek, 1957, pp. 65, 68. As an article two years later made clear, Stirling was particularly admiring nineteenth-century buildings here. In Stirling's view the *Architectural Review*'s so-called 'functional tradition' was 'perhaps a little narrow, faintly Georgian, and too nearly confined to early industrialism': James Stirling, 'The Functional Tradition and Expression', *Perspecta*, 6, 1959, p. 89.

2   James Stirling, 'A Personal View of the Present Situation', *Architectural Design*, 28, June 1958, p. 233.

3   James Stirling, 'An Architect's Approach to Architecture', *RIBAJ*, 72, May 1965, p. 233.

4   Ibid.

5   Interestingly, when the house was published at the time as well as later by Stirling, no such Victorian aspects were allowed into its representation: see 'House in Kensington', *Architectural Review*, 127, March 1960, pp. 191–93; Arthur Korn, 'The Work of James Stirling and James Gowan', *Architect and Building News*, 215, 7 January 1959, p. 23; Peter Arnell and Ted Bickford (eds), *James Stirling: Buildings and Projects*, London: Rizzoli, 1984, pp. 57–58. It was only when Gowan published the house much later that an image of the rear wall was reproduced: *James Gowan*, ed. David Dunster, Architectural Monographs 3, London: Academy Editions, 1978, p. 21.

6   Stirling, 'The Functional Tradition', p. 91.

7   Reyner Banham, *The New Brutalism: Ethic or Aesthetic?* London: Architectural Press, 1966.

8   In 1989 the scheme was substantially altered as a result of the government-sponsored Design Improvement Controlled Experiment. The DICE was based on the defensible space strictures of Alice Coleman: see http://www.odpm.gov.uk/stellent/groups/odpm_urbanpolicy/documents/page/odpm_urbpol_608114.hcsp. Accessed 29 March 2005. The scheme was demolished in 1999, save for the old people's housing.

9   There were 194 dwelling units in total. The layout was approved in June 1957 and the tender (for £386,129) was accepted in April 1959: Lancashire Record Office, CBP/27/5. The second phase was again a mixture of blocks and terraces, this time by the Building Design Partnership (1964–67). The whole clearance and redevelopment programme, based on a master plan made by the Preston Borough Architect's Department, was awarded to John Turner & Sons, a local Lancashire firm of contractors who brought in Lyons Israel Ellis: see David Hunt, *A History of Preston*, Preston: Carnegie, 1992, pp. 256–57; and John Brook and Duncan Glen, *Preston's New Buildings*, Preston: Preston Borough Council, 1975, unpaginated. Stirling and Gowan were thus working as private architects for a public housing scheme, though their responsibility was to the contractor. The original brief, according to James Gowan, specified the units of dwelling to be built but not the specific height of the buildings: James Gowan, interview with the author, 16 May 2005.

10 Photographs of these houses and their yards were taken by the council shortly before the slum clearance scheme: see Lancashire Record Office, CBP 4/1/37. There is a photograph, probably by James Stirling, of a nearby terrace in CCA DRCON 2000:-0027:022:002.

11 Gowan has stated that the three-storey terraces and old people's housing were largely

his designs and the four-storey block largely Stirling's: James Gowan, interview with the author, 17 May 2005.

12 Stirling later (1963) regretted this 'separation into age groups': James Stirling, 'Urban Redevelopment', in Mark Crinson (ed.), *James Stirling: Early Unpublished Writings on Architecture*, London: Routledge, 2009, p. 104.

13 Alison and Peter Smithson, *Urban Structuring*, London: Studio Vista, 1967, p. 10.

14 As Kenneth Frampton has pointed out, 'The vestigial "yard" . . . seems to have been conceived as being an addendum to the house that could be converted into closed living accommodation': Kenneth Frampton, 'Team 10, Plus 20: The Vicissitudes of Ideology', in *Labour, Work and Architecture: Collected Essays on Architecture and Design*, London: Phaidon, 2002, p. 337, n. 8

15 Stirling and Gowan quoted in Arnell and Bickford (eds), *James Stirling*, p. 61.

16 *Architecture Canada*, 45:4, April 1968, p. 44.

17 *Architect and Building News*, 221, 14 March 1962, p. 381.

18 These junctures seem to have fascinated, or perhaps worried, Stirling judging by the number of photographs he took of them: CCA 022:002 JS–007.

19 Stirling, 'Regionalism', p. 65.

20 For Gowan's later criticism of this open space see Ellis Woodman, *Modernity and Reinvention: The Architecture of James Gowan*, London: Black Dog, 2008, p. 192.

21 James Gowan, interview with the author, 16 May 2005.

22 'This gives better protection during transit and site handling': *Architect's Journal*, 133, 8 June 1961, p. 849.

23 See *Architecture Canada*, 45, April 1968, p. 44. 'I never select materials emotionally,' he wrote in 1965, 'they are chosen entirely at a practical level, but then, of course, they must be transformed to cohere at a level of significance': Stirling, 'An Architect's Approach', p. 240.

24 See Raphael Samuel, 'The Return to Brick', *Theatres of Memory, Volume 1: Past and Present in Contemporary Culture*, London: Verso, 1994, p. 123.

25 J. B. Priestley, *English Journey* (1934), London, 1997, p. 323.

26 On the good and bad everyday of bricks see Michael Fried, *Menzel's Realism: Art and Embodiment in Nineteenth-Century Berlin*, New Haven and London: Yale University Press, 2002, pp. 152–59.

27 Stirling had admired a similar 'quality of weightlessness', though achieved by different means, at Ronchamp: James Stirling, 'Ronchamp: Le Corbusier's Chapel and the Crisis of Rationalism', *Architectural Review*, 119, March 1956, p. 156.

28 Mark Girouard, 'Florey Building, Oxford', *Architectural Review*, 152, November 1972, pp. 260–77.

29 Nicholas Taylor, 'The Failure of Housing', *Architectural Review*, 142, November 1967, p. 346.

30 My attribution of these images to Stirling is based on the attribution given by the *Architect and Building News*, 221, 14 March 1962, p. 381, by James Gowan's testimony, and the negatives and prints that are now in CCA 022:002 JS–007; 022:002 JS–018; 022:002 JS–019. Stirling's photographs were reproduced in several other journals at this time: see, for instance, *Architectural Forum*, 116, March 1962, pp. 92–95; and *Architecture d'aujourd'hui*, 104, Oct.–Nov. 1962, pp. 72–75.

31 This appeared in 'Re-housing at Preston, Lancashire', *Architectural Design*, 31, December 1961, p. 538, and was later reproduced in Arnell and Bickford (eds), *James Stirling*. A print and negative is held in CCA 022:002 JS–007, which also has other views of Preston by Stirling.

32 'Re-housing at Preston, Lancashire', p. 538.

33 Other likely sources of inspiration were Mayne's images of Southam Street in Notting Hill, published in *Uppercase*, 5, 1961, as well

as Nigel Henderson's images of East End children which had appeared in Alison and Peter Smithson's photomontaged *CIAM Grille*, 1953.

34 Spender's pre-war photographs of Bolton had finally appeared in Tom Harrisson's *Britain Revisited* (1961) where they were used – contra-post-war planners – to claim that little had changed in working-class street life.

35 Stirling photographed these ramps many times: see CCA 022:002 JS–007.

36 Michael Young and Peter Willmott, *Family and Kinship in East London*, London: Penguin, 1957, p. 38.

37 'Re-housing at Preston, Lancashire', p. 538.

38 On this see Manfredo Tafuri, 'L'architecture dans le boudoir', *The Sphere and the Labyrinth: Avant-Gardes and Architecture from Piranesi to the 1970s*, Cambridge, Mass. and London: MIT Press, 1990, p. 271.

39 These statements appear in a number of journals, sometimes in edited or rearranged form: see 'Re-housing at Preston, Lancashire', pp. 538–45; *Architect and Building News*, 221, 14 March 1962, pp. 381–86; and *Architects' Journal*, 133, 8 June 1961, pp. 845–50.

40 On sociology and modernism in Britain see Miles Glendinning and Stefan Muthesius, *Tower Block: Modern Public Housing in England, Scotland, Wales and Northern Ireland*, New Haven and London: Yale University Press, 1994, pp. 101–3, 122; and Ben Highmore, 'Hopscotch Modernism: On Everyday Life and the Blurring of Art and Social Science', *Modernist Cultures*, 2:1, 2006, pp. 70–79.

41 Mass Observation was set up in 1937 by Humphrey Jennings, Tom Harrisson and Charles Madge. Both before and after the war the later Independent Group member Nigel Henderson had good contacts with Mass Observation's key thinkers: Victoria Walsh, *Nigel Henderson: Parallel of Life and Art*, London: Thames and Hudson, 2001, p. 9.

42 'Re-housing at Preston, Lancashire', p. 538.

43 Stirling, 'Urban Redevelopment', p. 102.

44 'Re-housing at Preston, Lancashire', p. 538.

45 *Architect and Building News*, 221, 14 March 1962, pp. 381–82.

46 *Lancashire Evening Post*, 19 April 1955 and 29 February 1958.

47 On this renovative approach in Stirling's later work see Robert Maxwell, *Sweet Disorder and the Carefully Careless: Theory and Criticism in Architecture*, New York: Princeton Architectural Press, 1993, p. 231.

48 As Nicholas Taylor argued, only a few years later, Stirling and Gowan's housing was implicated in the 'visual bedlam and environmental chaos' of Avenham as a whole: Taylor, 'The Failure of Housing', p. 346.

49 'A few critics have questioned why they should wish to force the affluent aircraft workers back into a visual echo of the lean days of the cotton trade': ibid. Taylor also argued that the architects had not done what they set out to do, losing Victorian walled yards to a 'meaningless and useless patch of grass': ibid.

50 'Visitors could not decide which was the front and back door of his flat': *Lancashire Evening Post*, 7 June 1961.

51 On this image of the north see Dominic Sandbrook, *Never Had It So Good: A History of Britain from Suez to the Beatles*, London: Little, Brown, 2005, pp. 212–13.

52 *Architectural Design*, 31, July 1961, p. 285.

53 *Housing Review*, 11, May–June 1962, p. 23.

54 *Daily Mail*, 18 October 1963.

55 Nikolaus Pevsner, *North Lancashire*, London: Penguin, 1969, p. 198. For Pevsner on historicism see his 'Modern Architecture and the Historian or the Return of Historicism', *RIBAJ*, 68, April 1961, pp. 230–37.

56 *Casabella*, 260, February 1962, pp. 26–27. The reproductions accompany a translation of the statement by Stirling and Gowan that appeared in 'Re-housing at Preston, Lancashire', p. 538. The Lowry image was also sent out by Stirling and Gowan but only *Casa-*

bella seems to have used it: CCA 022:002 JS–018.

57   Reyner Banham, 'Neo-Liberty: The Italian Retreat from Modern Architecture', *Architectural Review*, April 1959, p. 235.

58   See, for instance, Maristella Casciato, 'Neo-realism in Italian Architecture', in Sarah Williams Goldhagen and Réjean Legault (eds), *Anxious Modernisms: Experimentation in Post-War Architecture Culture*, Cambridge, Mass.: MIT Press, 2000, pp. 25–53.

59   Reyner Banham, 'Coronation Street, Hoggartsborough', *New Statesman*, 9 February 1962, p. 200. Interestingly, an extract from Banham's review was republished in Arnell and Bickford's monograph on Stirling's work. The article marks one of the few critical commentaries in Banham's many reviews of Stirling's work. His criticism was clearer two years later: 'at Preston, they seem to have decided the appropriate character subjectively on the basis of arbitrary sociological decisions': Reyner Banham, 'The Style for the Job', *New Statesman*, 14 February 1964, p. 261.

60   Banham, 'Coronation Street', p. 200.

61   Ibid.

62   Ibid.

63   Ibid.

64   Ibid., p. 201.

65   Ibid.

66   See Tafuri, 'L'architecture', p. 267.

67   See Jules Lubbock, *The Tyranny of Taste: The Politics of Architecture and Design in Britain 1550–1960*, New Haven and London: Yale University Press, 1995, pp. 333–37.

68   Pevsner was far more concerned by modernist apostates playing with historicism than he was by 'Georgian-Palladian diehards': Pevsner, 'Modern Architecture', p. 230. For the relation between disgust and the picturesque as it was revived by Pevsner and others see John Macarthur, *The Picturesque: Architecture, Disgust and Other Irregularities*, London and New York: Routledge, 2007, pp. 105–6.

69   Pevsner defended the *Architectural Review* from the charge of historicism by using the example of the Bride of Denmark, a Victorian pub reassembled in the *Review*'s basement. This he called a 'folly' and certainly not an incubus for a Victorian revival: Pevsner, 'Modern Architecture', p. 234. Similarly, the use of Victorian typography in the *Architectural Review* was 'not a recommendation to look *à la Victorienne* but rather a recommendation to spice with Victorian ingredients': ibid., p. 235.

70   On this see Elain Harwood, 'Butterfield & Brutalism', *Architecture Association Files*, Summer 1994, pp. 39–46; Macarthur, *The Picturesque*, pp. 106–8.

71   'Re-housing at Preston, Lancashire', p. 538.

72   This formulation is partly inspired by similar comments in Maxwell, *Sweet Disorder*, pp. 316–18.

73   This was published in 'Re-housing at Preston, Lancashire,' p. 538.

74   The statement was sent out by the architects and was also photographed and enlarged for display with other images of the scheme: CCA 022:002 JS–018. Gowan has since said that the use of the Chaplin statement was more Stirling's idea than his, and that he thought it 'glib': James Gowan, interview with the author, 4 January 2006.

75   Jean Starobinski, 'The Idea of Nostalgia', *Diogenes*, 54, 1966, pp. 86–87.

76   On the denigration of memory by modernism see Adrian Forty, *Words and Buildings: A Vocabulary of Modern Architecture*, London: Thames and Hudson, 2000, pp. 215–19. On the problems of the return of memory to intellectual respectability see Kerwin Lee Klein, 'On the Emergence of Memory in Historical Discourse,' *Representations*, 69, Winter 2000, pp. 127–50. For nuanced discussions of nostalgia one needs to look outside architectural discourse: see Wendy Wheeler, 'Nostalgia Isn't Nasty: The Postmodernizing of Parliamentary Democracy', in Mark Perryman (ed.), *Altered States: Postmodernism,*

Politics, Culture, London: Lawrence & Wishart, 1994; Kathleen Stewart, 'Nostalgia: A Polemic', *Cultural Anthropology*, 3, 1988, pp. 227–41; and Doreen Massey, 'Space-time and the Politics of Location', in James Lingwood (ed.), *Rachel Whiteread: House*, London: Phaidon, 1995. Charles Moore, when asked to provide another term than 'post-modernism' to describe the movement, suggested 'nostalgesque' on the basis that artistic movements stood a better chance of survival when they were given a term of opprobrium (like 'gothic' or 'baroque'): 'Charles Moore on Post-Modernism', *AD Profiles 4: Post-Modernism*, London: AD Magazine, 1977, p. 255.

77 For use of the term in the inter-war period see Christopher Lasch, *The True and Only Heaven: Progress and its Critics*, New York: Norton, 1991, pp. 106–13.

78 Stirling continued to use the word later in his career. In 1987, for example, he spoke positively about 'nostalgia for the cities' destroyed both by bombs and post-war reconstruction: 'Stirling Stuff: Conversation with Sunand Prasad and Satish Grover', *Architecture and Design* (New Delhi), 5, July–August 1987, republished in Robert Maxwell (ed.), *James Stirling: Writings on Architecture*, Milan: Skira, 1998, p. 233.

79 Stewart, 'Nostalgia', p. 227.

80 Anthony Vidler, *The Architectural Uncanny: Essays in the Modern Unhomely*, Cambridge, Mass, MIT Press, 1992, p. 7.

81 On Stirling's early years see Mark Girouard, *Big Jim: The Life and Work of James Stirling*, London: Pimlico, 2000, pp. 1–3. On Stirling's use of nostalgic elements in his *c.*1984 redesign of Albert Dock to serve Tate Liverpool see Richard J. Williams, *The Anxious City: English Urbanism in the Late Twentieth Century*, London: Routledge, 2004, p. 113. For a reading of some of Stirling's later buildings in terms of his memories of Liverpool see Brian Hatton, 'Shifted Tideways: Liverpool's Changing Fortunes', *Architectural Review*, January 2008, pp. 48–50.

82 Colin Rowe, *As I Was Saying: Recollections and Miscellaneous Essays*, 3 vols, Cambridge, Mass. and London: MIT Press, 1996, vol. 3, p. 355.

83 See Peter Fritzshe, 'Specters of History: On Nostalgia, Exile and Modernity', *American Historical Review*, 106:5, December 2001, pp. 1591–92, 1595.

84 Richard Hoggart, *The Uses of Literacy*, Harmondsworth: Penguin, 1958, p. 285; Young and Willmott, *Family*, pp. 198–99. This thesis has since been much debated and often accused of middle-class sentimentality: see Jennifer Platt, *Social Research in Bethnal Green*, London: Macmillan, 1971; Mark Clapson, *Invisible Green Suburbs, Brave New Towns: Social Change and Urban Dispersal in Postwar England*, Manchester: Manchester University Press, 1998, pp. 64–67. For an updating of Young and Willmott's book, demonstrating that the changes it had predicted have come about, see Geoff Dench, Kate Gavron and Michael Young, *The New East End: Kinship, Race and Conflict*, London: Profile Books, 2006.

85 Reyner Banham, 'Form Fuddles Function', *New Statesman*, 23 April 1965, p. 656.

86 James Gowan, interview with the author, 4 January 2006.

87 James Gowan, 'Notes on American Architecture', *Perspecta*, 7, 1961, p. 77.

88 CCA DR2000:025:002:001–006. Slightly different variations on this can be seen in the drawing in Gowan's possession.

89 James Stirling, *James Stirling: Buildings and Projects 1950–1974*, London: Thames and Hudson, 1975, p. 62.

90 James Gowan, interview with the author, 4 January 2006.

91 This would have been the case even had the service road, which separates the hall from the main school building, been removed as promised: Woodman, *Modernity*, p. 197.

92 Stirling, *James Stirling*, p. 58.

93 'School Dining and Assembly Hall, Camberwell', *Architect and Building News*, 225, 18 March 1964, pp. 485, 488.

94 CCA DRCON2000:0027:720:140–0512; James Gowan, interview with the author, 28 May 2009.

95 Arnell and Bickford (eds), *James Stirling*, p. 77.

96 See 'Deed of Dissolution of Partnership', CCA DRCON2000:0027:720.

97 Woodman, *Modernity*, p. 198.

98 Although the bricks were not chosen by Gowan but forced on him because the LCC's supply of London stocks was committed: James Gowan, interview with the author, 28 May 2009.

99 Ibid.

100 James Stirling, 'Anti-Structure', *Zodiac*, 18, 1969, republished in Maxwell (ed.), *James Stirling*, p. 112.

101 Ibid.

102 Ibid.

103 Gowan has recently recognised this problem: Woodman, *Modernity*, p. 198.

104 It was built as part of an LCC programme resulting in fifty-four new homes by 1964: LCC Welfare Department, *Homes for Old People*, London: LCC, 1964.

105 Banham, 'Form Fuddles Function', p. 656.

106 Ruth Owens, 'Beyond the 60s', *Architects' Journal*, 190, 11 October 1989, p. 44.

107 As Stirling reported, 'the LCC descended upon the Home and managed to wall-paper every bedroom in a different pattern': Stirling, 'An Architect's Approach', p. 233.

108 CCA DR2000:029:001–003, drawing dated 12 December 1962.

109 CCA DRCON:2000:0027:820, lecture notes, 'Berlin '64'.

110 James Stirling, notes for a lecture: CCA DR2007:0083.

111 See Quentin Hughes, *Seaport: Architecture and Townscape of Liverpool*, London: Lund Humphries, 1964, pp. 48–49.

112 James Gowan, interview with the author, 16 May 2005.

113 Robert Maxwell, *James Stirling Michael Wilford*, Basel: Birkhäuser, 1998.

114 John Jacobus, 'Introduction', in Stirling, *James Stirling*, p. 17.

115 Milan Kundera, *Ignorance*, trans. Linda Asher, London: Faber & Faber, 2002, p. 8. Homer's *Odyssey* is, in Kundera's words, 'the founding epic of nostalgia'.

116 Reinhold Martin, *Utopia's Ghost: Architecture and Postmodernism, Again*, Minneapolis: University of Minnesota Press, 2010, p. 29.

117 'The idea of modernity would like there to be only one meaning and direction in history, whereas the temporality specific to the aesthetic regime of the arts is a co-presence of heterogeneous temporalities': Jacques Rancière, *The Politics of Aesthetics*, trans. Gabriel Rockhill, London: Continuum, 2004, p. 26.

6 THE MECHANICAL HOBGOBLIN

1 The Murray Report (1948) and the Niblett Report (1957).

2 Joseph Rykwert, 'Universities as Institutional Archetypes of Our Age', *Zodiac*, 18, 1969, p. 61.

3 'We tried to make contact with the very few older, pre-war architects we admired. Leslie Martin was one of the very few in this category': 'James Stirling in Tokyo: Interviewed by Arata Isozaki', in Robert Maxwell (ed.), *James Stirling: Writings on Architecture*, Milan: Skira, 1998, pp. 199–200.

4 Martin passed on commissions to Gillespie Kidd and Coia (halls of residence at Hull University), the Architects Co-Partnership (Leicester), the Smithsons (the Economist building in London), and Denys Lasdun (University of East Anglia), as well as other jobs to Peter Womersley and Trevor Dannatt.

5 Stefan Muthesius, *The Postwar University: Utopian Campus and College*, New Haven and London: Yale University Press, 2000, p. 4.

6   For the Churchill College competition see Elain Harwood, 'The Churchill College Competition and the Smithson Generation', in Louise Campbell (ed.), *Twentieth-Century Architecture and its Histories*, London: Society of Architectural Historians of Great Britain, 2000, pp. 37–56; Muthesius, *Postwar University*, pp. 65–70; Mark Goldie, *Corbusier Comes to Cambridge: Post-War Architecture and the Competition to Build Churchill College*, Cambridge: Churchill College, 2007; Amanda Reeser Lawrence, 'Revisioning History: Modern Strategies in Stirling's Early Work', *Oase*, 79, 2009, pp. 86–90. Powell and Moya did not enter, so there were actually twenty competitors.

7   For the brief see Churchill College Archives, CCGB/211/3. Martin's preference was that Alvar Aalto be asked to design the college, but the jury insisted on a British practice: interview with Patrick Hodgkinson, Mark Girouard Collection.

8   CCA DR 2000:0042:023:002. This is a photograph of a drawing which was probably destroyed by Stirling in the mid-1970s. The four finalists did not have their first schemes published, unlike most of the other sixteen competitors.

9   The purpose of the drawing was confirmed in conversation with Gowan: James Gowan, interview with the author, 20 June 2006.

10 Ellis Woodman, *Modernity and Invention: The Architecture of James Gowan*, London: Black Dog, 2008, p. 194. Gowan has said that this was suggested by the quadrant version of the Expandable House: ibid., p. 195.

11 'Churchill College: Report and Outline Specification', file marked 'Older Projects 1950–60', CCA DRCON2000:0027:720.

12 James Gowan, interview with the author, 20 June 2006.

13 Kit Evans, correspondence with the author, 23 July 2006.

14 Colin Rowe, 'The Blenheim of the Welfare State', *Cambridge Review*, 31 October 1959, republished in Colin Rowe, *As I Was Saying: Recollections and Miscellaneous Essays*, 3 vols, Cambridge, Mass. and London: MIT Press, 1996, vol. 1, p. 146.

15 Churchill College Archives, CCAR/401/1/1, letter of 21 April 1959 from the Secretary of the Churchill College Trust Fund to the finalists. Several first stage schemes, like that by the Smithsons, had included sculptural memorials to Churchill. Howell Killick and Partridge's final scheme envisaged an island tomb for the great leader.

16 'Churchill College', 'Older Projects 1950–60' file, CCA DRCON2000:0027:720.

17 James Stirling, '"The Functional Tradition" and Expression', *Perspecta*, 6, 1960, p. 97.

18 This separation of living quarters was one of the new guidelines sent to the finalists: CCAR/401/1/1, letter to finalists 21 April 1959.

19 Stirling, 'Functional Tradition', pp. 96–97.

20 Ibid., pp. 95–97.

21 Muthesius, *Postwar University*, p. 68.

22 Stirling, 'Functional Tradition', p. 96.

23 On the medieval model in post-war universities see Iain Boyd Whyte (ed.), *Man-Made Future: Planning, Education and Design in Mid-Twentieth Century Britain*, London and New York: Routledge, 2007, p. 217.

24 James Stirling, lecture notes titled 'Berlin '64', 'Older Projects 1950–60' file, CCA DRCON2000:0027:720.

25 *Architect and Building News*, 216, 9 August 1959, p. 152.

26 Rowe, 'Blenheim', p. 151.

27 Selwyn College Archives, Governing Body Minutes, 24 June 1959, SEGB/3.

28 Woodman, *Modernity and Invention*, p. 197. Selwyn College Archives, Governing Body Minutes, 2 March 1960, SEGB/3.

29 Selwyn College Archives, Governing Body Minutes, report of a discussion between Stirling and the college bursar, 23 March 1960, SEGB/3. All the drawings for these schemes are in the Selwyn College Archives.

30 It was published in *Architectural Review*, 129, January 1961, pp. 12–13.

31 Muthesius, *Postwar University*, pp. 76–77.

32 *Selwyn College Calendar*, 1960–61, p. 22.

33 Ibid.

34 'Topics for Discussion', two sheets of notes in James Stirling's handwriting, CCA DRCON2000:0027:720.

35 James Stirling, 'An Architect's Approach to Architecture', *RIBAJ*, 72, May 1965, p. 233.

36 Woodman, *Modernity*, p. 197.

37 This intention is made very clear in a section across the whole site showing sight lines: drawing dated 26 October 1959, Selwyn College Archives.

38 The Yale University Art Gallery was also well known in Britain through Reyner Banham's article, 'New Brutalism', *Architectural Review*, 118, December 1955, p. 357. Stirling referred to the Richards building's 'organised pattern of accommodation' in his 1960 article: Stirling, 'Functional Tradition', p. 95.

39 The terraced housing scheme was shown at CIAM 10 Dubrovnik in 1956.

40 See, for instance, the apartment building for Oued-Ouchaia, Algeria (1933–1934): Le Corbusier, *Oeuvre complète 1929–1934*, Zurich: Erlenbach, 1946, pp. 160–69.

41 James Stirling, 'Black Notebook', in Mark Crinson (ed.), *James Stirling: Early Unpublished Writings on Architecture*, London: Routledge, 2009, p. 22.

42 John Jacobus, 'Introduction', in James Stirling, *Buildings and Projects 1950–1974*, London: Thames and Hudson, 1975, pp. 19–20.

43 Selwyn College Archives, Governing Body Minutes, 26 April 1960, SEGB/3.

44 *Architectural Review*, 129, January 1961, p. 13.

45 All the drawings for these schemes are in the Selwyn College Archives.

46 This was the scheme that appeared as the frontispiece to the *Selwyn College Calendar* for 1960–61.

47 Ibid., p. 23.

48 This is supported by the fact that the drawing is not in the Selwyn College Archives, whereas all the others are.

49 *Architectural Review*, 129, January 1961, p. 12.

50 Selwyn College Archives, Governing Body Minutes, 2 March 1960 and 26 July 1960, SEGB/3.

51 James Gowan, interview with the author, 24 November 2007.

52 *Selwyn College Calendar*, 1960–61, p. 22. In another account it is suggested that the university syndicate responsible for developing the nearby Sidgwick site objected to the siting of Stirling and Gowan's scheme, and that a new site was contemplated but the architects were not prepared to start again from scratch: W. R. Brock and P. H. M. Cooper, *Selwyn College: A History*, Bishop Auckland: Penland, 1994, p. 248.

53 The best historical accounts of the building are Peter Blundell Jones and Eamonn Canniffe, *Modern Architecture Through Case Studies 1945–1990*, London: Architectural Press, 2007; John McKean, *Leicester University Engineering Building*, London: Phaidon, 1994; and Irenée Scalbert, 'Cerebral Functionalism: The Design of the Leicester University Engineering Building', *Archis*, 5, 1994, pp. 70–80.

54 Leicester University Engineering building brief, James Gowan Collection. Despite mention of other briefs ('a few laconic sheets of foolscap': McKean, *Leicester*, p. 20) and references to them in the Leicester University Archives, this one-page brief is the only one that seems to survive.

55 *Architectural Design*, 34, February 1964, p. 63.

56 Stirling, 'An Architect's Approach', p. 239.

57 Stirling and Gowan to Parkes, 7 November 1959, file titled 'Leicester "Brief" etc', CCA DRCON2000:0027:720.

58 Woodman, *Modernity*, p. 199.

59 Leicester University Archives, Gowan to Registrar, 24 August 1959, EST/BUI/ENG/13/5.

60 Leicester University Archives, Buildings Advisory Committee Minutes, 4 November 1959.

61   Leicester University Archives, Parkes to Gowan, 16 November 1959, EST/BUI/ENG/13/5.

62   Leicester University Archives, Buildings Advisory Committee Minutes, 14 December 1959.

63   Leicester University Archives, Parkes to Vice Chancellor, 18 January 1960, EST/BUI/ENG/13/5.

64   Leicester University Archives, Parkes to Gowan, 31 December 1959, EST/BUI/ENG/13/5.

65   Leicester University Archives, Parkes to Vice Chancellor, 31 December 1959, EST/BUI/ENG/13/5.

66   He wrote to Gowan, 'please let us have the original admirable office block where it was, even at some sacrifice of proximities (I understand from my recent discussion with Mr Stirling that the proximity problems may be solved another way)': Leicester University Archives, Parkes to Gowan, 31 December 1959, EST/BUI/ENG/13/5.

67   Leicester University Archives, telegraph from Parkes to Vice Chancellor, 2 March 1960, EST/BUI/ENG/13/4; and Parkes to Stirling and Gowan, 7 March 1960, EST/BUI/ENG/13/4. Parkes's letter to the architects was fulsome in its praise but also, notably, continues the process of dialogue by arguing for several minor changes.

68   Leicester University Archives, Buildings Advisory Committee Minutes, 15 March 1960.

69   He mentioned these in the list of previous works submitted by both architects to the university: Leicester University Archives, EST/BUI/ENG/13/5.

70   James Gowan (ed.), *Projects: Architectural Association 1946–71*, London: Architectural Association, 1973, p. 42.

71   Leicester University Archives, Buildings Advisory Committee Minutes, 10 May and 17 May 1960.

72   Leicester University Archives, Buildings Advisory Committee Minutes, 26 September 1959 and 1 March 1961; McKean, *Leicester*, p. 22.

73   James Gowan, interview with the author, 29 July 2009; Michael Wilford, interview with the author, 30 July 2009. For accounts of the work of these assistants see McKean, *Leicester*, p. 29; Mark Girouard, *Big Jim: The Life and Work of James Stirling*, London: Pimlico, p. 107.

74   The 'approximate division of responsibility' described by Girouard is based on Newby's memory: Girouard, *Big Jim*, p. 115. However, this was only a brief separation of detailing tasks that coincided with Newby's first contact with the project in the spring of 1960: James Gowan, interview with the author, 29 July 2009; Michael Wilford, interview with the author, 30 July 2009.

75   DAM 246–001–011.

76   DAM 246–001–003. There are notes written on the drawing: 'This is structural slope [?] therefore *no* column required at end.'

77   DAM 246–001–005.

78   DAM 246–001–002.

79   Michael Wilford, interview with the author, 30 July 2009.

80   Michael Wilford, lecture at Yale University symposium, 'James Stirling: Architect and Teacher', 10 May 2009.

81   A specific source for this was cited by Gowan – Van Doesburg and Van Eesteren's artist's house project of 1923: Scalbert, 'Cerebral Functionalism', p. 78.

82   See Yve-Alain Bois, 'Metamorphosis of Axonometry', *Daidalos*, 1, 1981, pp. 40–58.

83   Anthony Vidler, *James Frazer Stirling: Notes from the Archive*, Montreal, New Haven and London: CCA, YCBA and Yale University Press, 2010, pp. 238–40.

84   Robert Maxwell, 'Frontiers of Inner Space', *Sunday Times* (colour supplement), 29 September 1963, p. 7.

85   James Stirling, 'Royaumont Talk', in Crinson (ed.), *James Stirling*, p. 91.

86   James Gowan, *Style and Configuration*, London: Academy Editions, 1994, p. 87.

87 'When I went to the US for the first time I found the asymmetric turn of the century stick houses of even a town like New Haven a revelation. Furness in Philadelphia and H. H. Richardson in Boston were superb': James Stirling, Cambridge Talk, 25 May 1980, Mark Girouard Collection. The talk is similar to the RIBA Gold Medal talk that Stirling gave in the same year, but the latter does not include the reference to Furness.

88 Le Corbusier, *Oeuvre complète 1929–1934*, p. 171.

89 CCA DRCON2000:0027:003:001–007.

90 See Mark Crinson, '*L'Architecte Anglais*: Stirling and Le Corbusier', in Crinson (ed.), *James Stirling*, pp. 108–39.

91 Such north-facing lights were not on Parkes's original brief: Leicester University Engineering building brief, James Gowan Collection.

92 Stirling, 'Royaumont Talk', p. 91.

93 This was worked out by Gowan using balsa wood models: James Gowan, interview with the author, 6 July 2007.

94 Interview with Edward Parkes, Mark Girouard Collection.

95 The link has been obscured rather than clarified by the sources usually pointed to as images for Melnikov's building. Girouard cites 'Bruno Zevi's *Architecture Moderne*', a book that appears not to exist, and the unnamed Russian books lent to Stirling by Paul Manousso: Girouard, *Big Jim*, p. 77. Scalbert cites 'Zevi's *Spazi dell'Architettura Moderna*', a book not published until 1973: Scalbert, 'Cerebral Functionalism', p. 74. Vidler cites Vittorio de Feo's *URSS architettura 1917–1936*, which was not published until 1963: Vidler, *James Frazer Stirling*, p. 127, n. 130. Vidler also mentions articles by Berthold Lubetkin in the *Architectural Association Journal* (May 1956, pp. 260–64), but these do not reproduce Melnikov's building. In general, publications on Russian constructivist architecture only began reappearing in the mid- and late 1950s, after a quarter-century gap: see the bibliography in

de Feo, *URSS*. If there is a possible relevant source it is Zevi's *Storia dell'architettura moderna* (Turin: Einaudi, 1950), which published a plan, section and photograph of Melnikov's building. While remaining open to the possibility that Melnikov's building was known to the architects at the time, two points need making here: first, that the link has not been definitively made, and, second, that the form of the lecture theatres does not depend upon this link anyway. Indeed, the constructivist affiliation brings in a range of associations that have obscured Leicester's own design evolution as well as its links to Stirling's previous work.

96 K. Melnikov, 'The Rusakov Workers' Club', in Rishat Mullagildin (ed.), *Architecture of Konstantin Melnikov 1920s–30s*, Tokyo: TOTO Shupan, 2002, p. 48.

97 DAM 246–001–011.

98 Colin Rowe, 'Mannerism and Modern Architecture', *Architectural Review*, 107, May 1950, p. 290.

99 James Gowan, interview with the author, 29 July 2009.

100 Although Newby had been appointed soon after Stirling and Gowan were commissioned, his active involvement only started in May 1960: I am grateful to David Yeomans for this and other information on Newby's Leicester contribution based on his research in Frank Newby's personal papers.

101 Girouard, *Big Jim*, pp. 82–83.

102 Ibid., p. 113; McKean, *Leicester*, pp. 24–29.

103 Parkes suggested the change in March 1960: Leicester University Archives, Parkes to Stirling and Gowan, 7 March 1960, EST/BUI/ENG/13/4. It might be assumed that Newby provided the solution to the problem identified by Parkes, but Parkes had already suggested the architects revert to the 'sloping brackets' that he had seen in an earlier design: Parkes to Stirling and Gowan, 7 March 1960, file titled 'Leicester "Brief" etc', CCA DRCON2000:0027:720. Parkes did not just see this as a practical change – '[the

sloping brackets] seemed to balance the raked lecture theatres on the north side': ibid.

104   The Department of Engineering, Oxford University (1960–62), by Ramsay, Murray, White & Ward.

105   Stirling, 'Black Notebook', p. 53.

106   Reyner Banham, 'Vehicles of Desire', *Art*, 1, 1 September 1955, p. 3.

107   Reyner Banham, 'The Style for the Job', *New Statesman*, 14 February 1964, p. 261.

108   *Architectural Design*, 34, February 1964, p. 63.

109   Ibid.

110   This is most apparent in the talk he gave to the Team 10 Group in 1962: Stirling, 'Royaumont Talk', pp. 85–100. This deference was one of the subjects of the discussion after the talk.

111   CCA DR2000:0027:006:001–004, DR2000:-027:004:001–005.

112   Leicester University Archives, Buildings Advisory Committee Minutes, 31 May 1961.

113   Michael Wilford, interview with the author, 30 July 2009; Woodman, *Modernity*, p. 200. For the problems with patent glazing see Alan Berman, 'Building the Future: Challenges and Failures of Postwar Architecture', in Alan Berman (ed.), *Jim Stirling and the Red Trilogy: Three Radical Buildings*, London: Frances Lincoln, 2010, pp. 71–72.

114   Stirling, 'An Architect's Approach', p. 236.

115   Peter Eisenman, 'Real and English: The Destruction of the Box I', *Oppositions*, 4, October 1974, p. 32, n.1. Eisenman mentions Stirling's Sheffield University competition design (1953) as a forerunner, but he can only mean this for its treatment of the implied wall planes as its composition is still that of a single box, even if stretched either side of a central corridor.

116   Ibid., pp. 7, 9 and 20.

117   Manfredo Tafuri, 'L'Architecture dans le Boudoir', *The Sphere and the Labyrinth: Avant-Gardes and Architecture from Piranesi to the 1970s*, Cambridge, Mass. and London:

MIT Press, 1990, pp. 267–71, originally published in *Oppositions*, 3, May 1974.

118   That the Churchill library was in Gowan's mind as a precedent is clear from contemporary comments: *Architects' Journal*, 139, 25 March 1964, p. 678.

119   On this see Claire Zimmerman, 'James Stirling's "Real Function"', *Oase*, 79, 2009, pp. 128–30.

120   Ulrich Beck, 'The Reinvention of Politics: Towards a Theory of Reflexive Modernization', in Ulrich Beck, Anthony Giddens and Scott Lash, *Reflexive Modernization: Politics, Tradition and Aesthetics in the Modern Social Order*, Cambridge: Polity, 1994, p. 2.

121   Leicester University Archives, Parkes to Gowan, 16 November 1959, EST/BUI/ENG/13/5.

122   The commission came via Basil Spence, who nominated the partners for this British Steel job as one of among twelve practices considered. Most of the design work was left to Gowan because of Stirling's teaching duties at Yale: James Gowan, interview with the author, 30 June 2006. A similar pattern, though in wooden boarding, was used in the partners' small refitting project for a school at Eltham. This project dates to 1957 and came to the partners because they were registered on the LCC's small works list: James Gowan, interview with the author, 22 February 2008. The project was mentioned in lecture notes *c.*1959 by Stirling – 'LCC Kitchen – Churchill   consolation – minor work': CCA DR2007:0083. There are negatives in CCA DR2006:0022:001 VIII James Stirling.

123   Gowan had designed factory prototypes before this at Stevenage and went on to design warehouses at Deptford, Hackney and Bermondsey after the partnership ended. Stirling made several designs for industrial clients in his later career, including for Dorman Long, Siemens, and Olivetti.

124   Although the decorative use of the corrugated pattern is reminiscent of the patterns

of weatherboarding on buildings in the 'functional tradition': see the special issue on 'The Functional Tradition', *Architectural Review*, 108, January 1950, p. 29.

125 This was the substance of his 1959 Rede Lecture, but had been trailed three years before in an article in the *New Statesman*, 6 October 1956, pp. 41–42.

126 Interestingly, he used Snow's anathematisation of the incomprehension of science to justify a respect for the specialist knowledge of his clients at Leicester. In this situation, Stirling suggested, the architect had to accept a modest role in determining the form of a building: Stirling, 'Royaumont Talk', p. 94.

127 Michael Sanderson, *The Universities and British Industry, 1850–1970*, London: Routledge and Kegan Paul, 1972, pp. 349–50.

128 One response came with Harold Wilson's new government setting up a Ministry of Technology in 1964, to which Snow was appointed as Parliamentary Under Secretary.

129 Donald Cardwell, *The Organisation of Science in England*, Melbourne: Heinemann, 1957. This aspect of Cardwell's argument has been supported by more recent historians: see David Edgerton, *Science, Technology and the British Industrial 'Decline', 1870–1970*, Cambridge: Cambridge University Press, 1996, p. 23.

130 Sanderson, *The Universities*, p. 364.

131 Jack Simmons, *Leicester and its University*, Leicester: Leicester University Press, 1957, pp. 41–42.

132 Leicester University Archives, Development Committee file, EST/BUI/ENG/13.

133 *Architects' Journal*, 139, 25 March 1964, p. 678; Stirling, 'Royaumont Talk', p. 86.

134 Stirling, 'Royaumont Talk', p. 86.

135 Leicester University Archives, report dated January 1962, EST/BUI/ENG/13.

136 Colin Rowe, 'James Stirling: A Highly Personal and Very Disjointed Memoir', in Peter Arnell and Ted Bickford (eds), *James Stirling: Buildings and Projects*, New York: Rizzoli, 1984, p. 14.

137 Interviews with Edward Parkes and Patrick Hodgkinson, Mark Girouard Collection.

138 Martin may have been persuaded that towers on the park side of the campus were a good way to solve problems of expansion, as the Wilson building (by Lasdun) and the Attenborough building (by Arup Associates) were both later approved.

139 Contemporary critics seized positively on this same effect. 'This . . . must cause acute embarrassment to the proponents of coherence through master planning. . . . its uniqueness only reinforces the impression that a kind of Darwinian, laissez-faire attitude is mandatory in the hammering out of vital new buildings. Especially at a time when so much contemporary design is compromised by exaggerated respect for locale': John Jacobus, 'Engineering Building, Leicester University', *Architectural Review*, 135, April 1964, p. 253.

140 I am deliberately reusing the language Beck deploys to describe what he calls the 'individualization' of reflexive modernisation: Beck, 'The Reinvention', pp. 13–14.

141 C. P. Snow, *The Two Cultures: And a Second Look*, Cambridge: Cambridge University Press, 1964, p. 31.

142 Beck, 'The Reinvention', pp. 2, 28–29; Ulrich Beck, *Risk Society: Towards a New Modernity*, London: Sage, 1992, p. 11.

143 'Eight Questions to Stirling and Gowan', *Polygon*, 5, 1960, republished in Crinson (ed.), *James Stirling*, pp. 79–80.

144 One of Wilford's tasks was to find 'gaps' like this – areas of the building undeveloped in the partners' designs – and resolve them: Michael Wilford, interview with the author, 30 July 2009. For Wilford's drawing see McKean, *Leicester*, p. 22.

145 Woodman, *Modernity*, p. 202.

146 Stirling, 'An Architect's Approach', p. 233.

147 Craig Hodgetts, 'Inside James Stirling', *Design Quarterly*, 100, 1976, p. 4.

148 This is the Portuguese architect Amancio Guedes's response during a discussion fol-

lowing a talk by Stirling: Stirling, 'Royaumont Talk', pp. 92–93.

149   Eisenman, 'Real and English', p. 10.

150   Ibid., p. 30. What I am suggesting implicitly here is that Eisenman's argument failed to follow its own logic through into non-formal aspects of the building.

151   Stirling might have remembered here the combination of monument and public lavatory (below it) in Liverpool's Queen Victoria monument: Stirling's undated drawing of this is reproduced in Arnell and Bickford (eds), *James Stirling*, p. 175.

152   In Gowan's words, the architects 'pulverised the doors to accept the consequences of the skin': *Architects' Journal*, 139, 25 March 1964, p. 678.

153   Peter St John in Berman (ed.), *Jim Stirling and the Red Trilogy*, p. 107.

154   I am grateful to Michael Farr for alerting me to this range of colours.

155   Banham, 'Style for the Job', p. 261.

156   *Architectural Design*, 34, February 1964, p. 85.

157   See, for instance, Charles Jencks, *Modern Movements in Architecture*, Harmondsworth: Penguin, 1973, p. 264.

158   Stirling, *Buildings and Projects*, p. 176.

7   AFTERMATH

1   For an account of Stirling's teaching at Yale see Mark Girouard, *Big Jim: The Life and Work of James Stirling*, London: Pimlico, 2000, pp. 116–36.

2   John McKean, *Leicester University Engineering Building*, London: Phaidon, 1994, p. 17. Stirling was also seeking to set up a practice in the States: Girouard, *Big Jim*, p. 127.

3   Girouard, *Big Jim*, p. 138; David Gray, interview with the author, 17 October 2005; James Gowan, interview with the author, 4 January 2006.

4   The *New Statesman* project was for a seven-storey office block. This got as far as prelimi-

nary designs, although none have survived. It was stopped by the refusal of planning permission after drawings were submitted in July 1963: CCA DRCON2000:0027:905/906/907/908/909; correspondence for 10/11 Great Turnstile, Holborn, in London Borough of Camden Planning Office.

5   CCA DRCON2000:0027:720, 'Deed of Dissolution of Partnership'. The deed also determined what would happen about copyright on drawings and access to them: 'The copyright in all designs, drawings and buildings at any time made or designed by the Partnership shall . . . from the dissolution date belong to the Partners as tenants in common in equal shares.' All letters, documents, designs and drawings relating to the partnership were to be made available to the other partner for inspection and copying. However, these provisos on the practice's drawings would not prevent later disputes about one partner passing off the other's drawings as his own rather than as joint work of the partnership. When Stirling exhibited drawings at the Heinz Gallery in 1974, Gowan claimed that Stirling had omitted to mention that some were by him: *Architects' Journal*, 159, 15 May 1974, p. 1062; *Architects' Journal*, 159, 29 May 1974, p. 1182. I see this as another demonstration of how easy it was to minimise Gowan's contribution. Stirling was not to blame for this, but rather a critic who wrote of the 'strong but fastidious quality of Stirling's draughtsmanship' beside a drawing of Churchill College that had been entirely Gowan's work: *RIBAJ*, 81, April 1974, p. 11. The effect of the exchange of letters and the adjustment to the catalogue's attributions was not so much to give greater credit to Gowan but to make him appear only one among many other draughtsman employed by Stirling: *RIBAJ*, 81, May 1974, p. 8; *RIBAJ*, 81, June 1974, p. 2.

6   James Gowan, 'Home: A Castle for an Englishman' (1977), republished in James Gowan,

Style and Configuration, London: Academy Editions, 1994, p. 56.

7 Robert Maxwell, 'Frontiers of Inner Space', *Sunday Times Magazine*, 29 September 1963, p. 7.

8 Reyner Banham, 'The Word in Britain: "Character"', *Architectural Forum*, August–September 1964, p. 119.

9 Nikolaus Pevsner, 'The Anti-Pioneers', BBC Third Programme talk given 3 December 1966, republished in Stephen Games (ed.), *Pevsner on Art and Architecture: The Radio Talks*, London: Methuen, 2002, pp. 299–300. Ironically, Pevsner compared Leicester's 'violent self-expression' with the 'calm outline' and 'beautiful grouping' of Gollins Melvin Ward's Sheffield University buildings.

10 Smithson's comments (which Alison Smithson supported) were made after a talk on Leicester given by Stirling to the 1962 meeting of Team 10 at the Abbaye Royaumont: see Mark Crinson (ed.), *James Stirling: Early Unpublished Writings on Architecture*, London: Routledge, 2009, pp. 94, 97.

11 Joseph Rykwert, 'Universities as Institutional Archetypes of Our Age', *Zodiac*, 18, 1969, p. 61.

12 Kenneth Frampton, 'Leicester University Engineering Laboratory', *Architectural Design*, 34, February 1964, p. 61.

13 James Stirling, 'Black Notebook' in Crinson (ed.), *James Stirling*, pp. 34, 37–39.

14 Stanley Mathews, *From Agit-Prop to Free Space: The Architecture of Cedric Price*, London: Black Dog, 2007, p. 195.

15 John McKean, 'The English University of the 1960s: Built Community, Model Universe', in Iain Boyd Whyte (ed.), *Man-Made Future: Planning, Education and Design in Mid-Twentieth Century Britain*, London: Routledge, 2007, pp. 205–22.

16 Mathews, *From Agit-Prop*, p. 238.

17 Stirling, 'Black Notebook', p. 26.

18 A cream coloured brick was originally intended, but this was changed to blue engi-neering brick when it was realised how tempting the retaining wall would be for graffiti: James Gowan, interview with the author, 28 May 2009.

19 The house has clear points of comparison with Frank Lloyd Wright's Richard Lloyd Jones house in Tulsa (1929), designed on a grid and with similar façades of alternating vertical windows and brick piers: see H.-R. Hitchcock, *In the Nature of Materials: The Buildings of Frank Lloyd Wright 1887–1941*, New York: Hawthorn, 1942, figs 297–301.

20 Gowan found Georgian precedents for the serrated forms: Ellis Woodman, *Modernity and Reinvention: The Architecture of James Gowan*, London: Black Dog, 2008, p. 109. The precedents are 'Leinster Square, the north end of Gloucester Terrace and Powis Square': *James Gowan*, ed. David Dunster, Architectural Monographs 3, London: Academy Editions, 1978, p. 70.

21 Banham defended Stirling by sidestepping the issue. It was Gowan, he said, not Stirling who invented the term 'style for the job': Reyner Banham, 'History Faculty, Cambridge', *Architectural Review*, 144, November 1968, p. 329. This ignores the fact that the term 'multi-aesthetic' – used by both architects – was interchangeable with 'style for the job'.

22 See Gavin Stamp, '"Stirling's Worth": The History Faculty Building', *Cambridge Review*, 30 January 1976, pp. 77–82; Gavin Stamp, 'The Durability of Reputation: The Cambridge History Faculty', *Harvard Design Magazine*, Autumn 1997, pp. 54–57; Nicholas Ray, 'The Cambridge History Faculty Building: A Case Study in Ethical Dilemmas in the Twentieth Century', in Nicholas Ray (ed.), *Architecture and its Ethical Dilemmas*, London and New York: Routledge, 2005; Girouard, *Big Jim*, pp. 152–55. A full account of the construction history of the Cambridge History Faculty building and the relative responsibilities of architect, client, builders and subcontractors for its failings must still

await full research exploiting the CCA's holdings: see CCA DRCON2000:0027:025, CCA DRCON2000:0027:023, CCA DRCON-2000:0027:022, CCA DRCON2000:–0027:020, CCA DRCON2000:0027:009, etc.

23 This is the gist of Eisenman's critique of the Florey and the Cambridge History Faculty buildings as not 'addressing the same issues critically . . . [they] are not in their compositional attitude invested with the same relational structure': Peter Eisenman, 'Real and English: The Destruction of the Box I', *Oppositions*, 4, October 1974, p. 30.

24 Colin Rowe and Fred Koetter, *Collage City*, Cambridge, Mass.: MIT Press, 1978, p. 149.

25 Woodman, *Modernity*, p. 203.

26 It was commissioned in 1963 after a limited competition in which Leslie Martin advocated Stirling and Gowan.

27 A doodle on the back of letter from Stirling to R. Arkwright shows him explaining the panopticon concept at the beginning of May 1963: CCA DRCON2000:0027:023. Among other examples of panoptic libraries are the British Library and the Manchester Central Library. The type is not to be found among other libraries in Cambridge.

28 William Fawcett, 'Understanding the History Faculty, Cambridge', in Alan Berman (ed.), *Jim Stirling and the Red Trilogy: Three Radical Buildings*, London: Frances Lincoln, 2010, p. 48.

29 All of them recently reiterated for Stirling in the evocative photographs of Quentin Hughes's *Seaport* (1964), two copies of which were in Stirling's library: Lady Stirling Collection. Stirling seems to have taken or collected a number of photographs of Liverpool's Lime Street Station in the early 1960s: CCA DR2006:0022 Stirling I and II.

30 CCA DR2006:0022.

31 James Stirling, 'An Architect's Approach to Architecture', *RIBAJ*, 72, May 1965, p. 236.

32 Stirling, 'An Architect's Approach', pp. 235–36; Banham, 'History Faculty, Cambridge', p. 330. See also the section drawings indicating

sightlines: James Stirling, *James Stirling: Buildings and Projects*, London: Thames and Hudson, 1975, pp. 88–89.

33 Alvin Boyarsky, 'Stirling "Dimostrationi"', *Architectural Design*, 38, October 1968, p. 455.

34 This was one of the criticisms made by Stamp: Stamp, 'Stirling's Worth', p. 79.

35 Concerning this offensiveness, there was something of a reprise of Stirling's criticism of the Festival of Britain; now his building itself could do the job of attacking its neighbour, Casson and Conder's 'effete' Faculty of Arts building (1952): Reyner Banham, 'Cambridge: Mark II', *New Society*, 26 September 1968, p. 454. Casson was actually on the committee that chose Stirling for the History Faculty. As Pevsner memorably wrote, 'Sir Hugh must have fully known that he voted for a shock for himself. . . . Perhaps if [Casson] had not been so playful, James Stirling might not have been so rude': Nikolaus Pevsner, *Cambridgeshire*, The Buildings of England, Harmondsworth: Penguin, 1970, pp. 216–17.

36 The visual links with the nearby tower of Magdalen College, as suggested in the Black Book, are, though, entirely spurious: Stirling, *James Stirling*, p. 118. So too is the hilarious background of palm trees collaged into a photograph of the opening ceremony: ibid., p. 124.

37 Le Corbusier, *Oeuvre complète 1934–1938*, Zurich: Girsberger, 1953, pp. 82–87. This was itself a variation on several schemes for apartment blocks with stepped back profiles: see, for instance, *Oeuvre complète 1929–1934*, Zurich: Girsberger, 1935, pp. 160–67. The stepped back form itself has several modernist precedents: see, for example, Marcel Breuer's hospital at Elberfeld (1928). On these precedents see also Claire Zimmerman, 'James Stirling's "Real Function"', *Oase*, 79, 2009, pp. 132–34.

38 This represents a reversal of Stirling's feelings about Aalto's building: Colin Rowe,

'Eulogy: Jim Stirling', *As I Was Saying: Recollections and Miscellaneous Essays*, 3 vols, Cambridge, Mass. and London: MIT Press, 1996, vol. 3, p. 344.

39 Robert Maxwell, 'A Rakish Dorm Confronts Oxford', *Architecture Plus*, 1, February 1973, p. 28.

40 A comparison with Trinity College's gate towers was sometimes made in Stirling's lectures: 'Jim the Great', *Casabella*, 399, 1975, p. 24.

41 Such ambiguities might include the demands made on the residents to operate environmental controls in order to adjust their living conditions. For the maintenance and operating problems with the building see Girouard, *Big Jim*, pp. 156–60; Igea Troiani, '"Stirling's Worth": Architectural Quality and the Florey Building, Oxford', *ARQ*, 11, December 2007, pp. 291–99.

42 The simplest of the 'red buildings' was the block of flats in Camden Town (1964–68). The red brick, glass and tile façades contrast starkly with the surrounding terraces of Victorian stucco. The building gains a certain justification for this rudeness in an older block of flats (1954–56) by Ernö Goldfinger that shares its bombsite and backs directly onto its garden. Although Stirling's planning is unexceptional, the building's elevations evoke Stirling's favourite 1950s precedents: it is Morettian in the central slot that divides the building at the back, and Corbusian in the Poissy-like circulation of cars in the basement parking or the Garches-like arrangement of stairs, ramp, canopy and *fenêtres en longueur* at the front.

43 James Stirling, 'Anti-Structure', *Zodiac*, 18, 1969, republished in Robert Maxwell (ed.), *James Stirling: Writings on Architecture*, Milan: Skira, 1998, p. 120.

44 Joseph Rykwert, 'Stirling in Scozia', *Domus*, 491, October 1970, pp. 5–15. See also Michael Spens, 'Stirling's Finale: The Two Roads to Melsungen', *ARQ*, 5, September 2001, especially pp. 338–43.

45 Manfredo Tafuri, 'L'architecture dans le boudoir', *The Sphere and the Labyrinth: Avant-Gardes and Architecture from Piranesi to the 1970s*, Cambridge, Mass. and London: MIT Press, 1990, p. 270.

46 Gowan's own entry to the Runcorn housing competition is reproduced in *James Gowan*, pp. 68–69.

47 Girouard, *Big Jim*, pp. 160–62.

48 Ibid., pp. 187–91.

49 Colin Rowe, 'James Stirling: A Highly Personal and Very Disjointed Memoir', in Peter Arnell and Ted Bickford (eds), *James Stirling: Buildings and Projects*, New York: Rizzoli, 1984, p. 21. See also Heinrich Klotz, *The History of Postmodern Architecture*, Cambridge, Mass.: MIT Press, 1988, p. 331. Krier still sees Derby (and the Siemens Headquarters project) as an integral part of his work, although when Maurice Culot attributed Derby to Krier it inspired a letter of complaint from Stirling: interview with Leon Krier, Mark Girouard Collection.

50 James Stirling, 'Architectural Aims and Influences', *RIBAJ*, 87, September 1980, p. 37.

51 The book was trailed by an article: Colin Rowe and Fred Koetter, 'Collage City', *Architectural Review*, 157, August 1975, pp. 65–91.

52 For Rowe see Anthony Vidler, *Histories of the Immediate Present: Inventing Architectural Modernism*, Cambridge, Mass.: MIT Press, 2008, pp. 80–81. One sign of a similar taste in Stirling is his collecting of Thomas Hope furniture, starting probably in the late 1960s.

53 Anthony Vidler, *James Frazer Stirling: Notes from the Archive*, Montreal, New Haven and London: CCA, YCBA and Yale University Press, 2010, p. 185.

54 William Ellis, 'Type and Context in Urbanism: Colin Rowe's Contextualism', in K. Michael Hay (ed.), *The Oppositions Reader*, New York: Princeton Architectural Press, 1998, p. 34.

55   Bruno Latour, *We Have Never Been Modern*, trans. Catherine Porter, Cambridge, Mass.: Harvard University Press, 1993, p. 43.

56   *James Gowan*, p. 70.

57   James Gowan, interview with the author, 22 February 2008.

58   *Architectural Review*, 148, September 1970, p. 192.

59   Ibid., p. 191; *Architectural Design*, 40, April 1970, pp. 187–205; *Architectural Review*, 178, August 1985, pp. 44–54; *Architecture + Design*, 11, March–April 1994, pp. 53–59.

60   'Amérique Latine: méthodes et problèmes', *Architecture d'Aujourd'hui*, 173, June 1974, pp. 300–2.

61   Something like 60 per cent according to one source: *Architectural Review*, 178, August 1985, p. 54.

62   In this formulation I am adapting Ben Highmore's discussion of the relation between aesthetics and everyday life: Ben Highmore, *Everyday Life and Cultural Theory*, London: Routledge, 2002, pp. 19–24

63   Stirling, 'An Architect's Approach', p. 231.

64   The nearest Stirling would come was to say, 'I feel on the fringe of postmodernism. . . . I don't feel part of it': *James Stirling*, video directed by Michael Blackwood, Michael Blackwood Productions, 1987.

65   Most obviously the two exhibitions, *Roma Interrotta* at the Mercato di Traiano, Rome (1978), and *The Future of the Past* at the Venice Biennale (1980).

66   The terms are from Frederic Jameson's classic essay, 'Postmodernism, or the Cultural Logic of Late Capitalism', *New Left Review*, 146, July–August 1984, p. 85.

67   'Nostalgesque' was a term suggested by Charles Moore to replace postmodernism: 'Charles Moore on Post-Modernism', *AD Profiles 4: Post-Modernism*, London: AD Magazine, 1977, p. 255.

Photograph credits

Sandra Lousada – 1

B. Szmidt (ed.), *The Polish School of Architecture 1942–1945* – 2

Liverpool University Archives – 3, 5

James Stirling/Michael Wilford Fonds, Collection Centre Canadien d'Architecture/Canadian Centre for Architecture, Montreal – 4, 6, 7, 8, 9, 10, 12, 13, 14, 16, 17, 20, 21, 22. 23, 38, 39, 40, 41, 42, 45, 47, 49, 52, 59, 60, 61, 64, 65, 66, 68, 71, 72, 74, 86, 87, 90, 104, 105, 107, 109, 113, 118, 119, 120, 122, 123, 125, 126, 127, 128, 131, 133, 137, 140, 141, 148, 152, 162, 182, 191, 192, 195, 198, 200

Architectural Review – 11 (March 1947), 43 (May 1950), 75 (September 1955), 76 (March 1956), 114 (March 1960)

FLC/ADAGP, Paris, and DACS, London – 15, 18, 159

Lady Stirling – 24, 25, 67, 70, 93

RIBA Library Photographs Collection – 26, 194

James Gowan – 27, 29, 30, 31, 32, 33, 34, 35, 91, 92, 108, 110, 112, 116, 130, 132, 135, 145, 153, 167, 183, 184, 185

Mark Crinson – 28, 48, 80, 82, 83, 84, 85, 88, 89, 111, 129, 136, 138, 149, 161, 163, 165, 170, 171, 172, 173, 174, 175, 176, 177, 178, 179, 180, 184, 188, 189, 190, 193

Architects' Journal – 36 (15 February 1951), 144 (13 August 1959)

Architect and Building News – 37 (7 January 1959)

Spazio – 44 (December 1952)

Architectural Design – 46 (January 1959), 55 (August 1954), 57 (November 1955), 100 (April 1956), 115 (December 1953), 121 (September 1961), 124 (September 1961), 160 (February 1964), 166 (February 1964)

M. J. Long – 50

Smithson family – 51, 56, 62

Eric Firley/RIBA Library Photographs Collection – 53

Architectural Press Archive/RIBA Library Photographs Collection – 54, 187

Vancouver Province – 58 (February 1955)

Design – 63 (March 1959)

J. M. Richards, *The Bombed Buildings of Britain* – 69

Architects' Year Book 8 – 73

Mark Girouard – 77

London Borough of Richmond on Thames – 78, 79, 81

Deutsches Architektur Museum, Frankfurt – 94, 95, 96, 97, 106, 134, 143, 155, 156, 157, 158, 168

House & Garden – 98 (April 1957), 101 (April 1957), 102 (April 1957)

Ideal Home – 99 (1954)

Wycombe District Council (redrawn by the author) – 103

Preston Borough Council – 117

Quentin Hughes, *Seaport* – 139

RIBA Library Drawings Collection – 142, 146

Selwyn College Archives – 147, 150, 151

James Gowan, *Projects: Architectural Association 1946–71* – 154

Vittorio de Feo, *URSS architettura 1917–1936* – 164

Leslie Martin, *Buildings and Ideas 1933–83* – 169

James Stirling, *James Stirling: Buildings and Projects 1950–1974* – 181, 199

John Donat/RIBA Drawings Collection – 196

Casabella – 197 (October 1972)

Index